The WTO and the Doha Round

The Changing Face of World Trade

Global Trade and Finance Series

VOLUME 4

The WTO and the Doha Round
The Changing Face of World Trade

Edited by

Ross P. Buckley

Professor and Executive Director
Tim Fischer Centre for Global Trade and Finance
Bond University, Australia

KLUWER LAW INTERNATIONAL

THE HAGUE / LONDON / NEW YORK

A C.I.P. Catalogue record for this book is available from the Library of Congress.

ISBN 90-411-9947-0

Published by
Kluwer Law International,
P.O. Box 85889, 2508 CN The Hague, The Netherlands
sales@kluwerlaw.com
http://www.kluwerlaw.com

Sold and distributed in North, Central and South America by
Aspen Publishers, Inc.
7201 McKinney Circle, Frederick, MD 21704, USA

Sold and distributed in all other countries
by Turpin Distribution Services Limited
Blackhorse Road, Letchworth, Herts.,
SG6 1HN, United Kingdom

Printed on acid-free paper

Printed and bound in Great Britain by Antony Rowe Limited

To Michael & Vera Seiden

Whose unstinting support of my family on so many levels
makes endeavours such as this possible

Contents

Acknowledgments

This book grew out of a colloquium into the future of the WTO held at Bond University in August, 2002. To facilitate dialogue and debate, presenters were encouraged to present their thoughts and ideas rather than a finished paper, and presentations were kept short, and question times long.

This strategy worked well and all credit for its success goes to the presenters and attendees. The result has been that most of the authors in this volume knew what their co-authors would be writing about and some read drafts of their co-authors' forthcoming contributions. I trust we have, by these means, produced a relatively coherent work.

Some of the ideas presented that day never made it into this volume for various reasons, and those that did have been joined by distinguished contributions from colleagues in China, Switzerland, and the United States. My thanks to all who participated or have since contributed – you have been a splendid bunch who have met deadlines admirably and done it all in good humour.

It is intended to make this colloquium, and the resulting book, a biennial event held shortly after the biennial Ministerial meetings of the WTO. Freer trade and fairer trade offer more hope than aid to the billions who today live in abject poverty. To this end, the WTO is a critical global institution, and we who have the time and training to highlight ways forward for the institution have an obligation to do so.

Particular thanks are due to two people. First to Professor Ken Moores, Vice-Chancellor and President of Bond University, for his role in the conception of, and ongoing support for, the Tim Fischer Centre for Global Trade and Finance. More personally, I would also like to thank Ken for his quite exceptional support of me as I have of late grappled with one of those steep challenges life at times throws at us. Second, my sincere thanks to the publisher of the Global Trade and Finance Series, Ms Sian O'Neill, of Kluwer Law International, London, for her unflagging support of the Series and my role in it.

Professor Ross Buckley
Tim Fischer Centre for Global Trade & Finance
Bond University, Gold Coast, Australia
February, 2003

Contributors

Ross Buckley is Executive Director of the Tim Fischer Centre for Global Trade and Finance, an interdisciplinary research centre at Bond University in Australia. He also serves as Series Editor of the series in which this book appears.

His principal areas of research interest are international finance, international trade, and globalization. He is particularly interested in capital flows to developing countries. He has written over 75 articles and chapters in Australian and foreign journals and collections and is the author of *Emerging Markets Debt* (Kluwer, London, 1999). Before joining Bond, he practised law in Australia, Hong Kong, and on Wall Street. He has been a Visiting Professor at Northwestern University in Chicago and a Visiting Fellow at Manchester College, Oxford and has served as a consultant to law firms, business, and foreign governments.

Ann Capling is Associate Professor in Political Science at the University of Melbourne. She teaches in the area of public policy, political economy, and international political economy. She has a particular interest in trade policy, global economic governance, intellectual property rights, and the political economy of sport.

Capling is one of Australia's leading authorities on the multilateral trade system. Her books include: *Australia and the Global Trade System: From Havana to Seattle* (Cambridge University Press, 2001); *Australian Politics in the Global Era* (Longman, 1998) with Mark Considine and Michael Crozier; and *Beyond the Protective State* (Cambridge University Press, 1992) with Brian Galligan.

She is Associate Dean (Academic Programs) in the Arts Faculty, and Director of the Bachelor of Public Policy and Management.

Teresa Chataway is a Research Fellow at the Key Centre for Ethics, Law, Justice, and Governance at Griffith University, Brisbane. She is currently part of a team working on an Australian Research Council funded project on the legal and ethical aspects of international intervention on humanitarian, pro-democratic, and anti-terrorist grounds, and also on a series of East–West Dialogue workshops supported by the Open Society Institute. She is a former ARC Postdoctoral Fellow (1998–2001) with a forthcoming book on *Norberto Bobbio: Law and Cosmopolitical Democracy*. She is also editing a volume of essays on recent international law developments, titled *Cosmopolitical Jurisprudence, and the Changing Universal Legal Order*. For the past decade she has been engaged in legal–political research drawing on European trends.

Chen Xuebin is a senior partner and associate director of Shanghai Asia & Great Wall, a Shanghai law firm, Associate President of AAPC & Great Wall, an alliance of Chinese law firms, a member of the Board of Directors of the All-China Lawyers Association, and a Senior Fellow of the Tim Fischer Centre of Global Trade and Finance of Bond University in Australia.

His prime interest is in international trade and investment law, and the WTO in particular. In this area, he has published over 40 papers. He was honoured as one of the 10-excellent Lawyers in Nantong in 1994 and in Jiangsu Province in 1995, and one of the 100-excellent Lawyers in China in 1997. He has held the title of First Class Lawyer since1998. He spent part of 1999 and 2000 as a visiting scholar with the Law School at Bond University.

Bradly J. Condon is Professor of International Law and Business at ITAM in Mexico City and a Senior Fellow of the Tim Fischer Centre for Global Trade and Finance, Australia. He has written over 50 articles on various business and legal topics. His books include *NAFTA, WTO and Global Business Strategy: How AIDS, Trade and Terrorism Affect Our Economic Future* (Quorum Books, 2002) and *Drawing Lines in Sand and Snow: Balancing Border Security and North American Economic Integration* (M. E. Sharpe, 2003) (with Tapen Sinha). His research focuses on international trade law and business strategy. He has served as Director of the Centre for North American Business Studies, as an expert witness before the Canadian Parliament, an advisor for the Commonwealth Law Association, and a guest of the United States Congress on international trade issues. In 2001, Professor Condon won the Lumina Award for Outstanding Research in law and regulation.

Rosita Dellios is Associate Professor of International Relations and head of the international relations department within the School of Humanities and Social Sciences, Bond University. She is author of *Modern Chinese Defence Strategy* (Macmillan, 1989) and has written numerous articles and chapters on Chinese affairs. She is a member of the London-based International Institute for Strategic Studies and a Council Member of the Australian Institute of International Affairs (Queensland branch). She has developed successful courses in global politics, and has lectured and travelled extensively in China, Eastern India, and Southeast Asia where she spent a number of years as a journalist. Her current research interests are Sino–global relations as well as the conceptualization and application of the mandala metaphor in international relations. This metaphor she regards to be of cosmopolitical significance in the globalising world. Her web-based articles may be found on <http://www.international-relations.com>.

Jeffrey L. Dunoff is the Charles Klein Professor of Law and Government and Director of the Institute for International Law and Public Policy at Temple Law School in Philadelphia. He serves on the US EPA's National Advisory Committee, as an Associate Editor of the Yearbook of International Environmental Law, and as Vice Chair of the International Economic Law Group of the American Society of International Law. He is co-author of *International Law: Norms, Actors, Process* (2002, with Ratner and

Wippman) and has published widely on international law, international trade, and international environmental law issues. In 2003, he will serve as a Visiting Professor of Public and International Affairs at the Woodrow Wilson School at Princeton University. He has previously served as a Visiting Fellow at the Center of International Studies at Princeton University and as a Visiting Research Fellow at the United Nations Asia and Far East Institute in Japan.

Angus Francis convenes the Masters program in international economic law at the University of Canberra, Australia. His research and teaching focuses particularly on China, having taught international trade law to attorneys and senior management across China. He is widely published in the area of comparative economic law.

Robyn Lui is a research assistant at the Key Centre. Her current projects include East–West Dialogues on Governance Values and Ethics of Intervention. Her research interests are contemporary responses to refugees and forced migration, ethics in international affairs, post-conflict reconstruction, and critical approaches to international relations. She is currently working on a monograph on a critical history of the international refugee regime and a number of papers on issues relating to the future of the protection regime for refugees. A critique on the discourse of human security and its ambiguous consequences for refugee protection will be published by the United Nations High Commissioner for Refugees (UNHCR) in late 2003.

Bryan Mercurio is Director of the Electoral Law Project in the Gilbert & Tobin Centre of Public Law at The University of New South Wales, Sydney. Previously, Bryan specialized in international trade law at a Sydney-based law firm and worked on international trade matters while with the Canadian Embassy, Washington, DC.

Jan McDonald is the John F Kearney Professor of Law and Head of the Law School at Griffith University, Brisbane and Gold Coast. Her research interests lie in environmental law, with a particular focus on the relationship between international trade law and environmental protection.

Margaret Palmer is a Research Fellow at the Key Centre for Ethics, Law, Justice and Governance at Griffith University, Brisbane. She is currently researching a book on deterring and defeating coups d'état with Charles Sampford. She is also part of a team working on an Australian Research Council funded project on the legal and ethical aspects of international intervention on humanitarian, pro-democratic, and anti-terrorist grounds. She has worked as a lawyer and policy officer for a number of Australian Government Departments and agencies, including the Environment Department, Foreign Affairs and Trade, ATSIC, and the Department of Primary Industries and Energy.

Charles Sampford is currently Foundation Director of the Key Centre for Ethics, Law, Justice and Governance and President of the International Institute for Public Ethics. Previous appointments have been in Law and Philosophy at Melbourne and Foundation Dean of Law at Griffith University (which he was invited to take up in 1991). He has held Senior

Visiting Fellowships at Oxford and Harvard (where he held a Fulbright Senior Award).

He has written over 60 articles and chapters in Australian and foreign journals and collections ranging through law, legal education, and applied ethics and has completed 18 books and edited collections. He has also won over twelve million dollars in grants, consultancies, and awards for research work he has led.

He has been consulted by business, government, and international organizations (including the World Bank and the World Council of Churches). He is currently a member of the US Council for Foreign Relations International Task Force for Responding to Threats to Democracy.

Patrick Weller is professor of politics and public policy and deputy director of the Key Centre for Ethics, Law, Justice and Governance at Griffith University. He is a graduate of Oxford and the Australian National University. He is author of a number of books on Australian and comparative politics, including *Malcolm Fraser PM* (1989), *First among equals: Prime Ministers in Westminster Systems* (1985), *Australia's Mandarin: the frank and the fearless?* (2001), and co-editor of *The Changing of Top Officials* (2001) and *The Hollow Crown: Countervailing Trends in Core Executives* (1996).

Xu Yi-chong is associate professor of political science at St Francis Xavier University in Nova Scotia and a Visiting Professor at the Key Centre for Ethics, Law, Justice and Governance at Griffith University from 2002–2003. Her research interests are international political economy and the reform of utilities in developing economies. She is author of *Powering China: Reforming the electric power industry in China* (2002).

Andreas Ziegler is Senior Officer at the Secretariat of the European Free Trade Association (EFTA) and a Professor of Law at the University of Lausanne. He was formerly head of the unit for International and European Economic Law in the State Secretariat for Economic Affairs and, prior to that, legal counsel in the Swiss Directorate for Public International Law. He also teaches regularly at the University of St Gallen and the University of New South Wales in Sydney, and has been invited to teach at the Chicago-Kent College of Law in Chicago and at the University of Pittsburgh.

1. Introduction: The Changing Face of World Trade and the Greatest Challenge Facing the WTO and the World Today

Ross P. Buckley

The Changing Face of World Trade was selected as the title of this volume to emphasize the significance of the appointment of Dr Supachai Panitchpakdi as Director-General of the World Trade Organisation (WTO) in 2002,[1] and to emphasize how significantly the trade challenges facing the world today have changed from those confronting it when the Uruguay Round commenced in 1986.

Dr Supachai is the first person from a developing country to head the WTO or, before it, the Secretariat of the General Agreement on Tariffs and Trade (the GATT).[2] This is of critical importance for, if the current Doha round of trade negotiations is to succeed, the developed world will have to address and resolve the sense of many developing and least developed countries that there is unfinished business and broken promises from the Uruguay round.

To the extent the that Director-General of the WTO can be considered the face of world trade, with Dr Supachai's appointment the face of world trade changed from a Western to an Asian face (though still a male one, we await that evolution).

The developing and least developed countries now represent an overwhelming majority of members of the WTO, over 100 of the current 144 members, and Dr Supachai's appointment reflects this reality in an organization which

---

[1] For more on Dr supachai's views, *see* Dr Supachai Panitchkpakdi, 'The Evolving Multilateral Trade System in the New Millennium' (2001) 33 *George Washington International Law Review* 419; and the self-published collection of his writing and speeches, Dr Supachai Panitchpakdi, *Reflections on World Trade, Finance and Development*, 1998.

[2] The Director-Generals of the GATT were Eric Wyndham White (1948–68), Olivier Long (1968–80), Arthur Dunkel (1980–93) and Peter Sutherland (1993–95). The Director-Generals of the WTO have been Renato Ruggiero (1995–99) and Mike Moore (1999–2002). Dr Supachai commenced his three-year term as Director-General in September 2002. For more on the term shared between Mike Moore and Dr Supachai *see* 'WTO member governments agree on Director-General succession', WTO PRESS/131 22 July 1999, available at <http://www.wto.org/english/news_e/pres99_e/pr131_e.htm>.

operates on the one country one vote principle (unlike the IMF in which voting rights are tied to quotas which are proportional to national GDP).

Many significant developing and least developed countries believe that they have been cheated in the way the Uruguay Round commitments have been implemented. The Uruguay Round represented a dramatic widening of the reach of trade liberalization as the GATT, which had formerly dealt almost exclusively with trade in goods, was supplemented by two further treaties: the General Agreement on Trade in Services (GATS) and Trade-Related Aspects of Intellectual Property Rights (TRIPs).

Neither of these latter two treaties particularly serves the interests of developing or least developed countries. Such countries have very little potential to export services, and the protection of intellectual property rights only tends to serve an economy when the economy is sufficiently advanced to be developing substantial amounts of intellectual property. Until that stage in economic development is reached, developing countries may well be better served by weak and ineffective intellectual property regimes that permit their industries to copy technological advances made abroad. Much of the impetus to trade liberalization under the GATT in the 1950s and 1960s was the economic theory that tariff reductions benefit an economy because, while they might cause a degree of economic dislocation to directly affected industries, they render inputs into many other industries significantly cheaper and thus enhance the international competitiveness of those industries. Furthermore trade liberalization exposes industries to global competition that is the best, and perhaps only, long-term guarantee of competitiveness and efficiency. Multilateral trade liberalization can thus be proven theoretically to be a win–win game.

However, it is not apparent that this reasoning applies to either the GATS or TRIPS. On their face these treaties offered far more to the developed, than to the developing, world. Accordingly, the developing countries needed a carrot to entice them to agree to this radical extension of the trade liberalization agenda, and that carrot was enhanced access to developed world markets for agricultural products and textiles, clothing and footwear. In large measure, so these developing countries argue, the carrot has failed to materialize – the US and EU have failed to keep their promises regarding increased access to their markets – and there is much to suggest these countries have a legitimate grievance in this regard.

Accordingly, the WTO faces a particular challenge in the Doha Round in redressing this sense of broken promises and unfinished business.[3] This was part of the reason the new trade round was not initiated, as planned, in Seattle in 1999, and part of the reason the protracted and difficult Doha Ministerial meeting in November 2001 in Doha, Qatar so nearly failed again to launch a new round.

---

3 *See*, for instance, Vandana Shiva, 'Poverty and Globalisation', 2000 BBC Reith Lecture, in particular the response of Vandana Shiva to the question of Bhoopinder Singh Hooda, available at <http://news.bbc.co.uk/hi/english/static/events/reith_2000/lecture5.stm>; accessed on 6 February 2003.

And so the face of world trade is changing also in this sense – the developing world is finding its voice and searching, often less than effectively, for its collective power – Dr Supachai's non-Caucasian face reflects the changing power realities at work within the WTO.

The title of this chapter also makes a huge claim – that the greatest challenge facing the WTO today is also the greatest challenge facing the world. That challenge is the ever-increasing inequality that characterises the division of income and assets on our planet.

Income inequality among the citizens of the world is massive.[4] The richest 1 per cent of people in the world earn as much as the bottom 57 per cent; in other words, less than 50 million of the richest people earn as much as the 2,700 million poorest people. Furthermore, income inequality is rising. For example, between 1988 and 1993 inequality increased by 5 per cent with the real incomes of the poorest 5 per cent decreasing and the real incomes of the top 20 per cent increasing.[5] If we look at assets rather than incomes, the richest 20 per cent of humanity owned 60 times as much as the poorest 20 per cent in 1990, and 74 times as much in 2000,[6] and three men, the two founders of Microsoft, Bill Gates and Paul Allen, and the investor Warren Buffet, own as much as the 600 million people in the world's 48 least developed countries.[7]

This massive and increasing income and asset inequality threatens trade liberalization. Trade liberalization is central to globalization. There is a tendency to assume globalization is a given, and inevitable. This is not so. The period from 1870 to 1913 was one of intense globalization in trade in goods and especially in capital flows. Indeed, measured as a percentage of GDP of the capital exporting nations, it is arguable that capital flows were more globalized in this period than they are today.[8]

The First World War changed all that. The war was followed by a period of withdrawal from world trade that led eventually to the Great Depression of 1929.

---

4 Income inequality is far higher than conventional measures indicate. Recently, for the first time, research by Branko Milanovic, of the Development Research Group at the World Bank, has taken account of individual incomes within each country as well as between countries (rather than assuming all people in one country earn the average income for that country). *See* B. Milanovic, 'True World Income Distribution, 1988 and 1993: First Calculations Based on Household Surveys Alone' (2002) 112 *Economic Journal* 51.

5 Milanovic, *ibid*. For an accessible introduction to trends in global inequality, *see* 'World Inequality', *BBC News*, 18 July 2001, available at <http://news.bbc.co.uk/1/hi/business/1442073.stm>, accessed 26 February 2003.

6 Sulak Sivaraka, 'Globalisation Represents Greed', *Bangkok Post*, 21 September 1999.

7 Walden Bello, 'Dark Victory: The United States and Global Poverty'.

8 Net capital outflows from the UK peaked at some 9% of GNP before 1914 and the proportion was almost as high for France, Germany, and Holland, the other major creditor countries. These proportions have not been achieved since. Likewise, current account deficits of the principal capital importing countries, Argentina, Australia, and Canada, were over 10% for long periods. These levels have only been achieved by developing countries for short periods, which typically have been followed by very difficult adjustments: B. Eichengreen and M. Mussa, *Capital Account Liberalization: Theoretical and Practical Aspects*, IMF Occasional Paper No. 172, 1998, at 31. While net capital flows relative to GDP of capital exporters were higher pre-1914 than now, gross flows are much higher today for today huge amounts of capital also flows from rich individuals in developing countries to developed countries (as safe havens for investment).

With these lessons fresh in their minds, John Maynard Keynes and Harry Dexter White crafted an international economic system for the post-Second World War period that encouraged trade and economic interdependency and that led directly to the prosperity of the 1950s, 1960s and 1970s.

So history tells us trade liberalization is not inevitable. It can be reduced, easily, by national governments erecting trade barriers. Politicians may well do this if they see electoral advantage in it; and, if a turn away from the world leads a political party to power in one nation, one can be fairly confident that parties in other like countries will emulate their policy settings.

Trade liberalization is a major part of globalization, and globalization remains very unpopular in many countries. While history tells us clearly that isolationism and policies aimed at economic self-sufficiency are in fact a prescription for poverty[9] – politicians often focus more on the short-term electoral impact of their policies than the long-term economic impact. It would be the most arrant folly of developed nations to assume increased trade liberalization is assured and not something that needs to be worked at, and hard.

Globalization and trade liberalization, in simple terms, increase the size of markets. Markets go from national to regional, and from regional to global. Larger markets tend to reward the successful participants in them more handsomely than smaller markets, while bringing more competition to those who lack special skills or expertise. Advertising experts, on the one hand, are now able to design global advertising campaigns and reap the corresponding rewards, whereas production line workers in Australia, on the other hand, are now competing with their peers in China or Indonesia, and likewise reaping the corresponding 'rewards'. Accordingly, globalization and trade liberalization tend to increase inequality between nations and between individuals within a nation.

If globalization and trade liberalization are permitted to continue to exacerbate inequality both between and within nations, they will be sowing the seeds of their own destruction. Accordingly, the greatest challenge facing the WTO, and the world, is to manage globalization in such a way that its benefits are shared far more equally among individuals than is today the case. This is not merely desirable on grounds of fairness or ethics, though it is utterly defensible on those grounds.[10] Rather this is essential if we are not to slide backwards into a less interdependent, and far poorer, world.

The developed nations, if they were able to see clearly, would argue for a fairer allocation of the benefits of globalization on grounds of strict self-interest. In trade terms, this means fair access to the markets of rich countries for the exports of poorer countries – which is no more than the same access that the rich countries themselves demand for their own exports to the poorer countries' markets.

---

[9] Witness the economic performance of virtually all Latin American nations in the twentieth century: De Ruyter Van Steveninck, 'Import Substitution and the Debt Crisis in Latin America' (1991) 3(2) *Tinbergen Institute Research Bulletin* 133.

[10] As the following chapter by Sampford, Chataway, Lui, and Palmer, argues persuasively.

But there is precious little clear sightedness among policy makers in the United States, the United Kingdom, or Australia today on foreign policy issues.

The causes of terrorism are many and complex. However it is difficult to deny that increasing inequality fuels the bitterness and sense of alienation that underpin much terrorist activity.[11] The educated, middle-class backgrounds of individuals terrorists do not disprove this thesis for these people, above all, die for a cause, and massive and increasing inequality fuels their hatred for rich countries, and renders their cause believable. Furthermore, history, from the time of the Bourbon Kings of France to Indonesia today, shows clearly that increasing inequality contributes to declining political stability. It is as if human beings can live with inequality, but gross inequality, or ever-widening inequality, provokes strong emotions of bitterness and resentment that are inimical to stable political processes and systems.

Accordingly, a better deal for the world's poor and decreasing inequality is the best recipe for the global political stability that will lead to still greater prosperity for all. This is the greatest challenge facing humanity today.

For the WTO to rise to this challenge will principally require better and fairer access to US and EU markets for agricultural produce and other exports of poor countries. Yet the opposition and influence of US and EU farmers in their nations domestic politics is massive and undiminished. The road ahead in the Doha round will be long and hard for developing countries.

For a quick reality check, take a look at the web site of Senator Max Baucus of Montana.[12] As Chair of the all-powerful Senate Finance Committee and senior member of the Senate Agriculture Committee, Max Baucus has tremendous influence on US trade policy. Indeed, it is highly likely that Senator Baucus' role in this regard is more significant than that of the US Trade Representative, Bob Zoellick, a member of the Bush cabinet and, on the surface, the principal US player on this issue. Yet while Senator Baucus plays a critical role in US trade policy formation, his website is utterly silent on the issue. Why? Because, of course, notwithstanding his position and power on Capitol Hill, Max Baucus' owes his job to the voters of Montana. There are only 900,000 people in Montana, and most of them are farmers. As the sign on Max Baucus' desk says, 'Montana Comes First'.

That is his job. Politics are essentially local. This is the reality of the long, hard fight that lies ahead in seeking sufficient new access to US and EU

---

11 *See*, in particular, the concluding comments of the distinguished Oxford development economist, Frances Stewart, in 'Horizontal Inequalities: The Neglected Dimension of Development', the WIDER Annual Lectures 5, UNU World Institute of Development Economics Research (UNU/WIDER), 2002. *See* also D. Bell and M. Renner, 'The War on Terrorism Needs a Marshall Plan', available at <http://www.net-about-town.com.au/imaginepeace/articles/marshallplan.htm>; accessed February 10, 2003; and Bradly Condon, *NAFTA, WTO and Global Business Strategy: How Aids, Trade and Terrorism Affect Our Economic Future* (Quorum Books, 2002), at 210.

12 *See* generally: <http://www.senate.gov/~baucus>.

markets for agricultural products, textiles clothing and footwear, and other exports of poorer countries.

The following 11 chapters examine various ways forward for the WTO in the Doha Round and beyond. They commence with a chapter by Sampford, Chataway, Lui, and Palmer that examines the promises that developed nations argue global trade offers to all. While noting these promises are much contested, this chapter argues that the key question is not one of fact – will trade liberalization make everyone better off? The key question is one of action – what must developed nations do to make these promises a reality and are they are willing to do it? The authors argue that there are three reasons why developed nations should ensure that the promises are fulfilled rather than undermined by their own action: normative issues of integrity; pragmatic issues of self-interest; and normative arguments about rights of human beings as members of a global community. The first two sets of reasons argue from the point of view of developed nation-states and their citizens. The final set of reasons argue from the global point of view – the point from which the arguments in favour of trade liberalization are made in the first place.

The following chapter, by Ann Capling, analyses three central challenges to the WTO: the decline of US leadership in the multilateral trade system; the pressure from non-governmental organizations (NGOs) for direct participation in the WTO; and internal governance issues of the WTO especially related to the concern of developing countries that the process marginalizes them. Her chapter highlights the importance of the WTO, as the administrator of a rules-based system, to developing countries – for otherwise global trade issues would be resolved by power politics.

Jeff Dunoff then similarly proceeds to make three central claims about the state of the international trade regime. He argues first that the trade regime is in a time of fundamental transition and transformation. He then analyses how the strategies used so far to address these transition issues have been relatively conventional and either ineffectual or counterproductive. He then examines how the pressures driving the WTO's transitional era illuminate the limits of our current understandings of the trade regime and call for new perspectives that more fully capture the realities of the international trading system.

Xu Yi-chong and Patrick Weller examine international civil servants and their role and impact on international politics through the lens of their role in negotiating the GATS. The authors find that the international civil servants played a critical role in securing progress in the negotiations. The civil service acted as both an honest broker and a source of ideas and potential compromises. To be able to play this role the Secretariat had to be seen to be the advocate of no country and the adherent to no cause. Indeed, the Secretariat often pursued much broader objectives than those advocated by the powerful and rich countries.

Bryan Mercurio examines the dispute settlement procedure in the WTO. He analyses the shortcomings of the implementation phase of the dispute settlement understanding and proposes solutions to its growing problems including the meaning of a 'reasonable period for implementation' and the apparent conflict between Articles 21.5 and 22 of the DSU. The author argues that, if left unaddressed, these problems could seriously undermine the effectiveness of the WTO.

The following chapter, by Jan McDonald, analyses trade and environment linkages in the Doha round and beyond. The author looks at the history of this linkage and the ways in which the WTO's appellate body has 'greened' WTO Agreements, particularly the GATT, and the institutional responses to this, including the 'environment' provisions of the Doha Ministerial Declaration. Jan McDonald argues that the conservatism of the Doha environmental mandate and the WTO Committee negotiations evidences a continuing resistance to linking trade and environment. She also finds clear evidence of this resistance in non-trade fora. She concludes that real progress on promoting mutually supportive trade and environment policies remains elusive and that the WTO's failure to deliver on the promises of trade liberalization for developing countries is one of the root causes of this stalemate.

Angus Francis reflects upon the long march of China's accession to the WTO. Francis analyses what can be learnt from China's accession in relation to the place of rights in the international trading system, looking in particular at the theoretical work of Ernst-Ulrich Petersmann.

A further timely contribution on China's accession comes from Chen Xuebin. His chapter on the Agreement on Trade Related Investment Measures as it applies to China highlights the long march still ahead for China's lawmakers and government if they are to, as now they must, conform their laws and rules to those required by TRIMS.

The cultural and political contexts for the future of world trade are critical at this time with a US administration that appears to care little for other cultures and that is adopting an increasingly unilateralist and interventionist approach to global problems. This cultural and political context and the imperative need for globalization to be managed in a sustainable manner are the topics of the next chapter by Rosita Dellios.

The chapter by Andreas Ziegler traces the evolution of bi- and multilateral trade negotiations since 1850 and analyses the relation between the two. The author, a Senior Officer in the Secretariat of the European Free Trade Association (EFTA), then proceeds to examine EFTA's bilateral agreements and analyses the lessons to be learned from EFTA's experiences in this regard with a particular focus on the new areas of interest to WTO members such as competition and investment.

The final chapter, by Bradly Condon, looks to the future and seeks to assess the likely impact of AIDS and terrorism on flows of trade, capital, people, and knowledge. This analysis is through two case studies. The first looks at the impact of September 11 on North American border management and highlights the differences between North–North and North–South border security co-operation. The second case study examines the controversy over patents and access to AIDS medicine in Brazil. This demonstrates how whether a developing country has the capacity to manufacture its own generic drugs may well ultimately determine the price it pays for imported drugs. Both case studies show how economic and institutional underdevelopment may limit the ability of developing countries to benefit from international trade and investment flows.

Conclusion

Each of the 11 other authors of this volume has identified problems or shortcomings in the architecture of the international trading system. However all are optimists – all have identified solutions to the respective problems. The challenge does not lie principally in knowing how to improve the multilateral trading system but in summoning the political will to do it. Global prosperity depends upon politicians of all nations putting the common good of all their constituents above the interests of selected groups of constituents. The peculiar political challenge is that in all countries vested interest groups will fight far, far harder to not be prejudiced by trade liberalization than the average person will fight to benefit from it. And when the vested interests are those of multinational corporations or other developed nation constituencies, and the common interests are of the poorer members of developing countries, the power imbalance leads to many of the problems identified in these pages.

2. Living up to the Promises of Global Trade

Charles Sampford, Teresa Chataway, Robyn Lui, and Margaret Palmer

2.1 Introduction: 'Have We Got a Deal for You!'

From Davos to Doha, western diplomats and company executives have been busy proclaiming the virtues of trade liberalization. Their message for the rest of the world is: if you embrace trade liberalization, you will be better off. They argue that trade liberalization alleviates poverty, promotes development, and increases GNP, personal income, and living standards. It fosters peaceful relations between and within states. Countries that have experienced the greatest integration with the world economy have managed to grow the fastest and reduce poverty the most. Trade liberalization improves the quality of goods produced and promotes competition and the efficient use of resources. Foreign investment brings much-needed managerial and technical expertise. The free exchange of ideas and the desire to attract investment encourages the development of effective political administration. In colloquial terms: 'have we got a deal for you!'.

Yet there are some skeptics in the developing and developed world who doubt these claims, and who argue that the deal is actually a bad one. From their view, trade liberalization is good for rich countries with strong and established economies but very damaging for emerging economies. Furthermore, and most importantly, they maintain that developed countries use their greater bargaining power and knowledge capital to extract very favourable terms for themselves out of trade negotiations.

Important promises are being made. However, they are not being fulfilled now, and there are risks that they will not be met in the future, because there is a rupture between the act of making promises and the act of implementing policies that work towards realizing them. This raises discrete ethical questions. We have to be careful that our own actions do not undermine our promises by securing for ourselves trading arrangements so favourable that we benefit at the expense of those to whom we have promised beneficial trade liberalization. We would be making liars of ourselves!

The question of whether trade liberalization benefits developing countries or disadvantages them is not just a simple empirical question. The attainment of such benefits depends on the behaviour of those involved.

While this point is often made about developing countries, it does not seem to be made often or consistently about western actors. As the dominant players and drivers in world trade – and especially in world trade negotiations – our actions have a significant influence on the outcome. The range of possible outcomes varies from a substantial realization of the free trade dream to the worst nightmares of free trade opponents; the difference will be largely determined by our actions. What is of concern is that we do not make the connection between our acts and our words. Globalization and trade liberalization are not primarily a question of what is and what will be but how we choose the processes that will produce the anticipated benefits. In this context, it is a matter of real concern that western nations promise that other nations will benefit from world trade while carefully calculating how their own citizens and corporations can benefit from a forceful push for some trade liberalizations and the opposition to others.

Accordingly, this chapter will examine some arguments for acting to ensure that we are not liars when we argue for trade liberalization. These arguments take two forms. First, there are ethical arguments about keeping promises. Second, there are pragmatic considerations relating to what will happen if the reality does not live up to those promises – what will happen if developing countries find they have been duped and why it is in our own interest to have prosperous (rather than poor and resentful) neighbours and trading partners. These arguments are within the standard framework of strong sovereign states and their interests. However, there is another set of ethical arguments that goes beyond the paradigm of the interests and ethical responsibilities of states as actors. This ethical position is based on what is good for human beings as co-habitors of a single planet rather than as citizens of competing sovereign states.

2.2 Promises and Potential Benefits of Global Trade Liberalization

In classic economic theory, trade liberalization brings benefits to the respective trading parties. This ideal has underpinned the drive to advance liberalization as the organizing principle of the global economy. Since the 1970s, the liberalization of the domestic market and integration into the global economy have become important development strategies for developing countries. The World Bank and the International Monetary Fund (IMF) regularly exalt the potential of trade liberalization to contribute to the objectives of economic growth and poverty reduction, and to the general practices of good governance. It would be useful, therefore, to explore the promises and potential benefits of trade liberalization.

The connection between trade liberalization and the alleviation of poverty can be considered to be positive by policy-makers from both North and South, because the reforms needed to be a player in the global market almost invariably bring changes that help to encourage the efficient use and allocation of resources and foster long-term growth. The success of countries like China, Brazil, Hungary and Mexico to generate growth and to reduce poverty can be attributed to their efforts to open up 'their economies as part of a broader development strategy that builds on two pillars: improving the investment climate for the private sector to generate jobs and empowering poor people, so they can participate in growth'.[1]

Liberalization has a positive effect on market structure and prices. Barriers to entry foster conditions where domestic companies become monopolies. This environment interferes with the workings of market mechanisms and leads to an inefficient use of resources. The opening of domestic markets weakens the possibility of monopolistic power. The liberalization of the domestic market can change the market structure, 'with more firms producing goods'; direct resources to the most productive areas; encourage greater innovation; and result in price reduction for goods and services.[2] Since 1980 the integration into the global economy of those developing countries with reasonable locations, policies, institutions and the infrastructure to harness their abundant labor has given them a competitive advantage in some manufacturing and services.[3] Entry into export markets can improve productivity. The increased export earnings finance more imports, intensifying competition.

Trade liberalization has the potential not only to maximize the allocation and use of economic resources, but also to improve education and skills standards. Foreign investment affects the labour market and creates employment in certain sectors. The demand for a good and competent labour market encourages the return to education and raises the skill premium. The increase in basic education tends to reduce inequality. In the long term, the presence of foreign companies and opening of the national economy improve wages, thus alleviating poverty. Poverty reduction raises life expectancy and spread of basic education and health.

Foreign investment flow brings capital, advanced technology and access to international markets. The domestic partners become part of the global economy network. Foreign investment also brings much-needed managerial and technical expertise. The presence of foreign banks in the local market can strengthen the financial infrastructure. In other areas, multinationals play a crucial role in research and development, technology transfer and generating new technologies. Moreover, with the appropriate incentives, foreign investment can be the means by which ports, roads, telecommunications and other business services are established efficiently in developing countries.

The potential benefits of global trade liberalization depend, among other things, on the robustness of domestic institutions and policies. When a country establishes an attractive investment-friendly environment, it is required to set up practices of good governance, that is, the control of corruption, the development of well-functioning bureaucracies and business

---

1 B. Hoekman, A. Mattoo, and P. English (eds), *Development, Trade, and the WTO. A Handbook* (The World Bank, Washington, DC, 2002), p. xi.

2 The World Bank, *World Bank Policy Research Report. Globalization, Growth, and Poverty* (World Bank and Oxford University Press, New York, 2002), p. 90.

3 *Ibid.*, p. 38.

regulation and the protection of property rights. An unstable investment climate, including inefficient and weak regulation, corruption and underdeveloped infrastructure, deters long-term capital and financial investment. This does not mean that countries must have strong institutions in place before liberalizing their markets and participating in the global economy. The combination of the exchange of ideas that often follows openness and integration can lead to the adoption of best practices in many industries and political administration. In other words, liberalization can spur wide-ranging reforms that increase the capacity and enhance the credibility of domestic institutions.

While trade liberalization holds many potential benefits, it is a complex process. We should keep in mind that there are also risks of these promises not being fulfilled, and that some people have lost out, particularly in the short run, in this current drive for openness. This reality requires us to be attentive to those who have gained little from the process, because if we do nothing to mitigate their concerns, we are sabotaging their welfare and in the long run, our own.

2.3 Threats to and Potential Damage from Global Trade Liberalization

The governments of developing and developed countries are seeking to reap more benefits than costs from the liberalization of trade and markets. But for some developing countries, the entry into the global trading system has had detrimental effects on their political, social, and cultural development. It seems that the 'invisible hand' of the market is insufficient to realize the economic and social benefits of trade. This is not to say that international trade is inherently opposed to the needs and interests of the poor. The benefits and risks of global trade are the results of choices that are made about the rules which govern its processes. The prospects of development and economic growth in many developing countries are constrained by, among other things, the asymmetrical structure of the world economy, weak domestic institutions and uncertain opportunities. The World Trade Organization (WTO) – the key multilateral trade institution – despite claims of equal membership, in practice reinforces the asymmetry of economic and political power among nations. Industrialized countries can and do set up trade barriers to protect their domestic industries and producers at great cost to countries of the South. These conditions translate into vulnerabilities that are often worsened by the South's limited power to decide its own pace of integration and forms of participation in the global trade system. The lack of accountability, transparency and appropriate ethical standards in the financial and corporate world is contributing to the growing number of obstacles preventing the fulfillment of the promises of free trade and greater liberalization. The current multilateral trading arrangements set up significant opportunities for the abuse of economic power, usually by developed countries. Such abuses undermine the promises of global trade and the integrity of liberal–democratic governments, and create distrust and resentment.

Not surprisingly, there is a rising tide of opposition, often labeled mistakenly as the 'anti-globalization' movement, supposedly hostile to free trade and the activities of the WTO, World Bank and IMF.[4] The public rallies in Seattle, Melbourne, Prague, Gothenburg, Genoa, Davos and the World Social Forum in Porto Alegre reveal a deep sense of disillusionment with the present world order. Social movement groups and non-government organizations from the North and South share many common concerns about the current character of the global trade regime. They oppose neo-liberal economics and corporate-driven globalization. In their view, many developing countries are being coerced into adopting an agenda of economic reforms that distort national priorities and subvert the needs of their own citizens. As these countries become caught up between WTO agreements, World Bank strictures, IMF conditions and the demands to be seen as stable financial and foreign investment-friendly locations, they are increasingly deprived of the time and space they need to design and implement their own strategies of poverty eradication and development.

2.3.1 Oxfam's fair trade campaign

Oxfam is one of the high profile international non-government organizations in the humanitarian-development realm that has long campaigned for fair trade as a means to alleviate poverty in developing countries. *Rigged Rules and Double Standards: Trade, Globalisation, and the Fight Against Poverty* is its latest attempt to reform a global trading regime that deprives many developing countries of the opportunity to reap the potential benefits of trade.[5]

The Report argues that although the market economy has helped to alleviate, and in some 'rare' cases, break the cycle of poverty, the prevailing levels of inequality and poverty in the world are unacceptable. The problem is not that international trade is inherently opposed to the needs and interests of the poor, but that the rules of engagement are perverted to favour the wealthy. The current world trade rules are contributing to the poverty problem in developing countries and the widening gap between prosperity and poverty.[6] According to Oxfam, the current international trade rules are

---

[4] These international economic organizations are the Bretton Woods institutions that were the outcomes of the inter-war dialogue between the American and British governments. The core objective of the Bretton Woods system was to establish an economic order that would prevent another political and economic collapse that led to the Second World War. The International Bank for Reconstruction and Development or the World Bank is the agency responsible for financing economic development. The International Monetary Fund provides financial assistance to its members in resolving short-term balance of payments problems. The General Agreement on Tariffs and Trade (GATT) and now the WTO is concerned with creating and preserving a liberal international trading system. It was hoped that the creation of a more open-trading system would lead to interdependence and so ensure peace through internationally shared prosperity.

[5] Oxfam, *Rigged Rules and Double Standards: Trade, Globalisation, and the Fight Against Poverty* (Oxfam, Oxford, 2002).

[6] *Ibid.*, p. 5.

impediments to economic growth and development for developing countries. The Report raises many issues relating to global trade, poverty and inequality. But the two key factors that contribute to the pauperisation of the developing world are the protectionism of developed countries and the practice of coerced economic liberalization of developing countries by the IMF and World Bank.

2.3.1.1 Protectionism and the lack of market access

Trade barriers obstruct the entry of developing countries' products into rich countries and thus their full integration into the global economy. When developing countries export to wealthy countries, they face tariff barriers that are four times higher than those encountered by developed countries.[7] The range of trade barriers confronting developing countries includes tariffs, tariff escalation, non-tariff barriers, product standards and anti-dumping actions.[8] When developing countries' export earnings are derived from selling their products to industrialised countries, the latter's protectionist practices undermine the potential benefits of global trade for already low-income countries. These barriers cost developing countries US$100 billion a year – twice as much as they receive in development assistance. Sub-Saharan Africa loses US$2 billion a year, India and China in excess of US$3 billion in foreign-exchange earnings, and these are only the immediate costs.[9]

According to Oxfam, subsidies to farmers in the European Union and United States amount to more than US$1 billion a day. According to OECD data, domestic subsidies in OECD countries have risen from US$275 billion between 1986 and 1988 to US$326 billion in 1999.[10] These subsidies often encourage environmentally damaging practices and over-production. The surplus is dumped on the world market, usually below the cost of production, thus driving the particular commodity's market price down and devastating the farmers of developing countries.[11] When the agricultural sector represents a substantial share of the economies of developing countries, such practices by Northern countries have grave consequences for agricultural labourers in the South (of whom 65 per cent are women) and their households.

2.3.1.2 Pressure from the IMF and World Bank to liberalize economies rapidly

As 'openness' becomes a catchword among the international civil servants at the IMF and World Bank and Northern government officials, import liberalization as an engine for growth in developing countries has become

---

7 *Ibid.*, p. 5.

8 *Ibid.*, pp. 102–105.

9 *Ibid.*, p. 100.

10 OECD, *Agricultural policies in OECD Countries: Monitoring and Evaluation 2000* (OECD Secretariat, Paris, 2002).

11 Oxfam, *Rigged Rules and Double Standards: Trade, Globalisation, and the Fight Against Poverty* (n. 5–9), p. 11.

the new model consensus. Developing countries have been encouraged through a system of incentives and penalties associated with IMF–World Bank loan conditions to adopt an import liberalization model of economic growth, with detrimental social, political and economic outcomes. World Bank–IMF loan conditionality creates a 'one system, two rules' approach to trade policy, and severs the link between trade policy and poverty-reduction strategies.[12] Too often international monetary and fiscal reforms undermine domestic public policies designed to alleviate poverty and redistribute income. Indeed, rapid import liberalization in developing countries has often intensified poverty and inequality.[13] The IMF and World Bank also have miscalculated the importance of strong and functioning state institutions to provide 'safety-nets' for those who might be adversely affected by the adjustment costs associated with trade liberalization, such as rising unemployment.[14] The speed of reform must be matched by the capacity of governments to manage the expected and unexpected outcomes. The inability of governments of the South to cope with the rapid transition to open markets jeopardizes efforts to build democratic institutions. But since both organizations function as gatekeepers to donor assistance, debt relief and financial rescue packages, developing countries have few options but to implement trade reforms when they request assistance.

The double standard of the current push for trade liberalization can be summed up as the pressure on developing countries to move to greater openness (import liberalization) while at the same time being denied access to markets in industrialized countries. Developed countries, however, have not lived up to their obligations to liberalize their markets. Their governments have found ways to comply with the international agreements to reduce the trade barriers, and at the same time introduce less visible barriers to avoid or postpone the adjustment involved for protected domestic producers. These various forms of tariffs and barriers are imposed mostly on labour-intensive agricultural commodities and manufactured goods from developing countries. When governments fail to honour international agreements in this way, the benefits from the agreements are lost.

2.3.2 Unfulfilled promises and power politics at Doha

Robert Zoellick, the US Trade Representative to the 2001 WTO meeting at Qatar, described the 'Doha development agenda' as an attempt to address the grievances aired by developing countries and mass protests at Seattle. But the issues raised by developing countries' representatives, such as the implementation of agreements on agriculture and textiles concluded at

---

12 *Ibid.*, p. 126–8.

13 *Ibid.*, p. 12.

14 *Ibid.*, p. 120. The World Development Movement's second report on resistance to IMF and World Bank policies in poor countries in 2001 documented protests in 23 countries, charting 77 separate civil protests directed at these international economic institutions. M. Ellis-Jones, *States of Unrest II: Resistance to IMF and World Bank policies in poor countries* (World Development Movement, London, 2002).

the Uruguay Round, were overshadowed by the ambition of developed countries to initiate a process that would lead to negotiations on the 'Singapore issues' such as investment, competition policy, government procurement, and trade facilitation, after the Fifth Ministerial meeting in 2003. According to NGOs observing the negotiations and representatives from developing countries, Doha continued the marginalization of third world concerns in trade liberalization discussions.[15]

One of the obstacles to getting a fair deal for developing countries is the current undemocratic international architecture for trade negotiations. It is not a forum where nations meet and negotiate rules of the trade for their mutual advantage. The system of decision-making and the lack of internal transparency within the WTO discriminate against developing countries. North–South diplomacy is marked by asymmetry of power between the two sides and the North makes the most of this good fortune during trade talks. The WTO functions largely in the service of the United States and some European countries. Trade ministers are under heavy pressure from the influential agribusiness, pharmaceutical and financial-services industries to lobby for their special interests. The familiar back room deals, exclusive 'high-level' meetings and threats to revoke preferential trade status of developing countries if they interfere or oppose the agendas of the North were evident again at the Doha round.

Walden Bello, Director of the Focus on the Global South points out that the key points of the Doha Declaration are not aligned with the interests of the developing countries. He notes, for example:

(1) There is only a superficial acknowledgement of the need to review implementation issues, which was the key agenda of the developing countries.
(2) The proposal to phase out agricultural export subsidies was weakened because of the strong objections by the European Union.
(3) Similarly, there is no assurance to phase out textiles and garment quotas by developed countries.
(4) The demand by a number of developing countries to promote issues of food security and development was disregarded.
(5) It took a very long time to secure any agreement to the variation of the Trade-Related Intellectual Property Rights (TRIPs) agreement to accommodate developing countries' overriding of patents in the interest of public health.
(6) The plea to change the TRIPs agreement so as to outlaw biopiracy and patents on life – a core concern of developing countries – was largely ignored.[16]

---

[15] *See* Global Exchange, *Doomed from the start, Doha round is a hollow victory for corporate-managed trade* <http://www.globalexchange.org/wto/gx111401.html>, 25 July 2002; and A. Kwa, *Power Politics in the WTO: Developing Countries' Perspectives on Decision-making Processes in Trade Negotiations* (draft paper only) (Focus on the Global South, Chulalongkorn University, Bangkok, 2002).

[16] W. Bello, *The Meaning of Doha* <http://www.tni.org/archives/bello/meaning.htm>, 1 July 2002.

The last point is very important because many communities in developing countries depend on natural resources, the environment and agriculture for their livelihood. The Declaration on the TRIPs Agreement and Public Health does not protect farmers' right to seed and the integrity of biodiversity and indigenous knowledge systems. On contrary, it has legitimated corporate monopolies on seeds and plant varieties.

2.4 'Making It so': Ethical Reasons for Keeping Our Word and Fulfilling the Promises of Trade Liberalization

In *Star Trek: The Next Generation*, a science fiction television series, the leadership team discusses a matter, makes a decision and the Captain, Jean-Luc Picard, and calmly directs 'make it so.' Like Star Trek, Western nations have come together to decide that trade liberalization benefits everyone. But unlike Star Trek, Western nations do not attempt to 'make it so.' Instead, the United States and other countries of the EU devote their far superior knowledge base and bargaining power to ensuring that every change to the system and every trade arrangement benefit them – even at the expense of others, including developing countries.

At the World Council of Churches colloquium on climate change in May 2000, David Hallmann claimed that the United States had developed a sophisticated model of the US economy that allowed the calculation of the effects of various climate control proposals in seconds. During the debates about different models and measures, the US negotiators were provided with real time information of the effects on US economic strength. Of course, the reliability of the model, like all economic models, would be open to question. But the point is that other countries lacked this facility, which put the US in a superior position during the negotiations. When the US representatives put forward a proposal dressed up in high principle, these other countries could not predict the likely implications for them. Furthermore, they were unaware that the proposal had been vetted beforehand to ensure that it advanced US interests.

For some such conduct is entirely acceptable. Is it not the role of our trade representatives to secure the best possible deal for us? Is it not the job of our diplomats to secure the best possible international treaties for us? In the name of 'national interests', it is the job of our diplomats and trade representatives to lie on our behalf – to say things that are untrue, or are only true under certain circumstances. The diplomats spout generalities, which are true under unlikely contingencies, and the trade representatives ensure that those contingencies are less likely to occur because they ensure that the interests of their nation are furthered at the expense of the other nations that the diplomats had said would benefit. To put it another way, the Foreign Minister makes general statements that world trade is good for other countries, purportedly using 'other regarding' arguments. At the same time, the trade representatives pursue self-regarding policies that capture as much benefit for their country as possible. To us, this kind of institutionalized duplicity is dishonest, unethical and ultimately self-defeating.

2.4.1 Trade negotiations as simple trade writ large

Trade liberalization is not a zero-sum game. Under most circumstances, it will be a positive sum game.[17] A trade is a Pareto efficient exchange in which one person swaps that which he has for that which he would prefer. For example, we have two bananas and you have two avocadoes and we prefer one of your avocados to one of our bananas and vice versa. If we are better at growing bananas than avocados this is a positive sum game.

However, what if we know all about bananas and avocadoes and you know nothing? Indeed, what if we have well-funded bureaucrats and think tanks that can tell us more than any avocado grower can ever know. What if we then claim, and persuade you, that bananas are the elixir of life and you cannot live without them, and if you want some bananas you must provide all the avocadoes you can grow in exchange for them. If we know this to be false, or are reckless as to the truth, we are acting unethically.

In most modern economies, we are guilty of an offence and may be prosecuted by a fair trading authority. All the advanced countries have domestic consumer protection institutions to protect their citizens from domestic and international snake oil merchants. It is generally an offence to deceive others to deliberately induce someone to sign a contract to his or her disadvantage. It is generally 'misleading and deceptive conduct' to say one thing to induce another to sign a contract and then act to ensure that the benefits that were promised in the inducement are not delivered, but received by the company offering the inducement.[18]

Unfortunately, there are no equivalent fair trading authorities to investigate the arguments put by diplomats and prosecute those who 'lie in state' or who engage in misleading and deceptive conduct. One response might be to say that, until a consumer protection institution is created, there is no obligation to avoid lying or recklessly telling untruths. However, this is to argue that there are no ethical obligations in the absence of enforceable legal obligations. It is also to argue that traders had no ethical responsibilities before fair trading laws were introduced. Such an approach suggests that there is no such thing as ethics and that there are no constraints on human behaviour other than law.

2.4.2 Ethical reasons for not misleading

If we see our trade representatives in the same light as domestic traders before the introduction of fair trading legislation, what kinds of ethical arguments do we think they should consider? To some, the question, if asked, does not need an answer. Of course, you tell the truth. There are many reasons for this answer – from the 'golden rule' that you do unto others as you would have them do unto you, to Kantian concerns that we should not treat others as means to our own ends. Followers of John Rawls will

---

[17] It is generally supposed that, when everybody pursues their self-interest the world is, on average, better off. Indeed, if markets are Pareto-efficient, then everyone is better off because each person has traded what he has for what he would prefer to have.

[18] Of course, these fair trading laws do not apply to their trade representatives.

judge such relations on the maximum principle that social and economic arrangements should be structured to be of the greatest advantage to the least well off. Utilitarians will look to the greatest happiness of the greatest number, tempered by the 'principle of diminishing marginal utility', which recognizes that a dollar in the hands of a poor person gives much more happiness than a dollar in the hands of a middle class westerner.

Applied ethicists have not confined themselves to the traditional ethical theories with their universalistic tendencies to treat all human beings with 'equal concern and respect'.[19] They also address the cynical, self-centred 'economic man' which neo-liberal economics imagines being at the centre of efficient markets. The applied ethicists argue that honesty is in the long-term self-interest of 'economic man'[20] who seeks to maximise profit for himself.[21] The honesty bestows credibility or trustworthiness. Others are more likely to want to do business with you and listen to your propositions rather than dismiss them all as self-serving nonsense.

(1) Honesty reduces the transaction costs of business because not everything has to be bargained, negotiated and written down in legally enforceable form.
(2) Honesty is simpler. As one of our fathers used to muse: 'if you tell the truth to everybody, you will not have to remember which lies you have told to which people'.
(3) Honesty is less risky – even if truth will not always out, there is a risk that it will – one day. Accordingly, prudent risk management suggests that you tell only the truth (though not necessarily all the truth).
(4) Deciding to be honest avoids a complicated and ultimately unresolvable consequential calculus. There may well be occasions when it would be in your self-interest to deceive or lie. However, the calculation of risks and potential benefits and the probability of their occurring, not to mention the unintended and unforeseen consequences, are impossible. Thus it is better to be honest as a rule than to spend the time and resources doing the sums.
(5) When we deceive (or lie to) others, we are also deceiving (or lying to) ourselves.
(6) If we support those who claim to help us to prosper by lying to others, do we have any basis for believing that they will not deceive or lie to us? Why should we believe that they would only lie to the citizens

---

19 One of Rawls most engaging claims was that the major theories of justice (and ethics) provide alternative ways of treating all persons with 'equal concern and respect' – acknowledging that utilitarians, from whom he had broken, reflected that concern by ensuring that every persons happiness counts equally.

20 We leave him in the male gender. No feminist we know would allow that women could be so crass or simple. However, some may suspect that they have married him.

21 This is, itself, a bastardized version of utilitarianism that saw morality in terms of the maximizing happiness. This was too complicated for their mathematics as happiness could be measured in so many ways. More corrosively for economics, utilitarianism took into account the distribution of wealth in calculating happiness where Bentham's subversive 'law of diminishing utility' meant that a shilling in the hand of a poor man produced more happiness than a shilling in the hand of a rich man.

> of other countries? This assumes that they do not believe only in self-interest – that they believe in patriotism – not only above truth telling but also above self-interest. We are not sure how many people have such a set of values. Oliver North certainly portrayed himself to be one such person – a not entirely reassuring example. If someone professes to have such values one must recall the fact that they have just eschewed truth telling as a value, and therefore one would wonder if the claim about patriotism is equally false. Samuel Johnson's quip that 'patriotism is the last refuge of a scoundrel' is more convincing than the idea that patriotism is the first virtue of the state-funded liar.

We should always be wary of an ethic that is founded on long-term self-interest. First, as the great economist John Maynard Keynes said, 'in the long run we are all dead'. A life lived solely for self-interest is ultimately self-defeating as all those efforts come to nought at death. Second, as pointed out above, it is not possible to work out what will actually maximize profit over the longer term. It is actually easier to follow ethical principles that you believe to be generally advantageous. Finally, if others think that you are only adhering to ethical values only because you believe that it is generally in your long-term self-interest to do so, they will always wonder if a particular instance is the exception. They will assume that this could be the case where you conclude that acting against ethical or other declared values will be more profitable than adhering to them. Under such circumstances, these people will have to take one of two kinds of precaution – either spend more time contracting to ensure that you do not have the opportunity to cheat them; or, more simply, just deal with someone else. This is why some have argued that this kind of 'fanatical ethical behaviour', stating values and living up to them, is likely to be more profitable.[22]

2.4.3 Asymmetric power

To have power raises immediate questions about the means by which it is used. Western nations have a particularly important form of power – knowledge. Not only is knowledge an increasingly important form of power in the modern world, it is particularly important in the economics of markets. The neo-liberal economic theory that informs most of the push for free markets assumes the symmetry of knowledge – or that sufficient players have sufficient knowledge so that real markets will reflect the behaviour and outcomes of theoretical markets. However, here we have a case where there is a systematic asymmetry of knowledge. The knowledge about the way that

---

[22] This is not unknown to economic theory. Those who advocate free markets argue that the profit motive is often a better way of achieving social goals than seeking to achieve them directly. This argument merely reverses it. Sometimes the best way to achieve profits is to further generally accepted goals – in particular, behaving ethically and seeking to further values other than your narrow self-interest. This argument was more extensively stated by Sampford in 'Ethical Investment: from oxymoron to tautology', a paper delivered to the Ethical Investment 2001 Conference, Brisbane, February, 2001. Simon Longstaff independently made a similar argument.

markets operate gives western countries a distinct leverage over countries with less knowledge capital. This knowledge can be used to design trade agreements that further our interests rather than theirs. As Nobel laureate Professor Stiglitz has emphasized, markets work very differently under asymmetric knowledge. This issue is fundamental for those claiming the benefits of markets as arguments in favour of trade liberalization. Either they ensure that information and knowledge are shared, or that, to the extent that it is not shared, developed countries should eschew using that asymmetric knowledge to advance their interests at the expense of developing countries.

At this point, the opportunistic free-trade proselytizer may seek to produce a raft of specially commissioned studies purporting to show that free trade is in the interests of the developing world. This again raises important ethical issues for those who fund and those who carry out such research. If it is to be relied upon by others to their potential detriment, it is critical that researchers recognize this and are especially careful about the accuracy of what they say. They should also seek to ensure that their findings are not used in a misleading fashion. In our view, to behave otherwise is dangerous and short-sighted because, as we will argue in the next section, it is in our long-term interests to live up to the promises of trade liberalization, that is, to 'make it so'.

2.5 Pragmatic Reasons for 'Making It so'

Enlightened self-interest on the part of developed countries offers pragmatic reasons why they should support the entry of developing countries into the world trading system. The Doha Round has an ambitious plan.[23] Development of poor countries is said to be the round's 'central objective'.[24] Paragraph 2 of the Doha Declaration states that '[i]nternational trade can play a major role in the promotion of economic development and the alleviation of poverty.... In this context, enhanced market access, balanced rules, and well targeted, sustainably financed technical assistance and capacity-building programmes have important roles to play'.[25] Recognition of the role of trade is helping developing countries is there. The challenge is to make it happen.

2.5.1 Trade and development

The World Bank Report *Globalization, Growth and Poverty: Building an Inclusive World Economy*[26] suggests that more trade is correlated with higher economic growth. As the World Bank Report says, 'Globalization generally

---

23 *See* Department of Foreign Affairs and Trade, 'WTO Doha Round of Trade Negotiations Background Paper' <www.dfat.gov.au/trade/negotiations/consultations/wto_doha_trade_negoatiations_background_paper.pdf> (undated).

24 J. Bhagwati and A. Meyer 'Special Report: The poor's best hope – Trading for development; By invitation', *The Economist*, 22 June 2002, 24.

25 Doha Ministerial Declaration, WT/MIN(01)/DEC/1 <www.wto.org>, 20 November 2001.

26 World Bank, 'Globalization, Growth and Poverty: Building an Inclusive World Economy' <www.econ.worldbank.org/prr/globalization/text-2857/>, 2002.

reduces poverty because more integrated economies tend to grow faster and this growth is usually widely diffused'.[27]

The report points to a range of statistics – some impressive and others frightening:

> Countries that strongly increased their participation in global trade and investment include Brazil, China, Hungary, India, and Mexico. Some 24 developing countries – with 3 billion people – have doubled their ratio of trade to income over the past two decades. The rest of the developing world actually trades less today than it did 20 years ago. The more globalized developing countries have increased their per capita growth rate from 1 per cent in the 1960s, to 3 per cent in the 1970s, 4 per cent in the 1980s, and 5 per cent in the 1990s. Their growth rates now substantially exceed those of the rich countries: they are catching up just as during earlier waves of globalization there was convergence among OECD countries. While the new globalizers are beginning to catch up, much of the rest of the developing world – with about 2 billion people – is becoming marginalized. Their aggregate growth rate was actually negative in the 1990s.
>
> About 2 billion people live in countries that are not participating strongly in globalization, many of them in Africa and the Former Soviet Union (FSU). Their exports are usually confined to a narrow range of primary commodities. Such a concentration has made them highly prone to terms of trade shocks. There is also evidence that dependence upon primary commodity exports increases the risk of civil war.

However, both the World Bank Report and the Oxfam Report have claimed that trade barriers erected by wealthy countries have limited the capacity of poorer countries to join the international trading system.[28] This will severely impede development in these countries.

2.5.2 Development and democracy

In its Millennium Declaration, the UN stated that 'We resolve ... to create an environment – at the national and global levels alike – which is conducive to development and to the elimination of poverty. Success in meeting these objectives depends, *inter alia*, on good governance within each country. It also depends on good governance at the international level and on transparency in the financial, monetary and trading systems. We are committed

---

27 *See also* B. Hoekman, A. Mattoo, and P. English (eds), *Development, Trade, and the WTO* (World Bank, Washington, 2002).

28 The UN Secretary-General has made the same criticism. *See* K.A. Annan, 'Road map towards the implementation of the United Nations Millennium Declaration: Report of the Secretary-General', A/56/326, para. 137 <www.un.org/documents/ga/docs/56/a56326.pdf>. But see 'Special Report: The poor's best hope – Trading for development; By invitation', n. 24, which argues that the trade barriers of the poor countries against one another are more significant restraints on their own development than those imposed by the rich countries.

to an open, equitable, rule-based, predictable and non-discriminatory multilateral trading and financial system'.[29] The declaration also states that 'Men and women have the right to live their lives and raise their children in dignity, free from hunger and from the fear of violence, oppression or injustice. Democratic and participatory governance based on the will of the people best assures these rights'.

The relationship between development and democracy is a complex one, with the direction of the relationship one of its most hotly debated aspects. The UN in General Assembly Resolution 'Promotion of a democratic and equitable international order' states that 'democracy, development and respect for human rights and fundamental freedoms are interdependent and mutually reinforcing ...'.[30]

There is no hard and fast rule here. In Lipset's words, 'the socioeconomic correlations point to probabilities'.[31] Other factors are also influential – whether the country in question was a former British colony (or, on the other hand a French, Belgian, or Dutch one); ethno-linguistic fractionalization; historical incidents, for example, the allocation of Eastern Europe to the Soviet Union after the Second World War; percentage of GNP on military expenditure; and cultural factors. But the literature does recognize that development and democracy are interlinked. Lipset claims that '[w]ith a significant rise in national income, consumption becomes more equal, the middle class grows, more people have access to health care, the level of illiteracy drops, and more teenagers stay in secondary school. This occurs whether the society is Islamic or atheist, Marxist or market-oriented, African, Asian, or European'.[32]

Lipset[33] concludes that economic development is the single most important predictor of political democracy when other variables are controlled for: further, the more well to do a nation is, the greater the chance it will be able to sustain democracy.[34] 'People with more income, in complex and widely interdependent work situations, with more education, and more access to health and other services are more likely to ask for increased political freedom'.[35] With more economic complexity, citizen demands become more visible and patterns of politics arise which can accommodate them.

---

29 A/RES/55/2 <www.un.org/millennium/declaration/ares552e.htm>.

30 A/RES/56/151.

31 S.M. Lipset, K.-R. Seong, and J.C. Torres, 'A comparative analysis of the social requisites of democracy' (1993) 45 *International Social Science Journal* 155.

32 *Ibid*, p. 166. However the authors concede that the oil rich states are the exception, where a sharp increase in income does not necessarily lead to these consequences.

33 'A comparative analysis of the social requisites of democracy' (n. 31).

34 Lipset's analysis also finds that the level of coerciveness, based on the level of military expenditure, is inversely proportional to political democracy (here the military in third world countries is more likely to be focused on maintaining internal order than on external defence). 'Ironically, therefore, in Third World countries, spending heavily on defence is associated with political instability, not civil order'. Lipset is also careful to emphasize that economic development alone will not produce democratization: other factors will influence this. These include historical experiences, for example, whether or not a new nation experienced British rule (as opposed to French, Portuguese, Dutch, or Belgian rule). British rule is more likely to lead to democracy (though not inevitably as is shown by the examples of Burma, Bangladesh, Pakistan, Kenya, Nigeria, Tanzania, Uganda, and Ghana).

35 *Ibid*, p. 166.

Others support the view that development causes democracy. Diamond concludes that 'the more well-to-do the people of a country, on average, the more likely they will favor, achieve, and maintain a democratic system for their country ... The effects of economic development are not only powerful and consistent but often literally overwhelming'.[36] Others agree, while recognizing that the relationship is complicated by other factors. Burckhardt and Lewis-Beck suggest that one variable that needs to be considered is a nation's position in the world system. If core economies are those characterized by high wages, high profits and a capital-intensive nature, and those on the periphery have low wages, low profits, and are labour-intensive, then although it is clear that economic development 'substantially improves a nation's democratic prospects', the 'full magnitude of that effect depends on the location of the nation in the world system. As the nation moves from the core ... to the periphery, the effect diminishes. Even in the periphery, however, the effect remains statistically and substantively significant'.[37] Even those who disagree that development must precede democratization concede that democracies, once established, 'are likely to die in poor countries and certain to survive in wealthy ones'.[38]

Thus, even though the relationship between development and democracy is a complex and contested one, the link between the two is affirmed overall. Further, the correlation between development and democracy may be useful in determining which democracies will break down: for example, Haiti, many of the poorest African countries and the ex-Soviet republics in central Asia 'are unlikely candidates for stable democracy'.[39] This view is supported by recent work by the World Bank.[40] In a review of 25 post-communist countries of Central and Eastern Europe and the former Soviet Union, the study concludes that democracy has been an important precondition for economic reform. Although the two processes – political and economic liberalization – are strongly complementary, those countries which entered the transition process with more democratic institutions and greater civil liberties (a 'vibrant civil society') were able to implement faster and more comprehensive reform policies. At the top of the range are countries such as Hungary, Estonia, the Czech Republic, and Poland, while at the bottom are Tajikistan, Turkmenistan, Uzbekistan, and Azerbaijan.[41]

---

36 L.J. Diamond, 'Economic Development and Democracy Reconsidered' (1992) 36 *American Behavioral Scientist* 450 at 468.

37 R.E. Burkhart and M.S. Lewis-Beck, 'Comparative Democracy: The Economic Development Thesis' (1994) 88(4) *American Political Science Review* 903 at 907.

38 A. Przeworski and F. Limongi, 'Modernization: Theories and Facts' (1997) 49(2) *World Politics* 155 at 167. *See also* G. O'Donnell, *Modernization and Bureaucratic Authoritarianism: Studies in South American Politics* (Institute of International Studies, University of California, Berkeley, 1979), who also disagrees with Lipset's development thesis.

39 'A comparative analysis of the social requisites of democracy' (n. 31). On this basis, East Timor's democratic progress should be closely monitored.

40 J.-J. Dethier, H. Ghanem, and E. Zoli, *Does Democracy Facilitate the Economic Transition?* <www.worldbank.org> (1999).

41 The authors suggest that this is because 'given the heavy short-term costs entailed by economic liberalization policies, only democratically elected governments have the legitimacy to carry them out'. Further, the emergence of democratic political institutions changes the

It is true that other factors are important in determining the survival of democracy, in particular where democracy occurs 'prematurely'.[42] These include socio-economic factors such as a democratic political culture (including civilian control of the military), an external orientation of the military, the presence of a civil society and a supportive international environment. Countries with these factors include Costa Rica and Botswana. Cases where the successful promotion of development has failed to sustain democracy include Argentina, Burma, Fiji, Ghana, Guatemala, Indonesia, Nigeria, Peru, the Philippines, South Korea, Thailand, and Turkey. Development in these countries could not compensate for 'serious weaknesses in non-socio-economic factors'.[43]

However the overall relationship between development and democracy makes successful participation in the international trading system essential for developing countries.

2.5.3 Democracy and peace

Both international organizations and the literature confirm the close link between democracy and peace. Regional organizations make this connection in the context of upholding democracy: the preamble to the Charter of the Organization of American States (OAS), for example, states that 'representative democracy is an indispensable condition for the stability, peace and development of the region'. Article 2(g) states that an essential purpose of the OAS is 'To eradicate extreme poverty, which constitutes an obstacle to the full democratic development of the peoples of the hemisphere'; Article 12 of the Inter-American Democratic Charter provides that '[p]overty, illiteracy and low levels of human development are factors that adversely affect the consolidation of democracy'.[44]

The literature points to a strong argument that the spread of democracy is conducive to world peace and thus that the international community

---

Contd.
incentives for rent-seeking by those in power, and market oriented reforms require the introduction of changes in the legal and constitutional framework. The study notes in particular that civil society institutions were weaker in the former Soviet Union countries (where there was more of a battle between reformers and elites) than in the Central and Eastern European countries.

42 A. Siaroff, 'Premature Democracies, the promotion of development and political-cultural factors,' (1999) 20(2) *Third World Quarterly* 405. 'Prematurity' is determined by measuring whether or not each particular country in the study passes the threshold for four variables of human development: adult literacy; infant mortality; GNP per capita; and the share of family farms, that is, the percentage of total land holdings which are either owned by individual families or leased by tenant farmers without making them socially and economically dependent on the landowner.

43 Siaroff in fact argues that the successful promotion of development only assists the survival of democracy in 'premature' democracies in a 'modest, statistically insignificant way', with these other factors at least as important

44 The OAS's AG/Res. 1782 (XXXI-O/01 of 2001 notes the 'marked interdependence of democracy, economic and social development, and human rights …' (preamble). The same recognition of a link between development and democracy is also evident in the documents of the UN.

should take an active role in its achievement.[45] Democratization does reduce the risk of a country being involved in war, either as a target or as an initiator. 'Shared power between the executive and legislature, each largely staffed by officials pressured by public opinion' is the aspect of democratization which reduces the probability of war: 'to the extent that changes towards democracy bring with them constraints on the executive branch of government, the attendant reduction in the risk of war appears quite robust'.[46]

Dixon suggests that 'just as important as the presence of competition is the presence of rules, procedures or guidelines for setting its boundaries which leads to 'the distinctively circumscribed nature of democratic competition'. An example is political competition for office where all players agree not to use physical violence or coercion to secure victory. Thus 'the prevailing mode of democratic competition, particularly among politicians and other political elites, is non-violent. The internalization of this norm of bounded competition in the realm of domestic affairs means that it is more readily adopted in the sphere of foreign affairs, where the competition, again, is over incompatible material interests and values. And politicians and other elites have routinely had much experience with the norm in domestic dispute resolution. This rationale 'offers an unambiguous explanation for the democratic peace based on the role of shared democratic norms in averting military hostilities'.[47] Further, it means that shared democratic norms directly enhance the prospects of peaceful settlement. Further, the most reliable path to stable *domestic* peace in the long run is to democratize as much as possible, even though, in the short run, a democratizing country will have to live through an unsettling period of change.[48]

Authoritarian, repressive regimes, on the other hand, are a threat to world peace. Not only do they create suffering and economic deprivation at

---

45 B. Bueno de Mesquita, J.D. Morrow, R.M. Silverson, and A. Smith, 'An Institutional Explanation of the Democratic Peace' (1999) 93(4) *American Political Science Review* 791 at 791. *See also* T.C. Morgan and S.H. Campbell, 'Domestic Structure, Decisional Constraints, and War: So Why Kant Democracies Fight?' (1991) 35(2) *Journal of Conflict Resolution* 187; J. Rawls, *The Law of Peoples* (Harvard University Press, Cambridge, Massachusetts, 1999) at p. 51; and J.M. Owen, 'How Liberalism Produces Democratic Peace' (1994) 19(2) *International Security* 87. There are some who contest the relationship between democracy and peace: *see*, for example, E. Mansfield and J. Snyder, 'Democratization and the Danger of War,' (1995) 20(1) *International Security* 5, who argue that states *undergoing* a democratization process are more war-prone (to interstate wars) than those who have not undergone a regime change. However these authors also conclude that 'in the long run, the enlargement of the zone of stable democracy will probably enhance the prospects for peace' (at 38). Critics of their analysis, who support the view that there is a positive relationship between democracy and peace, claim that they fail to take into account data on democratization after 1980 (when many Latin American military dictatorships democratized and when the communist countries of Eastern Europe did the same: *see* R. Wolf, 'Correspondence' (1996) 20(4) *International Security* 176; E. Weede (untitled) at 180 and A.J. Enterline, 'Driving while Democratizing (DWD)' 183, both in the same volume.

46 M.D. Ward and K.S. Glenditsch, 'Democratizing for Peace' (1998) 92(1) *American Political Science Review* 51. What is relevant is 'the universal trait of bounded competition'.

47 *See* W.J. Dixon, 'Democracy and the peaceful settlement of international conflict' (1994) 88(1) *American Political Science Review* 14.

48 H. Hegre, T. Ellingsen, S. Gates, and N. Petter Gleditsch, 'Toward a Democratic Civil Peace? Democracy, Political Change, and Civil War, 1816–1992' (2001) 95 *American Political Science Review* 33.

the domestic level, but also the rapidly expanding refugee flows from such countries have security implications for neighbouring countries.[49] As demonstrated by events in the Great Lakes Region of Central Africa, refugee warriors can regionalize the conflict of their country of origin by employing refugee camps in other countries as a base of operations and refugees as a shield.[50]

The international legal system is built around the notion of state sovereignty, with the corresponding requirement of non-intervention in the domestic affairs of states.[51] It is tempting, therefore, to see the failure of democracy within a state – and internal conflict in general – as affecting nobody else but the unfortunate population of the state concerned. Although this assumption has probably never been valid, the intensifying trend towards globalization has made it preposterous. In the context of considering action by the UN Security Council under Chapter VII of the Charter,[52] even cautious analysts argue that 'the Security Council may legitimately consider the threat to or removal of a democratically elected government by a force internal to the State in question as a factor which could, together with other factors such as mass killings or refugee flows,[53] in some circumstances *contribute* to a threat to international peace and security under recently expanded conceptions of that term'.[54]

The Security Council has in fact found a threat to peace and security in situations where the internal situation gave rise to massive refugee flows, for example, Iraq (repression of the Kurdish minority)[55] and a violent coup in Haiti.[56] In the latter case, following the failure of sanctions to dislodge

---

49 G. Loescher, *Refugee Movements and International Security* (Adelphi Paper 268, Brasseys, for the International Institute for Strategic Studies, London, 1992). Loescher concludes that 'Refugee warriors invite military retaliation, complicate relations with other states, and threaten the host states and the security of their citizens. As a result, host countries have often been unwillingly drawn into conflicts with their neighbours'. An example is the destruction wreaked on south Lebanon in Israeli reprisals for Palestinian raids. Warring factions have served as surrogates of the superpowers, from whom they have received assistance in the form of arms, economic assistance, and military training. Because of this, the number of people likely to cross borders due to a combination of political strife, economic hardship, and environmental degradation is likely to increase.

50 J. Milner, *Sharing the Security Burden: Towards the Convergence of Refugee Protection and State Security* (RSC Working Paper No. 4, Refugees Study Centre, University of Oxford, 2000).

51 *See* Articles 2(4) and 2(7) of the United Nations Charter.

52 Chapter VII provides for the UN Security Council to authorize coercive intervention by the UN in the event that the Council makes a determination that the conduct of a State amounts to a 'threat to (international) peace and security'.

53 Surely a matter of international concern in any case, since the obligations of countries are governed by the 1951 Convention for the Protection of Refugees.

54 *See*, for example, M. Byers and S. Chesterman ' "You, the People": pro-democratic intervention in international law,' in G.H. Fox and B.R. Roth (eds), *Democratic Governance and International Law* (Cambridge University Press, Cambridge, 2000), p. 259 at 283.

55 In the case of Iraq, most of the ten states supporting Security Council Resolution 688 of 5 April 1991 based this on the view that the refugee problem was a threat to peace and security: J.E. Stromseth, 'Iraq's Repression of its Civilian Population: Collective Responses and Continuing Challenges', in L.F. Damrosch (ed.), *Enforcing Restraint: Collective Intervention in Internal Conflicts* (Council on Foreign Relations Press, New York, 1993), p. 77. Further, both Turkey and Iran called for international assistance, characterizing the cross-border movements as a threat to the security and stability of the region.

56 For a description of the circumstances giving rise to large numbers of refugees *see* S. Zaidi, 'Humanitarian Effects of the Coup and Sanctions in Haiti', in T.G. Weiss, D. Cortright, G.A. Lopez,

the military regime over a period of three years, the Security Council passed Resolution 841 of 1993, which concluded that in these 'unique and exceptional circumstances' the continuation of the 'humanitarian crisis, including mass displacements of population' threatened international peace and security in the region.[57] Other situations in which the security council has found a threat to peace and security include starvation (Somalia),[58] genocide and serious humanitarian crises (Rwanda, Burundi, and Zaire), and civil wars (Liberia and Angola).[59] Such situations occur in countries where democracy is spectacularly missing or threatened. Consistently with this changing international landscape, the Security Council has expanded its definition of what constitutes a threat to the peace: 'The non-military sources of instability in the *economic*, social, humanitarian and ecological fields have become threats to peace and security'.[60]

2.5.4 The costs of conflict

Not enough work has been done on the economic costs of conflict. The standout publication by the Carnegie Commission, which considers the external costs of several conflicts,[61] points to the need for further work in this area.[62] While it is relatively straightforward to estimate military costs, economic costs are more difficult to quantify, even though they are there. A few examples highlight this. In the case of Bosnia, the Commission notes that at the end of the war exports had slipped to ten percent of

---

Contd.
and L. Minear (eds), *Political Gain and Civilian Pain: Humanitarian Impacts of Economic Sanctions* (Rowman & Littlefield Publishers, Lanham, MD, 1997), p. 189.

57 Although this finding has been open to some criticism: B. R. Roth, *Governmental Illegitimacy in International Law* (Oxford University Press, New York, 1999); *see also* ' "You, the People": pro-democratic intervention in international law' (n. 54). Byers and Chesterman think that the determination in the Haitian case was 'clearly an atypical conception of a threat to international peace and security'.

58 Amartya Sen hypothesizes that famines are less likely to occur in democratic countries: 'no substantial famine has ever occurred in any independent country with a democratic form of government and a relatively free press'. A. Sen, *Development as Freedom* (Alfred A Knopf, New York, 1999), p. 152. Sen notes the importance which political freedoms play through both instrumental and constructive roles: in providing both incentives and information relevant to solving economic problems, in conceptualizing economic needs through public debates and discussions, and in publicly pressuring governments to deal with economic disasters.

59 N.D. White, *Keeping the Peace: The United Nations and the maintenance of international peace and security* (2nd edn, Manchester University Press, Manchester, 1997).

60 *See* 'Note by the President of the Security Council' UN Doc S/23500, 31 January 1992, p. 3 (emphasis added).

61 Bosnia, Macedonia, Slovakia, the Persian Gulf, Cambodia, Rwanda, Somalia, Haiti, and El Salvador.

62 M.E. Brown and R.N. Rosecrance (eds), *The Costs of Conflict: Prevention and Cure in the Global Arena* (Carnegie Commission on Preventing Deadly Conflict, Rowman & Littlefield, New York, 1999). The Report notes that 'few analysts have attempted to estimate the costs of violent conflicts', but, in the case of internal costs, refers the reader to J.M. Richardson, Jr. and S.W.R. de A. Samarasinghe, 'Measuring the Economic Dimensions of Sri Lanka's Ethnic Conflict' in Samarasinghe and R. Coughlan (eds), *Economic Dimensions of Ethnic Conflict* (London, Pinter Publishers, 1991); and M. Cranna (ed.), *The True Cost of Conflict: Seven Recent Wars and Their Effects on Society* (New Press, New York, 1994).

their pre-war level, but states that the implications of the war for trade throughout the region were 'largely immeasurable'.[63] Similarly, in the case of Rwanda, the report notes that economic opportunity costs (e.g. tourism and agricultural losses and particularly environmental damage) are hard to quantify.[64]

The Gulf War caused severe environmental damage, with deliberately lit oil fires causing atmospheric poisoning from Eastern Europe to India, where acid rain destroyed crops.[65] The costs of this in lost production have not been quantified. In the case of Somalia, 'the refugee crisis disrupted trade, including non-monetarized trade, which is important in subsistence areas and inherently difficult to estimate'.[66] In very poor countries, such as Cambodia, Rwanda, and Somalia, the authors note that lucrative trade ventures are not affected by conflict because they do not exist in the first place.[67] What this may mean, however, is that opportunities for development have been foregone for the duration of the war. Cambodia's productivity must also be affected by its crippling legacy of landmines, and 'the rising level of foreign investment, particularly by the Association of Southeast Asian Nations (ASEAN), suggests that business and investment ventures were lost for the regional economy as a whole due to the instability of the war'.[68]

A study by the World Bank has already identified significant economic ripple effects from civil wars. In the source country, these destroy human capital, divert funds into weapons rather than into activities that have an investment return, drive away foreign direct investment and inhibit market exchanges. But neighbours are also affected: civil wars are likely to disrupt trade, sever supply lines for inputs, create collateral damage from battlefields, and generate refugee costs. The study concludes that civil war creates a significant (negative) influence on short-run growth within the country and its neighbours, with less clear-cut evidence of a long-run effect.[69]

The Carnegie Commission has identified economic costs among five main sets of costs of intrastate conflict to outsiders.[70] The Commission identifies direct economic costs and economic opportunity costs: lost investment in

---

[63] A.K. Talentino, 'Bosnia', in *The Costs of Conflict: Prevention and Cure in the Global Arena* (n. 62), p. 25 at 45.

[64] A.K. Talentino, 'Rwanda', in *The Costs of Conflict: Prevention and Cure in the Global Arena*, p. 53 at 68.

[65] M. Blakley, 'The Persian Gulf', in *The Costs of Conflict: Prevention and Cure in the Global Arena*, p. 109 at 124.

[66] M. Blakley, 'Somalia' in *The Costs of Conflict: Prevention and Cure in the Global Arena*, p. 83 at 86.

[67] See the entries by Talentino and Blakley (n. 63–65), and Talentino, 'Cambodia', in *The Costs of Conflict: Prevention and Cure in the Global Arena*, p. 173, at 190.

[68] A.K. Talentino, 'Cambodia' in *The Costs of Conflict: Prevention and Cure in the Global Arena*, at 191.

[69] *See* J.C. Murdoch and T. Sandler, *Economic Growth, Civil Wars and Spatial Spillovers* <www.worldbank.org/research/conflict/papers/spillovers.htm>, 2001. This paper was prepared for the World Bank's research program 'The Economics of Crime and Violence'.

[70] Others are refugee costs, military costs, instability costs and costs associated with international humanitarian operations, conflict resolution and management operations. The Commission does not analyse the costs of conflict to the parties themselves – 'in terms of loss of life, damaged facilities, or production foregone', these costs being hard to measure and because the study assumes outside powers become involved through selfish reasons. The inclusion of costs to the parties would make an even stronger case for early prevention. *Ibid.*, p. 2.

local and joint projects; lost imports (e.g. strategic resources such as oil); lost export markets; and disruptions to labour supplies. Indirect costs may affect the region as a whole: if the region is considered unstable then capital costs may be higher, loans be harder to get, inflation higher. Costs are not confined to the region but can impose a heavy burden on distant countries as well.

2.5.5 Hurdles for developing countries

Joining the globalization process is not without difficulties. On one view, '[t]he globalisation prescription being offered to poor countries shares many characteristics with the (structural) adjustment model. Just as aid has to be used to mitigate the social costs of adjustment, it is now being used to mitigate the costs of rapid globalization'.[71]

Where unpopular measures have to be taken to reform the economy (in particular where costs of basic commodities rise and there is less money for delivery of basic services such as health and education), it may seem that a stable and authoritarian government will be the most effective in implementing these: commenting on fledgling democracy movements in Africa, one analyst notes that '[t]he difficulty of performing a delicate balancing act between domestic demands for some economic relief and external pressures for austerity may very well exceed the capacities of some of Africa's recently elected leaders. Some may be tempted to revert to repressive and authoritarian methods ... Others may simply be swept aside, with military forces stepping back in to "restore order" or safeguard their own corporate interests ... For those inclined to give pre-eminence to structural adjustment over parliamentary forms of rule, a reversion to military government may appear unavoidable in certain circumstances'.[72] It is easy to overlook the fact that the economies of the developed world grew slowly and usually enjoyed considerable economic protection and/or privileged access to wider markets.[73]

Special measures are therefore required to assist developing countries to maintain the necessary pace of development and thus to maintain the momentum to democratize fully. This means providing aid programs that provide a social services safety net if harsh structural adjustment measures have to be put in place, or if exports fail. But the difficulties outlined above serve also to emphasise the priority to be put on reforming the trading system to allow developing countries to participate in ways beneficial to their economic development.

---

71 J. Randel, T. German, and D. Ewing (eds), *The Reality of Aid 2000: An Independent Review of Poverty Reduction and Development Assistance* (The Reality of Aid Project, Earthscan Publications Ltd, London, 2000), p. 16.

72 E. Harsch, 'Structural adjustment and Africa's democracy movements' (1993) 40(4) *Africa Today* 7 at 16. *See also* G. Joffe, 'Sovereignty and Intervention: The Perspective for the Developing World,' in M. Heiberg (ed.), *Subduing Sovereignty* (Pinter Publishers, London, 1994), p. 62.

73 *Ibid.*

2.6 Beyond the Nation State – Global Arguments for 'Making It so'

To date our argument has been framed within the familiar 'territory' of nation states. We have given reasons why individual states should live up to the promises they make. We have argued that it is in their interests to do so. However, the relative decline of sovereign states and the increasing emphasis on human rights suggest a different way of arguing for and against global policies such as trade liberalization, and the need for a redefined overarching policy, which takes into consideration the interconnectedness of all individuals and their well-being across the globe. Kant emphasizes such interconnectedness thus: 'national, international and cosmopolitical rights are so interconnected, that if any one of these three possible forms of the juridical relation fails to embody the essential principles that ought to regulate external freedom by law, the structure of legislation reared by the others will also be undermined, and the whole system would at last fall to pieces'.[74]

In this section, it is argued that the cosmopolitical idea can be usefully explored for its potential to provide a more inclusive approach to further reforms to the current global trade system. The present discussion on the 'new face of global trade' is consistent with the broader debate occurring in other major areas, such as democracy, peace, human rights and international law, over their models of governance.

The cosmopolitical (or cosmopolitan) idea is not a novelty, but rather it possesses an historical heritage that can be located in the intellectual climate of different ages.[75] Philosophers and contemporary theorists have engaged with the different strands of this extended tradition, which is generally identifiable with either Kant or the Stoics.[76] The tragedy of the Second World War prompted deep reflection and quite a deal of theorizing in various disciplines, especially on the issue of an open and inclusive society. This was to be based on the principles of liberty, equality and justice, and would help create, or rebuild, democracy within states.

The failure of historical communism in 1989 and consequent break-up in the former USSR generated a new impetus and attraction for the cosmopolitical idea. This found its place at the intersection of democratic politics and international relations, and was aided by expectations of an emergent new world order. The ensuing debate raised important questions about the type

---

[74] I. Kant, *The Philosophy of Law* translated by W. Hastie (T. & T. Clark, Edinburgh, 1887) p. 162.

[75] The use of 'cosmopolitical' derives from Kant's *ius cosmopoliticum, see* I. Kant, *The Philosophy of Law*, n. 74, pp. 226–228. This translation of the term is adopted both for its linguistic and philosophical nuances, and follows Bobbio's modern refinement of 'cosmopolitical right', which can be traced in a number of his major works in Italian, and in English, *The Age of Rights* (Polity, Cambridge, 1996). *See* T. Chataway, 'Where does the dove of peace fly?' (2001) 7(2) *CONVIVIO* 136–151; and D. Archibugi, 'Cosmopolitical Democracy' (2000) 4 *New Left Review* 137–150, where one author's reason for also preferring cosmopolitical is stated in footnote 7 on p. 143.

[76] T.J. Schlereth, 'Preface' and 'Prologue' in *The Cosmopolitan Ideal in Enlightenment Thought* (The University of Notre Dame Press, Notre Dame, 1977), pp. xi–xxv; and C.J. Friedrich, *The Philosophy of History in Historical Perspective* 2nd edn. The University of Chicago Press, Chicago & London, 1963), ch. IV, pp. 27–41.

of governance that would promote the extension of democracy between states.[77] Among the various definitions of the concept of democracy, which the Italian legal and political philosopher, Norberto Bobbio[78] provides, the following encapsulates some of the questions addressed in this chapter:

> If for democracy one understands, as it should to be understood, the system that allows the resolution of conflicts of interests and also of values peacefully, the solutions of the problems in today's society can only be found at a much broader level, which is the international. Today even the issue of distributive justice, and therefore of the correction to capitalist democracy… which remains the political program of social democracies, cannot be resolved other than on the international level, that is, in the relations between North and South. … Today, the future of democracy rests in its internationalization.[79]

More than internationalization, however, the cosmopolitical dimension of democracy indicates a model of political and legal organization that allows, or rather, requires citizens throughout the world to participate in the decision-making process in parallel with, and independently of, their own governments. Among those contemporary scholars who feature in this extended cosmopolitical tradition with its potential contribution to legal, political and moral philosophy, are Archibugi,[80] Bobbio, Derrida,[81] and Held.[82] In varying degrees they all take up the Kantian notion of 'cosmopolitical right'. Due limitations of space, only certain aspects by Bobbio and Held are discussed.

Bobbio maintains that one of the least studied aspects in Kant's *Perpetual Peace* is that of a third type of law designated as *ius cosmopoliticum*, or cosmopolitical right. This branch of law was introduced alongside domestic public law and public international law, which constituted the traditional partition. In his view, a *tertium genus* needed to be added to the traditional partition. The reason for this was that besides the relation between a State and its citizens, or the relation between a State and other States, the relation between each State and the citizens of other States, or conversely, the relation

---

[77] N. Bobbio, 'Il futuro della democrazia. Ci vuole un mondo che superi gli Stati' [The future of democracy. There is a need for a world beyond States] *La Stampa*, 16 November 1994.

[78] Bobbio (1909–) is Emeritus Professor at the University of Turin, and one of the leading theorists of democracy. On the question of 'unkept promises' see his *The Future of Democracy* (Polity, Cambridge, 1987), pp. 23–42; on human and social rights *The Age of Rights*, n. 75, and *Left and Right: The Significance of a Political Distinction* (Polity, Cambridge, 1996), pp. 60–71, and on ethics *In Praise of Meekness. Essays on Ethics and Politics* (Polity, Cambridge, 2000).

[79] N. Bobbio, 'Questioni di democrazia' [Questions about democracy] (1989) 17 *Sisifo* pp. 1–8.

[80] D. Archibugi, 'Cosmopolitical Democracy' (2000) *New Left Review* pp. 137–150; D. Archibugi and D. Held (eds), *Cosmopolitan Democracy. An Agenda for a New World Order* (Polity, Cambridge, 1995), and D. Archibugi, D. Held, and M. Köhler (eds), *Re-imagining Political Community. Studies in Cosmopolitan Democracy* (Polity, Cambridge, 1998).

[81] J. Derrida, 'The right to Philosophy from a Cosmopolitical Point of View' (1994) IV *Surfaces*, <http:///A | /Derrida on cosmopolitical_files/derrida.htm>.

[82] D. Held, 'Law of States, Law of Peoples: Three Models of Sovereignty' (2002) 8 *Legal Theory* 1–44.

between citizens of a State different from one's own with other States, must also be considered.

Another relevant and related aspect is that of the reciprocity relation between the right of entry of a foreign citizen and the duty of hospitality of the State visited. For Kant the fundamental principle of cosmopolitical right is that of 'universal hospitality', or what can also be defined as a duty of reciprocity. This consists on the one hand, of the right of every foreign citizen visiting another State not to be treated in a hostile way, and on the other, of the obligation of the visitor not to exploit such hospitality by transforming the visit into a conquest. These reciprocal rights and duties of States and individuals, respectively, are aimed at the establishment of universal peace. Moreover, allowing free access to citizens of other States would favour commerce and, as Kant argued, 'the commercial spirit cannot coexist with war and sooner or later this takes hold of every population'. From a reciprocal position, the duty of a visitor not to appropriate any territory of the host state without its consent eliminates one of the forms of excessive use of violence. At certain times, this process was justified by some colonizing populations as 'redounding to the world's benefit'. Kant also uses the principle of cosmopolitical right to condemn as inconsistent at law two extreme behaviours. The first is the behaviour of barbarians who do not respect the duty of active hospitality, and the other is that of civilized individuals who violate the obligation passive hospitality entails.

Kant prefigured the right all individuals to be citizens not only of their own State, but also of the whole world. He regarded the earth as a potential global city, precisely like a cosmopolis. Kant concludes that it is only with regard to the last type of relation, that is, the relation between States and individuals of other States, that the universal legal system, or cosmopolis, represents the fourth and final phase of his general legal system. He contended that following the state of nature (Hobbes), where no right exists other than the private, in a civil State there is a right between individuals, which is regulated by domestic public law; and by extension in the international system, this is regulated by international public law. Accordingly, through cosmopolitical right, individuals across the globe can become holders of rights and duties beyond their status as subjects or citizens of a particular country or state. In effect, the premises for individuals, and no longer only States, to become legal subjects at international law were established by the 1948 Universal Declaration of Human Rights, which enabled the transition to a new phase in international law to begin. This process also extended the right of all peoples to the right of all individuals.

Bobbio raises the suggestive force of cosmopolitical right by acknowledging its contemporary importance and implications for human rights, democracy, and peace, as follows: 'subjects become citizens when their fundamental rights are recognized. There will only be stable peace, peace that no longer has war as an alternative, when there are citizens not only of different states but also of the world that is organized into a legal and democratic system'.[83]

---

[83] N. Bobbio, 'Il futuro della democrazia. Ci vuole un mondo che superi gli Stati' [The future of democracy. There is a need for a world beyond States] *La Stampa*, 16 November 1994.

It is only through such recognition that all individuals can be guaranteed the basic social and economic well-being in a non-violent world. This would allow everyone to live in dignity and in peace within democratic states, which are also part of a fully democratized international community.

Held is also a supporter of the Kantian idea, which he refers to as 'cosmopolitanism'. In his most recently published piece, he defines cosmopolitanism as 'the moral and political outlook that offers the best prospects of overcoming the problems and limits of classic and liberal sovereignty'.[84]

In his 'Cosmopolitan Sovereignty' Held contends that 'human beings are in a fundamental sense equal and that they deserve equal political treatment, that is, equal care and consideration of their agency irrespective of the community in which they were born or brought up'.[85] He also provides a framework for delineating a set of 'Cosmopolitan Principles' by which to achieve such a goal. These are as follows:

(1) equal worth and dignity;
(2) active agency;
(3) personal responsibility and accountability;
(4) consent;
(5) reflexive deliberation and collective decision-making through voting procedures;
(6) inclusiveness and subsidiarity;
(7) avoidance of serious harm and the amelioration of urgent need.

After discussing the two well-known models of sovereignty, classic and liberal, and their transformations thus far, with respect to the third, or cosmopolitan, he contends that 'there are tendencies at work seeking to create new forms of public life and new ways of debating regional and global issues'.[86] These are gradually promoting changes to certain established practices of multinational corporations and other international institutions aimed at attaining greater accountability and transparency, which will contribute to the realization of a cosmopolitan order.

In similar vein, Sampford has argued that the processes of globalization should lead us to reconsider and reconceive liberal democratic values. He has argued that profound changes in national and international governance are being wrought by the forces of 'globalization'. These changes are as profound and far reaching as those of the seventeenth and eighteenth centuries which saw the rise of the strong sovereign state and its gradual and partial civilization by enlightenment and post-enlightenment liberal and social democratic values – liberty, equality, citizenship, democracy, the rule of law, human rights, and the environment. The technological, economic, and political forces collectively called 'globalization' have undermined the assumption of the strong state as the context for political debate about the balancing and realizing of liberal and social democratic values. This has led

---

84 Held, 'Law of States', n. 82, p. 39.
85 *Ibid.*, p. 23.
86 *Ibid.*, p. 39.

some to ignore important liberal democratic values and others to bolster the sovereign state as the only institutional means for defending those values. Others argue that we need new institutions or newly democratized institutions that can realize liberal and social democratic values on a global scale. However, there is a weakness in such arguments. Liberal democratic values were created in and for strong sovereign states. Citizenship, rights, democracy, welfare and community have clear reference to sovereign states but seem to lack apparent application in a larger, more diffuse global world. For him, the challenge facing us is to reconceive our liberal and social democratic values as genuinely global values and then frame the institutions that will sustain and advance them.[87]

Cosmopolitical approaches such as these have application to all areas of governance in a globalizing world – especially the governance of the global trade system. They provide an important alternative to the state-based arguments in the body of this chapter that are grounded in the normative obligations and national interests of nation states. Cosmopolitical discourse recognizes the interconnectedness of all human beings and their right to co-habit the globe. It encourages the parallel development of democracy within and among states, and the pursuit of peace through dialogic engagement and resolution of conflict. This process in turn requires that existing, as well as newly created international institutions, economic, political, or legal, be endowed with the necessary authority, democratically acquired, so as to enable implementation of a system of global governance underpinned by democratic principles and values. Among its core aims there are those of nonviolence, inclusiveness, accountability, and transparency, without which neither domestic nor global democracy can fulfil its objectives. With regard to the interconnectedness of cosmopolitical democracy, and the human rights protection that it can warrant, the following passage from Kant's *Perpetual Peace* has contemporary applicability: 'The peoples of the earth have thus entered in varying degrees into a universal community, and it has developed to the point where a violation of rights in *one* part of the world is felt *everywhere*'.[88]

Once we enter cosmopolitical discourse, arguments about the benefits of trade liberalization take on a new dimension. The reasoning shifts from the duties and interests of developed nations to the rights and interests of the citizens of developing nations. The arguments put forward in the body of the chapter remain. The representatives of developed nations should tell the truth and should not undermine their promises as a matter of integrity, because their citizens benefit if the citizens of developing nations are better off. However, the most powerful argument is the claim itself – that the impoverished peoples of the world are equally deserving of our concern and respect and their welfare is important to us all. If liberalizing global

---

87 Sampford, 'Sovereignty and Intervention,' in Campbell and Leiser (eds), *Human Rights in Theory and Practice* (Ashgate, London, 2001).

88 I. Kant, in H. Reiss (ed.), *Kant's Political Writings* (Cambridge University Press, Cambridge, 1977), pp. 107–8, original emphasis.

trade can benefit the least well off, then that is the strongest argument for trade liberalization and for making the promise so!

2.7 Conclusion

Diplomats and company executives from the developed world make big claims about the benefits of trade liberalization to the peoples of the developing world. However, at the same time, sophisticated trade negotiators from developed countries seek to maximize the benefits that their own countries achieve, potentially negating the promised benefits. This has the potential to make liars out of their proselytizing colleagues – and realize the nightmare scenarios portrayed by the opponents of trade liberalization. Whether the promises of trade liberalization are realized is not just a matter of prediction but of action.

We have argued that there are three sets of reasons why the developed world should work to ensure that trade liberalization lives up to its promises. First, there are normative issues of integrity – of not making liars of ourselves, of not deceiving those who are at a disadvantage in knowledge and power. Second, there are issues of self interest – the developed world will be a safer and more secure place if the lives of those in developing nations are secure and improving.

Thirdly, examining the link between trade and development, development and democracy, and the interconnection between democracy, peace, and human rights, it becomes evident that there is an urgent need to formulate policies that ensure the participation of *all* individuals in the benefits of globalization. Prosperous states should act to strengthen rather than undermine the promises of global trade, whose fundamental aim is to help create the basic social and economic conditions that will allow everyone to live with dignity and in peace. This would enhance the likelihood of national, regional, and global stability, and in the long term contribute to the attainment of the cosmopolitical ideal.

3. The Multilateral Trading System at Risk? Three Challenges to the World Trade Organization

Ann Capling

The architects of the postwar reconstruction had two main objectives with respect to the restoration of the multilateral trade system. Their first and most important aim was to prevent a retreat to the discriminatory economic blocs that had characterized international commercial relations before the war. Their second objective was to promote economic recovery and growth through the promotion of international trade. The challenge was to establish rules that enabled a compromise between the quest for open and non-discriminatory markets and the domestic welfare and development objectives of states. This compromise, which established a middle ground between various forms of Keynesian domestic interventionism and unfettered economic liberalism, has been aptly described by Ruggie as 'embedded liberalism'.[1]

These rules were embodied in the charter for the International Trade Organization (ITO), which was to be the third pillar of the Bretton Woods system alongside the International Monetary Fund (IMF), and the International Bank for Reconstruction and Development. Due to opposition in the US Senate, the ITO never came into being. Instead, rules on commercial policy were extracted from the ITO charter and incorporated into a General Agreement on Tariffs and Trade (GATT). As Gardner commented in 1956, the GATT was very much a 'slender reed' on which to base the establishment of the multilateral trade system.[2] With no formal organizational status, no administrative capacity to deal with problems between meetings of the 'contracting parties', and only a tiny secretariat to provide support for its activities, the viability of the GATT depended on the willingness of participants to adapt trade rules in response to the changing nature of the international political economy.

---

1 J.G. Ruggie, 'International Regimes, Transactions and Change: Embedded Liberalism in the Postwar Economic Order', (1982) 2 *International Organisation* 396.
2 R.N. Gardner, *Sterling Dollar Diplomacy* (Clarendon, Oxford, 1956), pp. 379–80.

Notwithstanding the GATT's impermanence, the 'slender reed grew into a strong plant'.[3] Its membership grew steadily from the original 23 contracting parties in 1947 to 103 countries by the commencement of the Uruguay Round of multilateral trade negotiations in 1986. Along with this steady expansion, new GATT rules were established in response to the interests of its signatories and transformations in the international political economy. From its origins as an agreement to discipline the use of tariffs, GATT rules grew to embrace non-tariff barriers to trade in the 1970s. During the Uruguay Round, the GATT was expanded to include new rules for agricultural trade, which had been effectively excluded from the rules that covered trade in manufactured goods. In addition, two new agreements were established to stand alongside the GATT: the General Agreement for Trade in Services (GATS), and the agreement on Trade-Related Aspects of Intellectual Property (TRIPs). Countries involved in the Uruguay Round also agreed to establish the World Trade Organization (WTO) in 1995, in order to provide a formal institutional structure for the GATT, GATS, and TRIPs, as well as the new dispute settlement process.

Like the GATT before it, the WTO's relevance will depend on its willingness and capacity to respond to the needs of its members and the problems and opportunities posed by globalization. Paradoxically, while the WTO enjoys a much stronger organizational footing than the GATT, it is struggling to contend with new pressures and challenges from both outside and within the organization. This chapter outlines the three most pressing and significant of these challenges. The first, and possibly most intractable of these, is the apparent decline of American leadership in the multilateral trade system. Since the mid-1980s, the United States has cast off its historic opposition to discriminatory trade agreements, in favour of regional and bilateral agreements. This has been underscored by the sharply unilateralist turn in American foreign policy since the election of President George W. Bush in 2000. The second challenge comes from outside the WTO from a wide variety of non-governmental organizations (NGOs), including civil society organizations and businesses, which are seeking opportunities for direct participation in the WTO and its processes. The third challenge comes from within, and relates to internal governance issues within the WTO, especially with respect to concerns among developing countries that the trade negotiation process marginalizes all but the most powerful members of the WTO.

Failure by the WTO and its member states to respond effectively to these challenges will have serious consequences for the legitimacy and viability of the multilateral trade system. The contemporary preoccupation with 'free trade' among defenders and detractors of the WTO alike has undermined a more general appreciation and understanding of the importance of a multilateral rules-based system for the conduct of international trade. Before turning to a discussion of the challenges confronting the WTO, it is worth reminding ourselves of what is fundamentally at stake here.[4]

---

3 G. Curzon, *Multilateral Commercial Diplomacy* (Michael Joseph, London, 1965), p. 33.

4 The following section is drawn from the introductory chapter in A. Capling, *Australia and the Global Trade System: From Havana to Seattle* (Cambridge University Press, Cambridge, 2001).

Despite its flaws, a multilateral 'rules-based' system of trade provides many benefits, especially for small and medium-sized countries, which lack economic and political power in the international economy. Perhaps the most important aspect of the multilateral trade system is the way that it helps to constrain the behaviour of the more powerful states. Indeed to the extent that multilateral rules for trade exist at all, the weak benefit. To be sure, the largest and most powerful states have exercised the most influence in the multilateral trade system. But it is also true that the system gives small countries a greater opportunity to pursue and protect their trade interests than would otherwise be the case. Of central importance here are the 'rules' for multilateral trade that give small states some protection against discrimination by large powers.

The norms of the multilateral trade system also help to protect small states. For instance, the emphasis on transparency insofar as the trade policies of members are concerned is a benefit to states that do not have the bureaucratic resources or capacity to dig out detailed commercial policy information about their trade partners. The Trade Policy Review Mechanism and other institutional processes allow smaller states to seek such information and to press for changes in the trade policies of other states, or in the rules of the system itself.[5]

Another benefit of the multilateral system relates to the fact that smaller countries rarely have the market power that enables them to negotiate improved market access on a bilateral basis. Thus the multilateral system with its norms of non-discrimination and reciprocity, and the Uruguay Round precedent of comprehensive negotiations across many different sectors, affords small and medium countries more opportunities for improved market access than they would otherwise be able to negotiate bilaterally.[6]

The most important aspect of multilateralism is the norm of non-discrimination: the principle that a nation treats all its trade partners equally and impartially. Non-discrimination has enabled the multilateral trade system to facilitate international economic cooperation by promoting trade, by introducing predictability and transparency in trade relations, and by providing mechanisms for the resolution of disputes. Thus, the system has played an important role in the management of conflict and the fostering of cooperation in the face of competing claims and demands.

But the WTO does not exist simply to provide 'order' in international relations: it also enables nation states to express and negotiate their differences, while understanding that these differences cannot always be fully reconciled. As Robert Wolfe has argued, the purpose of the WTO is to find ways to reconcile difference not to remove it, precisely because states 'want

---

[5] The Trade Policy Review Mechanism examines the impact on the trade system of the trade policies and practices of WTO members. The process involves the preparation of reports by the government under review and the WTO Secretariat, which are made available to all members. The objective is to provide information to other member states, not to challenge the WTO 'legality' of particular trade measures.

[6] For an exposition of the rules and norms of the multilateral trade system *see* J.A. Finlayson and M.W. Zacher, 'The GATT and the Regulation of Trade Barriers: Regime Dynamics and Functions' (1981) 4 *International Organisation*.

to retain the ability to regulate in the national interest, to allow the process of domestic dialogue to have a determinative influence on policy'.[7]

3.1 The Decline of American Leadership

The United States has played a central role in creating and driving forward the multilateral trade system since the Second World War. While the multilateral system has been collectively created and maintained, it has depended on American leadership, especially to give impetus to multilateral trade negotiations.[8] To be sure, the European Union and Japan have the capacity to effectively 'veto' American proposals, but neither of them has ever sought to set the multilateral trade agenda in the same manner that Washington has. And WTO newcomer China is not likely to seek to exercise any more power or influence in the system than the European Union or Japan presently does. In that sense, the United States remains the unchallenged superpower in the global trade system, which is precisely the reason why the decline of American interest in multilateralism is so troubling.

3.1.1 The shift away from multilateralism

This waning of American interest was first evident in the early 1980s as US trade policy became increasingly strategic, bilateral, and 'results-oriented'. In an historic departure from its traditional commitment to multilateralism, the United States negotiated two new discriminatory trade agreements. First was a bilateral agreement with Canada in 1989, which was followed in 1994 by the North American Free Trade Agreement (NAFTA) with Canada and Mexico. Since NAFTA, Washington has promoted the establishment of a Free Trade Area of the Americas, a hemispheric trade agreement that includes 34 countries in North and South America. Most recently, the United States has negotiated bilateral agreements with Singapore and Chile, and signalled its interest in negotiating similar agreements with countries in Latin America, Africa, and possibly Australia.[9] The very nature of bilateral agreements entails preferential access for parties to the agreement and discrimination against all others. This shift in American trade policy towards bilateral and regional trade agreements constitutes an unprecedented retreat from its commitment to multilateralism and its central principle of non-discrimination and most-favoured-nation treatment.

---

7 R. Wolfe, 'The World Trade Organisation', in B. Hocking and S. McGuire (eds), *Trade Politics* (Routledge, London, 1999), p. 222.

8 For an elaboration of this point *see* R. Higgott, 'Toward a Nonhegemonic IPE: An Antipodean Perspective', in C.N. Murphy and R. Tooze (eds), *The New International Political Economy* (Lynne Rienner Press, Boulder, 1991).

9 Robert Zoellick, United States Trade Representative, 1 August 2002, at <http://www.ustr.gov/releases/2002/08/02-80.htm>, 7 November.

3.1.2 The societal backlash against trade agreements

Until the early 1990s, US participation in the GATT aroused very little public concern or interest among Americans. To be sure, industries with a vested interest in the outcomes of trade agreements were periodically involved in multilateral trade negotiations, but otherwise the GATT attracted little attention. This began to change in the early 1990s as a broad range of environment, consumer, and citizen action groups began to question whether trade agreements undermined US norms and regulations. Their concerns were galvanized by a 1991 ruling by a GATT dispute panel against a US import embargo on tuna that was not caught using dolphin-friendly fishing practices. The decision by the dispute panel was not binding; moreover, the United States could have used other non-trade-related measures to promote dolphin-safe tuna fisheries. Nevertheless, many environment groups interpreted the panel's decision as evidence that multilateral trade rules undermined environmental protection and regulation.

The backlash generated by the tuna–dolphin case grew into a broad-based movement that included environmentalists, consumer rights advocates, trade unions, human rights organizations, and other advocacy groups. These groups took a close interest in the NAFTA negotiations that took place in 1992–93. Some sections of the trade union and environmental movement opposed the agreement outright, fearing that there would be a 'race to the bottom' effect as continental free trade created incentives for firms to relocate to Mexico to take advantage of cheap wages or lax environmental standards. Other critics of NAFTA pressed for side deals that addressed labour and environmental issues.[10]

Concerns about the implications of NAFTA spilled over into other aspects of trade policy, including US participation in the multilateral trade system. Many NGOs condemned the Uruguay Round, claiming that it focused too narrowly on economic benefits, while overlooking other policy goals such as environmental protection, public health, and economic development. Public campaigns against NAFTA, the GATT, and the Uruguay Round results soon merged into a new anti-WTO coalition, which has been deeply influential in American trade policy agendas since the mid-1990s. Under the banner of 'fair trade, not free trade', this social coalition was instrumental in preventing the Clinton Administration from securing fast-track negotiating authority in 1997. The same coalition was well represented at the Third WTO Ministerial meeting held in Seattle in November/December 1999, where its influence was evident among protestors in the streets and in the policy positions of the Clinton Administration.[11]

---

[10] S. Aaronson, *Taking Trade to the Streets: The Lost History of Public Efforts to Shape Globalisation* (University of Michigan Press, Michigan, 2001).

[11] Although the protesters at Seattle managed to severely disrupt the meeting, WTO ministers failed to launch a new round because of fundamental differences between governments on issues such as agriculture, textiles, and labour standards. Many participants believed that Clinton Administration promoted the 'fair trade' agenda in a way that was calculated to appeal primarily to their domestic constituencies. In particular, Clinton's insistence on pushing labour standards in the absence of any consensus within the WTO angered and alienated the

3.1.3 The preoccupation with dispute settlement

American enthusiasm for multilateralism has also appeared to wane with the introduction of the dispute settlement mechanism in the WTO. Certainly, it was the new process for dispute settlement that caused the most anxiety on Capitol Hill during congressional debate on the ratification of the Uruguay Round results and the establishment of the WTO. At the time, opposition to the new dispute settlement mechanism came from across the political spectrum. On the right, conservative nationalists claimed that the new process constituted an unacceptable violation of national sovereignty that circumscribed US freedom of action to use domestic trade legislation and remedies.[12] On the left, critics argued that it was incompatible with the American judicial process, on the grounds that dispute panels operated in secret and that appeals outside the system were prohibited.[13]

The WTO dispute settlement mechanism is meant to allow the clarification of existing rules and agreements; the preservation of the rights and obligations of members under these agreements; and the monitoring of compliance.[14] Unlike the GATT with its diplomatically-oriented approach to dispute resolution through negotiation and compromise, the WTO process is more legalistic and rules-oriented. The intention here is that members will pay greater attention to the rules, thus providing greater certainty and predictability in the multilateral trade system. Most scholars believe that the new dispute settlement mechanism is a great improvement over the GATT system, and is generally working well, while also acknowledging that it is not without problems.[15] Nonetheless, American anxiety about the system has continued into the present, especially with respect to the way that the WTO has curbed the ability of the United States to impose unilateral trade sanctions on other countries in the context of trade disputes.[16]

Contd.
developing countries while Gore was attacked for exploiting the Seattle process in pursuit of his own electoral ambitions. *See* R.G. Kaiser and J. Burgess, 'A Seattle Primer: How Not to Hold WTO Talks', *Washington Post*, 12 December 1999, and (1999) 48 *Bridges Weekly Trade Digest*, 15 December.

12 D.S. Cloud, 'Critics Fear GATT May Declare Open Season on U.S. Laws' (1994) 29 *Congressional Quarterly* 2005–2010, and G. A. Pigman, 'The Sovereignty discourse and the US debate on joining the World Trade Organization' (1998) *Global Society* 12.

13 R. Nader, 'Drop the GATT' (1994) *The Nation* 10 October, pp. 368–9.

14 J.H. Jackson, *The World Trade Organisation: Constitution and Jurisprudence* (The Royal Institute of International Affairs, London, 1998).

15 G. Winham, in A. Rugman and G. Boyd (eds), *The World Trade Organisation in the New Global Economy* (Edward Elgar, Cheltenham UK, 2001), p. 36. *See also* D. Steger's review of C.E. Barfield, *Free Trade, Sovereignty and Democracy: The Future of the WTO* (The AEI Press, Washington, 2001) in (2002) 2 *Journal of International Economic Law* 565–70.

16 *See* for instance the testimony to the US Senate Finance Committee Subcommittee on International Trade, 20 June 2000, by L. Wallach, Director of Global Trade Watch. Available at <http://www.citizen.org/trade/wto/Dispute/articles.cfm?ID=5581>, accessed on 7 November 2002.

3.1.4 Light at the end the tunnel? or the coming train?

Notwithstanding these troubling trends, there have been a number of positive developments that suggest some cause for optimism. The collapse of the Seattle Ministerial meeting in 1999 was a sobering experience for WTO members, and it provided a strong incentive to ensure that the subsequent Ministerial meeting did not blow up on the launch pad. In the intervening period, the Republican presidential candidate, George W. Bush was elected to office. The change of administration in Washington enabled the United States to significantly revise its demands in preparation for the Fourth Ministerial meeting, held in November 2001 at Doha in the Gulf State at Qatar. Clinton's agenda at Seattle had included a proposal for trade sanctions aimed at the enforcement of labour standards, which had been strongly opposed by developing countries since the mid-1990s. By contrast, the Bush Administration appeared to be more sympathetic to developing country concerns. At the Doha meeting, the United States announced a number of concessions to these countries in areas pertaining to industrial tariff peaks, non-tariff barriers, intellectual property, and implementation deadlines.[17]

Following the successful launch of the Doha 'Development' Round, the Bush Administration secured Trade Promotion Authority (TPA) from the Congress. TPA, formerly known as 'fast-track negotiating authority', is a mechanism that ensures that Congress cannot unpick the details of any trade agreement negotiated by the Administration: instead, Congress can only approve or reject an agreement in its entirety. In the absence of TPA, no country would be willing to enter serious trade negotiations with the United States because of the risk that Congress would unravel the entire package. Thus, the granting of TPA meant that WTO negotiations could finally begin in earnest.

However, TPA, which was granted in August 2002, came at a great cost. Having promised developing countries at Doha that the United States would open up its markets to imports of agriculture, steel, and textiles, the Bush Administration moved to shore up Congressional support with new forms of protectionism in precisely these sectors.[18] For example, despite the long-standing US commitment to reduce the use of trade-distorting subsidies in agriculture, the *Farm Security and Rural Investment Act of 2002* provides billions of dollars of subsidies and other forms of assistance to domestic producers. This adversely affects world markets by depressing prices.[19] The 'Farm Bill', announced in April 2002, was designed in part to

---

[17] The Ministerial Declaration from the Doha Meeting (WT/MIN(01)/DEC/1) agrees to place 'the needs and interests' of developing countries' at the heart of the new round of trade negotiations. The Declaration is available at <www.wto.org>. For journalistic commentary *see also* N. Guye, 'Sleepless in Doha' (2002) *European Business Journal* 46–50.

[18] J. Faux, 'A deal built on sand: at the Doha meetings, the World Trade Organisation got back on the fast track. But a train wreck lies just ahead' (2002) 1 *The American Prospect* 22–4.

[19] In 2000 alone, nearly US$30 billion was paid directly to US farmers and ranchers (representing 50 per cent of net farm income). *See* WTO, Trade Policy Review of United States, September 2001, Report by the Secretariat. Available at <http://www.wto.org/english/tratop_e/tpr_e/tp172_e.htm> (accessed on 8 November).

boost Congressional support for TPA in the farm states of Texas, Florida, and the mid-west. Similarly, in March 2002, the United States imposed new tariffs of up to 30 per cent on steel imports, in a move that was aimed at bolstering Republican support in the rust belt. Both of these measures were at odds with the thrust of US pledges at Doha, and sent out a very poor signal to other members of the WTO. On the other hand, most WTO members will also understand that this was the cost of securing TPA, without which there could be no successful WTO negotiations.

3.2 Accommodating Civil Society? NGOs and the WTO

The WTO is one of the most important institutions for global economic governance in the contemporary era. Its purview not only includes the regulation of cross-border trade in manufactured goods, services, and agriculture, but it also extends to intellectual property rights, foreign investment regulations, and cultural and environmental protection. In this context, it is little wonder that NGOs in both the profit and not-for-profit sectors have developed considerable interest in the WTO. In many cases, this has involved NGOs bypassing governments altogether and seeking to engage directly with the WTO. This activity has led to a lively debate about the merits, or otherwise, of expanding NGO participation in the WTO.

3.2.1 NGO involvement since the GATT

Opponents of greater NGO participation in multilateral trade system argue that the WTO is an *intergovernmental* organization that cannot accommodate NGOs in the same way that other international organizations have. But this argument is at odds with the original intentions of the architects of the multilateral trade system who clearly envisioned a role for NGOs. At the United Nations Conference on Trade and Employment (1946–48), several NGOs were involved in the drafting of the charter to establish an ITO. Reflecting the Keynesian flavour of the times, these NGOs included the World Federation of Trade Unions, the American Federation of Labour, and the International Chamber of Commerce. In addition, the Charter for the ITO included provisions for NGO participation in the organization.

The stillbirth of the ITO effectively stymied these early developments. The impermanent and insecure nature of the GATT, and its status as an intergovernmental treaty rather than an international organization, rendered it somewhat insular with respect to engagement with non-state actors.[20] Instead, GATT negotiations became strictly state-centric affairs. To the extent that NGO involvement occurred, it was at the national level, and was generally limited to those non-state actors who had a direct and vested

[20] S. Charnovitz and J. Wickham, 'Non-Governmental Organisations and the Original International Trade Regime' (1995) 5 *Journal of World Trade* 111–22.

interest in the outcome of trade negotiations – typically business and producer groups, and occasionally trade unions.

The Marrakesh Agreement of 1994 that established the WTO sought to restore the intent of the original ITO Charter with respect to NGO involvement by including an explicit commitment to consultation and cooperation with NGOs.[21] As yet, few formal mechanisms have been put into place to give substance to this vision. So far, attempts by the WTO to foster NGO participation – including quicker derestriction and release of documents, presentations to NGOs on WTO issues, and informal NGO involvement in ministerial meetings – have been largely an exercise in promoting better public relations. In that sense, the scope and level of NGO engagement in the WTO is still fairly shallow, especially when compared to similar efforts by the World Bank and the IMF.[22] One reason for this shallow engagement is that, compared to the other Bretton Woods institutions, the WTO has relatively few resources to devote to fostering relations with civil society organizations. And so far, WTO member states have demonstrated little interest in boosting their financial contributions to the organization, which would allow the secretariat to expand its operations with respect to NGOs. Nonetheless, there is a general acknowledgement within the WTO that civil society interest is not going to recede and that it will need to develop deeper forms of engagement with NGOs in the twenty-first century.

3.2.2 Arguments in favour of NGO involvement

Arguments in favour of NGO participation in the WTO can be broadly clumped into five categories. First is Daniel Esty's observation that NGOs can serve as connective tissue to help bridge the gap between state and non-state actors and between local and global politics.[23] Given that nation states are no longer the sole or primary actors in international politics, it is a mistake to assume that all societal interests are represented and played out through state to state negotiations. Thus NGOs may play a vital role in expressing minority views that may in fact represent a substantial body of opinion or a community of interest at the transnational level. Related to this connective role is the communicative role of NGOs, specifically their capacity to articulate particular concerns and views, which may not otherwise get a hearing, to the WTO and its members.

Second, NGOs can play a role in reducing transaction costs for both governments and the WTO itself. By providing expert information and

---

21 Article V.2 of the Agreement establishing the WTO provides that: 'The General Council may make appropriate arrangements for consultation and co-operation with non-governmental organisations concerned with matters related to those of the WTO'.

22 For instance, the World Bank has sought to engage directly with NGOs, especially with the well-resourced 'technical' NGOs that can provide sophisticated analysis and information in areas such as environmental policy and debt relief. Now more than half of the World Bank's projects directly involved NGOs and more than 70 NGO specialists work in the field offices of the Bank. 'The Non-governmental order', *The Economist*, 11 December 1999.

23 D.C. Esty, 'Non-governmental organisations at the WTO: Cooperation, Competition or Exclusion' (1998) *Journal of International Economic Law* 123–47.

advice on particular policy problems, monitoring compliance with agreements, and providing independent verification of self-reporting by states, NGOs enable governments to reallocate scarce bureaucratic resources to other activities. The role of NGOs as monitors may also help to assist states that do not have the bureaucratic or technical capacity to gather and analyse that information for themselves.[24]

Third is the educative role of NGOs, which can help to provide information about the WTO, and demystify and demythologize its operations and functions. NGOs can also disseminate information about the multilateral trade system, thus helping to contribute to securing public support for trade and sustainable development and, perhaps more importantly, helping to promote a better understanding of the benefits of multilateral institutions to promote collective action. The importance of these activities cannot be underestimated given the widespread public distrust of the WTO, and by contrast, the generally high public regard for NGOs, especially those in the not-for-profit realm.

Fourth is the role of NGOs in promoting alternative views to prevailing orthodoxies. NGOs can help to stimulate debate, formulate alternative perspectives, and challenge the WTO and its members to rethink entrenched positions.[25]

The fifth, and perhaps most controversial, argument in favour of strengthening NGO participation relates to concerns about the 'democratic deficit' associated with the emerging institutions of global governance. As the creature of its 145 member states, the WTO's 'legitimacy' is not in doubt. But not all WTO member states are themselves democratic. Moreover, the highly attenuated lines of delegation between national societies and the WTO means that multilateral trade agreements rest on a very circumscribed notion of public consent.[26] Many advocates of greater NGO participation in the WTO argue that enhanced opportunities for civil society contributions to global regulation should be one dimension of a broader strategy to democratize the institutions of global economic governance.[27]

3.2.3 Arguments against NGO involvement

There is also significant opposition to expanding the involvement of NGOs in the WTO. Many in the traditional trade policy community, including some trade diplomats, bureaucrats, and negotiators, have been resistant to the notion of enhancing or formalizing NGO participation in WTO processes.

---

[24] K. Raustiala, ' States, NGOS, and Environmental Institutions' (1997) 4 *International Studies Quarterly* 719–40. Raustiala's analysis is restricted to environmental agreements, but its application is equally salient for WTO agreements.

[25] J.A. Scholte, R. O'Brien, and M. Williams, 'The WTO and civil society', in B. Hocking and S. McGuire (eds), *Trade Politics*, p. 162.

[26] C. Bellman and R. Gerster, 'Accountability in the World Trade Organisation' (1996) 6 *Journal of World Trade* 31–74; and J. Nye Jr., 'Globalisation's Democractic Deficit – How to Make International Institutions More Accountable', *Foreign Affairs*, July–August 2001.

[27] J.A. Scholte, 'Civil Society and Democracy in Global Governance' (2002) *Global Governance* 281–304.

The views of Alan Rugman, a business studies scholar with considerable trade policy expertise, are not atypical of this group. Rugman described the decision to give standing to NGOs at the Seattle Ministerial Meeting in November 1999 as 'a dreadful mistake' and he claims that multilateralism is 'being killed by the presence of NGOs at the WTO'.[28]

This sort of hostility is not surprising: multilateral trade negotiations have been typically shrouded in secrecy, in large part because of the complexity, compromises, and trade-offs that are an inherent part of international commercial diplomacy. Many governments fear that opening up negotiation processes to non-government actors would make it virtually impossible for difficult deal-making to occur, as negotiators would be overwhelmed by domestic constituencies seeking to undermine national positions. In this view, NGOs should not be given the opportunity to take a 'second bite of the apple', having already had an opportunity to promote their position at the domestic level.

A second argument against greater NGO participation in the WTO is informed by public choice and collective action theories. In this view, groups that have special interests to defend – typically business/producer groups and trade unions seeking to defend their sector against imports – will organize and lobby more effectively than those who gain from the diffuse benefits of more open markets.[29] Thus, opening WTO processes to NGOs will result in 'special interest' capture of the WTO by protectionist groups.[30]

A third argument focuses on fears about the nuisance effect of NGO participation. There is a concern that interventions from NGOs could be misdirected or ill-informed, and therefore disruptive and resource-diverting. At the national level, many bureaucrats fear that greater public participation will result in overload and chaos in the policy-making process. Similarly, the WTO is already significantly under-resourced and under-staffed, compared to other multilateral economic institutions and can ill afford to divert resources to dealing with NGOs, no matter how well-intentioned.[31]

The fourth argument against the expansion of NGO participation relates to concerns about representativeness and equity. Many developing countries are suspicious of the desire of the United States and other developed countries to accord greater status to NGOs in the WTO. The influence of the 'Teamster–Turtle' coalition in American trade politics underlines the concern

---

28 A. Rugman, 'The World Trade Organisation and the International Political Economy', in Rugman and Boyd (eds), *The World Trade Organisation in the New Global Economy*, pp. 19–20.

29 P.M. Nichols, 'Extension of Standing in World Trade Organisaiton Disputes to Nongovernment Parties' (1996) *University of Pennsylvania Journal of International Economic Law*.

30 This is probably the least defensible argument against enhancing NGO participation in the WTO. Special interests, including well organized protectionist interests, have always played a significant role in the development of national negotiating positions.

31 In 2002, the WTO Secretariat had 560 staff members, compared to 2,633 at the IMF. *See* WTO *Annual Report* 2002, p. 154, and IMF *Annual Report*, 2002, p. 87. In the mid-1990s, the WTO's entire administrative budget was only slightly larger than the IMF's travel budget. B. Hoekman and M. Kostecki, *The Political Economy of the World Trading System* (Oxford University Press, Oxford, 1995), pp. 40–1.

among developing countries that some trade unions and green groups represent self-interested protectionism garbed in the clothes of workers' rights or environmental protection. Developing countries have also expressed reservations about the impact of NGO participation in the dispute settlement process. In recent dispute panels, environmental NGOs were allowed to submit *amicus curiae* (friends of the court) briefs, raising concern among developing countries that well-funded lobbyists from developed countries could begin to exercise disproportionate control of dispute settlement processes, thus further tilting the playing field against developing countries.[32]

On balance, the arguments in favour of developing more effective measures for NGO participation in WTO processes outweigh those against. The reality is that NGOs already play a significant role in WTO policy-making through their organizational and lobbying efforts at the national level, which translate into national negotiating positions. As Jeffrey Dunoff has noted, NGOs that are already involved in trade policy-making 'typically represent business and industry interests, to the near exclusion of labor, consumer, environmental and other relevant interests'.[33] Indeed, opening these processes to a broader range of interests may help to overcome the existing problems of government capture by narrow business interests. Given the far-reaching nature of WTO agreements and their impact on regulation in areas such as culture, environmental protection, and public health, it is appropriate and desirable that a broader range of NGOs should be engaged in the development of global trade regulation.

3.2.4 The way forward?

The real challenge for the WTO is to develop appropriate modalities for NGO engagement in the each of the three areas of WTO activity: (i) regular meeting activity, including meetings of the General Council and Ministerial Conferences; (ii) Dispute Settlement; and (iii) multilateral trade negotiations.[34] There is already a very robust debate about the participation of NGOs in the dispute settlement process, and WTO practices are likely to evolve in response.[35] The issue of NGO participation in trade negotiations is more problematic: only governments have the authority to make 'concessions' in trade negotiations that involve the amendment of domestic regulatory policies and practices, and only governments can make these agreements stick. Governments can seek advice from NGOs, include them

---

32 'Shrimp–Turtle Ruling Gets Lukewarm Reaction from All Sides' (1998) *Bridges Weekly Trade News Digest*, 19 October.

33 J.L. Dunoff, 'The Misguided Debate over NGO Participation at the WTO' (1998) 3 *Journal of International Economic Law* 433–56.

34 For a good overview of current WTO practices with respect to NGO involvement in these three key activities *see* G. Marceau and P.N. Pedersen, 'Is the WTO Open and Transparent? A Discussion of the Relationship of the WTO with Non-governmental Organisations and Civil Society's Claims for more Transparency and Public Participation' (1999) 1 *Journal of World Trade* 5–49.

35 For a good overview *see* E. Hernández-López, 'Recent Trends and Perspectives for Non-State Actor Participation in World Trade Organisation Disputes' (2001) 3 *Journal of World Trade* 469–98.

in their national delegations, and give them a place in their negotiating teams. It is hard to see any rationale for giving NGOs additional representation on top of their participation through national processes. Indeed, this would raise serious equity issues for developing countries. As Jagdish Bhagwati notes, giving NGOs a 'second shot independent of governments ... serves to give the rich-country negotiators added weight because it is the rich-country NGOs that are effectively going to have a great voice, given their greater resources of money, clout, and lobbying experience'.[36]

In any case, these issues are complex and change is likely to be slow given the diversity of WTO membership and the need to develop a consensus-based approach to reform. Indeed, given the difficulties of achieving consensus within the WTO, it is imperative that the member states themselves develop more participative and effective means of engaging with the diverse interests of contemporary civil society. While much of the academic debate has focused on the need for the WTO to engage directly with global social movements,[37] efforts to redress the democratic deficit in global institutions must surely begin at the national level. As Paul Hirst and Grahame Thompson point out, nation states are still the 'crucial agencies of representation' in a system of global governance; it is national governments that have primary responsibility for the promotion of social cohesion within their territories.[38] Only national governments have the authority and legitimacy to represent the interests of pluralistic national societies and to commit those societies to international agreements.

In effect, it is national governments that ensure, albeit in a mediated way, that global institutions are ultimately accountable. Thus, whether the WTO adequately addresses the civil society challenge depends, to a great extent, on the responsiveness of democratic governments to public concerns about global trade issues. National governments will need to develop more widely consultative and participatory approaches to the development of trade policy objectives; this necessarily entails a greater role for a diverse range of NGOs than has previously been the case.

3.3 WTO Governance

For an organization that is alleged by its detractors and defenders alike to have sweeping power and authority, the WTO is a surprisingly fragile institution. Like most international organizations, one of its most important roles is to promote international cooperation between nation states. But the WTO differs from other international organizations in its approach to promoting cooperation. Most organizations typically rely on collective action,

---

36 Jagdish Bhagwati, 'After Seattle: Free Trade and the WTO' (2001) 1 *International Affairs* 15–29.

37 This view is exemplified by R. O'Brien, A.M. Goetz, J.A. Scholte, and M. Williams, *Contesting Global Governance: Multilateral Economic Institutions and Global Social Movements* (Cambridge University Press, Cambridge, 2000).

38 P. Hirst and G. Thompson, *Globalisation in Question* (Polity Press, Cambridge, 1996), ch. 6.

which is often based on decisions made by limited membership councils. By contrast, the WTO promotes cooperation through a system of contractual rules, enforced by its individual member states through their own domestic legislation.[39] The significance here is that the WTO is a genuinely member-based institution, where decisions are generally reached by consensus among member states, with minimal involvement by the secretariat.[40]

With its contractual nature and its emphasis on consensual decision-making, the WTO affords a great deal of autonomy and sovereignty to its members. Nonetheless, developing and least developed countries have called for significant reform of WTO internal governance, and the introduction of greater transparency and wider participation in its decision-making processes. This is partly driven by the recognition that decision-making processes that were once appropriate to the GATT with its much smaller membership no longer work in an organization that has more than 140 members. But demands for internal reform in the WTO are also driven by a deeper feeling that the multilateral trade system does not satisfactorily recognize and accommodate the needs and concerns of developing and least developed countries. In that sense, these two issues – internal governance and developing country problems in the WTO – are intrinsically linked. This section explores some of the key dimensions of developing country dissatisfaction with the WTO, and outlines the major areas where reform is sought.

3.3.1 Developing country concerns

In the 1980s, the traditional view of the GATT as a 'rich man's club' softened as many developing countries adopted more liberal trade and investment policies, and became more appreciative of the benefits of the multilateral trade system for the 'non-great' powers.[41] During the Uruguay Round, a small group of developing countries was closely involved in negotiating agreements in agriculture, tropical products, services, textiles and clothing, TRIMs, and dispute settlement. Rather than acting en bloc as they had in the past, these countries more often operated within coalitions or 'ginger groups' that typically consisted of developing and small industrialized countries. Two notable examples of this type of activity were the Cairns Group of agricultural fair traders and the Rolle Group in the services negotiations.[42]

Although the Uruguay Round process helped to build their confidence in multilateral trade negotiations, developing countries are deeply dissatisfied

---

[39] G. Winham, 'The World Trade Organisation: Institution-Building in the Multilateral Trade System' (1998) 3 *The World Economy* 349–68.

[40] For a contrasting perspective on this issue, see the chapter in this book by Patrick Weller and Xu Yi-chong.

[41] *See* R. Hudec, *Developing Countries in the GATT Legal System* (Trade Policy Research Centre, London, 1987); and T.N. Srinivasan, *Developing Countries and the Multilateral Trade System: From the GATT to the Uruguay Round and the Future* (Westview Press, Boulder Colorado, 1998).

[42] Capling, *Australia and the Global Trade System*, chs 5 and 6.

with many aspects of the WTO. Many of their concerns were aired at the Seattle Ministerial Meeting where developing countries were deeply critical of the major powers for failing to advance liberalization in key areas of interest to them; for tackling too many new and controversial topics such as labour standards, competition, and investment policy while developing countries still had 'unfinished business' from the Uruguay Round; and for shutting developing countries out of the important 'Green room' processes where the real deals were being worked through.

Part of the problem has been the failure of Uruguay Round agreements to live up to some of their promise, especially with respect to the delivery of significant market openings to developing countries. As a quid pro quo for agreeing to negotiate services and intellectual property during the round, developing countries had expected to receive significant improvements in market access for their exports, especially in farm products, and textiles and clothing.[43] However, the Uruguay Round results have fallen short of developing country expectations in these key areas. For instance, while the Uruguay Round Agreement on Agriculture included reductions in the use of farm export subsidies and domestic producer subsidies, as well as increases in import market access, the reality is that these commitments involve very modest liberalization.

Equally disappointing for developing countries was the agreement on textiles and clothing. Although WTO members agreed to phase out the use of discriminatory import quotas, these commitments were 'backloaded' so that most of the liberalization was put off until the end of the implementation period in 2004. Even if the major importing countries do eventually honour their Uruguay Round commitments, tariffs on textiles and clothing will remain significantly higher than average tariffs in most high-income countries.[44] Failure by the industrialized countries to liberalize their markets in agriculture and clothing/textiles has been a source of great frustration for developing countries, and it has contributed to their feeling that the global trade system is stacked against them.

Developing countries have also experienced significant difficulties in implementing many of their obligations arising from the Uruguay Round, particularly in relation to commitments involving domestic regulation, such as intellectual property rules, quarantine measures, and technical standards.[45] The case of the Uruguay Round Agreement on TRIPs provides a good example of these difficulties. The origins of the TRIPs agreement can be traced to a desire by the United States to secure a comprehensive international agreement that establishes minimum standards for the protection and enforcement of a wide variety of intellectual property rights, including patents and copyright.

---

43 The Uruguay Round results were negotiated and implemented as a single undertaking; it was tacitly understood that trade-offs and linkages would be made across a wide variety of different negotiating areas.

44 Hoekman and Kostecki, *The Political Economy of the World Trading System*, p. 209.

45 C. Michalopoulos, 'Developing Country Strategies for the Millenium Round' (1999) 5 *Journal of World Trade* 1–30; and A. Mukerji, 'Developing Countries and the WTO: Issues of Implementation' (2000) 6 *Journal of World Trade* 33–74.

The TRIPs agreement was highly controversial and many developing countries, along with many trade experts, have argued that the new regime is better suited to industrialized country economies than it is to developing countries.[46] Moreover, the implementation of the TRIPs agreement, which entails significant reform of administrative and legal systems, has placed enormous additional burdens on developing countries.[47]

While transitional provisions allowed developing countries additional time to bring their domestic regulatory regimes into conformity with TRIPs, many of them have found the task so great that they have yet to meet their deadlines.[48] Thus, in the lead-up to the Seattle Ministerial meeting, a major objective for developing countries was to secure an extension of the implementation deadlines for the TRIPs agreement.[49] The response at Seattle was largely negative: there appeared to be little concern or understanding among industrialized countries about the difficulties that confronted developing countries with respect to TRIPs. For its part, the United States was neither willing to extend the implementation deadlines, nor renegotiate aspects of the agreement to address developing country concerns.

3.3.2 Ownership and capacity-building

The WTO has some 100 members that are developing countries, transition economies, or least-developed countries. Many of these feel little 'ownership' of the rules and reforms that they are meant to be implementing. As Michael Finger and Philip Schuler observe, ownership of the rules is especially important in an institution like the WTO where the organization itself has limited power to enforce rules. Creating this sense of ownership begins with effective participation in the WTO decision-making processes where rules are made.[50] However, significant resource constraints severely limit the capacity of the majority of developing countries in the WTO to participate fully in these processes. For instance, many developing and least developed countries members do not have delegations in Geneva. Among those that do, their delegations are typically very small and under-resourced compared to those from industrial countries.[51] Thus, one or two

---

46 A. Capling, 'Intellectual Property Rights', in Hocking and McGuire (eds), *Trade Politics*, p. 79.

47 For discussion *see* C.A.P. Braga and C. Fink, 'Reforming Intellectual Property Rights Regimes: Challenges for Developing Countries,' (1998) 4 *Journal of International Economic Law* 537–54.

48 Developing countries and transition economies were given until 1 January 2000 to comply with their TRIPs obligations. An exception exists in cases where developing countries provide patent protection to processes rather than products, in which case, product protection can be delayed until 2005. Least developed countries must comply with TRIPs by 2006, although some extensions are possible.

49 'No new issues without redress of Uruguay Round imbalances' (1999) *Bridges Weekly Trade News Digest*, 24 November.

50 J.M. Finger and P. Schuler, 'Implementation of Uruguay Round Commitments: The Development Challenge', in B. Hoekman and W. Martin (eds), *Developing Countries and the WTO: A Pro-active Agenda* (Blackwell Publishers, Oxford, 2001), pp. 115–30.

51 For instance, when the Uruguay Round commenced, nearly one-third of the 65 developing country members of the GATT did not have delegations in Geneva. Moreover, developing

people may have to attend to all matters pertaining to the WTO, along with other Geneva-based international institutions, making it virtually impossible for them to participate in a meaningful way in WTO processes. This problem of ownership and participation helps to explain why developing countries have begun to push for reform of WTO decision-making processes, especially in the areas of internal decision-making.

In response, the WTO Secretariat has proposed a number of 'confidence-building' measures to address developing country concerns about their capacity to participate fully in WTO processes. These measures include the provision of technical assistance and support for 'capacity-building' for developing and least-developed countries. In addition to the provision of resources, technical assistance includes WTO assistance to developing countries to identify their own trade policy agendas; WTO cooperation with the IMF and the United Nations Conference on Trade and Development (UNCTAD) to create a macro-economic framework to promote investment in developing countries; and World Bank assistance to help developing countries diversify their production. WTO Director-General Supachai Panitchpakdi has also spoken of the need to provide 'legal aid' to help the poorest countries access the dispute settlement mechanism.[52] The message appears to be getting through. The Doha Ministerial declaration includes multiple references to technical assistance and capacity-building, although only time will tell whether the Doha negotiations live up to their commitment as the 'development round'.

3.3.3 Reform of decision-making processes

Developing countries have also demanded more 'internal transparency' in WTO decision-making processes, as well as enhanced opportunities to participate in those processes themselves. There are three major forums for decision-making in the WTO: the General Council, the Ministerial Meeting, and the Trade Negotiations committee, which oversees periodic rounds of multilateral trade negotiations.

In the General Council, each member state holds a single vote, and with a very few exceptions, decision-making in the General Council is traditionally by consensus. While this robustly democratic approach makes change very difficult to achieve, it does mean that where change is agreed, it is far more likely to be implemented by member states. Votes in the General Council are taken only on amendments relating to general principles such as most-favoured-nation (where unanimity required); interpretations of the provisions of WTO agreements and waivers (three-quarters or 75 per cent

---

Contd.
country delegations were very small compared to those from industrial countries. *See* C. Michalopoulos, *Developing Countries' Participation in the World Trade Organisation*, Policy Research Working Paper 1906 (The World Bank, Washington DC, March 1998).

52 'Global Trade Liberalisation: Coordination and Coherence,' Speech given by Supachai Panitchpakdi at the University of Melbourne, 5 July 2000.

majority required); and amendments relating to issues other than general principles (two-thirds or 66 per cent majority required).

Developing countries are relatively satisfied with this aspect of WTO governance: the principles of one member/one vote and the tradition of consensus are appropriate for an organization that has such a broad diversity of membership. Indeed, these processes give developing countries more leverage than they have in other multilateral economic institutions where weighted voting is the norm. However, the major challenge for the WTO is to ensure that developing and least developed countries are able to represent themselves in the General Council, as discussed in the previous section.

But there are also concerns that these robustly democratic processes could also prevent the WTO from responding quickly and effectively to changes in the global political economy. Legal scholars have also drawn attention to some of the problems involved in trying to clarify WTO rules during the periods between multilateral trade negotiations. In response, there have been a number of proposals for some sort of steering group that could help to give direction, clarify rules, provide advice to the Director-General, or develop recommendations for the General Council. One proposal is to grant more powers to the Secretariat, but WTO members are hostile to this prospect.[53] Notwithstanding the reality that the WTO Director-General and Secretariat do sometimes play a role in policy development,[54] members are strongly wedded to the notion of the WTO as a member-based organization (without the pathologies associated with the bloated secretariats of some other international organizations). Another proposal is to create some sort of Executive Committee chaired by the Director-General, with a rotating membership, to steer the activities of the General Council.[55] This would bring WTO practices into line with the IMF and the World Bank. An effort by the GATT to develop an informal executive process in the early 1980s quickly floundered and was abandoned after a few years,[56] but perhaps the dramatic growth in membership of the WTO (145 in November 2002) makes the idea more feasible now. If any sort of steering group were to be established, it would be wise to trial it for a limited period of time in the first instance.[57]

The area of internal governance that poses the greatest concern for developing countries is the multilateral trade negotiating process itself. During the Tokyo Round (1973–79) and the Uruguay Round, multilateral trade negotiations were formally overseen by a Trade Negotiations Committee (TNC) consisting of all GATT members and chaired by the Director-General.

---

53 M.C.E.J. Bronckers, 'Better Rules for a New Millenium: A Warning Against Undemocratic Developments in the WTO' (1999) 4 *Journal of International Economic Law* 547–66.

54 *See* chapter by Xu Yi-chong and Patrick Weller in this volume.

55 J. Soloway and A. Anishchenko, 'Agenda setting for a Millennial Round: challenges and opportunities', in Alan Rugman and Gavin Boyd (eds), *The World Trade Organisation in the New Global Economy* (Edward Elgar, Cheltenham UK, 2001), p. 60.

56 This was the Consultative Group of 18, established to keep momentum in the GATT after the end of the Tokyo Round in 1979.

57 J. Jackson, 'The WTO "Constitution" and Proposed Reforms: Seven "Mantras" Revisited' (2001) 1 *Journal of International Economic Law* 67–78.

Meetings of the TNC were usually conducted as 'set pieces' for a general stock-taking of progress in the round, but they were too large and cumbersome to allow for any substantial negotiation.[58] Issue-specific negotiating groups were similarly conducted as formal meetings for the purpose of tabling proposals and elaborating national positions. But in these meetings, progress was often difficult to achieve, especially in difficult or highly conflictual areas such as agriculture. In situations where formal negotiations bogged down or became deadlocked, the Director-General would often convene an informal meeting in his private conference room (the 'Green Room'). These meetings, which brought together a small group of countries that were in conflict over a particular issue, were typically frank, robust, and off-the-record. Sometimes breakthroughs were achieved, but more importantly, the Green Room process highlighted negotiating decisions demanded political intervention in home capitals. Attendance at Green Room meetings varied depending on the issue, but it was usually limited to less than 30 countries.

At the Seattle Ministerial meeting, Director-General Mike Moore adopted the Green Room process, and invited a small number of developed and developing countries to participate in drafting an agreement to launch a new round of multilateral trade negotiations. However, there were no agreed criteria for participation in the Green Room, and many of the new WTO members were deeply dismayed to be excluded from this process. Indeed, Green Room meetings typically consisted of the Quads – namely the United States, the European Union, Canada, and Japan – with a few hand-picked developing countries. The vast majority of developing countries were not invited to participate in the Green Room process, had little knowledge of what was transpiring, and felt completely excluded from the Seattle process.[59] As a result of this experience, developing and least-developed countries have sought to reform this Green Room process, with a view to creating more open and representative mechanisms for these informal discussions.

A demand by the least-developed countries that no Green Room sessions be allowed in the Doha Round[60] is simply not feasible. But there is going to have to be some reform of the Green Room process for informal closed door negotiating sessions to accommodate the reality of a much bigger WTO membership. One alternative could be through the development of issue-based coalitions of like-minded countries, which could delegate authority to a single country with respect to participation in informal, high-level negotiations. This approach worked well with the Cairns Group during the Uruguay Round, and developing countries have already shown they can act cohesively in the Doha Round with respect to TRIPs reform. The challenge is to develop effective forms of 'minilateralism' that are both representative and participatory, but are still small enough in size to ensure that real discussion and progress are possible. This will not overcome the reality

---

[58] J. Croome, *Reshaping the World Trading System: A History of the Uruguay Round* (World Trade Organization, Geneva, 1995), p. 163.

[59] D.K. Das, 'Debacle at Seattle: The Way the Cookie Crumbled' (2000) 5 *Journal of World Trade* 181–201.

[60] 'Countries Struggle Over How to Negotiate WTO Doha Mandate' (2002) 1 *Bridges Weekly Trade Digest* 16 January.

of great power dominance in multilateral trade negotiations, which has been described as 'pyramidal bargaining', 'minilateral great power cooperation', and 'vertical minilateralism'.[61] But most supporters of the multilateral trade system see this is as a necessary if unfortunate aspect of ensuring the sustainability of the system, for without it the major powers would simply defect and the system would fall apart.

In the end, it is important that reform of internal governance in the WTO not be seen as a substitute for addressing the legitimate concerns that many developing and least-developed countries have in relation to WTO rules and agreements. There is the need for a broader agenda that goes beyond the provision of support for the implementation of WTO agreement; the enhancement of national trade policies and negotiating skills and capacities of developing and least-developed countries; and internal governance reforms to enhance their participation in WTO processes. In recent years, the WTO has focused on the need to lower market access barriers to exports from low income countries. But this puts the 'free-trade cart' ahead of the 'development horse'. Trade liberalization will not resolve the more fundamental problems of lack of transport infrastructure, limited access to credit and trade finance, deficient informational networks, and inadequate public support services for agricultural and industrial production.[62]

The architects of the ITO understood that international trade could only be mutually advantageous if supported by domestic policy and international collaboration to promote full employment in industrialized countries and the promotion of production and productivity in developing countries.[63] But in narrowing its focus to free trade, the WTO seems to have lost sight of this bigger picture. In his work on the role of the WTO in poverty reduction, Milton Churche warns that: 'If the push to confine the WTO's mission to a narrow trade liberalization agenda is sustained ... there is likely to be increasing public questioning of whether it is promoting shared social goals of the international community'.[64] This view challenges the WTO to rethink its role in addressing poverty and development more generally.

3.4 Concluding Comments

The WTO provides a forum for the expression of fundamental differences in national cultures, values, and economic systems; the representation of

---

[61] *See* G. Winham, *International Trade Negotiations and the Tokyo Round* (Princeton University Press, Princeton, NJ, 1986) and M. Kahler, 'Multilateralism with Small and Large Numbers' in J.G. Ruggie (ed.), *Multilateralism Matters* (Columbia University Press, New York, 1993).

[62] M. Churche, 'Trade Liberalisation, Trade Policy and Poverty Reduction' Paper presented to the Conference on Globalisation, Growth and (In)Equality at the Centre for the Study of Globalisation and Regionalisation', University of Warwick, 15–17 March 2002.

[63] *See* Capling, *Australia and the Global Trade System*, chapter 1; W.A. Brown, *The United States and the Restoration of World Trade* (Washington, 1950); J.G. Ruggie, 'International Regimes, Transactions, and Change: Embedded Liberalism in the Postwar Economic Order,' (1982) 2 *International Organisation*; and Clair Wilcox, *A Charter for World Trade* (New York, 1945).

[64] M. Churche, 'Trade Liberalisation, Trade Policy and Poverty Reduction'.

competing claims and demands; and the management of trade-related disputes between nations. Governance in the era of globalization depends on the existence of global political institutions like the WTO that can help to influence behaviour and regularize civil interactions between nations. To view the WTO narrowly as a vehicle for free trade, as both its critics and supporters are wont to do, is to miss the real importance of this institution.

Like the GATT before it, the WTO exists as a 'contract' among nations, where international economic cooperation is achieved primarily through consensually negotiated rules. Although this makes decision-making slow and cumbersome, the GATT nevertheless developed a capacity to be flexible, adaptive, and responsive to changes in the international political economy. Those who resist change on the grounds that 'things must remain as they were in the GATT', may be overlooking the fact that the GATT also evolved to meet the times. Similarly, the future relevance of the WTO will depend to a great extent on the willingness of its members to continue to evolve in response to political, social, and economic change.

A failure to meet these challenges head on will not only jeopardize further trade liberalization, but something that is far more important – namely the WTO's capacity to regulate the global trade system, and in particular to promote rules that help to protect small and middle-sized countries against the use of unilateral measures by the major powers in the global economy. At stake is not the future of free trade, but rather a system of multilateral rules that prevents the law of the jungle from operating in the global economy.

4. The Post-Doha Trade Agenda: Questions About Constituents, Competence, and Coherence

*Jeffrey L. Dunoff**

4.1 Introduction

The Seattle and Doha Ministerial meetings mark a watershed for the international trading system. In this short essay, I want to reflect on the failure to launch a new round of trade negotiations in Seattle and the halting progress of negotiations after Doha, and outline three claims about the state of the international trade regime.

The first claim is that the trade regime is in a time of fundamental transition and, perhaps, transformation. The issues driving this transition are at once political, institutional, and jurisprudential. While the Seattle Ministerial's failure and the post-Doha difficulties are more a symptom than a cause of this transition, they raise both the visibility and the political salience of the pressures driving this transitional era.

The second claim is that the strategies used to date to address these transition issues have been, for the most part, relatively conventional strategies. But, as demonstrated more fully below, these strategies have been, at best, ineffectual, and, at worst, counterproductive.

The third claim is that the pressures driving the World Trade Organization's (WTO) transitional era illuminate the limits of our current understandings of the trade regime. Hence, they highlight the need for new understandings that more fully capture the realities of the international trading system.

I will develop these claims through examination of a few simple-sounding questions, namely who, what, and where? By asking 'who', I mean to raise a question about constituencies: Who does the trade system serve? Who has a meaningful voice in the system? By asking 'what', I mean to raise a question

---

* Charles Klein Professor of Law and Government and Director, Institute for International Law and Public Policy, Temple University School of Law. An earlier version of this essay appeared in the George Washington International Law Review.

about competencies. What subject areas fall within the trade regime? Labor? Competition? Environment? What principle defines the line that distinguishes the issues that are properly within, and those properly without, the trade regime? Finally, by asking 'where', I mean to raise a question about institutional and doctrinal coherence. Where does the WTO fit within the larger universe of international law and international organizations? Is the WTO one among many international organizations? Or does WTO law have a 'constitutional' dimension, rendering trade law superior to other forms of international law and the WTO more equal than other international organizations?

These questions help to define the scope and dimensions of the current transitional era. But exploration of these questions will, in turn, raise two other, fundamental questions: why and how? Why is the trade system in the midst of a dramatic transition period now, especially so soon after the lengthy bargaining that produced the Uruguay Round Agreements? And finally, how? How are the various problems at issue during the transition related, and how might they be solved? Discussion of these questions will show that, ironically, many of the issues driving the transition result from past successes of the trade regime. But they will also show why the strategies that were successful in the past are unlikely to be so in the future, as the transition issues signal that what is at stake in trade disputes has significantly changed.

4.2 Who?

To understand the present transition period, we should start with the 'who' question. This question asks who benefits from, and who drives, the trade system? Who sets the agenda, and who has a meaningful voice in the WTO? While each of these queries deserves attention, for present purposes I will focus on the question of who meaningfully participates in the WTO as a proxy for the larger 'who' question.

Until the 1990s, there was a short and simple answer to the question of who meaningfully participates in the trade regime. Until then, the General Agreement on Tariffs and Trade (GATT) was primarily driven by the US–EU relationship. Major proposals for change often originated with one of these parties, and any proposal, to be successful, invariably required the support, or at least acquiescence, of both these parties.

But, after the Uruguay Round, increasing pressure from both inside and outside the WTO signaled that this succinct answer to the participation question was no longer adequate. From inside the WTO, developing countries advanced two related concerns about the nature and quality of their participation. First, they raised a *procedural* concern that they had been largely shut out of the most important aspects of the Uruguay Round negotiations. In addition, they raised a *substantive* concern that the Uruguay Round Agreements favoured developed states at their expense. In particular, since 1995, developing states have increasingly perceived that the Uruguay Round Agreements are being implemented, to their detriment, in a strikingly asymmetrical manner. For example, since the Marrakesh meeting, there has been relatively little progress on the industrialized states' principal Uruguay Round commitment to progressively phase out import quotas on textiles and apparel over 10 years. At the same time, developed nations have exerted increasing pressure on developing states for timely implementation of their principal Uruguay Round commitments, including commitments in the intellectual property area. From the developing state perspective, the Uruguay Round's 'grand bargain' has increasingly been perceived as a bum deal.[1]

As a result, developing states resolved not to be effectively shut out of the process again. In retrospect, the lengthy and acrimonious dispute over the naming of a new WTO Director-General in 1998 and 1999 was a signal that developing nations were no longer willing to conduct business as usual. Moreover, developing states adopted an extraordinarily proactive role in the run-up to Seattle. For example, of the over 250 specific formal proposals submitted for consideration by WTO Members, over half were submitted by developing states.

At Seattle, the developing states protested to an unprecedented extent their exclusion from the 'green room' process.[2] In response, the Conference Chair, Ambassador Charlene Barshefsky, created working groups designed to afford developing nations greater participation than they had at the Singapore Ministerial. However, developing states believed that they were still (*de facto*) excluded from the decision-making process, and deemed Ambassador Barshefsky's efforts inadequate. To demonstrate their concern, the OAU, AEC, CARICOM, and a group of Latin American and Caribbean nations issued communiqués rejecting Ambassador Barshefsky's approach to Ministerial decision-making. In particular, they objected to Ambassador Barshefsky's statement that she reserved the right to use a 'more exclusive process to achieve a final outcome' in the event the working groups were unable to reach consensus.[3] The Latin American and Caribbean communiqués also expressed strong objection to the 'parallel course of action' in which a course of 'limited and reserved participation by some Members' had been created separate and apart from the working groups.

In addition to the complaints of the developing states about the quality of their participation, the WTO has been under dramatic external pressure from non-governmental organizations (NGOs) and other sectors of civil society. Complaints from these groups focused on their *exclusion* from WTO processes. While NGOs were not terribly concerned about this exclusion for

---

1 Sylvia Ostry, WTO: Institutional Design for Better Governance 10 (unpublished manuscript, on file with author).

2 At various times during the Uruguay Round negotiations, after disagreement on particular issues had been limited to small but very significant differences among negotiators, the GATT's Director-General would hold informal sessions to crystallize and to agree on the specific boundaries of disagreement and then to seek a common ground to resolve them. These came to be known as 'Green Room' negotiations because the conference room next to the Director-General's office in the GATT building, where such meetings took place during the Round, is painted green.

3 US Trade Representative Charlene Barshefsky, 'Press Briefing, World Trade Organization Conference, Seattle, Washington' <www.ustr.gov/speech-test/barshefsky/barspb.pdf>, 2 December 1999.

the first 45 years of GATT's existence, the Tuna–Dolphin I panel report dramatically illustrated how trade rules can significantly impact a number of diverse regulatory areas where NGOs are active. This realization has sparked a multi-pronged attack on the WTO. One of the most important components of this attack has focused on the WTO's closed system of dispute resolution, and NGOs have insistently demanded public access and input into WTO decision-making processes.

These internal and external trends coalesced in Seattle, where NGO street theatre captured public and media attention, and the developing states loudly and pointedly claimed that their demands for greater inclusion were not adequately met. More particularly, developing states submitted formal declarations stating that they would not accept any consensus that had been reached without their full and effective participation. At the close of the Ministerial, Ambassador Barshefsky acknowledged that the WTO needs a process which has 'a greater degree of internal transparency, and inclusion to accommodate a larger and more diverse membership'.[4] This acknowledegement reflects the fact that the developing nations' insistence on meaningful participation – and willingness to block progress until this demand is satisfied – marks a sea change from earlier periods of GATT's history.

Since Seattle, there has been much activity in the effort to improve the nature and quality of developing states' participation. For example, at its February 2000 meeting, the WTO General Council identified the issue of internal transparency and effective participation of Members as a priority issue to be addressed in the first six months of the year. Since then, the Chairman of the General Council has conducted an intensive series of open-ended consultations on how to improve internal transparency.

Similar activities continued during the run-up and aftermath of the Doha Ministerial, with a particular focus on helping developing states participate more fully in the WTO system. For example, the WTO Secretariat supported weekly meetings of the least-developed country (LDC) Consultative Group and meetings of other informal groups such as the African Group. In addition, the Secretariat began to offer, through a new WTO Training Institute, training courses outside of Geneva. The first two courses were offered in July 2002; one for Francophone Africans at the University of Casablanca in Morocco and the other for Anglophone Africans at the University of Nairobi in Kenya. In addition, the WTO established WTO Reference Centres connecting LDCs' capitals to WTO sources of information through the Internet; started a new programme to fund interns within country missions in Geneva; and supported increased participation of developing countries, especially LDCs, in international standard-setting bodies. Other initiatives related to technical assistance include creation of the Doha Development Agenda Global Trust Fund and the entering into agreements with other international organizations, including the Asian Development Bank and the

---

4 US Trade Representative Charlene Barshefsky, 'Remarks, Closing Plenary, World Trade Organization Conference' <www.ustr.gov/speech-test/barshefsky/barshefsky_57.pdf>, 3 December 1999.

Arab Monetary Fund, to cooperate on joint technical assistance programmes and capacity building designed to enhance developing state participation. The WTO has sponsored a series of 'Geneva weeks' (in November 1999; October 2000; September 2001; and April 2002) where WTO Members without permanent representation in Geneva come to WTO headquarters for a week-long session of briefings from chairs of various WTO committees and councils, all designed to enhance their participation in the WTO. Finally, at the Doha Ministerial, a decision was made to establish the Agency for International Trade Information and Cooperation as an inter-governmental organization, to provide information, training, and personalized assistance services for developing state delegations.

In part as a result of these efforts, developing states have played an active role in post-Doha negotiations. In the agriculture negotiations, for example, more than 150 proposals and other written contributions had been presented through August 2002. Of these proposals, half were tabled by developing countries, either individually or in different groupings (such as the African Group). The developing countries and LDCs have taken the initiative in the negotiations on trade in services by tabling a large number of proposals (including, for example, an important LDC Group proposal on negotiation modalities). Similarly, developing states have submitted, as of October 2002, nearly 90 proposals regarding the expansion of special and differential treatment.

The Doha Ministerial did not use the 'Green Room' process. Instead, a 'Committee of the Whole' approach was used, which permitted all interested WTO Members to participate in plenary meetings, as well as in six working groups dealing with the major outstanding issues. The Chairs of the working groups reported regularly to the committee of the whole (i.e. the heads of delegations). There is a general sense that this system worked reasonably well, and was a major improvement over processes used at Seattle.

Moreover, the WTO has also taken steps to enhance the quality of developing states' participation in WTO dispute resolution proceedings. The most visible means of doing so is through creation of an Advisory Centre on WTO Law. The Centre began operations in July 2001. In its first year of operations, the Centre provided written legal analyses to six countries (three Members, one least developed country and two non-member developing countries). Three Members have requested an analysis of the merits of bringing a WTO case. In addition, two non-members requested legal opinions; one requested an opinion on the WTO consistency of trade policy proposals that its government was considering tabling as legislation. The Centre provided a written opinion on the vulnerability of such legislation to challenge by other WTO Members. Another state received a written opinion on the relationship between the General Agreement on Trade in Services (GATS) and proposed investment provisions in a free trade agreement. In addition, the Centre provided legal advice, upon request, in six WTO disputes during its first year.

Efforts on this front continue. While there can be little doubt that there has been substantial activity, whether or not this activity will translate into an enhanced quality of participation at the WTO is, at this point, an open question.[5] The post-Doha fight over who ought to serve as Chair of the Trade Negotiations Committee was a hint that developing states still feared that they could be marginalized in future negotiations.

Moreover, as this is written (November 2002), it is not clear that developing states have much to show as a result of the efforts to enhance their participation. For example, agriculture is, for many developing states, the key to the Doha Round. To date, despite a large number of proposals on the table, there has been little progress beyond pre-negotiation positions. More urgently, it appears that the Chair of the agriculture negotiations will not complete a draft modalities paper by the original December 2002 deadline, which may mean that a March 2003 deadline for 'modalities in further commitments' may slip as well. In addition, a July 2002 deadline for the Committee on Trade and Development to report its recommendations on strengthening 'special and differential' (S&D) treatment provisions came and went with no decision except a deadline extension to 31 December, 2002. The missed deadline reflects a deadlock between developed and developing states on S&D provisions. An October 2002 meeting revealed that developed states find many developing state proposals on S&D provisions to be impractical and developing states find developed states to be 'intractable'. The Doha Declaration on Trade-Related Aspects of Intellectual Property Rights (TRIPs) and Public Health was surely an important achievement for developing states. However, it does not solve all of the problems associated with intellectual property protection and public health. In particular, it leaves open the problem of states that lack manufacturing capacity to produce medicines under compulsory license, and progress on this issue since Doha has been limited. While it is surely too soon to expect substantial progress in negotiations on all of these issues, the present situation calls into question the assumption that enhanced participation will produce more favourable outcomes for developed states in the Doha Round. A fair conclusion is that the jury is still out on this issue.

There has similarly been much activity in the effort to facilitate and formalize the participation of non-state actors at the WTO. The Marrakesh Agreement specifically authorized the General Council to 'make appropriate arrangements for consultation and cooperation' with NGOs.[6] The General Council has since adopted a set of guidelines designed to define WTO–NGO relations.[7] Pursuant to these guidelines, the WTO Secretariat has organized a number of initiatives designed to improve the dialogue with civil society. For example, the Secretariat has organized three Symposia on trade and the environment, one on trade and development, and yet another on trade facilitation. These meetings have provided NGOs the opportunity to formally

---

5 *See*, for example, 'Implementation and Transparency Issues Make Slow Progress in WTO's General Council' (July–August 2000), 4 Bridges 5.

6 Marrakesh Agreement Establishing the World Trade Organization, Annex, 2, *in* Results of the Uruguay Round of Multilateral Trade Negotiations, The Legal Texts 404 (1994), reprinted in (1994) 33 ILM 1226.

7 Guidelines for arrangements on relations with Non-Governmental Organizations, Decision adopted by the General Council on 18 July 1996, WT/L/162.

discuss specific issues with representatives of WTO Member countries. In addition, the WTO's website provides access to much of the documentation that under GATT was deemed 'restricted' and therefore not available to the public. Finally, the WTO has webcast important meetings and hosted web-based discussion forums on topics of wide interest. These have been important moves to increase the WTO's transparency.

There have also been interesting developments in the context of dispute resolution that are commonly understood as efforts to increase the formal participation of non-state actors in the WTO dispute settlement system. Perhaps the most dramatic development occurred in the Shrimp–Turtle dispute,[8] where the Appellate Body (AB) explicitly rejected the panel's legal determination that amicus briefs submitted by NGOs could not be considered as a matter of WTO law. The AB held that 'a panel has the discretionary authority either to accept and consider or to reject information and advice submitted to it, whether requested or not'.[9] However, the AB expressly approved the panel's decision to permit parties to append NGO briefs to their own briefs, and adopted a similar procedure itself. The United States accepted this invitation, and appended NGO briefs to its submission. The AB then specifically asked the United States to state whether it 'agree[d] with or adopt[ed]' the legal arguments set out in the three non-governmental organization briefs appended to its own submission.[10] The United States replied that '[it] agrees with the legal arguments in the submissions of the non-governmental organizations to the extent those arguments concur with the US arguments set out in our main submission'.[11] The AB proceeded to largely ignore the NGO arguments and instead 'focus' solely on the arguments the United States presented in its 'main submission'.[12]

In the British Steel case, the American Iron and Steel Institute submitted an amicus brief to the panel, but it was rejected as not being timely filed.[13] Before the AB, both the American Iron and Steel Institute and the Speciality Steel Industry of North American submitted amicus briefs; both were rejected. The AB's reasoning, in its entirety, is as follows:

> We are of the opinion that we have the legal authority under the DSU to accept and consider amicus curiae briefs in an appeal in which we find it pertinent and useful to do so. In this appeal, we have not found it necessary to take the two amicus briefs filed into account in rendering our decision.[14]

---

8 United States – Import Prohibition of Certain Shrimp and Shrimp Products, WT/DS58/AB/R (12 October 1998).
9 *Id.*
10 *Id.*
11 *Id.*
12 *Id.*
13 United States – Imposition of Countervailing Duties on Certain Hot-Rolled Lead and Bismuth Carbon Steel Products Originating in the United Kingdom, at para. 6.3, WT/DS138/R (10 May 2000).
14 United States – Imposition of Countervailing Duties on Certain Hot-Rolled Lead and Bismuth Carbon Steel Products Originating in the United Kingdom, at para. 42, WT/DS138/AB/R (10 May 2000).

The next important development on this front occurred in the Asbestos case.[15] At the panel stage of this dispute, five NGOs submitted amicus briefs. The EC incorporated by reference two of these briefs, which the panel considered. The other three NGO briefs were rejected, again with minimal discussion.[16] On the appeal of this case, it quickly became apparent that many NGOs wanted to submit briefs. The AB issued a 'communication' setting out a procedure whereby interested entities could file a petition for leave to file a written brief with the AB. In response, the WTO's General Council scheduled a special meeting to discuss this communication and the larger issue of NGO participation. At this meeting, the large majority of WTO Members who spoke criticized the AB for issuing this communication. The Chair of the General Council stated that he would forward a note to the AB urging it to exercise 'extreme caution' on this issue. The AB denied each of the 17 applications for leave to file an amicus brief that had been submitted. Amicus briefs have been filed in a number of subsequent cases. In many cases they have not been considered.

EC – Trade Description of Sardines is the AB's most recent opportunity to examine this issue.[17] In this action, Morocco submitted an amicus brief, causing the AB to confront, for the first time, whether WTO Members can submit such briefs. The AB found that such briefs are 'admissible' in theory, but that this particular brief was not of assistance in deciding the dispute before the AB. The AB, therefore, did not consider Morocco's arguments. The AB similarly found an amicus brief submitted by a US law professor to be 'admissible' in theory, but not helpful to the resolution of the case, and the arguments in this submission were not considered. A European-based NGO, the UK Consumer's Association, working with a British law firm, prepared a lengthy letter challenging the legality of the EC regulation. Peru attached this letter to its submission. The panel considered this letter in its deliberations and even cited to the letter in its report. The AB affirmed the panel's use of this letter as evidence.

So, on the doctrinal front, there is an apparent advance – panels and the AB now clearly have legal authority to accept NGO submissions. But, paradoxically, the resulting practice is actually a step backwards for those who urge greater NGO involvement. In practice, NGO submissions are frequently rejected. In those few instances when they are even considered, they typically are considered only when adopted by a party.[18] In these cases, NGOs do not participate as independent actors, but rather as 'appendages'

---

15 European Communities – Measures Affecting Asbestos and Asbestos-Containing Products, WT/DS135/AB/R (12 March 2001).

16 *Id.* at paras 6.1–6.4.

17 European Communities – Trade Description of Sardines, WT/DS231/AB/R (26 September 2002).

18 A potentially important counter-example is the panel's acceptance of an amicus brief submitted by the Interior Alliance, an NGO representing indigenous peoples in United States – Preliminary Determinations with Respect to Certain Softwood Lumber from Canada, WT/DS236/R (27 September 2002). It remains to be seen whether this heralds a new trend or is aberrational. In this regard, I note that the panel in this dispute rejected three other amicus briefs, on the grounds that they were not timely filed. *Id.* at para. 7.2.

to the parties' submissions. In practice, they participate at the sufferance of the parties to the dispute. But by effectively turning NGOs from independent actors into entities that simply echo government arguments, the panels eliminate the potential advantages of NGO participation.

Moreover, this process reinforces many of the conventional arguments against NGO participation – that NGOs most appropriately participate at the domestic level, that states are free to adopt or reject NGO positions, and that NGOs should not have 'two bites at the apple' by participating at the international level. While doctrinal developments deprive NGOs of a powerful rhetorical argument about the closed nature of WTO dispute resolution, actual practice effectively keeps NGOs excluded from WTO dispute resolution.[19]

In short, despite substantial activity, there is a real question whether meaningful progress has been made on the inclusion front. Do we, in practice, have only the illusion of inclusion?

Things are little better on the transparency front. WTO hearings still remain closed to the public. The United States has offered a proposal to permit private parties to attend oral proceedings before panels. A number of WTO Members, including Japan and the European Union, have repeatedly opposed such proposals. For example, a day before oral argument in the British–Steel case, the United States requested that private parties be permitted to attend the hearing. The European Union objected, and the panel denied the United States' request. As is the case with efforts to improve the quality of developing nation participation, activity purportedly designed to enhance NGO participation in WTO processes has yet to bear significant fruit.

For these reasons, there is a broad consensus that the efforts to improve the quality of developing state participation and to improve the transparency of WTO processes have not been sufficient. Moreover, the failure to make greater progress on these issues has important implications. As a political matter, it is likely that only limited progress can be made in the new negotiating round unless and until these demands for greater inclusiveness are satisfactorily addressed. The paradox is that at the same time the WTO decision-making processes must become more inclusive, they must also become more efficient. Moving ahead on both of these apparently inconsistent fronts is one of the key challenges facing the WTO in this time of transition.

4.3 What?

A second inquiry that sheds light on this transitional era is the 'what' question. What issue areas are properly in the trade regime? What topics are – or

[19] This is particularly disturbing when one considers the access the other types of non-state actors have to WTO dispute resolution proceedings. *See*, for example, Jeffrey L. Dunoff, 'The Misguided Debate Over NGO Participation at the WTO' (1998) 1 *Journal of International Economic Law* 433 (outlining the considerable roles that business entities play in WTO dispute resolution).

should be – considered in other international fora? What are the principles that enable one to distinguish issues that are properly within from those properly outside the WTO's ambit?

As with the 'who' question, there are internal and external components to the 'what' question. The public component of this debate tends to centre on the inclusion of social issues, most prominently including environment and labour issues. During the last decade, the 'trade and environment' debate captured extraordinary public attention.[20] A series of controversial panel decisions, starting with Tuna–Dolphin I, kept the topic on the public agenda, and the resulting polarized debate assumed a self-perpetuating quality.

In the months preceding the Seattle Ministerial, the 'trade and labour' issue gained increased prominence. In response, both the United States and the European Union called for greater cooperation between the WTO and the International Labour Organization (ILO). In addition, the United States called for a WTO working party to examine possible links between trade and labour issues. President Clinton also devoted much of his Seattle speech to labour issues.

Of course, in a newspaper interview at the start of the Seattle Ministerial, the President suggested that labour rights should be incorporated into trade agreements and, ultimately, be enforceable through trade sanctions. Developing states, which had opposed the earlier US proposals, expressed a very strong negative reaction to the President's comments, and many consider that this interview helped seal the fate of the Seattle Ministerial.[21]

But these social issues do not exhaust the 'what' question. Other issues, which form part of the 'internal' debate at the WTO, include questions over whether the trade regime should include rules on, for example, competition policy, bribery, foreign direct investment, and other 'economic' issues.

Both within and outside of the WTO, there is an utterly fascinating and frustrating dissensus on the issue of what areas should be considered to be 'within' the trade system. Many trade experts, including I.M.Destler, urge that the social issues, such as labour and environment, are simply the next natural step in the long GATT journey from tariffs to quotas to services to intellectual

---

20 *See*, for example, Daniel C. Esty, Greening the GATT: Trade, Environment, and the Future (1994); C. Ford Runge, Freer Trade, Protected Environment: Balancing Trade Liberalization and Environmental Interests (1994); Steve Charnovitz, 'Free Trade, Fair Trade, Green Trade: Defogging the Debate' (1994) 27 *Cornell International Law Journal* 459; Jeffrey L. Dunoff, 'Institutional Misfits: The GATT, the ICJ, and Trade-Environment Disputes' (1994) 15 *Michigan Journal of International Law* 1043; Jeffrey L. Dunoff, 'Reconciling International Trade with Preservation of the Global Commons: Can We Prosper and Protect' (1992) 49 *Washington and Lee Law Review* 1407.

21 President Clinton suggested that, at some point, it might be appropriate to enforce labour standards through trade measures. The reaction of India's Commerce and Industry Minister was representative of many developing nations: 'The threat of sanctions,' said Murasoli Maran, 'was the last straw. It was a nakedly protectionist act by a clique of developed countries behaving like a "kangaroo court"'. There is, of course, some irony surrounding the debate over the inclusion of labour issues at the WTO, given that Article 7.1 of the original ITO Charter provided that 'The Members recognize that unfair labour conditions, particularly in production for export, create difficulties in international trade …'

property, and hence should be brought into the WTO system.[22] On the other side, equally distinguished commentators, including Columbia University economist Jagdish Bhagwati and former White House official Dan Tarullo, argue that the 'trade and' issues should be kept out of the trade system, enabling the WTO to focus on what it does best, removing border barriers to trade.[23] Experienced trade officials, including the former Director of the WTO Secretariat's Legal Affairs Division, argue that inclusion of 'trade and' issues will undermine both the trade order and the attainment of non-trade objectives.[24] Others, including World Bank economist Keith Maskus, argue for the inclusion of some of the 'trade and' issues within the WTO, but not others.[25] Still others, including trade officials such as WTO Director-General Supachai and academics such as Yale Law Professor Daniel Esty have urged the creation of new international bodies, such as a Global Environment Organization, to address the new issues.[26] Finally, Harvard political economist Dani Rodrik, Brookings Institution scholar Bob Litan and others look to domestic solutions to the 'what' issue, and urge governments to co-opt opposition to trade liberalization by enlarging domestic social safety nets.[27]

The Doha Ministerial launched negotiations on the relationship between WTO rules and multilateral environmental agreements and the reduction of barriers to trade in environmental goods and services. Ministers also reaffirmed the decision taken at the 1996 Singapore Ministerial that labour standards issues are best addressed at the ILO. They also agreed that negotiations on investment and competition would 'take place after the Fifth Session of the Ministerial Conference on the basis of a decision to be taken, by explicit consensus, at that Session on the modalities of negotiations'. Doha's ambiguous outcome on future negotiations over investment and competition, and the lack of post-Doha progress on environmental

---

22 *See*, for example, I.M. Destler and Peter J. Balint, The New Politics of American Trade: Trade, Labor, and the Environment (1999).

23 *See*, for example, Jagdish Bhagwati, 'What *Really* Happened in Seattle' <www.columbia.edu/~jb38/really.pdf>, Daniel K. Tarullo, 'Norms and Institutions in Global Competition Policy' (2000) 94 *American Journal of International Law* 478.

24 Frieder Roessler, 'Domestic Policy Objectives and the Multilateral Trade Order: Lessons from the Past', in A. Krueger (ed.), *The WTO as an International Institution* (1998), p. 213.

25 Keith E. Maskus, Regulatory Standards in the WTO: Comparing Intellectual Property Rights with Competition Policy, Environmental Protection, and Core Labor Standards, Institute for International Economics Working Paper 00-1 (January 2000).

26 Supachai Panitchpakdi, 'The Evolving Multilateral Trade System in the New Millennium,' (2001) 33 *Geroge Washington International Law Review* 419. Other trade officials have made similar calls. *See*, for example, Renato Ruggiero, 'Opening Remarks to the High Level Symposium on Trade and the Environment' <http://www.wto.org>, 15 March 1999. *See* also Daniel C. Esty, Greening the GATT: Trade, Environment and the Future (1994). I have endorsed the call for a new global environmental organization, albeit for different reasons. Jeffrey L. Dunoff, 'From Green to Global: Toward the Transformation of International Environmental Law' (1995) 19 *Harvard Environmental Law Review* 241. The EU has recently expressed renewed interest in this idea. European Union: EU Working Group Formed to Examine Creation of World Environment Organization, *BNA International Environment Daily*, 18 July 2000.

27 Robert E. Litan, 'The "Globalization" Challenge: The U.S. Role in Shaping World Trade and Investment' (2000) 18 *Brookings Review* 35; Dani Rodrik, 'Five Simple Principles for World Trade' <www.ksg.harvard.edu/redrik/papers>, 29 November 1999.

issues indicates how controversial these issues remain. As I've discussed the various ways that incorporation of the new 'trade and' issues challenge our most fundamental understanding of the trade system elsewhere,[28] in the final section of the chapter, I will limit my remarks to a few comments on why the 'trade and' debate generates such radically incompatible arguments, and why this ongoing debate is unlikely to reach closure anytime soon. For now, however, the salient point is that, absent progress toward a consensus on the 'what' issues, negotiations in the new round are unlikely to make significant progress.

4.4 Where?

A third inquiry asks where the WTO and international trade law fit into the larger international law universe. It is, in part, a question about the relationship of WTO law to other areas of international law, and in part a question about the relationship of the WTO to other international organizations.

4.4.1 The doctrinal dimension

There is substantial debate over whether the WTO is or should be a 'self-contained regime'. Under the GATT system, dispute resolution panels tended to ignore public international law when interpreting the General Agreement. While WTO panels and the WTO AB are much more likely to rely upon non-WTO law, this trend is not complete and there are important counter-examples.

GATT practice is well illustrated by the Tuna–Dolphin I report. In that dispute, the US's argument that the Convention on International Trade in Endangered Species (CITES) and various other international environmental agreements were relevant to the dispute was summarily dismissed. The panel stated that 'the agreements cited by the parties to the dispute were bilateral or plurilateral agreements that were not concluded among the contracting parties to the [GATT], and that they did not apply to the interpretation of the [GATT] or the application of its provisions'.[29]

But more recent panels have, for the most part, followed a rather different path with respect to the use or incorporation of non-WTO international law.[30] Perhaps the most striking example is the Shrimp–Turtle AB report.

---

[28] Jeffrey L. Dunoff, 'The Death of the Trade Regime' (1999) 10 *European Journal of International Law* 733.

[29] United States – Restrictions on Imports of Tuna, GATT Doc DS29/R (16 June 1994), at para. 5.19.

[30] The texts of several of the Uruguay Round Agreements explicitly refer to other international agreements, and which may therefore serve as direct sources of law in WTO dispute settlement proceedings. For example, the TRIPs Agreement refers to several of the major international intellectual property conventions, including the Paris Convention, the Bern Convention, the Rome Convention, and the Treaty on Intellectual Property in Respect of Integrated Circuits. Agreement on Trade Related Intellectual Property Rights, Article I.3.

That panel had to determine whether the phrase 'exhaustible natural resources' in Article XX(g) of the GATT included living resources. Declaring that this phrase must be read 'in the light of contemporary concern of the community of nations about the protection and conservation of the environment',[31] the AB reviewed relevant provisions of the Convention on the Law of the Sea,[32] Convention on Biological Diversity,[33] Agenda 21[34] and other international environmental law instruments. Similarly, in determining whether the US measure constituted 'unjustifiable discrimination' for purposes of Article XX, the AB relied heavily upon numerous international environmental documents, including the Rio Declaration, expressing a preference for multilateral over unilateral actions.

WTO panels have also applied bilateral agreements in the context of WTO dispute resolution. For example, in the Brazil – EC dispute over poultry exports to Europe, Brazil argued that a bilateral agreement between it and the Community was applicable to the dispute.[35] While the EC did not object to having the panel consider this agreement, the United States, as a third party, argued that the bilateral agreement was not within the panel's terms of reference.[36] The panel noted that the agreement had been negotiated within the framework of GATT Article XXVIII, and decided to consider the agreement 'to the extent relevant to the determination of the EC's obligations under the WTO agreements *vis-à-vis* Brazil'.[37] The AB found 'no reversible error in the Panel's treatment' of this bilateral agreement.[38]

The AB also had to decide whether to use non-WTO customary international law on several occasions. For example, in the Beef–Hormones dispute, the United States and Canada challenged a European ban on meat and meat products from cows injected with certain hormones. The case turned, in part, on the scientific justification offered for this ban, and the panel faced the question of whether the precautionary principle is part of customary international law. The panel held that 'even if' the precautionary principle is considered customary international law, it would not override

---

Contd.
Similarly, the DSU refers to the 'customary rules of interpretation of public international law', which has been held by the Appellate Body to refer to rules of treaty law set out in the Vienna Convention on the Law of Treaties. See United States – Standards for Reformulated and Conventional Gasoline, WT/DS2/AB/R at 17 (29 April 1996). For purposes of this essay, instances like this, where the covered agreements explicitly reference other international legal agreements or norms, are not considered a use of 'non-WTO law'.

31 Shrimp–Turtle AB Report, *supra* note 9.

32 United Nations Convention on the Law of the Sea, 10 December 1982, reprinted in, 21 *International Legal Materials* 1261 (entered into force 16 November 1994).

33 Convention on Biological Diversity, June 5, 1992, reprinted in, 31 *International Legal Materials* 818 (entered into force 29 December 1993).

34 United Nations Conference on Environment and Development, Agenda 21: Programme of Action for Sustainable Development, UN Doc. A/CONF.151/26 (1992).

35 European Communities – Measures Affecting the Importation of Certain Poultry Products, WT/DS69/R (13 July 1998).

36 *Id.* at para. 197.

37 *Id.* at para. 2.02.

38 European Communities – Measures Affecting the Importation of Certain Poultry Products, WT/DS69/AB/R, at para. 85 (13 July 1998).

explicit provisions of the WTO Agreements.[39] The AB affirmed, noting that the status of the precautionary principle in international law is the subject of debate.[40] The AB also stated that while the precautionary principle may have crystallized into a general principle of 'customary international environmental law', it was not clear whether it has been widely accepted as a principle of 'customary international law'.[41]

In the Bananas case, the AB addressed the issue of whether parties to a dispute could be represented by private counsel. St. Lucia, one of the intervening states, sought to include two private lawyers on its delegation before a panel. The United States and others objected, and the Panel excluded from the hearing those delegates who were not governmental employees.[42] This decision was challenged on appeal.

The parties and the AB understood this as raising a question of general international law rather than a question of WTO law. St. Lucia argued that 'as a matter of customary international law, no international organization ha[d] the right to interfere with a government's sovereign right to decide whom it may accredit as officials and Members of its delegation, absent rules to the contrary'. Canada and Jamaica endorsed this argument, but the United States and others opposed, essentially on the grounds that it was contrary to established WTO practice and was not required by general international law.

Noting that neither the WTO Agreement, the Dispute Settlement Understanding (DSU), nor the Working Procedures addressed the issue, the AB framed the issue not as a question of what international law permitted but, rather, of what it did not prohibit. The AB concluded that 'we can find nothing in ... customary international law or the prevailing practice of international tribunals, which prevents a WTO Member from determining the composition of its delegation in AB proceedings'.[43]

The conflicting positions reflected in these various reports on whether, and how, WTO panels should incorporate non-WTO law find expression in trade scholarship as well. Scholars such as Joel Trachtman argue that '[t]he mandate to WTO dispute resolution panels, to the AB, and to the Dispute Settlement Body is clear: apply (directly) only WTO law'.[44] This argument finds support in several provisions of the DSU. For example, DSU Article 3(2)

---

39 EC – Measures Concerning Meat and Meat Products (Hormones), WT/DS26/AB/R, WT/DS48/R, para. 8.157 (16 January 1998); *Id.* at para. 8.160.

40 EC – Measures Concerning Meat and Meat Products (Hormones), WT/DS26/AB/R at para. 123 (16 January 1998).

41 *Id.*

42 *See* EC – Regime for the Importation, Sale, and Distribution of Bananas, WT/DS27/AB/R, para. 7.11 (9 September 1997).

43 *Id.* at para. 10. The AB view has since been followed by subsequent panels. In the Indonesia–Autos dispute, the panel found 'no provision in the WTO Agreement or the DSU which prevents a WTO Member from determining the composition of its delegation to WTO panel meetings'. Indonesia – Certain Measures Affecting the Automobile Industry, WT/DS54/R, WT/DS55/R, WT/DS59/R, WT/DS64/R, para. 14.1 (2 July 1998). In the Korea Alcohol Case, the panel held similarly, allowing Korea to be represented by private counsel. Korea – Taxes on Alcoholic Beverages, WT/DS75/R, WT/DS84/R, para. 10.31 (17 September 1998).

44 Joel P. Trachtman, 'The Domain of WTO Dispute Resolution' (1999) 40 *Harvard International Law Journal* 333.

provides that the dispute settlement system 'serves to preserve the rights and obligations of Members under the covered agreements, and to clarify the existing provisions of those agreements in accordance with customary rules of interpretation of public international law', and that '[r]ecommendations and rulings of the DSB cannot add to or diminish the rights and obligations provided in the covered agreements'. In addition, Article 7 standard panel terms of reference provides for reference only to law arising from the WTO agreements. Finally, Article 11 of the DSU states that the function of panels is to make an objective assessment of the matter before it, including the applicability of and conformity with the covered agreements. Trachtman argues that these specific references to the 'covered agreements' identify and limit the law applicable in WTO dispute resolution proceedings: 'WTO dispute resolution panels and the AB are limited to the application of substantive WTO law and are not authorized to apply general substantive international law or other conventional international law'.[45]

In contrast, scholars such as Thomas Schoenbaum and David Palmeter and Petros Mavroidis argue a contrary position. Schoenbaum, for example, relies upon language in the DSU granting panels and the AB authority to 'make such other findings as will assist the DSB in making the recommendation or in giving the rulings provided for in the covered agreements'.[46] Schoenbaum argues that this should be read as an 'implied powers' clause which, broadly interpreted, would allow panels to decide all aspects of a dispute, and to avoid piecemeal decision-making.[47] The logic of this argument would greatly expand the subject matter jurisdiction of panels beyond a determination of whether a particular measure is GATT-consistent, and direct panels to use non-WTO substantive law when that law is relevant to some portion of the dispute between the parties.

Palmeter and Mavroidis reach a similar conclusion via a different argument. They argue that, while the DSU does not explicitly include an analogue to Article 38(1) of the ICJ Statute,[48] setting forth a list of sources of law, the terms of Article 38(1) are 'effectively brought into WTO dispute settlement' by the DSU.[49] Palmeter and Mavroidis rely, in particular, on DSU Article 7, which specifies that the terms of reference for panels shall be '[t]o

---

[45] *Id.* at 347–48.

[46] DSU, Article 11.

[47] Thomas Schoenbaum, 'WTO Dispute Settlement: Praise and Suggestions for Reform', (1998) 47 *International and Comparative Law Quarterly* 647, 653.

[48] This article provides: The Court, whose function is to decide in accordance with international law such disputes as are submitted to it, shall apply:

(a) international conventions, whether general or particular, establishing rules expressly recognized by the contesting states;
(b) international custom as evidence of a general practice accepted as law;
(c) the general principles of law recognized by civilized nations;
(d) ... judicial decisions and the teachings of the most highly qualified publicists of the various nations, as subsidiary means for the determination of rules of law.

[49] David Palmeter and Petros Mavroidis, 'The WTO Legal System: Sources of Law' (1998) 92 *American Journal of International Law* 398.

examine, in the light of the relevant provisions in (the covered agreement(s) cited by the parties to the dispute), the matter referred to the [panel]', and to 'address the relevant provisions in any covered agreement or agreements cited by the parties to the dispute'. According to Palmeter and Mavroidis, this article serves as 'the WTO substitute, mutatis mutandis, for Article 38 [of the ICJ Statute]'.[50]

It would appear that those who argue against the incorporation of non-WTO law have the better of the textual argument. Nevertheless, there is a strong trend in recent panel and AB reports toward incorporation. Many have applauded this development as a way of aligning WTO law with the mainstream of international law. However, as I argue in Section 4.6, there is reason to question whether the incorporation of non-WTO law by panels represents an integration of WTO law with other areas of international law.

4.4.2 The institutional dimension

The GATT had relatively little interaction with other international institutions during its existence. As a result, during the Uruguay Round negotiations, a negotiating group on the Functioning of the GATT System (FOGS) was created. One of the goals of FOGS was to improve the linkages between the GATT and the Bretton Woods institutions. After seven years of negotiations, FOGS work product consisted entirely of a largely rhetorical Ministerial Declaration on the Contribution of the WTO to Achieving Greater Coherence in Global Economic Policymaking. The Declaration included an 'invitation' to the WTO Director-General to seek greater coherence in global economic policymaking with the World Bank and International Monetary Fund (IMF).

The WTO has since concluded agreements with the IMF, in 1996, and with the World Bank, in 1997. These agreements address information exchange, provide access for staff from one organization to meetings at the other organization, authorize staff consultation and cooperation, and provide for the possibility of consultation on trade policy-related issues. In many ways, the agreements formalize the consultations and working linkages that had developed informally over the years. While the notion of coherence in play here is rather vague, these agreements, in effect provide a framework for these institutions to explore the precise mechanisms for strengthening institutional cooperation. The WTO has also entered into agreements with, *inter alia*, the World Intellectual Property Organization and the Office International des Episzooties.

It is instructive to compare these attempts at cooperative interactions with the WTO's interactions with other international organizations, particularly those concerned with 'social' issues. In 1997, the WTO approved an Integrated Framework with five other international organizations (UNCTAD, ITC, IMF, World Bank, and UNDP) to provide assistance to

---

[50] *Id.*

least-developed nations.[51] However, to date, little has come from this initiative. In the period before the Seattle meeting, the United States, Canada, Norway, Denmark, Switzerland, and Sweden all submitted proposals to expand cooperation among international institutions on trade and development issues. The European Union submitted the most detailed of these proposals.[52] Yet even this document revealed a reluctance to expand the substantive relationships between the WTO and other international institutions.

While these interactions have been relatively benign – if unproductive – at other times relations have been markedly less harmonious. In one infamous example, the WTO invited the Director-General of the ILO, which addresses international labour issues, to address the WTO's Singapore Ministerial. However, in response to pressure from several developing nations, including India and Pakistan, this invitation was later withdrawn.

More recently, the WTO engaged in a war of words with the UN High Commissioner for Human Rights. A draft report prepared for the Subcommission on the Protection of Human Rights states that the WTO is a 'veritable nightmare' for certain sectors of humanity and criticizes WTO rules as 'grossly unfair and even prejudiced'.[53] In a strongly worded response, the WTO secretariat sharply criticizes the report's 'language, methodology, and main conclusions'. The letter expresses surprise that the WTO was not approached during preparation of the report, and criticizes the report for drawing sweeping conclusions about the WTO that are unsubstantiated by empirical evidence. Finally, the letter suggests a meeting with WTO officials to correct the 'significant misunderstandings' included in the report.[54]

To be sure, it is reasonable for the WTO to seek greater coherence between itself, the IMF and the World Bank. The three bodies share similar philosophies and objectives. All are dedicated to expanding international trade, promoting high levels of employment, and increasing standards of living and real incomes. Moreover, while neither the Fund nor the Bank have direct regulatory authority over international trade, they do have important responsibilities in this area. For example, the level of a nation's trade barriers and its trade policies may affect the viability of specific projects financed by the Bank, as well as the success of the Bank's non-project lending. Similarly, the Fund's role in regulating the use of exchange restrictions and in exercising surveillance over monetary and financial

---

51 WTO, High Level Meeting on Integrated Initiatives for Least-Developed Countries Trade Development, WT/LDC/HL/1/Rev. 1, 23 October 1997.

52 Addressing the Challenges of Globalization: The Role of the WTO in Cooperation with Other International Organizations, Communication from the European Communities, WT/GC/W/391, 12 November 1999.

53 The Realization of Economic, Social and Cultural Rights: Globalization and its impact on the full enjoyment of human rights, E/CN.4/Sub.2/2000/13.

54 Letter from Miguel Rodriguez Mendoza, WTO Deputy Director-General to Mary Robinson, UN High Commissioner for Human Rights, 18 August 2000.

policies gives the Fund significant direct and indirect influence over trade matters.

But the pattern of interactions outlined above raises troubling questions. Why should the WTO's relations with international bodies concerned with labour and human rights issues be markedly less harmonious than its relations with the Bretton Woods institutions? Does the WTO interact with international financial and monetary bodies as co-equals, but treat international bodies that focus on social issues as hierarchical inferiors? In short, will the WTO help spearhead – or resist – moves towards integrated decision, making with international bodies other than the Bretton Woods institutions?

4.5 Why?

Examination of the 'who', 'what', and 'where' questions illuminate the nature and scope of the transitional issues facing the WTO. But they also raise additional questions, particularly the 'why' question. Why is the WTO in transition now? Ironically, each of the transition issues outlined above can be understood as a direct result of the trade regime's successes over the past 50 years.

GATT's negotiating rounds produced significant decreases in tariffs and other barriers to trade, and hence contributed to the dramatic expansion of global trade in the post-War era. But trade liberalization and expansion greatly increase the domestic economic importance, and hence the political salience, of international trade policy. This heightened political importance of international trade policy, in turn, produces the demands for inclusion from NGOs and other groups that previously displayed little interest in the international trade system, and the complaints that the trade regime suffers from a 'democratic deficit'.

Moreover, the GATT's extraordinary success at lowering tariffs and other 'border' barriers to trade has raised the importance and the scrutiny given to 'behind the border' barriers to trade. But GATT scrutiny of and disciplines on these behind the border barriers such as technical standards, sanitary and phytosanitary standards, lax competition laws, and health and safety regulations, impose restraints on the policy tools that governments can use to achieve both economic and, increasingly, non-economic policy objectives. And public dissatisfaction with these constraints has given rise to the 'trade and' agenda and the debate over 'what' issues should and should not be part of the WTO system.

Expanded trade also results in increased government attention to issues of international competitiveness and increased pressures to challenge alleged barriers to trade in other markets. Both of these heighten the clashes between trade and other policy areas, giving rise to the 'trade and' issues. In addition, these clashes – and panel reports deciding that domestic laws are incompatible with the GATT – raise public concern over the apparent priority of trade law over other areas of law, giving rise to questions as to 'where' international trade law fits in the larger international law universe.

4.6 How?

Finally, how are the issues reviewed above related? How might these issues be solved? While a complete discussion of these questions is well beyond the scope of this essay, I will identify three of the most important links between the various transition issues: (a) each of the three questions discussed above raise issues that transcend the trade regime and raise fundamental questions about the international legal order; (b) each of the questions discussed above reveals a 'myth' about the trade system; (c) each of the questions has an important expressive dimension. Finally, I will outline a few suggestions intended to redirect the debate over how these issues might be resolved.

4.6.1 The 'who', 'what', and 'where' issues are not only central to the WTO's transition, but also raise fundamental questions about the nature of the international legal order

One link among the 'who', 'what', and 'where' questions is that they do not present questions of mere negotiating strategy or diplomatic ingenuity. Rather, they involve issues that transcend the WTO's current transition era and raise fundamental questions about the nature of the international legal order as a whole. Thus, we can usefully understand the 'who' question in the trade context, for example, as an instantiation of ongoing debates over the status, roles, and functions of both states and non-state actors that runs throughout international legal discourse.

Similarly, the 'what' question can be understood to call into question the current conventional vision of public international law as consisting of a series of substantive fields (e.g. trade, human rights, environment, etc.) that exist as independent and autonomous areas, each subject to its own rules practices, norms, and institutional structures.

Indeed, the 'what' question implicitly emphasizes that our present way of organizing the disciplines of international law is a historically contingent phenomena. While international trade today is one of the most visible areas of international law, treatises, and scholarship from 50 or 60 years ago taught that international law consisted entirely of two categories, the 'Law of Peace' and the 'Law of War', and were largely silent regarding trade. As recently as the mid-1960s, international trade law was widely considered to be outside the mainstream of international law.[55] Indeed, in 1971, the

[55] Hence, leading international law treatises and casebooks from the time largely ignore international trade law. *See*, for example, 1 Oppenheim's International Law 971 ('the details of commercial treaties are, for the most part, purely technical, and are, therefore, outside the scope of a general treatise on International Law') (8th edn, H. Lauterpacht (ed.), D.P. O'Connell, International Law (1965)) (leading Canadian casebook, which does not list 'international trade' in its comprehensive index). For a fascinating account of the 'creation' of the field of international trade law in the United States, *see* David Kennedy, 'The International Style in Postwar Law and Policy: John Jackson and the Field of International Economic Law' (1995) 10 *American Journal of International Law & Policy* 671.

Societe Francaise de Droit International sponsored its famous debate on whether international economic law was part of international law or an autonomous discipline.[56] All of this suggests that there is nothing necessary or natural in the field's current doctrinal divisions, which consider, for example, international 'labour' issues to constitute a distinct doctrinal category from international 'trade' issues.

Finally, the 'where' question raises the related foundational question of whether the international legal order is a 'bric-a-brac' or a 'system'?[57] Is international law an aggregate of disparate elements or an organized and coherent structure?

4.6.2 The 'who', 'what', and 'where' questions reveal myths about the trade system

A second link among the 'who','what', and 'where' questions is that each reveals and subverts a fundamental myth about the trade system. For example, it is a truism among trade officials and scholars that the WTO is an intergovernmental body. This is frequently offered as a justification for not providing NGO and civil society access to WTO legislative and dispute settlement processes. The argument is that providing NGO access would not only undermine the intergovernmental status of the WTO, but also open the door to 'special interest' capture of WTO processes.[58]

While this truism is undoubtedly correct as a formal, textual matter, examination of the 'who' question problematizes this dominant understanding of the WTO. In fact, non-state actors have long played a significant, albeit informal and unofficial, role in both the legislative and dispute resolution aspects of the trade system. Thus, non-state actors had an enormous impact on the shape of the Uruguay Round negotiations. For example, in the late 1970s a small group of enterprises led by American Express and AIG invented the new term, 'trade in services', with the intention of bringing investment within the framework of multilateral trade rules. This private sector initiative ultimately resulted in the GATS and its 'commercial presence' commitments. Similarly, the pressure for including IPRs into the trading system was led by the software and pharmaceutical industries which argued, inter alia, that WIPO lacked an adequate enforcement mechanism, and that lax enforcement of intellectual property rights distorted international trade. Other examples abound, including the influential roles

---

56 Societe Francaise Pour le Droit International, Colloque d'Orleans, Aspects du droit international economique, Paris, editions Pedone (1972).

57 *See* Jean Combacau, 'Le Droit International: Bric–Brac ou Systeme?' (1986) 31 Archives de Philosophie du Droit 85.

58 Philip M. Nichols, 'Extension of Standing in World Trade Organization Disputes to Nongovernment Parties' (1996) 17 *University of Pennsylvania Journal of International Economic Law* 295; Philip M. Nichols, 'Realism, Liberalism, Values, and the World Trade Organization' (1996) 17 *University of Pennsylvania Journal of International Economic Law* 851; *See also* Steve Charnovitz, 'Participation of Non-Governmental Organizations in the World Trade Organization' (1996) 17 *University of Pennsylvania Journal of International Economic Law* 331.

played by private and industry actors in shaping GATT and WTO rules on agriculture, maritime transport, fish products, and anti-dumping actions.

Non-state actors have similarly played a significant role in WTO dispute resolution processes for a number of years.[59] Indeed, a number of WTO disputes – including the US–Japan dispute over photographic film[60] and the Reformulated Gasoline dispute[61] are only nominally between WTO parties, and can be more fruitfully understood as components of complex international corporate battles.[62] Other times, one of the real parties in interest is a WTO member, but the other nominal party is, in effect, espousing the claims of a private party. A good example of this phenomenon is the Bananas case,[63] where the United States, in effect, espoused the cases of private parties Chiquita Brands International and the Hawaiian Banana Industry Association. Hence, the examination of the 'who' question reveals the truism that 'the WTO is an intergovernmental body' is a myth.

Similarly, the 'what' question undermines the apparent tautology that the trade regime is a trade regime. But this seeming truism is also a myth; the WTO is not (only) a multilateral organization that deals exclusively with trade issues. The Uruguay Round Agreements contain rules on, *inter alia*, intellectual property, services, investment, technical barriers to trade, sanitary and phytosanitary standards, and competition rules. For these and other reasons, it is now conventional wisdom that inclusion of new issues in the Uruguay Round Agreements marked a watershed in the evolution of the global trading system, and signaled an era of deeper economic integration.

But the trade regime's transformation has been, if anything, even more profound. While there are many differences among the new issues, they often share a number of common characteristics. For present purposes, one of the similarities is their focus on the institutional infrastructure of domestic economies. Thus, for example, TRIPs requires WTO members to enact relatively comprehensive intellectual property regimes and to provide effective domestic fora for foreign parties who believe their intellectual property rights have been infringed. As this example suggests, the central domain of international 'trade' policy is increasingly domestic regulation and legal systems. Hence, the trade system, which used to focus on border measures and celebrate regulatory heterogeneity, increasingly focuses inside the border and urges regulatory harmonization. Much of the debate over 'what'

---

59 *See*, for example, Jeffrey L. Dunoff, 'The Misguided Debate Over NGO Participation at the WTO' (1998) 1 *Journal of International Economic Law* 433; Judith H. Bello, 'Some Practical Observations About WTO Settlement of Intellectual Property Disputes' (1997) 35 *Virginia Journal of International Law* 357, 360–1 (detailing various ways that private parties assist US government in the presentation of cases in WTO dispute resolution proceedings).

60 Japan – Measures Affecting Consumer Photographic Film and Paper, WT/DS44/R (31 March 1998).

61 United States – Standards for Reformulated and Conventional Gasoline, WT/DS2/AB/R (29 April 1996).

62 For an extended discussion, see Dunoff, Misguided Debate, *supra* n. 59.

63 European Communities – Regime for the Importation, Sale and Distribution of Bananas, Complaint by the United States, WT/DS27/R (22 May 1997); European Communities – Regime for the Importation, Sale and Distribution of Bananas, WT/DS27/AB/R (9 September 1997).

issues fall within the trade system fails to adequately account for this radical transformation of the 'trade' system. Hence, much of the 'what' debate proceeds from an outdated 'myth' about the nature of the trade system.

Finally, the 'where' question presupposes the myth that there exists a neat line that divides international 'trade' issues from other sorts of issues, such as international 'environmental' or 'competition' law issues. But the myth that we can usefully slice up the international legal domain into separate, self-contained subject matter areas, while probably never true, is increasingly false. Today, legal norms arising out of different subject matters can and do overlap, interact and, increasingly, clash. Indeed, the complex interactions between heretofore distinct subject areas, such as trade and environment, or development and human rights, present many of the most challenging and important international legal issues of our time.

Like many myths, each of the myths identified above served several purposes. For example, over the years, they helped to explain and justify the trade regime and to orient and provide focal points for diplomats and scholars as the trade community faced new challenges. Moreover, like many myths, each of these myths contained elements of truth. The question posed by the current transitional era is whether these myths – again, like many others – have now outlived their usefulness. I believe that, as the doctrinal and practical pressures felt in this time of transition illustrate, these myths no longer adequately capture underlying social and political realities, and may serve to frustrate, rather than advance, efforts to move ahead on the WTO's transition issues.[64]

4.6.3 The 'who', 'what', and 'where' questions contain an important expressive dimension

Finally, and perhaps most importantly, what is at stake in the 'who', 'what', and 'where' questions differs in important respects from what is at stake in more traditional trade issues. In conventional trade disputes, state A imposes a barrier to goods from state B. If state B prevails in WTO dispute resolution, state A is instructed to remove the offending trade measure. However, although state A 'lost' the particular dispute, the conventional understanding is that state A actually 'wins' because removing the trade restriction increases its aggregate welfare. To be sure, removing a trade barrier might harm an inefficient domestic producer, but, from a systemic perspective, it is a gain to both A and B to have more efficient producers successfully compete against less efficient domestic producers. Thus, while losing a case might present the losing government with some political difficulties, there was a rough consensus within the trade community that eliminating a trade measure because it was deemed GATT-inconsistent was a win–win action.

---

[64] For a more general claim about the obsolescence of many of international law's current doctrinal categories, *see* Jeffrey L. Dunoff, 'International Legal Scholarship at the Millennium' (2000) 1 *Chicago Journal of International Law* 85.

I believe that for many of the most highly charged of the current disputes, this conventional understanding of the 'win–win' nature of trade disputes is inapposite. Consider, for example, the debates over whether NGOs and civil society should have the right to participate in WTO dispute resolution; over intellectual property rights in the traditional knowledge of indigenous peoples; over bans on trade in genetically modified organisms; over the 'multifunctional' character of agriculture; or over trade in cultural products. Why do disputes over these issues attract so much more attention, and seem so relatively intractable, compared to, for example, disputes over Argentina's safeguards measures on footwear imports,[65] or Turkey's restrictions on the import of textiles from India,[66] or the Guatemala–Mexico dispute over sales of portland cement?[67]

I believe that the debates in the controversial areas are unlike debates in more conventional areas because they are largely not about expanding the size of the economic pie. They are largely not about maximizing aggregate welfare. What are these debates really about? I believe that many of the debates in these and other areas are largely debates over the social and moral standing of competing subcommunities, whether regional or racial, cultural or economic. Those most directly affected by these debates, whether a farming community or indigenous people, as well as other interested parties, often understand the choosing of one or another legal doctrine as a signal about the political and social standing of the affected groups, as a signal of whose stock is up and whose is down. The traditional, consequentialist rhetoric of trade law and doctrines is unlikely to accurately or adequately capture this important 'expressive' dimension of the 'who', 'what', and 'where' issues.

4.7 The Need for New Approaches

As many of the new problems facing the WTO in this time of transition grow out of earlier successes, it may be tempting to believe that the strategies that worked so successfully in the past will work again. In this short section, I outline why I believe that such conventional strategies are unlikely to be successful.

4.7.1 The limits of conventional decision-making processes

The GATT worked extraordinarily well. Governments worked together through negotiating rounds to significantly reduce barriers to trade and produce concrete benefits to all participants. But the system seems to have broken down. Why?

---

65 Argentina – Safeguards Measures on the Import of Footwear, WT/DS121/R (25 June 1999).

66 Turkey – Restrictions on Imports of Textile and Clothing Products, WT/DS34/R (31 May 1999).

67 Guatemala – Anti-Dumping Investigation Regarding Portland Cement from Mexico, WT/DS60/R (19 June 1998).

First, as the presence of some 20,000 protesters at Seattle made abundantly clear, the old days of multilateral trade negotiations being conducted by a small group of trade cognoscenti out of sight of the general public are forever gone. The creation of trade policy is now a high-profile enterprise. The WTO has been slow in adjusting to this new reality.[68]

Second, the WTO's membership has greatly increased, including many developing nations that previously were bystanders to trade negotiations. The GATT had 23 signatories when it came into effect in January 1947, 84 signatories at the end of the Tokyo Round in 1979, and more than 100 Members when the WTO was formed in 1994. As of this writing, the WTO has 144 Members, with the former Yugoslav Republic of Macedonia expected to become a Member before the end of 2002.

The previously impassive majority can no longer 'free ride' on negotiated agreements. Starting with the Uruguay Round, parties must participate in all negotiated agreements as part of a 'single undertaking'. This means that developing states have to commit to substantially greater reforms of their trade practices than in the past.

The old system worked because there were fewer players at the table and because there was no need for all countries to adhere to the results. Consensus building required the consent of only a small group of states; the rest went along. But this process is victim to the GATT's success at bringing developing states into the trade system and requiring them to be partners to the full range of new trade agreements.

4.7.2 The limits of conventional understandings of the trade system

Second, a classic understanding of trade politics is that trading states face a 'prisoner's dilemma' where each is tempted to pursue individually rational strategies (i.e. mercantilist trade policies) that produce sub-optimal outcomes. Under this understanding, the WTO helps solve this collective action problem and produce collectively optimal outcomes. But as analysis of the TRIPs Agreement suggests, the new issues undermine this vision of the trade regime as a mechanism for simply expanding the size of the pie.

Conventional border restrictions on trade amount to inefficient taxes on particular forms of economic activity. Hence, their restriction via trade liberalization is widely understood to be a move towards national and global welfare maximization. Granting greater protection to IPRs, in contrast, creates greater incentives for innovation while raising the costs of gaining access to the benefits of innovation. Such rules are unlikely to increase aggregate welfare in all countries. Moreover, many of the other 'trade and' issues, such as environment, and labour, present primarily distributional issues. Thus, the conventional game theoretic understanding that international cooperation to reduce trade distortions and expand trade will always

---

68 Daniel C. Esty, 'An Environmental Perspective on Seattle' (2000) 3 *Journal of International Economic Law* 176.

increase the domestic welfare of both the liberalizing nation and the global community will be unable to generate acceptable solutions to the 'what' questions.

Finally, conventional approaches to the 'who', 'what', and 'where' questions are likely to fail for another reason as well. Debates within and about the WTO tend to be consequentialist. That is, they tend to argue over what results will follow from adopting this or that rule, and whether such results are desirable. In this context, the 'desirable' outcome is typically understood to be the outcome that maximizes economic welfare.

But it is surely a mistake to understand the new trade issues exclusively in consequentialist terms. As noted above, these issues are so highly charged precisely because they have a largely expressive or symbolic importance. The traditional, consequentialist rhetoric of trade law and doctrines is unlikely to accurately or adequately capture this important expressive dimension of these issues.[69]

4.7.3 The limits of legalism

To make significant progress on the 'who', 'what', and 'where' questions, trade diplomats and reformers must not focus exclusively upon the texts of the Uruguay Round agreements, but instead must take cognizance of the larger conceptual, political, and institutional factors that shape each of the transition issues. Formalized legal analysis simply will not produce meaningful progress on these issues. This has less to do with any perceived inadequacies in legal reasoning than with the nature of the current problems facing the WTO.

For example, as suggested above, debate on whether to incorporate non-trade law into the trade regime is focused on whether the texts of the DSU and other Uruguay Round Agreements authorize or require such an incorporation. But this scholarly debate increasingly seems to be excessively formalistic, as it appears that the advocates for incorporation have, de facto, the upper hand. Indeed, in its very first opinion, the Appellate Body relied upon DSU language calling for WTO provisions to be clarified 'in accordance with customary rules of interpretation of public international law', to claim that: 'that direction [in Article 3.2] reflects a measure of recognition that the [GATT] is not to be read in clinical isolation from public international law'.[70]

But while the trend toward incorporation of non-WTO law seems strong, I wonder if important conceptual and practical considerations have been

---

69 The debate over the expressive meaning of law is voluminous. For a discussion of the relationship between consequentialist rhetorics and expressive theories of law, *see* Jane B. Baron and Jeffrey L. Dunoff, 'Against Market Rationality: Moral Critiques of Economic Analysis in Legal Theory' (1996) 17 *Cardozo Law Review* 431; I discuss the expressive function of international law in Jeffrey L. Dunoff, 'Some Costs and Benefits of Economic Analysis of International Law' (2001) *Proceedings of the Annual Meeting of the American Society of International Law* 185.

70 WTO Appellate Body, United States – Standards for Reformulated and Conventional Gasoline, WT/DS2/AB/R, at 17 (29 April 1996).

left out of the rather formalized and textual debate over whether WTO panels ought to incorporate non-WTO law. For example, in many ways, international trade law and international law are based upon different, if not conflicting, assumptions. Hence, international trade law, based upon the concept of 'comparative advantage', requires states, at times, to act in ways precisely opposite to what international law – based upon the notion of state sovereignty – would permit. For example, under a sovereignty-based regime, states are designed to protect the interests of its citizens, even at the expense of those outside the country; states pursue 'national' interests. But, international trade law is premised upon a notion of non-discrimination between like domestic and imported products; the pursuit of 'national interest' is understood as protectionism. Hence, '[a] sovereign state is inherently a mercantilist institution. This is implicit in the idea of sovereignty. But mercantilism is the antithesis of a liberal trade order'.[71] To date, the incorporation debate has not addressed the problems that flow from the fact that these two doctrinal areas start from different, nearly conflicting assumptions.[72]

Second, participants in the 'what' and 'where' debates have paid insufficient attention to the fact that the WTO now has, in effect, a highly functioning judicial law making process that is unique in international law. For many years, debate raged between those who argued that GATT dispute resolution was (or should be) mediatory and conciliatory, or whether it should be adjudicative. The advent of the DSU marked an end to this debate, and a decisive victory for those who urged use of an adjudicative model.

But the WTO dispute resolution system goes much further than simply supplying a 'rule-based' way of resolving disputes. Despite 'myths' to the contrary, the WTO dispute resolution system has developed into a system of de facto precedent.[73] Otherwise stated, with the Uruguay Round agreements, the WTO firmly moved towards the legalization of international trade relations and the institutionalization of a law-making function through the dispute resolution process. This unprecedented judicial law-making process is all the more extraordinary given the lack of a functioning legislative capacity in the WTO.[74]

---

71 Donald M. McRae, 'The WTO in International Law: Tradition Continued or New Frontier?' (2000) 3 *Journal of International Economic Law* 27.

72 For a fuller defense of this argument, *see* Donald M. McRae, 'The Contribution of International Trade Law to the Development of International Law,' (1996) 260 *Recueil Des Cours* 99. For a contrary view, *see* Georg Schwarzenberger. 'The Principles and Standards of International Economic Law,' (1966) 87 *Recueil Des Cours* 1; Ignaz Seidl-Hohenvelderen, *International Economic Law* (1989).

73 Raj Bhala, 'The Power of the Past: Towards De Jure Stare Decisis in WTO Adjudication (Part Three of a Trilogy)' (2000) 33 *George Washington International Law Review* 873; Raj Bhala, 'The Precedent Setters: *De Facto* Stare Decisis in WTO Adjudication (Part Two of a Trilogy)' (1999) 9 *Journal of Transnational Law & Policy* 1; Raj Bhala, 'The Myth About Stare Decisis and International Trade Law (Part One of a Trilogy)' (1999) 14 *American University International Law Review* 845.

74 Indeed, recent reports have raised concern that the panels and Appellate Body are encroaching upon the appropriate domains of the Ministerial Conference and General Council. *See*, for example, Bhala, The Power of the Past, *supra* n. 73, at 146–47; Frieder Roessler, 'The Institutional Balance between the Judicial and the Political Organs of the WTO' (unpublished

To the extent that other bodies of law are incorporated into the WTO system, then these other bodies of law may be developed by WTO tribunals. This is problematic in several respects. First, those who advocate the incorporation of non-WTO law into WTO dispute resolution have been notably reluctant to address the ability or competence of panels to correctly interpret non-WTO law. Review of the AB's reports demonstrates that panelists often have difficulty in correctly interpreting international trade law, their field of expertise. There is little reason to believe that they would be more successful in correctly interpreting non-WTO law. To the contrary, there is a strong argument that there may be other institutions with equal or greater expertise in interpreting non-WTO law.

In addition, there may be reason to fear that the incorporation of non-WTO law will be a 'selective' incorporation. Thus, while the Shrimp–Turtle AB used international environmental law to interpret Article XX, it did not, for example, examine whether the complainants had any duties under international environmental law towards endangered sea turtles. Nor did the AB directly address whether the US embargo was either authorized or required by international environmental law even though this issue was squarely presented in an amicus brief submitted by the Worldwide Fund for Nature. So the critical question here is whether the use of non-WTO law will be 'wholesale' or 'retail'. More pointedly, will future panels rely on non-WTO law where to do so does not interfere with the trade regime's goal of market access and trade liberalization, but fail to do so where non-WTO law impedes these objectives?

Perhaps most significantly, it may not be the case that legal doctrine in other issue areas should be developed by adjudicatory bodies in a common law manner. While international affairs have become increasingly legalized in recent years, the degree of legalization in various international institutions varies widely.[75] The unevenness of the spread of legalization across various areas of international relations gives rise to a number of interesting questions. For present purposes I assume that, in certain issue areas at certain times, international actors choose a less-legalized approach because that approach is superior.[76] For example, a less-legalized approach may make more sense when the underlying issues pose difficult challenges to state sovereignty.[77] Lower levels of legalization may also be appropriate when inter-state agreement is limited to a relatively high level of abstraction, or when the underlying issue has high levels of uncertainty. Finally, lower forms of legalization may 'facilitate compromise, and thus mutually beneficial cooperation, between actors with different interests and values, different time horizons and discount rates,

---

Contd.
manuscript, on file with author). For more on the political problems associated with the perception of judicial overreaching in the WTO context, *see* Dunoff, Death, *supra* n. 28.

[75] Kenneth W. Abbott and Duncan Snidal, 'Hard and Soft Law in International Governance,' (2000) 54 *International Organization* 421; Robert O. Keohane, Andrew Moravcsik and Anne-Marie Slaughter, 'Legalized Dispute Resolution: Interstate and Transnational' (2000) 54 *International Organization* 457.

[76] Abbott and Snidal, *supra* n. 75, at 422–24.

[77] *Id.* at 423.

and different degrees of power'.[78] Hence, the incorporation of other bodies of international law into the WTO dispute resolution process runs the risk of greatly heightening the legalization of those other bodies, even if these are areas in which increased legalization is not appropriate.

Finally, two general points about transitions may be relevant to the WTO's time of transition. First, many of the issues driving the difficult transition issues have a strongly procedural character. On the surface, the key transitional debates focus on 'who' has a meaningful voice in WTO processes, 'what' bodies of law WTO panels will apply, and 'where' the WTO fits into the larger international legal universe. But underneath the surface of each of these debates is a concern that all of the appropriate voices or values are being heard and appropriately valued. In this sense, at least in the short term, it may be less important that the resolution of any of these questions is 'correct' in any substantive sense, than that the resolution ensures that all the relevant interests are identified and taken into account.

Second, given the dramatic developments in the international economy, the increasing pressures of globalization, and the significant institutional transformations flowing from the Uruguay Round Agreements, we should not be surprised that the trade regime is in a time of transition. But even without these dramatic changes, we might expect the WTO to be in transition.

Trade scholars often rely on philosophic insights when examining the trade system.[79] Perhaps the Heraclitean aphorism that 'you cannot step into the same river twice' may be apt here.[80] If, as Heraclitus suggests, change is constant, then we should not be surprised to see the WTO in transition, even though it is a relatively new institution. Like people, legal doctrines and institutions have life cycles. They are born of practical need. If well designed, they flourish for some time. But inevitably, changing conditions pose new challenges. When the tensions between a doctrine and social necessity finally becomes too great, the doctrine will expire and be superseded by another doctrine that is destined to experience the same fate. So it may be that we will come to see that for the WTO, or other international institutions, to be in a time of transition is more a norm than an aberration, and more an opportunity than a crisis.

4.8 Conclusion

The Seattle and Doha Ministerials signal that the WTO has entered an important transitional era. I have suggested that we can understand the

---

78 *Id.*

79 *See*, for example, Frank J. Garcia, 'Building a Just Trade Order for a New Millennium' (2001) 33 *George Washington International Law Review* 1015; Frank J. Garcia, 'Trade and Justice: Linking the Trade Linkage Debate' (1998) 19 *University of Pennsylvania Journal of International Economic Law* 391; Raj Bhala, 'Hegelian Reflections on Unilateral Action in the World Trading System' (1997) 15 *Berkeley Journal of International Law* 159.

80 G.S. Kirk and J.E. Raven, The Presocratic Philosophers (1963) p. 197. Cratylus is supposed to have replied that you cannot step into the same river even once. *Id.*

issues driving this transition by focusing on the 'who', 'what', and 'where' questions. Given their centrality to the operation – and our understanding – of the trade system, these questions are likely to drive the Doha Development Round negotiations. Moreover, I have discussed 'how' these three transition questions are related. In particular, I have detailed a number of ways that these transition questions differ from those traditionally considered by the trade regime and how they reveal a number of myths about the trade system. In this way, reflection upon the three transition questions can enhance our understanding of the trade system. Finally, I have outlined 'why' conventional approaches to these questions are unlikely to be effective. In this way, I intend to illuminate the pragmatic, as well as the conceptual, challenges that the three transition questions pose to the trade regime.

5. International Civil Servants and Multilateral Trade Negotiations

Xu Yi-Chong and Patrick Weller

In the midst of protests against the World Trade Organization (WTO), the strongest complaint is that the General Agreement on Tariffs and Trade (GATT)/WTO, like the other two international economic institutions, the International Monetary Fund (IMF) and World Bank, has been a rich countries' club, helping the rich impose free trade on smaller and poorer countries. Meanwhile, others argue that the GATT/WTO is the most democratic international organization because it operates on consensus and all arguments must be made and agreements reached by states and states alone. Which side is right? Has the GATT/WTO as an international organization played any role at all in pursuing the liberalization of trade in goods and services? If so, what role has it been? Has it been pursuing the interest of the rich only? Or has it had influence in developing the multilateral trade rules and regulations and facilitating multilateral trade cooperation in its own right? Demystifying the GATT/WTO is paramount because its legitimacy and effectiveness are threatened by many misperceptions of the organization, what it does and how it operates.

To do so, the role played by international civil servants (ICS) must be examined. The best way is to take a case study, explain how the ICS fit within the GATT/WTO and then extrapolate from that experience to explain how ICS have had and can have influence on policy outcomes. Such an analysis permits an appreciation of the available opportunities and the skill with which they were used. Even though the position of the Secretariat may have altered as the GATT became the WTO, the essential challenges of servicing multilateral, rule-making negotiations remain very similar. An analysis of the options taken during the Uruguay Round of multilateral trade negotiations (MTN) may assist in appreciating what is possible for the Doha Round.

This chapter examines the role of the GATT Secretariat in negotiating the General Agreement on Trade in Services (GATS) during the Uruguay Round MTN. It will show that ICS play an important role in international politics. In the field of international trade, the GATT Secretariat, despite its lack of legal status, actively defended and promoted the multilateral trading system and seldom hesitated to expand into areas that might have had some relevance to international trade.

The first section of this chapter discusses briefly the role of ICS in comparison with that of their domestic counterparts. The second section discusses the development of the GATT Secretariat and the functions and roles it played in defending and promoting the multilateral trade system. Accepting that ICS have a range of accepted behaviours as professionals in pursuit of political outcomes, how they shape their advice, the degree to which they seek to promote a common philosophy or agenda and the way they intercede are matters for empirical research. The third section assesses the role of the GATT Secretariat in bringing about the GATS during the Uruguay Round. Our finding is that GATS would not have come out the way it did without the influence of the Secretariat that literally designed the new framework for trade in services, which was different from the traditional and original GATT approach.

This is a study of ICS and their role and impact on international politics, not an economic evaluation of the world trading system under the auspices of GATT/WTO. The multilateral trading system is examined only to the extent that the role of the ICS can be discussed. In examining the negotiation over trade in services in general, this chapter hopes to clarify the role and influence of the GATT Secretariat in MTN and its relationship with state delegates. It is not the intention of this chapter to make a moral judgement on GATT/WTO. Neither is it to challenge or confirm often held conspiracy theories behind the development of international trading system. Nor does it lend its support to the contention that international organizations can be treated as unitary entities and blamed for global social and economic ills. Its finding, however, shows that, contrary to the conspiracy claim about international organizations, ICS often pursue much broader objectives than those advocated by the powerful and rich countries. Balancing the interests of all contracting parties and being impartial are the prerequisites for the success of any international organizations, including GATT/WTO, in the sense that they not only survive despite constant crises but also expand despite criticism often coming from all sides. Indeed, before any judgement can be made on GATT/WTO as an organization and as an international trading system, we need to understand how the system works, who the players are (including this group of anonymous and often ignored civil servants), how the players interact, and what role ICS play in facilitating and promoting international cooperation.

5.1 International Civil Servants

At the heart of all modern administration are the civil servants. The public fate of governments lies with the elected representatives; domestic civil servants are supposed to serve the government of the day. The nature of this link between civil servants, politicians, and the public, and the role played by civil servants in the political process, have long been the subject for debate. The ever-increasing complexity of governments has demanded civil servants provide the sinews and muscle that make the body politic work. Civil servants directly shape policies and influence national policy development by bringing their expertise to the consideration of issues. They have a collective memory that can draw on the expertise of earlier events. They turn often-vague aspirations of politicians into practical propositions that are economically and administratively feasible. They often have a life of their own. The other side of the coin is that there is always an issue of accountability. That is, who are civil servants accountable to? How can the elected representatives ensure that the machinery of government implements their wishes? Are civil servants sufficiently powerful that they have a degree of independence? The civil service is necessary; it can also be troublesome for the representative government if ministers take an instrumental approach that assumes that civil servants work like a machine.

International civil servants play a role similar to their domestic counterparts in influencing the outcomes of political process and multilateral negotiations through their unique positions, identified strategies, and their skills and expertise. ICS by definition are those individuals selected on the basis of merit (at least in theory), working for international organizations. An international organization is a treaty-bound, multilateral body, whose identity, as Inis Claude pointed out years ago, 'is lodged in its professional staff'. ICS help shape the performance and character of the organization. While states may control the organization, 'they cannot be it; the staff is the organization'.[1] Compared to their domestic counterparts, their number is minuscule, their background is much broader, and their obligations are much more vaguely defined. Their influence in international politics varies depending on the organizations they work for (whether they are comprehensive, such as the United Nations, or single-issue organizations, such as the IMF, the World Bank, and the World Health Organization), the nature of the issues involved (whether program-oriented, such as the UN Environmental Program, service-oriented, such as the UN Food and Agricultural Organization, or policy-oriented such as the GATT or IMF), or whether they involve high politics (NATO) or low politics (focusing on economic and social issues).

Like their domestic counterparts, ICS have the knowledge and skill to have a direct impact on those to whom they provide support and give advice. It is also reasonable to assume that ICS are driven by the similar incentives as domestic civil servants – incentives that relate to career promotion, the advancement of a cause, or simply job satisfaction. They play a pivotal role in facilitating international cooperation and in 'fulfilling the purpose of the organization, of spending money, or raising standards of living or of performing other tasks of a social, cultural, humanitarian, financial or educational nature – tasks innumerable and continually changing according to the requirements of the [international] community'.[2]

---

1 Inis L. Claude, *Swords into Plowshares: The Problems and Progress of International Organization* (3rd edn, Random House, New York, 1964), p. 174. Also see Charles P. Kindleberger, 'Economists in International Organizations' (1955) 9(3) *International Organization* 338–52.

2 George Langrod, *The International Civil Service: Its Origins, Its Nature, Its Evolution* (Oceana Publications, New York, 1963), p. 62.

In domestic politics, the line of responsibility is clear – civil servants serve their political masters and they work to the instructions of the politicians in power. On the international scene, international civil servants exist in a different environment – there is no party in power and there is no cabinet to direct policy. They do not have a single master to serve. Their masters are states that are not only sovereign in making their domestic and foreign policies but also always carefully guard their sovereignty from any real or perceived encroachment. ICS owe their loyalty not to the countries where they are from but to the missions of the organization and the organization itself. They, as the first Secretary-General of the League of Nations, Sir Eric Drummond, declared, are 'supposed to act *only* on the instructions of the Secretary-General and in the interests of the League, without regard to the policy of [their] own government'.[3] Their loyalty to the international community and international organizations creates a base for their independence, impartiality, and influence in international politics in their own right.

As an administrative undertaking, ICS must manage on two fronts – internal and external. Internal management is the supporting function, covering 'planning, organization, direction, coordination, information, finance, the handling of staff and the administration of property'.[4] It ensures the smooth operations of the organization and successful accomplishment of the designated objectives. International collective actions cannot take place until internal management is in place. The larger and more complex the organization is, the more important and difficult this internal management becomes. That is why, one of the four 'pillars' of priorities identified by the new WTO Director-General, Supachai was to strengthen the WTO as an institution, especially to boost the morale of the dispirited staff, whose loyalty had been challenged in his predecessor Michael Moore's departing salvo. The leadership of the Director-General and his relationship with directors of different divisions is often vital to ensure smooth internal operations.

External management is a matter of fulfilling the objectives of the organization. It directly produces outcomes, whether policies, regulations or negotiation results. These include technical operations, particularly planning, organization, command, coordination, and supervision that are often designed to achieve political objectives of the organization. For example, ICS are required to prepare for international meetings, chair meetings, and write the minutes and reports of those meetings. These seemingly technical supports provided by ICS are part of the external administration because they ensure the continuation of the international negotiations. The influence of ICS can be substantial when they are asked to engage in fact-finding, policy analyses, policy recommendation, and sometimes in implementation. The more technical the issues an international organization deals with, the more its member states rely on the permanent and professional staff of the secretariat to conduct background studies and analyses. Indeed, as international organizations are

---

3 Quoted from Thomas G. Weiss, *International Bureaucracy: An Analysis of the Operation of Functional and Global International Secretariats* (D.C. Heath and Company, Lexington, MA, 1975), p. 35.

4 Langrod, *International Civil Service*, p. 61.

increasingly involved in pursuing social and economic objectives, ICS are increasingly called upon to recommend practices and policies. In doing so, 'impartiality in collecting and marshalling solid facts and letting them speak for themselves to avoid the controversial short-cut of value judgements largely accounts for the much-criticised length and dullness of secretariat report'.[5] However, collecting and presenting 'solid facts' always requires a selection process in which certain objectives are pursued by ICS.

In theory, international negotiations and decision-making at the policy level are normally not matters for ICS, unless they are called upon to do so. The more complicated the issues are, the more likely ICS are called upon to assist negotiations and decision-making processes and consequently the more influence ICS can exert in deciding the final outcome. International civil servants often exert their influence when they conduct the following activities:

- the definition and delineation of problems,
- the synthesizing of national positions, drawing out the common points and areas of difference,
- the drafting of alternative options,
- note taking from meetings and the presentation of outcomes,
- the steering of negotiations towards a possible and generally acceptable outcome,
- the use of bargaining making machinery,
- the scheduling of meetings and negotiations,
- the drafting of the final agreements,
- the mediation and settlement of disputes.

In doing so, ICS serve as policy initiators. They are also bridge-builders and crisis preventors, conflict managers and mediators, identity facilitators and consensus builders, and public educators. International politics inevitably involves conflicts and struggles for national self-interest; no international negotiation is problem-free. What is important is the capacity of an international organization to handle the problems and to change its course without destroying the basis for international political and economic cooperation and stability. This role of an active mediator 'requires a good deal of creativity, expertise, or authority on the part of the ICS'.[6] By presenting alternative positions for states to break stalemates, ICS have an opportunity to exert their influence on the outcome of the negotiation. Furthermore, in doing so, ICS can and do pursue the interests of the international community as a whole rather than those of rich and powerful states or specific groups of

---

[5] Jacques Lemoine, *The International Civil Servant: An Endangered Species* (Kluwer Law International, Boston, 1995), p. 57.

[6] Hans Mouritzen, *The International Civil Service: A Study on Bureaucracy: International Organizations* (Dartmouth, Alderson, 1990), p. 20. For the negative view on international civil servants without political masters, *see* Robert Ramsay, 'UNCTAD's Failure: The Rich Get Richer' (1984) 38(2) *International Organization* 387–97.

states. Their survival, existence, and expansion depend on their impartiality and active efforts in pursuing their mandates.

As globalization faces increasing criticism for all the social and economic ills, international civil servants are more concerned than ever to portray themselves merely as 'clerks' rather than as important players in international politics to avoid politicizing what they do. But that need not reflect the reality of their influence nor suggest that it is not proper and legitimate to use that influence to further the objectives of the organization for which they work.

5.2 International Civil Servants at the GATT/WTO

The General Agreement on Tariffs and Trade was a provisional contract signed by 47 states in 1947 and joined by other countries gradually through negotiations. GATT was also an organization, despite its lack of legal status as a formal international organization, first and foremost because it was created to 'govern' the economic relations among states. After all 'international governance is whatever international organizations do; and the formal attributes of international organizations, such as their charters, voting procedures, committee structures, and the like, account for what they do'.[7] GATT was created by a multilateral treaty to pursue 'reciprocal and mutually advantageous arrangements directed to the substantial reduction of tariffs and other barriers to trade and to the elimination of discriminatory treatment in international commerce'.[8] It created a set of rules and obligations, and a set of procedures for its member states to follow. It gradually developed a full-fledged organizational structure, with the Contracting Parties as a decision-making body; its Council, created by the Contracting Parties in 1960, responsible for the business between regular meetings of the Contracting Parties; committees, working parties, and other subsidiary bodies created either by the Contracting Parties or the Council, dealing with specific affairs; and the Secretariat, built out of the Interim Committee of the International Trade Organization (ICITO).[9]

The Secretariat of GATT/WTO has always been small; it had six staff when it was created in 1947 and only 550 in 2001. Like a domestic bureaucracy, it is organized vertically into a hierarchy. At the top is the Director-General, whose views on international cooperation in general and international trade

---

7 Friedrich Kratochwil and John Gerard Ruggie, 'International Organization: A State of the Art on an Art of the State', in Friedrich Kratochwil and Edward D. Mansfield (eds), *International Organization: A Reader* (Harper Collins College Publishers, New York, 1994), p. 5.

8 'Preamble of the General Agreement on Tariffs and Trade'.

9 For the history and the development of the GATT and its Secretariat, *see* Kenneth W. Dam, *The GATT: Law and International Economic Organization* (The University of Chicago Press, Chicago, 1970); Olivier Long, *Law and its Limitation in the GATT Multilateral Trade System* (Kluwer Academic Publishers Group, Boston, 1985); John H. Jackson, *World Trade and the Law of GATT* (The Bobbs-Merrill Company, Inc., New York, 1969); Robert Hudec, *The GATT Legal System and World Trade Diplomacy* (Praeger, New York, 1975).

specifically have been crucial in shaping the organization. As Confucius once said, 'the perfect system of the law of nations is to constitute an international association [composed] of delegates chosen amongst the most virtuous and most capable citizens [in order] to apply international good faith and ensure the reign of concord between States'.[10] The Director-General was entrusted with the responsibility to be a guardian of the General Agreement. He was expected to exert whatever influence he could on governments to observe the rules and to 'look beyond current problems and to reflect on, and anticipate, the best course for the organization and its member countries to follow in pursuit of their objectives'.[11]

The first Director-General, then called the Executive Secretary, Eric Wyndham White, piloted the GATT in its early years and paved the way for it to become a full-fledged international organization. For White and later Director-Generals, 'the success of the GATT would depend largely upon unobtrusive but continuous and firm guidance from the Secretariat'.[12] The importance of the GATT Secretariat was not based on its legal status but on its impartiality and its effectiveness in providing the contracting parties with the so-called 'intellectual products – ideas, information, institutional assistance, and policy influence'.[13] The GATT Secretariat had a group of international civil servants of the highest standards of efficiency, competence, and integrity, responsible for the mandate of the GATT and the GATT as an organization. Competence and the trust of the contracting parties were the fundamental prerequisites for effectiveness and influence in pursuing and facilitating international cooperation through MTN. Their belief in freer and fairer trade, their professionalism and dedication to pursuing the objectives defined the characteristics of the organization and its development.

There was an inseparable relationship between the GATT as an international trading system and the GATT Secretariat. As the international trading system expanded, so did the GATT Secretariat. The GATT was consolidated throughout the years because of 'the persistence and resourcefulness of a dedicated and pragmatic secretariat'.[14] The GATT Secretariat gradually grew in significance despite its ambivalent legal position for several reasons. First, its evolution was 'the consequence of the increase in GATT's membership and, in particular, its heterogeneity as regards the levels of development of its member countries, their economic structures, and their conception of what the international trade system should be like'.[15] The membership of the GATT had grown steadily. The earlier GATT rounds of trade negotiations involved only 20–30 countries. The number of countries increased to 62 in the Kennedy Round (1964–67) and 99 countries completed the Tokyo Round in 1979. When the Uruguay Round was launched,

---

10 Quoted from Langrod, *International Civil Service*, p. 33.

11 Long, *Law and its Limitations in the GATT Multilateral Trade System*, p. 53.

12 Sidney J. Wells, *Through the Eyes of the GATT: The Speeches and Writings of Eric Wyndham White, 1948–1964* Vol. 57:1 (GATT Archives), p. 5.

13 Devesh Kapur, John P. Lewis and Richard Webb (eds), *The World Bank: Its First Half Century* (Brookings Institution Press, Washington, DC, 1997), p. 2.

14 Dam, *The GATT*, p. 335.

15 Long, *Law and its Limitations in the GATT Multilateral Trade System*, pp. 43–44.

103 countries participated in the negotiation in 1986. The more states participated in international trade negotiations, the closer links they developed, the greater the possibility of friction. Faced with the interplay of political forces, with the action of various pressure groups, with conflicting interests and controversies, any deliberate and continuous action would have been impossible without a Secretariat 'emancipated' from direct dependence on the parties to the dispute.

Active involvement in mediating and settling differences among contracting parties in turn expanded the power and influence of the GATT Secretariat. From the very beginning, White believed that 'the crucial importance of the role of the Secretariat [was] to use its good offices in cases where there [were] some serious disputes in regard to the application of the Agreement or the manner in which negotiations should be conducted'.[16] In addition to the role of good offices, the Director-General, with the support of the Secretariat, conducted informal consultations – a practice by the 1980s that had become a standard procedure known as the 'Green Room' consultations and used frequently by the Director-General Arthur Dunkel. In 1952 when the chairman of the Contracting Parties, with the strong support of White, created panels consisting of experts to handle all the complaints about the violation of the General Agreement, the GATT Secretariat assumed more important responsibilities as the guardian of the Agreement and the trading system. Indeed, the effectiveness of the GATT Secretariat in facilitating international cooperation depended on its ability to mediate conflicts among contracting parties. This ability was based on the credibility, impartiality, and trust the Secretariat had *vis-à-vis* the contracting parties. The dispute settlement procedure, however imperfect and unbinding, was one of the important developments to ensure the continuation of the multilateral trading system and also became an essential vehicle to expand the responsibilities of the GATT Secretariat.

Second, the importance of the GATT Secretariat grew as the result of the expansion of issue areas in the MTN. The system started the pursuit of freer and fairer trade through negotiating tariff concessions (it is important to note that under the original treaty, no contracting party was 'required to lower tariff, or even to refrain from raising any tariff'[17]) and creating 'even' playing fields among trading partners. Negotiations gradually moved from creating rules regulating movements of goods to taxation, to trade behaviour, such as dumping, countervailing duties, government procurement, and eventually to subsidies and other domestic regulations which might have effects on trade in goods. By the beginning of the 1980s, more issue areas were brought into the GATT negotiations – all forms of protection (tariffs, subsidies, non-trade-barriers), as well as safeguards and exceptions, and technical standards; trade in services, trade-related intellectual property rights, trade-related investment measures, dispute settlement procedures, etc. All three Director-Generals under the study, Eric Wyndham White, Olivier Long, and Arthur Dunkel (1947–69, 1968–80, and 1980–93),

---

[16] Wells, *Through the Eyes of the GATT*, p. 8.
[17] Dam, *The GATT*, p. 17.

actively sought to expand the coverage of the international trade regulations negotiated under the auspices of the GATT. It is said that, 'although he was careful to give the appearance of playing the role of the typical international civil servant, to be neutral among all parties, and to avoid the appearance of taking initiatives which should be left to the nation-state participants, nevertheless, Sir Eric had a profound sense of the "possible" while continuously working toward the basic goals of the GATT agreement'.[18] Director-General Long admitted, throughout its history, the GATT Secretariat had 'no hesitation in extending the scope of its negotiations when the situation in trade negotiations demand[ed] it'.[19] The expansion of issues in the GATT negotiations greatly increased the opportunities for the ICS to play a more active role in facilitating liberalization of trade as well as international cooperation in trade relations. In addition to the technical supports, such as providing the internal services for the meeting concerned (minutes and records of meetings, organization of premises, distribution of documents, translation, material organization of debates), the Secretariat gradually extended its responsibility to provide a sort of liaison not only between the different meetings of the one session, but also between two or more successive sessions.

Third, the GATT staff became the main source of new approaches to international trade and the impetus for new ideas and compromises in its own right, pursuing international trade liberalization and cooperation. Like all international secretariats, the GATT Secretariat was the permanent working cell of the GATT as an organization and an irreplaceable instrument of liaison and transmission of the international trading system. It planned, persuaded, and reminded member states of their obligations. Over time, it helped the organization become *differentiated, durable*, and *autonomous*. '*Differentiation* refers to the development of organization distinctiveness from its environment ... autonomy for international organizations means the development of political organizations and procedures that are not simply expression of the interests of particular states or other international actors'.[20]

Finally, since the GATT was a multilateral treaty and international regulations and rules over trade relations were the outcomes of MTN, facilitating the negotiation process was the most important responsibility of the GATT Secretariat. Changing negotiation techniques to meet the increasing complexity of the negotiations also strengthened the role and influence of the GATT Secretariat. When the contracting parties in 1964 replaced the traditional product-by-product and country-by-country negotiation procedure with the 'linear reduction technique', it became the responsibility of the Secretariat to compile a working hypothesis for contracting parties to work on. During the Uruguay Round when a 'single undertaking' was set as the objective for achieving the successful conclusion of the Round, it was the Secretariat's responsibility to balance all the issues and ensure the totality of

---

18 John H. Jackson, *The World Trading System. Law and Policy of International Economic Relations* (The MIT Press, Cambridge, MA,1991), p. 38.

19 Long, *Law and its Limitations in the GATT Multilateral Trade System*, p. 24.

20 Robert O. Keohane, 'Institutionalization in the United Nations General Assembly' (1969) 23(4) *International Organization* 861–62.

the final agreement. No one country was able to do so because of self-interest as well as the lack of professional expertise and information on all issues and on all positions.[21]

The package negotiation also granted the Secretariat more responsibility to keep the negotiation going no matter how difficult it might be. The bicycle theory is widely hailed by international negotiators – negotiations must continue to avoid a permanent collapse of the international cooperative system. The GATT Secretariat historically played a crucial role in peddling the bicycle to prevent it from falling over because 'the international civil service is composed of persons who, by their permanence, their technical knowledge and their autonomy, can attempt to act as catalysts of the international spirit'.[22] MTN under the auspices of the GATT, however, have always involved the GATT Secretariat because of the complexity of the legal and technical matters. The GATT rules were said to be so complicated that anyone who read them was 'likely to have his sanity impaired'.[23]

For instance, during the Uruguay Round negotiation, in order to reach an agreement on trade in services, the GATT secretariat, led by Arthur Dunkel, is known to have replaced the text on which agreement had proved impossible among the negotiating parties. He produced a new draft that brought together recognition of the importance of the trade in services for many states, recognition that it was a key sector in the Round and should contribute to trade liberalization, a commitment to begin substantive negotiations, and agreement on major points to be taken into consideration.[24] MTN under the Uruguay Round was a complicated process when not only were there multiple states (in the early 1980s, over 100 states were GATT Members) but also multiple issues. Bargaining and compromising were inevitable. The more complicated and more entangled issues are, the easier it is for ICS to suggest alternative views on the matter and the greater affect they may have on the outcome eventually. By presenting the third party positions, the secretariat was able to keep the negotiations going. This was seen as beneficial to the participants, as well as the multilateral trading system as a whole.

5.3 Assisting the Negotiations

The agenda for the Uruguay Round negotiations under the GATT was massive, making it by far the most ambitious trade negotiation ever. It encompassed not only trade in goods, but also trade in services, trade-related

---

21 John W. Evans, *The Kennedy Round in American Trade Policy: The Twilight of the GATT?* (Harvard University Press, Cambridge, MA, 1971) and Anwarul Hoda, *Tariff Negotiations and Renegotiations Under the GATT and the WTO: Procedures and Practices* (Cambridge University Press, New York, 2001).

22 Langrod, *The International Civil Service*, p. 48.

23 Quoted from Jackson, *World Trade and the Law of GATT*, p. vii.

24 John Croome, *Reshaping the World Trading System: A History of the Uruguay Round* (Kluwer Law, Boston, 1995), p. 176.

aspects of intellectual property rights (TRIPS), and trade-related investment measures (TRIMS). Within these broad areas came such knotty issues as subsidies, dumping and anti-dumping, agricultural supports, rules of origin, safeguards or escape clause action, the creation of a new institution and the provision for settlement of disputes. All of these subjects are important and all are quite technically complex.

Negotiations over trade in services are chosen for examination here for several reasons. Trade in services was a new subject brought to Geneva in the early 1980s when the issue had support of a single country – the United States. By the time negotiations concluded in 1993, the GATS was accepted by all member states even though not all issues were settled – countries did agree to disagree in several sectors of services. The process of taking a highly controversial issue unknown to many trade experts to one known even to the general public within a decade provides a good opportunity to conduct some solid empirical research on the impact the services division of the GATT Secretariat had in the negotiations. This section will identify the conditions in which the intervention of ICS in the process of MTN was the most significant and identify the strategies used by the ICS to contribute to the development of the GATS. To do so, it is necessary to examine ICS at the GATT/WTO as an administrative undertaking, pursuing collective objectives with their expertise, professionalism, long-term international experience, and highly praised impartial views. It is also important to examine the roles played and contributions made by ICS in the three stages of MTN on trade in services in the Uruguay Round: the preparatory (1981–86), stalemate (1986–92), and negotiation stage. It will also assess where and when they chose to provide support, what the nature of that support was, what impact it might have had on determining the content and speed of the negotiation, and how ICS were able to maintain the momentum of the negotiations.

There are two views on who was important in bringing about the agreements at the Uruguay Round. One suggests that 'the dominant actors throughout [the Uruguay Round] were the member governments; it was their attitudes and decisions that decided at each stage the agenda for the officials working in the GATT in Geneva – Secretariat and delegates alike – and largely determined what it was possible for them to achieve or even to attempt'.[25] The other proposes that 'while the wheels of an international organization are set in motion by the spokesmen of the national governments represented in it, only the international civil service... is composed of persons who, by their permanence, their technical knowledge and their autonomy, can attempt to act as catalysts of the international spirit'.[26] Like ICS in other international organizations, the GATT Secretariat played an active and important role in facilitating cooperation, informing the member states of their options, bridging the gap between countries' demands, managing the

---

25 David Henderson, 'International Agencies and Cross-Border Liberalization: The WTO in Context', in Anne O. Krueger (ed.), *The WTO as an International Organization* (The University of Chicago Press, Chicago, 1998), p. 102.

26 Langrod, *The International Civil Service*, p. 48.

delicate negotiation process and shaping the direction of the negotiations. The role of international civil servants at the GATT was often overshadowed by the diplomatic, political, and economic struggles which occupied the forefront of the international scene. Drawing attention to the role played by the secretariat is not to ignore the role played by the participating delegates, but to show that the outcomes of MTN depend not only on interactions among participants but also on the context within which such interactions take place.

Soon after the Tokyo Round negotiations were concluded, contracting parties started discussing whether another round of MTN was needed to complete unfinished issues and to save this endangered institution at the time of economic difficulty. The GATT Secretariat took a lead in pursuing this objective for the interests of the international community as well as its own survival. One of the stumbling blocks for the new round of negotiations was whether trade in services should or could even be discussed in this international arena. We can arbitrarily divide the negotiation process into three stages – the preparation period (1981–86), stalemate stage (1986–92), and negotiation stage. The Secretariat played different roles in each of the three periods. In the preparatory stage, the new Director-General Arthur Dunkel travelled around the world's capitals to persuade countries of the necessity of engaging in a new round of MTN. He also 'carried through a series of "brainstorming" sessions with his own senior staff',[27] who then actively engaged in 'fact finding', 'education', and recruiting support by organizing 'independent' experts in shifting the dominant thinking about the issues of trade in services. The impact, however, was limited because the GATT Secretariat itself at the time did not have sufficient experts in the area.

In the second stage, while the negotiation was painstaking, the GATT Secretariat, especially its newly expanded services division, played a significant role in drawing the parameters and establishing a framework for negotiations. It carried out its normal responsibility to steer the negotiation – by organizing meetings, summarizing, and presenting the positions (states as well as the chair of the negotiation group), proposing compromise alternatives for the delegates, and mediating differences. It also launched a 'truly educative process for the negotiators, with surely more balanced results than those that would have been produced by passive acceptance of the initial proposals'.[28] It worked closely with the chairmen of the negotiation group on the issue and provided state delegates with a clear definition of the issues at hand, background studies and, more importantly, a framework for negotiation. The uncertainties of the delegates about their countries' positions gave greater power to the Secretariat in general and the services division that could absorb uncertainty by promoting its cause.

In the final stage after the framework for negotiations had been accepted, states started submitting their country tariff concessions on the trade in services. The GATT Secretariat assisted individual states in preparing their

---

27 Croome, *Reshaping the World Trading System*, p. 8.

28 Rubens Ricupero, 'Integration of Developing Countries into the Multilateral Trading System', in Jagdish Bhagwati and Mathias Hirsch (eds), *The Uruguay Round and Beyond: Essay in Honor of Arthur Dunkel* (The University of Michican Press, Ann Arbor, 1999), p. 16.

country's submissions and concessions and reaching some agreements on what they could or could not do by mediating the differences and presenting feasible compromises. The complexity of the issues created opportunities for the Director-General, to 'play a personally central role at every turning point in the Round, starting with the compromise of the Punta del Este Declaration, through the resolution of the two major crises to the Montreal Mid-term Review in December 1988 and the hoped for but frustrated conclusion in Brussels in December 1990 – up to the drafting and presentation of the Draft Final Act, the basis for the final outcome'.[29] In sum, the negotiation of the Uruguay Round was a complex affair involving a melange of cross-cutting interests, coalitions, and hidden agendas, which created a good opportunity for the ICS to play an important and independent role in facilitating and directing international cooperation.

5.3.1 Preparatory stage

In the preparatory stage, the Secretariat adopted three strategies to bring the issue of trade in services to the new round of MTN. One was the shuttle diplomacy conducted by the Director-General Arthur Dunkel; he travelled to capitals in Asia, Europe, and the Western Hemisphere, to convince the so-called 'like-minded' countries to support the US' initiative. The second strategy was to use and strengthen the existing institutional capacity to bring in line the general thinking. The GATT Consultative Group of Eighteen was the primary battlefield for the issue of trade in services. Director-General Dunkel held a series of meetings of the Group of Eighteen to sound out the views of GATT Members on the state of international trade relations, and discover what could be done to improve them. Dunkel acted as a main mediator and facilitator in resolving differences throughout the first half of the 1980s in preparation for launching another round of MTN. The third one was to 'educate' the country delegates by its own studies and fact findings. A group of 'independent' economic experts, who had published extensively on trade in services as academics or consultants, were brought in to 'report on the problems of the trading system, and how these might be overcome',[30] and to inform the participants of the policy options. Later they were recruited into the GATT Secretariat as the new round of negotiation started.

The Consultative Group of Eighteen had been created by the GATT Council of Ministers 'on a temporary basis on 1 July 1965 and made permanent since 1979' to 'provide guidance for the organization'[31] under the Director-General Long. It was set up to facilitate the work of GATT by (1) following international trade development with a view of pursuing and maintaining trade policies consistent with the objectives and principles of the General Agreement; (2) forestalling, whenever possible, sudden disturbances that could represent a threat to the multilateral trading system and to international trade relations

---

[29] Ricupero, 'Integration of Developing Countries into the Multilateral Trading System' p. 9.

[30] Croome, *Reshaping the World Trading System*, p. 18.

[31] Long, *Law and its Limitations in the GATT Multilateral Trade System*, p. 50 and Jackson, *The World Trading System*, p. 65.

generally; and (3) participating in the international adjustment process and co-ordinating actions between the GATT and the IMF. The Group was known as 'the embryo of a Steering Committee',[32] whose existence provided a good opportunity to avoid direct confrontation by discussing new and controversial issues before they were put on the negotiation table. The number of members in the Group was coincidentally the same as the Executive Board of the International Trade Organization (ITO), designed in the Havana Charter. The rationale then was that a small group of countries would find it easier to reach an agreement before any major decisions could be made within the whole organization. Even though the representation of the Group was well balanced between developed and developing countries, they were from major trading countries in the world. In the early 1980s, the membership included representatives from Argentina, Australia, Brazil, Canada, Czechoslovakia, Egypt, European Community, India, Japan, Malaysia, Nigeria, Pakistan, Peru, Switzerland, Sweden, Turkey, the United States, and Zaire. A consensus among the major trading partners in the Group over a specific issue was the prerequisite for it to be repeated and find expression in the Council and at sessions of the Contracting Parties, even though the Group was not to impinge on the competence or authority of the Council nor of the permanent GATT committees.

Between 1980 and 1986, the Consultative Group of Eighteen held a series of meetings to discuss the important issues of the day, such as structural adjustment following the debt crisis in developing countries, as well as new issues which were introduced by developed as well as developing countries. When the US delegates brought the issue on trade in services to the Group, even developed countries objected to the idea of liberalizing trade in services. While recognizing the growing importance of services in world trade, they argued that it was necessary to complete the learning process before deciding how the issue might be discussed under the auspices of the GATT, particularly because services was such a complex and heterogeneous field. Many countries simply rejected the relevance of trade in services to the GATT. Yet, none was opposed to further work on services by the GATT Secretariat in order to improve the members' knowledge and understanding of the issues, so it was requested to provide a study in order to identify the issues related to trade in services and their relevance to the GATT. At the beginning of 1981, the Secretariat presented a preliminary analysis of services to the Group. While admitting that the study did not deal with all the questions that might be posed, the study demonstrated that certain services were indissolubly linked with trade in goods and were therefore not only a proper, but also a necessary concern of the GATT.[33] This position was much ahead of most countries at the time. As the former Director-General, Olivier Long pointed out, the GATT Secretariat was 'always ready to investigate matters which, although possibly in some cases not its primary concern, might have effects on trade'.[34] Providing background studies

---

32 Long, *Law and its Limitations in the GATT Multilateral Trade System*, p. 51.
33 GATT document, CG.18/W/49, 1981.
34 Long, *Law and its Limitations in the GATT Multilateral Trade System*, p. 24.

is one way for ICS to influence the direction of international development. Impartiality still remains one of the most important requirements for the GATT Secretariat to have any influence at all. This was a balancing act – pursuing freer and fairer trade while being impartial to all.

The GATT Secretariat, while indirectly under the authority of all contracting parties – which were represented in the deliberative organs – was not, as regards to the performance of its task, subordinate to any of them, not even to the state of which individual staff were a national. As impartiality is undoubtedly a necessary quality of ICS, their independent status is also a *sine qua non* of their non-representative character. This attitude could be found in the studies done by its economists as position papers in the negotiation process:

> This revised analytical summary is based on the information contained in sixteen national examinations of the issues in the sector of services circulated through GATT pursuant to the Ministerial Decision of November 1982, as well as on information provided to date by relevant international organizations. In drawing up this summary, the secretariat has endeavoured to classify the information in a matter consistent with the presentations adopted in most national examinations, though the order in which the material is arranged does not necessarily correspond to the order followed in the examinations. Although careful attention has been paid to nuance, individual points made in national examinations may not be reflected in the text.[35]

All international actions take place as a result of a complex process of fact-finding, policy recommendation, consultation, negotiation, decision-making, and operation. Fact-finding is the very first stage on which all other actions are built. 'Since the supply of fact is infinite', pointed out Kindleberger, 'finders must exercise discrimination on their accumulation, or in other words, choose facts with a view to their analytical arrangement'.[36]

In 1985, the GATT Secretariat submitted an analysis of information exchanged among contracting parties to 'clarify the information in a manner consistent with the presentations adopted in most national examinations'.[37] This 100-page report included the concepts that encapsulated trade in services, the issues raised for possible multilateral action and the actions taken by other international organizations. In a meeting in April 1985, this summary acted as a basis for discussion among contracting parties that were looking for some common elements in the information. In September, the Secretariat submitted another summary of information on the subject matter, given by other international organizations.[38] Later, these analytical summaries of information were revised and re-circulated in November 1985 to allow contracting parties to focus their negotiations. In February 1986,

---

35 GATT Secretariat, 'Services: Analytical Summary of Information Exchanged among Contracting Parties', MDF/7/Rev. 2 (23 November 1985), p. 1.

36 Kindleberger, 'Economists in International Organizations', p. 339.

37 GATT document, MDF/7 (19 April 1985).

38 GATT document, MDF/7 (16 September 1985).

the Secretariat submitted another report about regulations that affected international transactions in services, allowing a subsequent meeting to discuss the concept of tradability of services. The papers provided by the Secretariat thus helped to define complicated concepts and identify the common ground on which nations could then make progress. They also brought the issue to the attention of the international community and improved other governments' awareness of the opportunities that existed for improving the cross-border flow of services. Yet, the issue was not completely resolved. Resistance to bringing trade in services to the negotiation remained so strong that it was said that the Secretariat was even prohibited from having any files on services in their offices.

The road to a new round of MTN was paved and the issue could not be ignored. Two small countries took the lead in working out a compromise for the launch of a new round of MTN. On September 20, 1986, 92 GATT contracting parties launched the eighth round of MTN at Punta del Este. The Declaration was divided into two sections. One covered negotiations on trade in goods and the other on trade in services. It was agreed that trade in services would be negotiated in parallel with trade in goods and other institutional matters, such as dispute settlements and the functioning of the GATT system. The Punta del Este Ministerial Declaration was known as the 'café au lait' compromise because of the joint efforts of the Swiss and Columbian delegate in bringing about the support of over 40 countries for an acceptable agreement. Yet, there would not have been any agreement at all if the Secretariat had not worked out the issues and options for countries to debate.

Three organizations were established – the Trade Negotiations Committee (TNC), the Group of Negotiations on Goods (GNG) and Group of Negotiations on Services (GNS). TNC was to oversee the new round of MTN as a whole. The GNG would '(i) elaborate and put into effect detailed trade negotiating plans prior to 19 December 1986; (ii) designate the appropriate mechanism for surveillance of commitments to standstill and rollback; (iii) establish negotiations groups as required; (iv) also decide upon inclusion of additional subject matter in the negotiations; (v) co-ordinate the work of the negotiation groups and supervise the progress of the negotiations; and (vi) the GNG shall report to the Trade Negotiations Committee'.[39] GNS would deal with matters concerning trade in services and report to the TNC as well. Despite bitter opposition to bringing trade in services into the negotiation, all participants became members of the GNS as well as GNG. The dual track was designed to ensure the progress in negotiations on goods and services would not be subject to each other, or rely on the success of the other issues.

The organizational arrangement had a direct effect on the result of the negotiations. Countries disagreed over the powers to be vested to the TNC, GNG, and GNS. The first two TNC meetings broke down because the two sides (EC vs. the United States) had sufficient support from smaller countries to block the other's proposal. This set the tone of the whole negotiations for the next 7 years – major trading countries did not see eye to eye on many issues and each was able to rally enough support from other smaller

---

39 'Ministerial Declaration on the Uruguay Round' (October 1986) *GATT Focus* 5.

countries. These stalemates created good opportunities for the 'third party' – the GATT secretariat – to appear as an agent of mediation and compromise. In this case, in mid-January 1987, GATT Director-General Arthur Dunkel produced a compromise proposal, suggesting a mechanism for surveillance of the standstill and rollback of protectionist measures; the surveillance body would report directly to the TNC. This proposal put the three bodies, the Surveillance Body, the GNG and the GNS on an equal standing while the TNC was given the overall authority for steering the negotiation in the right directions. The successful launch of the Uruguay Round, including trade in services, confirmed the observation of Keohane and Nye some time ago, 'international secretariats can be viewed both as catalysts and as potential members of coalitions'.[40]

5.3.2 Negotiation stage

When the Uruguay Round was launched in September 1986, the GNS was formed in parallel to the GNG. Felipe Jaramillo (Columbia), chairman of the Council at the time, was elected to chair the GNS and worked closely with the economic officers at the GATT Service Division. Gary Sampson, an Australian academic and a former staff member at the United Nations Conference on Trade and Development (UNCTAD) became the director of the newly expanded Services Division. Its officials had worked in this issue area and had already written during the early negotiation on trade in services and continued to do so. GATT and negotiations were virtually synonymous; and therefore the relationship between the chairmen of negotiation committees and the GATT Secretariat was crucial to the successful conclusion of trade negotiations as well as the GATT system as a whole. In theory, the amount of power and influence of chairmen of committees in international politics is limited because, after all, states are supposed to make the final decisions at international negotiation tables. In practice, however, collective actions are difficult to achieve without a group of international 'elite' facilitating the process.[41] The elected chairmen during GATT negotiations were almost without exception senior diplomats with extensive experience of international trade. This combination means that they were often also in charge of their state delegations; they also often shared the view of the GATT Secretariat that they were there to promote and defend the system rather than their national interests. Their busy schedules and heavy national responsibilities meant they relied on the assistance of the GATT Secretariat. The GATT Secretariat was there to be at disposal of the chairmen and was also known to have the ear of the chairmen regarding substantive and specific matters of the negotiation. It provided the chairmen with normal assistance to run the meetings. More importantly, it briefed the chairmen on the tactics that could be adopted, on the possible roads ahead and on how they

---

40 Robert O. Keohane and Joseph S. Nye, 'Transgovernmental Relations and International Organizations', *World Politics* (1974) 21(1) 53.

41 For the discussion, see Johan Kaufmann, *Conference Diplomacy: An Introductory Analysis* (2nd edn, Martinus Nijhoff, London, 1988).

might react to any eventualities. The Services Division undoubtedly had its footprint on the outcome of the negotiation by just 'helping' the chairmen to run the negotiation.

But it did more. After the negotiation started, the first things the contracting parties had to decide were the objectives and the range of elements open to negotiations. The Secretariat was asked to prepare a document on the objectives and content for the coming negotiations. At the time, a major difficulty at the GNS, itself a problem for negotiation, was to get a concrete proposal on the table. At the GATT, any contracting party could put forward a proposal. Yet, this could be a complex and delicate affair in all international negotiations. On the one hand, it was usually to the country's advantage to have the negotiations start from its own draft because the first draft often set the range and the tone for the negotiations. On the other hand, once written, a proposal often limits a party's subsequent freedom of action and so could reduce its bargaining strength. This dilemma often makes major states cautious about forwarding proposals as their own. It sometimes leads to proposals being put forward anonymously, that is, 'by certain delegations'. There was a strong tradition that, before doing so, the contracting party would hold informal and private discussions with a number of other parties and obtain assurances from them that they would support at least the major thrust of the proposal. Because of their economic and political interests, large countries (both developed and developing countries) played an active role in putting forward proposals either individually or jointly. No decisions on the agenda for negotiation could be taken if either of the large groupings actively opposed. However, neither of them could by itself (including the United States), even in combination, force the GATT to take any action in the face of stated and strong opposition by several of the other trading countries. The GATT Secretariat consequentially was often asked to put forward proposals as a neutral and compromise position.

Furthermore, serious multilateral negotiations on trade matters could not go forward unless there was a single document before the negotiators. This was commonly accomplished by having the Secretariat produce a document which incorporated parts of several, often conflicting, proposals, with the disputed paragraphs in square brackets. This editorial device was used to make clear what had and had not been agreed upon. It also served the very useful purpose of pinpointing the areas where further negotiations must still take place. Even then, in any event, it was almost always understood that in trade negotiations acceptance of a proposal was a 'basis for negotiation', that is, nothing was agreed until all was agreed. Incorporating proposals into a single document was often the responsibility of the Secretariat that therefore might set the direction of the negotiations.

The service division, on behalf of the chairman of the GNS, worked out a 'Program for the Initial Phase of Negotiations' which stated the negotiating objectives:

> Negotiations in this area shall aim to establish a multilateral framework of principles and rules for trade in services, including elaboration of possible disciplines for individual sectors, with a view to expansion of such trade under conditions of transparency and progressive

liberalization and as a means of promoting economic growth of all trading partners and the development of developing countries. Such framework shall respect the policy objectives of national laws and regulations applying to services and shall take into account the work of relevant international organizations.[42]

Since some countries at the time had not developed their services industries and many had not realized the significance of the existing services industries and what could be contributed to trade in services, the Secretariat provided a list of elements for negotiation, which included definitional and statistical issues, concepts on which principles and rules for trade in services might be based; coverage; existing international disciplines and arrangements; and measures and practices contributing to or limiting trade in services. This document provided a basis for countries to start their negotiation journey on trade in services.

In the following year, relevant international organizations, such as UNCTAD, IMF, and UN Statistical Organization (UNSO), were called in to present the GNS with information on existing multilateral disciplines. The Secretariat consequently provided a summary of objectives, coverage, and main features of existing international disciplines and arrangements relevant to trade in services.[43] Various countries submitted their positions on the negotiating objectives and elements. By the summer of 1988, the GNS had held 15 meetings in which governments, the GATT Secretariat and international organizations had produced over 30 written submissions and the background document. It was time for the chairman to take stock and clarify some issues. Even though some 'countries were reluctant, in the early stages of the Round, to authorize the Secretariat to produce documentation other than (exhaustive) reports on the meetings of the GNS',[44] the Service Division was asked in the summer 1988 first to provide a comprehensive list of definitions and then a draft glossary of terms.[45] The range of issues confronting contracting parties was both broad and complex; the terms and concepts used in their debates and submissions sometimes carried different or even conflicting meanings. By submitting its own definitions and glossary, the Secretariat not only identified differences in the use of those terms and concepts but, more importantly, made choices in its presentation of those concerns by providing its own definitions. Fundamental concepts for any trade negotiations were on the list – across-the-border trade, establishment/commercial presence, exceptions/escape clauses; market access; most-favoured-nation (MFN) treatment; national treatment; non-discrimination; reciprocity; restrictive business practices, etc. The Secretariat's list set the parameters for negotiations on trade in services.

At the end of 1988, the Service Division on behalf of the chairman of the GNS compiled a report on the trade negotiation on services and submitted it in November for informal consultation and then to the whole GNS for

---

42 GATT document, MTN.GNS/5 (2 February 1987).
43 GATT document, MTN.GNS/W/16 (6 August 1987).
44 Croome, *Reshaping the World Trading System*, 124–25 and MTN.GNS/W. 43 (8 July 1988).
45 GATT document, MTN.GNS/W/38 (16 May 1988) and MTN.GNS/W/43 (8 July 1988).

approval before submitting it to the Montreal Ministerial midterm review. This report recognized that (1) familiar GATT concepts related to goods could not be simply applied to trade in services and new definitions were needed; (2) there was a natural linkage between definition and coverage of trade in services; (3) the existing international disciplines and arrangements must be taken into consideration; (4) the natural connection between trade in services and development; and (5) distinction between negotiable and non-negotiable regulations.[46] It received a mixed reception:

(1) Canada – a great effort made in terms of summarizing and simplifying the contents of the Chairman's report;
(2) EC – disappointed but acknowledged that 'failing to complete any part of it should ultimately jeopardize the whole';
(3) Malaysia – not consulted but hoping guidance as to the future work could be offered in Montreal;
(4) US – acknowledgement of the complexity and diversity;
(5) Switzerland – disappointed because the report was not a consensus paper, nevertheless was a 'significant and useful' one and would show Ministers the scope of the work undertaken so far in the GNS.[47]

But it did provide a basis for a report to the TNC meeting in Montreal.

At the Montreal ministerial meeting, the stalemate over trade in services was overshadowed by the impasse over agriculture safeguard issues. This meant that the services negotiations were 'on hold' and the GNS did not hold any meeting until April 1989. Once again, the Secretariat was asked to compile a list of sectors which were relevant to trade in services. 'And a response to a request for policy guidance may be tinged with varying degrees of *real politik*, from the exact compromise on which conflicting short-run interests can agree to the long-run ideal which no country feels it can afford to accept'.[48] When the Secretariat submitted to the GNS a 'reference list of sectors' to facilitate negotiation, it provided a general framework within which participants could consider. This list provided 14 categories of services and over 100 specific areas of services. For example, under professional services, there were agriculture, forestry and fishing services; mining and oil-field services; legal services; accounting and taxation services; management and administration services; architectural services; market research and opinion polling; surveying and exploration services; advisory and consultative engineering services; industrial engineering; engineering design services; project management services; urban planning services; interior design services; R&D, lab, testing and certification; computer-related services; software development; travel agents and tour operators; economic and behaviour research; labour recruitment and provision of personnel; investigation and security activities; public relations services; photographic

---

[46] Mario A. Kakabadse, 'Trade in Services and the Uruguay Round' (1989) 19(2) *Georgia Journal of International and Comparative Law* 384–91.
[47] GATT document, MTN.GNS/20 (30 November 1988).
[48] Kindleberger, 'Economists in International Organizations', p. 339.

services; and miscellaneous professional services.[49] The significance of providing the information and analysis in an international organization rests on the fact that 'they have an audience which is under some obligation to take note of their analysis'.[50]

After Montreal, Director-General Dunkel, in his capacity as the TNC chairman, conducted 'high-level' consultations on the four outstanding negotiating areas, agriculture safeguard, textile, services, and TRIPS. The Services Division staff also attended public conferences, trying to convince the public that the success of the Uruguay Round was very important for the GATT in relation to two of its main functions: the GATT as an institution and that GATT as a negotiating forum. Negotiation on trade in services was part of the single undertaking and must be kept going.[51] Indeed, 'after Montreal, the battle line of the services negotiations ceased to be drawn on exclusively North–South line. Instead, there was a sharpening of differences on many issues among the developed countries'.[52] This new division on the one hand slowed down the negotiation. On the other hand, however, it created a new opportunity for the 'third party' – the Secretariat – to play a more active role in shaping the negotiation. The rest of 1989 was dominated by the submission of reports by the Secretariat on telecommunication (May), transport (July), tourism (July), professional services (August), financial services (September), safeguards and services (September), and Development (November). In December, the Secretariat submitted another document for negotiation as instructed by the agreement reached at the Montreal ministerial meeting 'in order to provide a structure and focus for the discussion in the GNS at assembling by the end of 1989 the necessary elements for the negotiation of a draft framework on services'.[53] Claiming that this material was drawn from national submissions as well as presentations made by the delegates during the discussions, this proposal was apparently a selection of the positions, ideas, concepts and terms on trade in services. In 1989, six meetings were held by the GNS for countries to discuss these submissions. Meanwhile both informal and formal consultations were held, sometimes led by the Director-General Dunkel through 'Green Room' sessions, to 'hammer out solutions to some of the most difficult problems that arose in the negotiating groups'.[54] Consultation was also sometimes conducted by the chairman of the GNS with or without the presence of the people from the Services Division. Yet, the latter was always available to 'service' the chairman.

In 1990, negotiation on trade in services was speeding up. Ten meetings were held to discuss country submissions but more importantly submissions of the Secretariat and other international organizations. In February, Latin American countries (Brazil, Chile, Colombia, Cuba, Honduras, Nicaragua, Mexico, Peru, Trinidad and Tobago, and Uruguay) proposed a structure for a

---

49 GATT document, MTN.GNS/W/50 (13 April 1989).
50 Kindleberger, 'Economists in International Organizations', p. 339.
51 Kakabadse, 'Trade in Services and the Uruguay Round', pp. 292–293.
52 Croome, *Reshaping the World Trading System*, p. 242.
53 GATT document, MTN.GNS/W.90 (18 December 1989), p. 1.
54 Croome, *Reshaping the World Trading System*, p. 164.

multilateral framework for trade in services as a counter submission to the one submitted by the United States earlier.[55] In May, seven Asian and African countries submitted their own positions. The chairman in July introduced his own 'Draft Multilateral Framework for Trade in Services', prepared by the Services Division, and submitted it to the TNC. In the following meeting, the chairman urged delegates to take stock of their work and see how they would proceed further in order to achieve, by November, a full draft text of a services framework. While pointing out that his report was open for consideration, the chairman emphasized that he had made further revisions to his version of the framework and the timetable agreed upon would not allow them to tear the framework apart. He suggested delegates consider the question of submitting to legal experts agreed texts in order to meet the deadline. 'This chairman's proposal cut usefully through a large number of sectoral questions, but – as an internal Secretariat note pointed out – most of the major issues remained open'.[56]

To facilitate the negotiation, the chairman broke the GNS into working groups on various sectors – working groups on financial services (including insurance), telecommunication, construction and engineering, and transport services, and labour mobility all started their first negotiation meeting in June 1990. As agreed in the July meeting, the *Secretariat* had prepared two informal documents: one containing draft texts on the articles appearing under Parts V and VI of the draft framework text and the second document containing a checklist of issues arising from discussion on the draft framework. Despite the differences, the GNS was able to compile a draft agreement entitled 'General Agreement on Trade in Services' to be submitted to the Brussels Ministerial meeting in December 1990. By then, however, the United States refused to accept a general obligation to give MFN treatment to all signatories of the new GATS. Only another round of 'Green Room' negotiation in early December saved the draft agreement, which was days later again stalled as the result of the collapse of the negotiation on agriculture.

At this stage, both the GNS and the Services Division had changed their leader. These changes were typical examples of the politics in the international trading system. That is, contracting parties expect the chairman of a committee or a negotiation group and the Secretariat to take the lead in pushing through the agenda and arriving at some kind of agreements towards liberalization of trade. Meanwhile, they were suspicious of any sign that the Secretariat or the chairman might take the initiative. Australian delegate, David Hawes replaced Jaramillo as the chairman of the GNS primarily because of the perceived inability of Jaramillo to bring countries in line in reaching an agreement. Meanwhile a former British civil servant and long time GATT veteran, David Hartridge, replaced Sampson to lead the Services Division primarily because of its successes in initiating a framework that was different from that regarding trade in goods and with which tariff reductions could be negotiated among contracting parties. While delegates accepted the framework, they also saw this as a threat to their control of the negotiations.

---

55 GATT document, MTN.GNS/W/95 (26 February 1990).
56 Croome, *Reshaping the World Trading System*, p. 249.

The focal points of disagreements were (1) whether the MFN principles would be applicable to the services sector, and (2) whether liberalization of trade in services would be feasible for those countries that had not even developed such sectors. Taking both issues into consideration, the Services Division worked out a draft framework that included two components – the general principles guiding the trade in services and the schedules of initial commitments based on different modes of delivery. This package adopted what is known as a 'two-track' approach. The approach can be explained in two ways. All participating countries must accept the general principles and the framework of GATS. Meanwhile, they would opt in rather than opting out of the agreement regarding the specific sectors they want to liberalize in the initial stage according to different modes of delivery. In other words, those countries that had already developed certain services sectors and were ready to liberalize them could exchange their concessions while those whose services were to develop or in the process of developing did not have to make any concessions at all.

At the final stage of the negotiation (1991–93), countries started preparing for country concessions on each specific service sector and the Secretariat worked closely with the contracting parties in negotiating and preparing for their initial schedules, based on the framework designed by the Services Division. The emphasis was on the general obligations, some of which were applicable to all sectors (e.g. MFN, transparency) and some only to scheduled commitments (e.g. payments and transfers), of trade in services and those aspects both developing and developed countries were interested in. For example, the interests of large developing countries were taken into consideration when the fourth mode of delivery, natural persons, was included.[57] So they would be able to select only those sectors or activities for which they were ready to negotiate concessions. The Secretariat provided a services sectoral classification list that contained 11 categories (business, communication, construction and related engineering, distribution, education, financial, health related and social, tourism and travel related, recreational, cultural and sporting, transport, and other services not included elsewhere) and hundred of sub-sectors.[58] Some countries opted in all while others listed only two or three categories in their initial schedule. In each category, countries must specify the limitation on modes of delivery.

Take the category of communication as an example. There are five subsectors under the category of communication services – postal, courier, telecommunication (that itself contained a further 15 sub-sub-sections), and audiovisual services. Tables 1 and 2 indicate how just two countries

---

[57] The obstacles to trade in services vary greatly, mainly because of the different modes of supply. 'If the service was to be delivered across national borders, with no movement of capital or labour, the way to liberalization might lie in the removal of communications barriers, regulations on materials and on payments. Movement of consumers might require easing of foreign exchange rules for tourists. Commercial presence could for instance involve rules on non-portfolio investment and foreign exchange. Movement of natural persons raised the kind of issues discussed above in connection with the proposed annex on labour services, as well as rules on professional qualification' (Croome, *Reshaping the World Trading System*, p. 274).

[58] GATT document, MTN.GNS/W/120 (10 July 1991).

Table 1 Schedule of Uruguay

Sector	Mode of delivery	Limitation on market access	Limitation on national treatment	Additional limitations
Courier services Private mail and courier services	1. Cross border supply	None	None	
	2. Consumption abroad	None	None	
	3. Commercial presence	None	None	
	4. Movement of natural persons	The entry and temporary stay of services suppliers is not bound, except in the case of senior and specialized personnel of enterprises in the sector by this offer		

Source: GATT document, MTN.GNS/W/128/Rev. 1 (29 November 1993).

Table 2 Schedule of Argentina

Sector	Mode of delivery	Limitation on market access	Limitation on national treatment	Additional limitations
Courier services	1. Cross border supply	None	None	
	2. Consumption abroad	None	None	
	3. Commercial presence	None	None	
	4. Movement of natural persons	None		
Telecommunication				
a. Electronic mail	1. Cross border supply	None	None	
b. Voice mail				
c. On-line information	2. Consumption abroad	None	None	
d. Value-added fax services	3. Commercial presence	None	None	
	4. Movement of natural persons	Not bound, except for senior personnel (managers, executives, and specialists)		

Source: GATT document, MTN.GNS/W/125/Rev. 3 (26 November 1993).

responded. Uruguay decided only to 'opt in' to the category of courier services, with some limitations. But it did not choose to list any telecommunications. Argentina opted in to courier services and 4 of the 15 sub-sub-categories listed under telecommunications. It did not list the other 11 which were therefore not to be part of the commitment the country made for liberalization. Neither country (indeed no country) subjected their postal services for liberalization. Nor did either list audiovisuals services. This capacity to 'opt in' made the services agreement different from those on trade in goods. This framework had been designed by the Secretariat and was a vital step in allowing a final agreement to be reached.

In the final stage of the Uruguay Round, there were a fewer meetings of the GNS while many concrete actions were taken on reaching agreements on submissions from the participants. Preparing the schedules turned out to be quite difficult for countries that had neither sufficient knowledge nor manpower to do so. The Secretariat not only helped countries prepare for their schedules but also provided guidelines along the way regarding clarifying issues arising in the process. More importantly, it compiled and evaluated offers in the services context to 'assist in the preparation of offers, requests and national schedules of initial commitments'.[59] Negotiations on trade in services during the Uruguay Round left many sectors unsettled. Yet, they did reach a final agreement and agreed to continue the negotiation over specific services sectors in the future.

5.4 Conclusion

This chapter explores the role that the GATT Secretariat played in the development of the agreement on trade in services. Legal-institutional studies stress the limited formal power granted by the treaty to the Secretariat and the Secretariat itself always downplayed its role. It often portrayed itself as the servant of the contracting parties and therefore with little influence on either the positions taken by the parties or the outcome of the MTNs. The degree to which the ICS may use whatever treaty opportunities they have to expand their *de facto* sphere of initiative and influence varies depending on the skills of the civil servants, the leadership role of the executive head, the issues under debate, and the interest participating countries have over the issue. Even this preliminary account of the occasions in which the Secretariat in general and the service division in particular played a role suggests that their presence was vital in securing progress in the international negotiations. Whether defining terms, suggesting alternative wordings, or bringing together disparate views, the Secretariat can act as honest broker and intellectual powerhouse. Without its diplomatic skill, political understanding, drafting aptitude, knowledge of its exponents and, most importantly, its assistance and facilitation, there might have been no agreement. Its very professionalism allowed progress in an area where initially it

---

59 GATT document, MTN.GNS/W/164 (3 September 1993).

seemed none was likely. Finally, to achieve that the Secretariat itself has to be seen as the advocate of no country and the adherent to no cause. In this case that stance worked effectively.

Negotiations on trade in services may have been fertile ground for assistance from the Secretariat because the subject was a completely new issue when negotiations began. The case in this chapter may have described the GATT Secretariat and its role in facilitating international cooperation in MTNs. The findings, however, are applicable to the WTO, which inherited the GATT Secretariat. With the creation of a formal international organization, the WTO, of course circumstances have changed. There may be greater rhetoric about the WTO as a 'member-driven organization'. There may be more regular and institutionalized ministerial meetings as part of the fabric of the negotiation process. There may be greater emphasis on the relationship between trade and development. There may be more members with very different political and economic systems. The responsibilities of the Secretariat remain, so does the potential it has to influence the development of international trade. Essentially the core business of the Secretariat is the same – providing support, advice, ideas, service, drafts, and mediation. Indeed as the member states expand in number, so does the need for technical advice on the WTO-compatibility of their economic policies and practices. The Secretariat cannot be taken for granted, nor is it wise to write its staff off as 'mere clerks'. The evidence suggests they were, and are, more than that.

Indeed, the lessons that may be drawn from this study emphasize how important the Secretariat will be for the success of the Doha Round of MTN. The Director-General, Supachai, has stressed on a number of occasions the need to strengthen the Secretariat. Given the increasing range of relationships that must be serviced and the increasing visibility of the WTO, the enhanced Secretariat may be an essential requirement to bring complex and multifaceted negotiations to a conclusion.

To conclude, no international organizations can simply be reduced to a collective voice of their participating states. Development of international organizations and procedures are not simply the expressions of the interests of particular states or other international actors. All international organizations have some degree of independence in making their own decisions without dictation from outside actors; the outputs of the system therefore do not merely reflect inputs from the environment but also bear the mark of the organization's values. As Keohane pointed out some time ago the outcomes in international organizations depend *not only* on government interaction *but also* on the context within which such interaction takes place.[60] Since an international organization is not a straightforwardly determined vector of member states' interests and power, organizational variables become important in explaining the choices of the organization. International civil servants are particularly important in helping to define the context where decisions are made.

---

[60] Keohane, 'Institutionalization in the United Nations General Assembly', pp. 859–96.

6. Dispute Settlement in the WTO: Questioning the 'Security' and 'Predictability' of the Implementation Phase of the DSU?

Bryan Mercurio

6.1 Introduction

When the Uruguay Round of Multilateral Trade Negotiations (Uruguay Round) concluded with the creation of the World Trade Organization (WTO), the procedures for settling international trade disputes were dramatically altered.[1] The creation of a broader, more efficient, rule-based dispute resolution process has been widely hailed as an improvement over the rules and procedures of its predecessor, the General Agreement on Tariffs and Trade (GATT). The WTO eliminated much of the shortcomings, delay, and subsequent lack of compliance associated with the GATT dispute settlement mechanism, however, several recent cases have highlighted numerous deficiencies in the textual language and processes of the WTO Understanding on Rules and Procedures Governing the Settlement of Disputes (DSU) that threaten to weaken the WTO as an international trading system.[2]

WTO Members recognise the deficiencies in the DSU and, as part of the full review of dispute settlement rules and procedures required by the Uruguay Round (DSU Review),[3] prepared several draft proposals to amend the DSU. Unfortunately, the Review, which was to have concluded in October 1998, stalled due to strong differences of opinion among Members. The Dispute Settlement Body (DSB) agreed to continue the review process until the end of July 1999,[4] but the 1999 Seattle Ministerial Conference ended without agreement. The DSU seemed permanently 'suspended' until the Doha Ministerial

---

1 Final Act Embodying the Results of the Uruguay Round of Multilateral Trade Negotiations, 15 April 1994, in 'The Legal Texts: The Results of the Uruguay Round of Multilateral Trade Negotiations' (1999) 33 *International Law Magazine* 1125 (WTO Agreement).

2 *See* Understanding on Rules and Procedures Governing the Settlement of Disputes, 15 April 1994, Marrakesh Agreement Establishing the World Trade Organization, Annex 2, *Ibid.*, 1226.

3 *See* Decision on the Application and Review of the Understanding on Rules and Procedures Governing the Settlement of Disputes, *Ibid.*, 1259.

4 *See* DSB meeting, 'Extension of the deadline for review of the DSU', WT/DSB/M/52 (3 February 1999).

Conference negotiations revived the DSU Review with the aim of concluding an agreement by May 2003.[5] The Doha Declaration states that the DSU Review is separate to, and will not be tied to the overall success or failure of, the other negotiations mandated by the declaration, giving Members the perfect opportunity to reach consensus on a number of troubling aspects of the DSU.

While slight changes are needed to most areas of dispute settlement in the WTO, this chapter analyses the shortcomings of the implementation phase and proposes solutions to address the growing problem.[6] The chapter seeks to show certain amendments are needed to address the shortcomings of the implementation phase that, left unaddressed, could seriously undermine the effectiveness of the WTO. Section 6.2 introduces the history of the international trading system. Beginning with the origins of the GATT, the section traces the GATT's development, its dispute settlement mechanism and ultimately its failure as a world trading system. The section then introduces the WTO and its dispute settlement system and reviews its rules and procedures. Section 6.3 examines the implementation phase of dispute settlement in the WTO. The section begins by reviewing DSB compliance and continues to scrutinize the dispute settlement procedures. Section 6.4 targets the implementation problems caused by textual ambiguity and oversight, specifically the 'reasonable period for implementation' and the apparent conflict between Articles 21.5 and 22 of the DSU. Section 6.4 critiques the leading DSU draft amendment proposal and recommends that more drastic reform is needed to maintain the DSU's credibility as a dispute settlement mechanism.

6.2 History of International Trading Systems

In order to fully understand and analyse the current international trading system, one must first appreciate the history of modern international trade negotiations and agreements. This process begins with the origins and evolution of the GATT and continues to the workings of the WTO and its dispute settlement process.

6.2.1 The GATT

6.2.1.1 The origins

In the aftermath of the Second World War, western leaders did not want a repeat of the economic isolationism that played a large part in deepening

---

[5] *See* Doha Declaration; DSB Negotiations, Statement by the Chairman, WT/DSB/W/181 (18 December 2001).

[6] For commentary and analysis of other DSU Review issues, such as panel status, length of panel decisions, NGO participation, timelines, transparency, etc. *See* T. Stewart and A. Karpel, 'Operation of Panels: Review of the Dispute Settlement Understanding: Operation of Panels' (2000) 31 *Law and Policy in International Business* 593; K. Van der Borght, 'The Review of the WTO Understanding on Dispute Settlement: Some Reflections of the Current Debate' (1999) *14 American University International Law Review* 1223.

the Great Depression and leading to the start of the war. Attempting to create new world political and economic institutions necessary to promote and maintain peaceful international relations, world leaders united in 1944 to negotiate the Bretton Woods agreement, which established the charters for the International Monetary Fund and the International Bank for Reconstruction and Development. A year later, the United States proposed the creation of a world trade system in the form of the International Trade Organization (ITO).

The proposed Charter for the ITO (Geneva Draft) included specific provisions on trade, development, commodity agreements, and other economic issues. It also mandated consultation, arbitration and referral to the International Court of Justice (ICJ) as part of dispute settlement. On 21 November 1947, 57 nations met in Cuba to finalize drafting of the proposal, which would became the Havana Charter.[7]

During that time, 25 of those nations agreed on the GATT trade agreement.[8] Seeking to liberalize international trade and reduce tariffs internationally negotiated, the Contracting Parties intended the GATT to be a temporary measure until absorbed by the ITO. The American Congress, however, in a move reminding some of the Treaty of Versailles and the League of Nations, refused to ratify the ITO negotiations and the organization never materialized.[9]

Consequently, eight signatories agreed to provisionally apply the GATT as of 1 January 1948.[10] The Protocol of Provisional Application (PPA) terms allowed for full application of Parts I and III of the GATT[11] and applied Part II only 'to the fullest extent not inconsistent with existing legislation'.[12] This

---

[7] T. Stewart (ed.), *The GATT Uruguay Round: A Negotiating History* (Kluwer Law International, London, 1993), pp. 2671–72.

[8] Negotiated between 1946 and 1948, the GATT is a multilateral treaty, with norms that bind Members and the ability to create law and develop custom. The GATT, however, lacks many of the provisions of the ITO Charter and does not include rule-oriented language or recourse to arbitration or the ICJ, meaning the GATT is not self-autonomous and Members must drive for organisational change. *See* J. Kasto, *The Function & Future of the WTO* (Kall Kwik, Kingston, 1996), p. 4.

[9] In hindsight, the ITO was probably too ambitious a proposal for the times. The ITO required significant changes in the law (such as requiring implementation and governed compliance with rules regarding trade barriers, restrictive trade practices, international commodity arrangements and international labour policies) and many signatories were not ready to abandon domestic laws in favour of implementing ITO consistent language. *See* Stewart, *supra* n. 7, at 2670.

[10] This group consisted of Australia, Belgium, Canada, France, Luxembourg, The Netherlands, United Kingdom, and United States.

[11] Parts I and III set basic policy for trade liberalization based on (i) preference for tariffs over other forms of protection (such as quotas or quantitative restrictions); (ii) abolition of quotas; (iii) application of quotas only under exceptional circumstances and with multilateral permission; (iv) most-favoured nation status to all GATT parties (with narrow exceptions); and (v) national treatment to all products of GATT parties that lawfully clear customs.

[12] Part II contains the substantive portion of the GATT, consisting of Articles III–XXIII. The provisions, which provide the necessary market access complement to Part I, include topics such as national treatment, antidumping and countervailing duties, custom valuation, origins, quotas and limitations, balance of payment restrictions, subsidies, emergency action, and exceptions to the GATT (including exceptions necessary to protect human, plant and animal life, health and safety, and national security).

clause became known as 'grandfather rights', allowing parties with these rights to continue applying measures inconsistent with the GATT obligations.

Article XXIX:2 of the GATT evidences just how fleeting the PPA was designed to be, providing '(p)art II of this Agreement shall be suspended on the day which the Havana Charter comes into force'. As the Havana Charter was expected to come into force rather quickly, GATT inconsistent legislation was not supposed to be tolerated for long. But the Havana Charter never came into force and the GATT survived for 47 years on a 'provisional' basis. Thus the GATT alone, without a constitutional or institutional foundation, was left to function as the world forum for international trade matters. The result of this unanticipated scheme was an organization ill equipped to regulate the broad issues presented in world trade. As a result, the Contracting Parties continuously sought revisions, codifications and improvements to the system, leading to constant improvisation and uncertainty.

6.2.1.2 Dispute settlement under the GATT

Articles XXII[13] and XXIII[14] provide the entire foundation of the GATT dispute settlement system. The GATT contained limited procedural rules because the Contracting Parties anticipated the detailed provisions of dispute settlement under the ITO soon would apply. Consequently, without any clear procedural rules, the GATT was forced to discover them through practice.

One unambiguous rule in the GATT was a preference for negotiated settlements. The GATT diplomatically referred to the dispute settlement process as 'conciliation', and Contracting Parties were mandated to enter into consultation and negotiation. Notably lacking from the articles, however, were any guidelines or procedures to guide the consultation and negotiation process. Failing to agree to a mutual solution, the dispute would be submitted to a panel to take evidence, hear arguments, rule on the legal issues and merits of the complaint, and submit its decision to the GATT council. Once more, the GATT provided no operational guidance or procedures.[15]

---

13 Article XXII:1 merely requires a party afford other parties adequate opportunity for consultation with respect to any matter affecting the operation of the Agreement. Article XXII:2 authorizes the Contracting Parties, as a whole and acting jointly, at the request of a party to the Agreement to consult with another party on matters not resolved through Article XXII:1 consultations.

14 Article XXIII:1 provides that a party can make a written representation or proposal to another party when it believes that a benefit directly or indirectly emerging from the Agreement is being nullified or impaired by that other party. If a satisfactory conclusion is not reached, then Article XXIII:2 authorizes the complaining party to refer the matter to the Contracting Parties (as a whole), who are required to investigate and make appropriate recommendations. In addition, Article XXIII:2 permits the Contracting Parties to authorize the complaining party to suspend tariff concessions or other GATT obligations to the party found to be acting inconsistent with its Agreement obligations.

15 In fact, the GATT experimented with the panel, with it first consisting solely of the GATT Chairman and eventually evolving to working parties consisting of the complainant, respondent, and any other interested party to solve the dispute before finally settling on a neutral panel. In 1952, a dispute between Norway and Germany saw a neutral panel used for the first time. M. Pryles, J. Waincymer, and M. Davies, *International Trade Law: Commentary & Materials* (CBC Information Services, Sydney, 1996), p. 787.

After receiving the written decision of the panel, a unanimous vote of the GATT Council was needed to adopt the panel decision.[16] In other words, a defendant could block, or essentially veto, an adverse panel decision. Therefore, the very nature of the GATT's quasi-voluntary procedure decreased its ability to effectively adjudicate international trade disputes.

For all its obvious shortcomings, the GATT successfully resolved many trade disputes and even thrived during its early years of existence. A leading scholar accounts for the early success of the GATT in the following way:

> Governments understood the legal rulings implicit in its vaguely worded decisions, and once these rulings were approved by the GATT Contracting Parties, defendant governments almost always felt it necessary to comply. The reason these impressionistic half-decisions were successful was that the early GATT of the 1950s was essentially a small 'club' of likeminded trade policy officials who had been working together since the 1946–1948 ITO negotiations... Thus they did not need a very elaborate decision-making procedure to generate an effective consensus about what particular governments were expected to do.[17]

Eventually the challenges of the changing conditions of international trade, which brought not only more complex cases but also a larger, more diverse group of nations, caught up with the GATT process. The GATT was no longer a small club of like-minded nations, but a large group with diverse viewpoints on numerous trade issues. Textual and procedural weaknesses continued to reveal themselves in the difficulties and failures of the GATT dispute resolution system and increasingly led to a large number of disputes which it could not effectively resolve.

The most glaring shortcoming of the GATT dispute resolution system stemmed from the voluntary nature of the process. Every organizational decision required complete consensus, meaning a defendant essentially had a veto right at every step of the process, from the appointment of a panel to the adoption of the panel's legal ruling and authorization of trade sanctions for non-compliance. As a result, smaller and developing nations found it impossible to obtain a successful resolution to a dispute.

Other procedural shortcomings of the GATT further undermined the coherence of the system and many contracting parties grew increasingly frustrated and disenchanted with the lack of coordination, guidance, and stability of the system.[18] Furthermore, increased GATT Membership introduced differing

---

16 Article XXIII requires all matters be decided by the 'Contracting Parties', meaning the GATT was a multi-party contract to be amended, interpreted, or modified only by consent of all the parties. D. Palmeter and P. Mauroidis, *Dispute Settlement in the WTO: Practice & Procedure* (Kluwer Law Institute, The Hague, The Netherlands, 1999), p. 9. This interpretation is consistent with Article 40 of the Vienna Convention on the Law of Treaties, which requires unanimity among contracting parties absent specific rules stating otherwise.

17 R. Hudec, 'The New WTO Dispute Settlement Procedure: An Overview of the First Three Years' (1999) 8(1) *Minnesota Journal of Global Trade* 5–6.

18 *See* K. Stiles, 'The New WTO Regime: The Victory of Pragmatism' (1995) 4(3) *Journal of International Law and Practice* 3, 5–8. Competing codes, alternative dispute settlement arrangements, forum shopping, panel delays, and transparency problems all contributed to the growing

views on international trade and thus, international trade law. This resulted in inconsistent panel decisions, an unsound body of case law and an increase in the number of Contracting Parties failing to comply with panel decisions. In fact, by the 1990s compliance with GATT panel decisions was under 60 per cent.[19] Maybe more importantly, many contracting parties began abandoning or withdrawing cases from the GATT dispute resolution panel in the growing belief that the system was ineffective. Despite six rounds of negotiation to improve the system, it became obvious that a larger, comprehensive effort incorporating wholesale changes was needed.

In retrospect, the GATT was simply too ambitious a proposal and doomed to failure at the moment of its inception. The formal structure of the organization, as well as its dispute resolution procedure, was weak and the process procedurally flawed and underdeveloped. These textual shortcomings may have been due to the fact that the GATT was not intended to be a permanent international trade body, but a stopgap measure until the ratification of the ITO. Nevertheless, the textual and procedural deficiencies in the GATT directly contributed to the ultimate failure of its dispute resolution process.

6.2.2 A new system: The WTO

The Uruguay Round set to resolve the textual and procedural shortcomings uncovered in the GATT and reach an agreement as to the solutions, with the Ministerial Declaration setting the broad negotiating objectives as to (1) strengthen rules and procedures and (2) enhance surveillance with a view to increase compliance. Formally concluded by 15 December 1993 in Marrakech, Morocco, the negotiations addressed the above issues and created the WTO as the new international trading system.

6.2.2.1 The fundamentals of the WTO

The WTO came into force on 1 January 1995, replacing the GATT as the authority on world trade relations, negotiations, and dispute resolutions. Essentially functioning exactly as the ITO was supposed to in the late-1940s, the WTO serves as the legal and institutional foundation of the international trading system. As the WTO implements the rules negotiated in the Uruguay Round, however, it is guided by past GATT decisions, procedures, and practices. A condition of entry to the WTO is that nations must accept the entire package of substantive agreements; therefore a nation cannot

---

Contd.
ineffectiveness of the GATT's dispute settlement procedures. So to did the fact that most GATT 'judges' were diplomats, not lawyers, and their decisions were often vague, diplomatic, and elusive. *See* R. Hudec, *Enforcing International Trade Law: The Evolution of Modern GATT Legal System* (Butterworth Legal Publishing, Salem, 1993), p. 12.

[19] *Ibid.*, 278. Forty complaints were filed between 1952 and 1958, only 10 were filed between 1960 and 1969 and only 3 were filed between 1963 and 1970. Stewart, *supra* n. 7, at 2679. Between 1979 and 1986, only 29 disputes were filed, resulting in 21 panel reports (with five decisions going unadopted due to the losing party's refusal to accept the decision). *Ibid.*, 2732. Parties simply thought the GATT rules were outdated, easy to evade through other trade measures, unbalanced and eventually led to unilateral retaliation. *Ibid.*, 2679.

'pick and choose which rules to follow and which to ignore'.[20] This requirement is a substantial improvement over the voluntary nature of the GATT.

The Uruguay Round intended that the WTO serve five main functions: (1) facilitate the implementation, administration and operation, and further the objectives of the agreement; (2) provide a forum for negotiations among its members concerning matters addressed under the agreement; (3) administer the Understanding on Rules and Procedures Governing the Settlement of Disputes; (4) administer the Trade Policy Review Mechanism; and (5) cooperate with the International Monetary Fund, International Bank and related agencies for reconstruction and development with a view towards achieving greater coherence in global economic policy.[21]

6.2.2.2 Differences between the WTO and GATT

One of the most significant differences between the GATT and the WTO are the rules governing trade disputes. The WTO entrusts the DSB to handle disputes in accordance with the DSU. The DSB meets regularly and has the authority to establish dispute settlement panels, adopt panel and appellate body reports, maintain surveillance of implementation rulings and suspend concessions and other obligations covered under any WTO Agreement if not implemented by an infringing member.

The agreement creates unique international law which confers compulsory jurisdiction on the DSU for purposes of resolving disputes. The importance of the DSU is stated in Article 3.2, which reads, 'the dispute settlement system of the WTO is a central element in providing security and predictability to a multilateral trading system'. In fact, the sections relating to dispute settlement may be the most significant achievement of the Uruguay Round.

Unlike the informal dispute settlement procedure of the GATT, the DSB adjudicates international legal disputes according to formal procedures. The DSU and its appendices set not only the basic institutional and jurisdictional scope of WTO dispute settlement but also rules and procedures for panels. The DSU continues to rely on Articles XXII and XXIII of the GATT, but extensively expands the procedure's legal powers.

Additionally, and unlike the GATT, the DSU creates a standing Appellate Body to review panels' legal decisions. Moreover, the DSB automatically adopts panel and Appellate Body reports unless the DSB decides by consensus otherwise. This eliminates the ability of one Member, namely the losing party, to block a panel decision using its veto power. Similarly, the

---

[20] W. Scanlan, 'A Test Case for the New World Trade Organization's Dispute Settlement Understanding: The Japan-USA Auto Parts Dispute' (1996) 45 *University of Kansas Law Review* 591, 598. The first 13 agreements of the WTO incorporated the GATT 1994. The topics for negotiation included tariffs, non-tariff measures, tropical products, natural resource-based products, textiles and clothing, agriculture, GATT articles, safeguards, MFN Agreements and Arrangements, subsidies and countervailing measures, dispute settlement, trade-related aspects of intellectual property (TRIPs) and trade-related investment measures (TRIMs). *See Ministerial Declaration on the Uruguay Round*, GATT Doc. No. MIN(86)/6 (20 September 1986), 5–8.

[21] *See* WTO Agreement, *supra* note 1, at Article II, para. 1–5, 1144.

DSU seeks to eliminate much of the delay and lack of compliance associated with the GATT's dispute settlement mechanism by making panel decisions valid at the moment of inception.

6.2.2.3 WTO dispute settlement

The DSU consists of five stages: consultations, panel, appellate review, arbitration, and compensation. The following describes each stage's intended purpose.

Consultation:[22] The first step to dispute settlement in the WTO is consultation. When a dispute arises pursuant to a covered agreement a member must first request a consultation. The consultation phase attempts to obtain a satisfactory resolution of the matter. If an implicated member does not respond within 10 days or enter into consultation within 30 days, or if the parties fail to settle the dispute within 60 days, the complaining party may request a panel.

The panel phase:[23] In order to prevent some of the problems associated with the GATT, a panel will be convened upon the request of a complaining party unless the DSB decides by consensus not to establish one.[24] Generally, panels are composed of three well-qualified individuals (generally academics or present or former members of non-party delegations to the WTO). Panelists are nominated by the Secretariat and parties to the dispute can only oppose the nominations for compelling reasons. If the parties cannot agree to the composition of the panel within 20 days, the Director-General, in conjunction with the DSB and the relevant Council or Committee, appoints the panellists. Panelists serve in their individual capacity, not as a representative of their government, who is prohibited from instructing or influencing panellists in any manner.

The panel is highly legalistic and strikingly similar to a court. The panel makes an objective assessment of the matter by examining the facts of the case and the relevant covered agreements. Its purpose is to assist the DSB in making recommendations or giving rulings. The panel accomplishes this through confidential analysis of written submissions, oral arguments, expert witnesses, and other relevant sources. The panel process is to last no more than 6 months.

Following oral arguments and rebuttal submissions, the panel submits its findings to the parties. The parties then submit comments regarding the findings. Next, the panel responds with an interim report. This report includes the panel's findings and conclusions. Unless a party requests that the panel review specific aspects of the interim report, it will be considered the final report and is circulated to Members. Twenty days after circulation Members may consider the report adopted, but may submit objections

---

22 *See* DSU Article 4.

23 *See* DSU Articles 6–8, 11–12.

24 DSU Article 6 mandates a panel be established no later than the second meeting after the request for a panel first appears on the DSB agenda. Thus, a party complained against can and often does 'block' establishment of a panel for one DSB meeting.

10 days prior to the meeting at which the report will be considered. Unless a party to the dispute notifies the DSB of its intention to appeal or the DSB decides by consensus not to adopt the report, the report is automatically adopted.

Appellate Review:[25] A party can appeal the panel report. When this occurs, the panel report is referred to the Appellate Body. The Appellate Body is composed of a standing body of seven persons of recognized authority, with three serving per case. The appeal is limited to the issues of law covered in the panel report and should not exceed 60 days in length. The proceedings of the Appellate Body are confidential and the opinions expressed are anonymous. Unless the DSB decides by consensus not to adopt the Appellate Body report, it will be adopted within 30 days following its circulation to Members.

Binding arbitration:[26] Upon consensus by all parties to a dispute, binding arbitration may be an alternative means of dispute resolution. The parties involved must agree on the procedures and abide by the arbitration award. Arbitration awards are subject to the agreement's other provisions regarding implementation and compensation.

Implementation and compensation:[27] The DSU requires compliance with recommendations or rulings of the DSB within a reasonable time. The reasonable time can be a period proposed by the member concerned and approved by the DSB, a period mutually agreed upon by the parties to the dispute, or a period determined through binding arbitration 90 days after the date of adoption of the recommended rulings. In arbitration, DSU Article 21 provides that 'a guideline for the arbitrator should be that the reasonable period of time to implement panel or Appellate Body recommendations should not exceed 15 months from the date for adoption of a panel or Appellate Body report'.

Disagreements as to the adequacy of compliance with WTO rulings are decided through recourse to the dispute settlement procedures, 'including wherever possible resort to the original panel'.[28] The panel circulates its report within 90 days after the date of referral of the matter. The DSB monitors the implementation of adopted rulings to ensure that it occurs within a reasonable time. If a party fails to implement the recommended measures, the member may be requested to enter into negotiations with the complaining party in order to develop mutually acceptable compensation. If no agreeable compensation plan can be reached and agreed to, the complaining party that invoked the dispute settlement procedures may request authorization from the DSB to suspend the application of concessions or other obligations under the covered agreements to the offending member.

---

25 DSU Article 17.
26 DSU Article 25.
27 DSU Articles 21–22.
28 *See* Article 21.5.

6.3 Implementation Issues

6.3.1 Compliance in the WTO

Despite the above procedures, issues regarding dispute settlement implementation in the WTO are still fiercely debated. This section examines the implementation procedures and cases that have caused the present debate and concern for the future of dispute settlement in the WTO.

Contrary to popular opinion, dispute settlement in the WTO is not subject to never-ending litigation and mass non-compliance with DSB rulings and recommendations. In fact, only approximately 33 per cent of the 275 cases filed in the WTO have reached the panel stage, with less than 15 per cent of cases reaching the point where DSU implementation procedures apply. A great majority of those cases reaching dispute settlement were fully implemented by the losing party or an agreement acceptable to the winning party was reached. In fact, only 10 cases have led to Appellate Body and Panel Reports on implementation of WTO rulings. Somewhat surprisingly, the WTO has only authorized the suspension of concessions in six cases. Looking at the statistics, the WTO dispute settlement system appears to be operating smoothly. This assessment, however, fails to account for the problems the recent, well-publicized cases of non-compliance have raised about the adequacy of the rules and procedures of the implementation phase of the process.

While the number of cases leading to non-compliance action may be few, the cases have caused many to question the textual-sufficiency of the WTO implementation process. The most significant cases are: *Australia–Salmon*,[29] *EC–Bananas*,[30] *Brazil–Export Financing Programme for Aircraft*,[31] *Canada–Measures Affecting the Export of Civilian Aircraft*,[32] *EC–Beef Hormones*,[33] *Australia–Leather*,[34] *Canada–Dairy Products*[35] and *US–Foreign Sales Corporations*.[36]

These contentious cases required full recourse to WTO implementation procedures and are useful in assessing what procedures need revision. The

---

29 *See* WTO Panel Report, Australia – Measures Affecting Importation of Salmon, WT/DS18/R (12 June 1998) *et al.*

30 *See* WTO Panel Report, European Communities – Regime for the Importation, Sale and Distribution of Bananas, WT/DS27/R (22 May 1997) *et al.*

31 *See* WTO Panel Report, Brazil – Export Financing Program for Aircraft, WT/DS46/R (14 April 1999) *et al.*

32 *See* WTO Panel Report, Canada – Measures Affecting the Export of Civilian Aircraft, WT/DS70/R (14 April 1999) *et al.*

33 *See* WTO Panel Report, EC Measures Concerning Meat and Meat Products (Hormones), WT/DS26/R/USA (18 August 1997) *et al.*; WTO Panel Report, EC Measures Concerning Meat and Meat Products (Hormones), WT/DS48/R/CAN (18 August 1997) *et al.*

34 *See* WTO Panel Report, Australia – Subsidies Provided to Producers and Exporters of Automotive Leather, WT/DS126/R (25 May 1999) *et al.*

35 *See* WTO Panel Report, Canada–Measures Affecting the Importation of Milk & the Exportation of Dairy Products, WT/DS/103, WT/DS/113 (17 May 1999) *et al.*

36 *See* WTO Panel Report, US – Tax Treatment for 'Foreign Sales Corporations', WT/DS/108/R (8 October 1999) *et al.*

cases expose a glaring need for reform of a system fraught with ambiguities, drafting omissions, and errors in the text of the DSU. In order to maintain confidence and credibility in the system, the timeframe for completing the process must to be shortened considerably. Moreover, the system needs some form of improved incentives or sanctions in order to achieve 'prompt compliance' with recommendations or rulings of the DSB, which DSU Article 21.1 declares 'is essential in order to ensure effective resolution of disputes to the benefit of all Members'.

6.3.2 The DSU implementation procedures: Cause for concern

As previously stated, the DSU rules governing dispute settlement were intended to strengthen the world trading system so Members could no longer avoid implementing a negative decision, as was common in the later years of the GATT. The system attempted to accomplish this through three separate procedures. First, the DSU created procedures and guidelines to be used in establishing a deadline for complying with an adverse ruling. Second, the DSU established 'compliance review' procedures to be used when a winning and losing party disagree as to whether the losing Member has come into compliance with the DSU ruling. Third, the DSU created procedures for the suspension of concessions if the losing party is found to have failed to implement the WTO rulings and recommendations or otherwise satisfy the winning party by the expiration of the deadline.

Considerable interpretive problems and concerns have been exposed in all three procedures. First, the guidelines and procedures in establishing a deadline for a losing party to come into compliance have caused considerable tension in the system. Article 21(3)(c) provides a guideline that a losing party should be given 'reasonable period of time… not exceed(ing) 15 months' to comply with the adopted decision, but then goes on to state that the implementation time may be 'shorter or longer, depending upon the particular circumstances'. Surprisingly, no more guidance on the timeline or what is required of the losing party during the 'reasonable period' is provided. Second, all aspects of the 'compliance review' procedures have been criticised. Controversy stems from the uncertain beginning of the process, to the uncertain procedures of the process and covers everything in between. Third, the procedures governing the suspension of concessions created an interrelated controversy over when a nation can request the suspension of concessions (retaliation) if there is a disagreement over compliance.

Compliance review and the request to suspend concessions have been the most contentious and disruptive issues to the WTO system. While progressive jurisprudence has had moderate success in interpreting and resolving the 'reasonable period of time' issues, the textual shortcomings and inconsistencies of compliance review and retaliation provisions have only been addressed through *ad hoc* arrangements among the parties. All of the previously mentioned issues and concerns prevailing in the three-implementation procedures, as well as the cases that have brought the problems to the fore, are evaluated below.

6.3.2.1 *Reasonable period of time to implement*

6.3.2.1.1 Article 21

The open-ended timeframe for compliance in the GATT proved to be a giant loophole in the system. In order to close the loophole, the DSU established procedures for a losing party to follow in implementing dispute settlement rulings and recommendations. DSU Article 21(1) states its preference for 'prompt compliance' on the part of the losing party, describing it 'essential in order to ensure effective resolution of disputes to the benefit of all Members'. It recognizes, however, that immediate compliance may be impracticable and, in those circumstances, Article 21(3) permits members to have a 'reasonable period of time' to implement the rulings.

Article 21(3) outlines three ways of deciding what the 'reasonable period' is in a particular case: (1) the losing party proposes a period that the DSB thereafter approves; (2) the winning and losing parties agree on an implementation period within 45 days following adoption of the ruling; or (3) if neither of the first two methods occur, the period can be set by binding arbitration, to be completed within 90 days following adoption of the ruling.

Article 21, however, leaves the definition of the phrase 'reasonable period' rather ambiguous. The article states that 'prompt compliance' is essential and suggests that the reasonable period should not exceed 15 months from the date the ruling was adopted, but besides further adding that the period 'may be shorter or longer, depending upon the particular circumstances', it does nothing to clarify the terms.

Article 21(6) additionally requires the DSB to keep the losing party 'under surveillance' from the onset of the 'reasonable period'. This requirement however, involves very little actual surveillance. To assist the DSB fulfilling their responsibility, Article 21(6) provides that 6 months into each implementation period, the losing member must begin providing regular 'status reports' at all scheduled DSB meetings. Nothing more than these reports are required of the losing member during its compliance period and no progress must be shown in the reports.

6.3.2.1.2 The Establishment of the Reasonable Period

Of the cases that have reached the stage of establishing a 'reasonable period of time' to implement, most set that period by mutual agreement, but a good number are decided by arbitration. Although the reasonable periods set by arbitration and those set by agreement have followed a gradual trend towards shorter implementation periods, the driving force behind that change has been the arbitral rulings.

Early in the process, arbitrators uniformly established a 15-month period to implement. These decisions created concern from Members who felt granting losing parties an automatic entitlement to a compliance period of 15 months seemed contrary to the 'prompt compliance' standard of Article 21 and an unfair extension of the dispute settlement process. For instance, in *Japan–Taxes on Alcohol*, the USA argued that Japan could comply with the decision by a simple tariff-scheme change, which could be effectuated under Japan's legal system within 5 months. Therefore, the United States requested compliance within five months. Conversely, Japan requested a 5-year implementation period. The arbitrator summarily rejected the United States' request for the shortest period possible. In setting the period at 15 months, the arbitrator stated he was 'not persuaded that the "particular circumstances" advanced by Japan and the United States justified a departure from the 15-month "guideline" '.[37]

The *EC–Bananas* case next established a 15-month implementation period. The ruling in that case, however, was slightly more beneficial in explaining why an implementation period of 15 months plus one week was proper. The EC defended its request for 15 months plus one week for compliance primarily on the difficulty it had reconciling the differences between its obligations under the WTO and Lome Convention, as well as the complexity of its legislative procedures. The arbitrator accepted the EC's requested period, giving dispositive weight to the complexity of the EC's implementation process.[38]

Although the next arbitral decision, the *EC–Beef Hormones* case, did not deviate from the 15-month 'guideline' of Article 21, its reasoning created the analytical framework for shorter implementation periods in future cases. Contrary to the arbitral outcome in *Japan–Taxes on Alcohol*, the *EC–Hormones* ruling stated, 'the reasonable period of time, as determined under Article 21.3(c), should be the *shortest period possible* within the legal system of the Member to implement the recommendations and rulings of the DSB'.[39] The ruling made clear that 'the shortest period possible' could not be used by the losing party as a second chance to develop additional justifications for its inconsistent measures. The enunciation of a new standard, however, did not result in a shorter implementation period. Instead, the arbitrator reaffirmed the reasoning in *EC–Bananas* that an important 'particular circumstance' to consider in setting the reasonable period is the complexity of the administrative process the Member must follow to implement the ruling. The arbitrator ruled that in the case of the beef hormone ban, the EC's 'co-decision' procedures required to change its legislation justified a 15-month period.[40]

The first arbitral decision to award a 'reasonable period' of less than 15 months was the *Indonesia–Automobiles* case.[41] The arbitrator in that case adjusted the 'shortest period possible' standard to the special circumstances of Indonesia and established a reasonable period of 12 months. While Indonesia's internal measures enabled it to conform within 6 months, the arbitrator relied heavily on DSU Article 21.2 to pay 'particular attention… to matters affecting the interests of developing country Members with

---

37 *See* WTO Arbitrator's Report, Japan – Taxes on Alcoholic Beverages, WT/DS8/15, WT/DS10/15, WT/DS11/13, p. 27 (14 February 1997).

38 *See* WTO Arbitrator's Report, European Communities – Regime for the Importation, Sale and Distribution of Bananas, WT/DS27/15, p. 27 (7 January 1998).

39 WTO Arbitrator's Report, EC – Measures Concerning Meat and Meat Products (Hormones), WT/DS26/15, WT/DS48/13, p. 26 (29 May 1998) (emphasis added).

40 *See Ibid.*, 48.

41 *See* WTO Arbitrator's Report, Indonesia – Certain Measures Affecting the Automobile Industry, WT/DS54/15, WT/DS55/14, WT/DS59/13, WT/DS64/12 (7 December 1998).

respect to measures which have been subject to dispute settlement'. For that reason, the arbitrator gave 'full weight' to the fact that Indonesia's economy was 'near collapse' in authorizing an additional 6 months to comply.[42]

Another case to undergo reasonable-period arbitration, *Korea–Alcoholic Beverages*, reaffirmed that 'the shortest period possible' standard was 'the most important factor in establishing the length of the reasonable period of time'.[43] In establishing a compliance period of 11 months, the arbitrator noted that the requirement to choose the 'shortest period' within the legal system 'does not require a Member ... to utilize an *extraordinary* legislative procedure, rather than the normal legislative procedure'.[44] The arbitrator added '(that) choosing the means of implementation is, and should be, the prerogative of the implementing Member, as long as the means chosen are consistent with the recommendations and rulings of the DSB and the provisions of the covered agreements'.[45]

The shortest 'reasonable period' arbitration award occurred in *Canada–Pharmaceutical Products*, where the arbitrator expressly agreed with the *EC–Hormones* arbitrator's interpretation of Article 21 and noted the 15-month 'guideline' is a '*maximum*' period for implementation, 'not an average, or usual, period'.[46] In establishing a 6-month implementation period, the arbitrator evaluated the shortest period required under the Canadian legal process to effectuate compliance and placed great weight on the fact that Canada could comply through administrative and regulatory procedures.

Recent jurisprudence clearly favours defining the 'reasonable period' as the 'shortest period possible', adjusted to the 'particular circumstances' of the case. The 15-month 'guideline' no longer assumes a 15-month norm and the amount of time needed to pass legislation is often considered a 'particular circumstance' which receives great deference.[47] The recent arbitral cases have also affected the reasonable periods set by agreement. This trend is shown in the agreements reached by the parties. For instance, early reasonable-period agreements reached in *US–Reformulated Gasoline*,[48] *Canada–Periodicals*,[49] and *India–Patent Protection for Pharmaceutical and*

---

42 *See Ibid.*, 26.
43 WTO Arbitrator's Report, Korea – Taxes on Alcoholic Beverages, WT/DS75/16, WT/DS84/14, p. 41 (June 1999).
44 *Ibid.*, 46.
45 *Ibid.*, 49 (citing the awards of the Arbitrator in *EC–Hormones* and *Australia–Salmon*).
46 *See* WTO Arbitrator's Report, Canada – Patent Protection of Pharmaceutical Products, WT/DS114/13 (18 August 2000), p. 12.
47 Recent arbitral cases have awarded implementation periods ranging from 10 to 15 months. *See* US – Hot Rolled Steel from Japan, WT/DS184 (19 February 2002) 15 months; Argentina – Bovine Hides, WT/DS/155 (31 August 2001) 12 months, 12 days; US – Anti-Dumping Act of 1916, WT/DS162/1 (28 February 2001), Canada – Patent Protection Term, WT/DS170/1 (28 February 2001).
48 *See* US – Standards for Reformulated and Conventional Gasoline, Status Report by the USA, WT/DS2/10 (10 January 1997).
49 *See* Canada – Certain Measures Concerning Periodicals, Status Report by Canada, WT/DS31/9 (13 March 1998).

Agricultural Chemical Products[50] consistently adopted 15 months for compliance. The agreements after *EC–Beef Hormones* announced its 'shortest period possible' standard resulted in much shorter implementation periods, including the *Argentina–Footwear* agreement for 242 days (8 months),[51] the *Japan–Agricultural Products* agreement for 9 months and 12 days,[52] and the *US–Shrimp-Turtle* agreement for 13 months.[53] More recently, most agreements have been even shorter, such as *Argentina–Definitive Anti-Dumping Measures on Imports of Ceramic Floor Tiles from Italy* for 5 months,[54] *India–Measures Affecting the Automotive Sector* for 5 months[55] and *US–Anti-Dumping and Countervailing Measures on Steel Plate from India* for 5 months.[56]

The widespread concern that the 'reasonable period' rules conferred an unintended, automatic 15-month compliance period to the losing party has been quieted with the recent arbitral rulings and agreements adopting the 'shortest period possible' standard. The trend towards shorter periods, however, does not altogether end the concern. Until the reference in the DSU text to a 15-month 'guideline' is replaced, losing parties will continue to claim to be entitled to the extended grace period following adoption of a WTO decision.

6.3.2.1.3 "Surveillance" during the Reasonable Period

Article 21(3) requires the losing Member 'inform the DSB of its intentions in respect of implementation of the recommendations and rulings of the DSB' at a DSB meeting held within 30 days after the date of adoption of the panel or Appellate Body report. Surprisingly, not much more is required of that Member until the expiration of the reasonable period.

The Member is not required to identify the changes, such as the offending measures it will remove or implementing legislation that will bring it into compliance with the ruling. Members are not even required to specify any sort of implementation schedule or consult with the winning party over implementation. Put simply, no good faith need be shown during the entire implementation period. The only obligation a losing Member must comply with during the implementation period is providing a 'status report' 6 months

---

50 *See* India – Patent Protection for Pharmaceutical and Agricultural Chemical Products, Status Report by India, WT/DS50/10 (12 November 1998).

51 *See* Argentina – Measures Affecting Imports of Footwear, Textiles, Apparel and Other Items, Communication from Argentina, WT/DS56/14 (7 July 1998) (reporting Argentina's agreement to conform its duties on textiles and apparel within 180 days and its statistical tax within 242 days).

52 *See* Japan – Measures Affecting Agricultural Products, Agreement Under 21.3(b) of the DSU, WT/DS76/9 (18 June 1999).

53 *See* US – Import Prohibition of Certain Shrimp and Shrimp Products, Status Report by the USA, Agreement Under 21.3(b) of the DSU, WT/DS58/15, P1 (15 July 1999).

54 Argentina – Ceramic Floor Times, Agreement Under 21.3(b) of the DSU, WT/DS189/7 (4 January 2002).

55 India – Automotive Sector, WT/DS146/13, Agreement Under 21.3(b) of the DSU, WT/DS175/13 (24 July 2002).

56 US – Anti-Dumping and Countervailing Measures on Steel Plate, Agreement Under 21.3(b) of the DSU, WT/DS206/7 (3 October 2002).

into the reasonable period and continuing at regular intervals. The report, however, is of little use as there is no requirement as to how specific or vague the losing Member must be in reporting. All the DSB can insist upon for purposes of fulfilling its obligation under Article 21(6) to 'keep under surveillance the implementation of adopted recommendations or rulings' is the report itself. The only other requirement on the losing party is ultimately coming into compliance at the expiration of its reasonable period.

Despite the lax requirements imposed on the losing party, the losing party often actively consults with the winning party during the implementation period to ensure compliance is reached.[57] On the other hand, a less compliant Member can elect to use its reasonable period to delay the process and evade its obligations. Two notorious cases against the EC best illustrate the permissiveness of the current DSU rules in this area. In *EC–Bananas*, the EC repeatedly refused to specifically address its implementation intentions and continuously exhibited a reluctance to correct the violations identified in the ruling. Four months into the reasonable period, after refusing to consult with the complaining parties, the EC issued a new banana proposal. The complaining parties repeatedly claimed the new proposal would not constitute compliance,[58] but the EC insisted that no substantive changes could be made to its proposal. Six months before its reasonable period expired and over strong objection from the original complaining parties (Ecuador, Guatemala, Honduras, Mexico, and the United States), the European Commission adopted the proposal. All the while, the EC's status reports to the DSB merely noted that 'significant progress' was being made towards implementation.[59]

In *EC–Beef Hormones*, the EC showed a similar unambiguous reluctance to lift its ban from the beginning of the reasonable period. Interestingly, the reasonable period arbitrator warned 'it would not be in keeping with the requirement of prompt compliance to include in the reasonable period of time, time to conduct studies, or to consult experts to demonstrate the consistency of a measure already judged to be inconsistent'.[60] The EC did not heed the warning, as its first status report noted only that the EC decided to

---

57 *See*, for example, US – Standards for Reformulated and Conventional Gasoline, Status Report by the USA, WT/DS2/10/Add.1 (14 February 1997); US – Standards for Reformulated and Conventional Gasoline, Status Report by the USA, WT/DS2/10/Add.2 (10 March 1997); US – Standards for Reformulated and Conventional Gasoline, Status Report by the USA, WT/DS2/10/Add.3 (18 April 1997); US – Standards for Reformulated and Conventional Gasoline, Status Report by the USA, WT/DS2/10/Add.4 (13 May 1997); US – Standards for Reformulated and Conventional Gasoline, Status Report by the USA, WT/DS2/10/Add.5 (12 June 1997); US – Standards for Reformulated and Conventional Gasoline, Status Report by the USA, WT/DS2/10/Add.6 (18 July 1997); US – Standards for Reformulated and Conventional Gasoline, Status Report by the USA, WT/DS2/10/Add.7 (26 August 1997).

58 Those representations were made at the DSB meetings on 22 January 1998, 12 February 1998, 25 March 1998, 22 April 1998, 22 June 1998, 23 July 1998, 22 September 1998, 21 October 1998, and 25 November 1998.

59 *See*, for example, European Communities – Regime for the Importation, Sale and Distribution of Bananas, Status Report by the European Communities, WT/DS27/17, P1 (13 July 1998).

60 *EC–Hormones, supra* n. 30, p. 39.

launch numerous scientific studies 'with a view to assessing the implications thereof for the Community's import prohibition'.[61] At no time did the report mention anything about lifting the ban. In fact, EC officials informally stated that its ban was certain to be maintained[62] and future official status reports continued to state only that the scientific studies were underway and progressing.[63] Therefore, the complainants were not surprised when the reasonable period ended and the EC admitted that the it would not lift its ban and would continue to study its scientific results in more depth 'to consider what steps may be necessary'.[64]

Developed counties are not the only members to abuse the system. In *Brazil–Export Financing Programme for Aircraft*,[65] Brazil announced to the complaining party, Canada, as well as to the DSB meeting of 19 November 1999, that it had removed offending measures and complied with the recommendations and rulings of the DSB. Canada disagreed and requested an Article 21.5 panel to review the measures for compliance purposes. The Panel Report declared Brazil had not complied with the rulings. Canada subsequently received authorization to suspend concessions in the amount of $CND344.2 million. At that same meeting, Brazil again unilaterally announced changes to its scheme that would bring the scheme into compliance with the rulings. Canada insisted the scheme still was non-compliant and, on 22 January 2001, again requested an Article 21.5 panel to review the measure. Six months later, the panel ruled for the fifth time that Brazil's measures were inconsistent with its obligations. In June 2002, the parties began negotiating a settlement with regards to reaching a 'voluntary settlement' regarding the inconsistencies of Articles 21.5 and 22.6. Therefore, some 6 years after initially requesting the establishment of a panel and nearly 3 years after securing its first ruling against Brazil, Canada has still not implemented any retaliatory measures against Brazil. The case demonstrates the ability of a losing nation to frustrate implementation of a negative ruling with minor changes and stall tactics.

At present, parties can, irrespective of good or bad faith, use the implementation period in any way they choose with little oversight from the

---

61 European Communities – Measures Concerning Meat and Meat Products, Status Report by the European Communities, WT/DS26/17, WT/DS48/15, p. 4 (14 January 1999).

62 C. Gleason and P. Walther, 'Operation of the Implementation Process: The WTO Dispute Settlement Implementation Procedures: A System in Need of Reform' (2001) 31 *Law and Policy in International Business* 709, p. 721.

63 European Communities – Measures Concerning Meat and Meat Products, Status Report by the European Communities, WT/DS26/17/Add.1, WT/DS48/15/Add.1 (5 February 1999); European Communities – Measures Concerning Meat and Meat Products, Status Report by the European Communities, WT/DS26/17/Add.2, WT/DS48/15/Add.2 (9 March. 1999); European Communities – Measures Concerning Meat and Meat Products, Status Report by the European Communities, WT/DS26/17/Add.1, WT/DS48/15/Add.1 (5 February 1999); European Communities – Measures Concerning Meat and Meat Products, Status Report by the European Communities, WT/DS26/17/Add.3, WT/DS48/15/Add.3 (16 April 1999).

64 European Communities – Measures Concerning Meat and Meat Products, Status Report by the European Communities, WT/DS26/17/Add.4, WT/DS48/15/Add.4 (11 May 1999).

65 Brazil – Export Financing Programme for Aircraft, WT/DS46 (19 November 1999) *et al.* *See* also, Canada – Measures Affecting the Export of Civilian Aircraft, WT/DS70/R (14 April 1999) *et al.*

DSB. There is no recourse to the complaining parties during the reasonable period, even if all the evidence suggests non-compliance from the losing party.

6.3.2.2 *The conflict between DSU Articles 21.5 and 22*

In the past few years, the 'reasonable period' and related 'surveillance' conflicts and concerns have been dwarfed by the multilateral debate over DSU Articles 21.5 and 22. Beginning as a textual dispute over the interpretation of, and relationship between, compliance review and the suspension of concessions, the so-called 'sequencing' conflict 'evolved into a near-constitutional crisis over the systemic implications of the issues involved'.[66] The *EC–Bananas* case brought the conflict to the fore and the issue immediately became the priority in the DSU Review. Until the DSU Review is completed and can add legal certainty and predictability to the procedures, non-compliance cases arising after *EC–Bananas* are forced to proceed through 'voluntary understandings' to negotiate around the textual shortcomings.

6.3.2.2.1 Articles 21.5 and 22: The Text

The DSU supplies two possible procedural options if the losing party fails to fully comply with the DSB, but fails to clarify the relationship between the two procedures. The first non-compliance procedure, articulated in Article 21.5, provides 'where there is disagreement as to the existence or consistency with a covered agreement of measures taken to comply with the recommendations and rulings such dispute *shall be decided through recourse to these dispute settlement procedures*, including wherever possible resort to the original panel (emphasis added)'. Other than to call upon the panel to circulate its report within 90 days, the DSU provides no other explanation of exactly what 'these dispute settlement procedures' entails or when those procedures may or must be invoked and who may invoke them.

The second procedure, articulated in Article 22, specifies the consequences if the losing party fails to implement the WTO ruling within the compliance period or negotiate mutually acceptable compensation within 20 days after the 'reasonable period' expires. Under those circumstances of non-compliance, Article 22.6 states 'the DSB, upon request, *shall grant authorization to suspend concessions or other obligations within 30 days of the expiry of the reasonable period* (emphasis added)', unless there is a consensus otherwise or the losing party refers the requested suspension amount to arbitration. If the amount is referred to arbitration, Article 22 instructs the original panel, if available, to determine whether the request is 'equivalent to the level of nullification or impairment' and issue its determination within 60 days after the expiration of the reasonable period. The DSB, upon request, must then authorize a suspension of concessions consistent with that decision. What is not clear is how the drafters intended the Article 22 timetable to be reconciled with the potentially protracted compliance review pursuant to Article 21.5.

---

66 Gleason, *supra* n. 62, at 721.

6.3.2.2.2 EC–BANANAS

The conflict between Articles 21.5 and 22 that occurred in *EC–Bananas* arose during an already tense period partly due to years of EC non-compliance in GATT dispute settlement and partly due to the EU's general unbending stance in agricultural cases.[67] The WTO ruling in *EC–Bananas* was the first WTO case testing whether the EC would begin honouring agricultural dispute settlement rulings. Therefore, when the EC, 6 months before the expiration of the reasonable period, approved seemingly inconsistent reforms, the United States swiftly moved to prevent the new measures from taking effect.

Attempting to work within Article 21.5, the United States proposed that the parties return to the original panel under Article 21.5 procedures for a ruling on the compatibility of the new measures. The EC rejected that and numerous similar requests, insisting an Article 21.5 compliance review could not be undertaken until the EC's reasonable period had expired.[68] The EC went so far as to ridiculously suggested that, even upon expiration of the reasonable period, Article 21.5 requires the United States to recommence *normal* WTO dispute settlement procedures in order to challenge the new measures (i.e. consultations, request for a panel, a 90-day panel review consistent with the one specific requirement of Article 21.5, an Appellate Body review and another reasonable period).

In response to that suggestion, the United States stated that it would request the suspension of concessions immediately upon the ending of the reasonable period (irrespective of whether an Article 21.5 review was undertaken). Only with that threat did the EC negotiate over compliance review. No agreement was reached, however, as the EC was unwilling to commit to a firm closing date to the panel review or change its view that the suspension timetable mandated under Article 22 must be waived.

Attempting to undermine the anticipated Article 22 request, the EC made several procedural efforts to compel its interpretation of Article 21.5. These efforts included filing a motion with the panel asking that it require the complaining parties to join in an action that Ecuador (one of the original complaining parties in *EC–Bananas*) unilaterally filed requesting compliance review of the new EC banana policy under Article 21.5.[69] When

---

[67] For instance, of the 13 agriculture cases filed in 1980, 10 were against the EC. *See* Stewart, *supra* n. 7, at 2706. In addition, the EC twice blocked adverse GATT rulings regarding its banana regime. *See* GATT Panel Report, *EEC – Member States' Import Regimes for Bananas*, DS32/R (3 June 1993) (unadopted); GATT Panel Report, *EEC – Import Regime for Bananas*, DS38/R (11 February 1994) (unadopted). The EC has also refused to comply with other adverse GATT panel rulings regarding its agricultural policies. *See* GATT Panel Report, European Community – Tariff Treatment on Imports of Citrus Products from Certain Countries in the Mediterranean Region, L/5776 (7 February 1985) (unadopted); GATT Panel Report, Brazil – Refunds on Exports of Sugar, L/5011 (7 October 1980); European Economic Community – Payments and Subsidies Paid to Processors and Producers of Oilseeds and Related Animal-Feed Proteins, L/6627 (14 December 1989).

[68] *See* EC Record of Delay, July–November 1998. Attachment to Rebuttal Submission of the USA, European Communities – Regime for the Importation, Sale and Distribution of Bananas (DS27) Arbitration under Article 22.6 of the DSU (18 February 1999).

[69] *See* European Communities – Regime for the Importation, Sale and Distribution of Bananas, Recourse to Article 21.5 of the DSU, WT/DS27/41 (18 December 1998) (communication from Ecuador).

the panel balked at that request, the EC unexpectedly requested Article 21.5 non-compliance review of its own measures and petitioned to require the complaining parties to participate in that proceeding.[70] That request was denied, as the panel realized that would entrap the complaining parties in a review that would prevent the exercise of Article 22 rights.

As expected, when the EC's reasonable period expired, the United States requested DSB authorization to suspend concessions. Both parties then accused the other of attempting to destroy the multilateral system. The EC insisted that the United States was ignoring the explicit mandate of Article 21.5, which states any disagreement over compliance '*shall* be decided through recourse to these dispute settlement procedures' and insisted the invocation of Article 22 rights is conditioned upon this requirement.[71] Moreover, the EC claimed that if the United States request were approved, 'the consequences for the multilateral dispute settlement would be grave, since the entire system is built on the premise that Members will refrain from such unilateral determinations [of non-compliance]'.[72]

Conversely, the United States contended that Article 22 implied the only legally guaranteed way to receive authorization to suspend concessions under the negative-consensus rule was if it made that suspension request within 20 days following the end of the compliance period. The United States further stated that the EC's interpretation would lead to another compliance period after the first review was concluded, followed by additional minor changes and another review, another compliance period, and so on, *ad infinitum*. The United States argued that the WTO did not intend for such an interpretation and insisted that, having already engaged in nearly 3 years of legal procedures, it should not have to wait any longer to exercise its right to suspend concessions.

When the United States authorization request came before the DSB, the EC requested Article 22 arbitration of the requested suspension amount and, together with the United States, agreed with the DSB Chairman's statement that Ecuador's Article 21.5 panel and the Article 22 arbitrators, being the same individuals, would 'find a logical way forward'.[73]

On 6 April 1999, the Article 22 arbitrators (and Article 21.5 panelists) resolved the textual failings by compressing a review of the EC's new measures into their analysis of whether the United States request amount was equivalent to the level of nullification or impairment. The arbitrators reasoned that they could not complete their Article 22 task of assessing the

---

[70] *See* European Communities – Regime for the Importation, Sale and Distribution of Bananas, Request for the Establishment of a Panel by the European Communities, WT/DS27/40 (15 December 1998).

[71] *Ibid.* Citing, European Community, *US Threat of Unilateral Action on Bananas puts Multilateral Dispute Settlement System at Risk* (29 October 1998), P6 (EC memorandum circulated to the DSB).

[72] *Ibid.* (citing p. 2).

[73] WTO Arbitrator's Report, European Communities – Regime for the Importation, Sale and Distribution of Bananas, Recourse to Arbitration by the European Communities under Article 22.6 of the DSU, WT/DS27/ARB, P4.9 (9 April 1999) (citing to DSB Chairman's statement of 29 January 1999).

equivalence between the proposed suspension and the nullification or impairment at issue without deciding whether the revised EC regime was WTO-consistent. Thus, three and a half months after the expiration of the EC's reasonable period of time (almost 2 months beyond the DSU's deadline for the arbitral ruling), the arbitrators issued tandem decisions in the Articles 21.5 and 22 proceedings. Both rulings established that the new EC regime was inconsistent with WTO obligations.[74] The panel, in its Article 22 analysis, further authorized the suspension of concessions in the amount of $US191.4 million.[75]

Thus, a fragile and improvised solution was found to end a conflict that threatened to disrupt the entire multilateral trading system. WTO Members, not wanting a repeat of these proceedings, immediately referred the interpretive dispute to the DSU Review.

6.3.2.2.3 Subsequent Creative Non-Compliance Cases

Since DSU Review has not been completed, several subsequent cases used equally creative and improvised solutions to solve the textual deficiency of the DSB. Examination of the 'voluntary agreements' reveals two approaches have developed which Members use to resolve the sequencing issue. *Australia–Salmon* developed a method whereby the parties agreed to initiate concurrent procedures under Articles 21.5 and 22.6. In this approach, Article 22 proceedings are suspended until the Article 21.5 procedure is complete.[76] If after the Article 21.5 hearing the respondent fails to comply with the ruling, then the complainant can re-commence Article 22 proceedings. Other cases to follow this approach include *US–Foreign Sales Corporations*[77] and *Canada–Dairy Products*.[78]

The second method of producing 'voluntary agreements' involves the parties undertaking an Article 21.5 review *prior* to initiating procedures to suspend concessions, thereby waiving the Article 22 timetable. A condition of those understandings, however, was that if non-compliance were found,

---

74 *See Ibid.*; WTO Panel Report, European Communities – Regime for the Importation, Sale and Distribution of Bananas, Recourse to Article 21.5 by Ecuador, WT/DS27/RW/ECU (12 April 1999). These decisions brought the number of adverse rulings against the EC's banana policy to seven.

75 *See* EC – Bananas Arbitrator's Report, *supra* n. 73, para. 8.1. The US requested $US520 million in concessions. On 18 May 2000, Ecuador suspended concessions in the amount of $US201.6 million.

76 Arbitrators subsequently indicated that their review would not produce a ruling until 7 months after the expiration of the reasonable period of time. Thus, Canada (the complaining party) accepted a delay in its right to suspend concessions well beyond the timetable currently laid down in Article 22. *See* Australia – Measures Affecting the Importation of Salmon, Recourse to Article 21.5 of the DSU by Canada, Communication from the Chairman of the Panel, WT/DS18/17 (13 December 1999).

77 US – Tax Treatment for 'Foreign Sales Corporations', Recourse to Arbitration by the European Communities under Article 21.5 of the DSU, WT/DS/108/R (20 August 2001).

78 *See* Canada – Measures Affecting the Importation of Milk and the Exportation of Dairy Products – Recourse to Article 21.5 of the DSU, WT/DS/103, WT/DS/113 (3 December 2001).

the losing party would not object to a suspension request (even though it was made outside the time-period), but could contest the level of suspension. Interestingly, the first of these voluntary agreements, arising in *Australia–Leather*, involved the United States, which, only months before, had fought the *EC–Bananas* non-compliance conflict.[79] The EC derided the United States decision to proceed to Article 21.5 before going to Article 22, but the United States defended its position by stating that in this case, unlike in *EC–Bananas*, an acceptable voluntary agreement was possible and insisted that it was not departing from its position that the DSU allows a party to request authority to retaliate before seeking an Article 21.5 review.[80] Other examples of this approach include the parallel cases of *Brazil–Aircraft*[81] and *Canada–Aircraft*[82] and *EU–Bed Linen from India*.[83]

Thus far, only one case, *EC–Beef Hormones*, involved an admission of the losing party that it had failed to come into compliance. That admission enabled the United States to proceed directly to Article 22 following the expiration of the reasonable period of time.[84]

The current non-compliance procedures lead to unpredictability and improvization to the system and, as the situation exists, non-compliance procedures can only be applied without conflict or mutually agreed arrangements in the rare situation where the losing party admits the DSB rulings and recommendations have not been implemented.

6.4 Suggested Reforms

Given the complexity of current WTO cases, plus the clear textual shortcomings of the DSU, disagreement and strife concerning implementation will only increase. In addition, the EC's refusal to implement adverse rulings in a timely manner appears unlikely to cease. The EC's resolve is even more evident when one considers their unbending stance in the face of substantial United States retaliation in *EC–Beef Hormones* and *EC–Bananas*. Further, more challenging trade disputes, such as health and safety issues over genetically modified foods, will most likely soon enter the WTO dispute settlement process.

---

79 *See* Australia – Subsidies Provided to Producers and Exporters of Automotive Leather, Recourse by the USA to Article 21.5 of the DSU, WT/DS126/8 (4 October 1999).

80 Gleason, *supra* n. 62, at 727, citing *WTO Backs United States Bid for Panel to Check Australian Compliance with Leather Ruling*, DAILY REP. FOR EXEC, 15 October 1999, p. A-1. In fact, the United States position proved correct, as the parties reached a mutual solution 5 months after the final report.

81 *See* Brazil – Export Financing Programme for Aircraft, Recourse by Canada to Article 21.5 of the DSU, WT/DS46/13 (26 November 1999).

82 *See* Canada – Measures Affecting the Export of Civilian Aircraft, Recourse by Brazil to Article 21.5 of the DSU, WT/DS70/9, Annex (23 November 1999).

83 European Communities: Anti-dumping measures on imports of cotton-type bed-linen from India, Recourse to Article 21.5 of the DSU, WT/DS/141 (29 November 2002).

84 On 3 June 1999, the USA suspended concessions in the amount of $US116.8 million (after requesting $US202 million) and Canada suspended concessions in the amount of $CND11.3 million (after requesting $CND75 million).

In contrast to the European Union, the United States has, by and large, consistently has come into compliance with adverse WTO rulings.[85] *US–Foreign Sales Corporation* marked the first blemish on the American performance record.[86] More worrying, however, is the fact that more challenging implementation obligations lie ahead and have the potential of further marring the American record of compliance.[87]

As disputes get progressively more intertwined with local policies and politics, and as new Members enter the WTO, Members will even more frequently challenge the WTO's implementation procedures. China's accession to the WTO, in particular, with its massive developing economy and a tradition of non-transparent regulations, is a substantial challenge for the implementation procedures.[88]

The current articles governing the reasonable period, compliance review and suspension of concession procedures are clearly not sufficient to deal with the future challenges on the horizon. The implementation procedures can be improved with small, yet effective, reforms meant to fortify existing operations and goals of the system. First, the ambiguities between Articles 21.5 and 22 need to be clarified. Second, the procedural tools for scrutinizing and inducing prompt compliance need to be strengthened.

6.4.1 Clarifying the conflict between Articles 21.5 and 22

The DSU continues to examine the textual conflict between Articles 21.5 and 22 and the conflict should be resolved, even though the DSU Review has not completed its task by its May 2003 deadline. The issue has received

---

85 *See* WTO Appellate Body Report, USA – Standards for Reformulated and Conventional Gasoline, WT/DS2/AB/R (29 April 1996); WTO Appellate Body Report, US – Restrictions on Imports of Cotton and Man-Made Fibre Underwear, WT/DS24/AB/R (10 February 1997); WTO Appellate Body Report, US – Measure Affecting Imports of Woven Wool Shirts and Blouses from India, WT/DS33/AB/R (25 April 1997); WTO Panel Report, US – Anti-Dumping Duty on Dynamic Random Access Memory Semiconductors (DRAMS) of One Megabit or Above From Korea, WT/DS99/R (29 January 1999); WTO Appellate Body Report, US – Import Prohibition of Certain Shrimp and Shrimp Products, WT/DS58/AB/R (12 October 1998).

86 WTO Appellate Body Report, US – Tax Treatment for 'Foreign Sales Corporations', WT/DS108/1 (17 November 2000). After a WTO Panel deemed a USA measure inconsistent in March 2000, the USA amended its laws to comply with the ruling. In January 2002, the new measure was again deemed inconsistent with WTO obligations. In August, an arbitrator established under Article 22.6 ruled that the European Union is entitled to impose $US4.043 billion in retaliatory measures. The United States is in the process of amending the legislation and the European Union has not yet imposed sanctions. *See* WT/DS108, *supra* n. 36.

87 *See*, for example, US – Anti-dumping measures on stainless steel plate in coils and stainless steel sheet and strip from Korea, WT/DS179; US – Anti-Dumping Measures on Certain Hot-Rolled Steel Products from Japan, WT/DS184/13; US – Section 110(5) of the US Copyright Act, WT/DS160/1; US – §211 Omnibus Appropriations Act of 1998, WT/DS/176; US – Anti-dumping Act of 1916, WT/DS/136, WT/DS/162; US – Anti-Dumping Measures on Certain Hot-Rolled Steel Products from India, WT/DS/206; and US – Offset Act (Byrd Amendment), WT/DS/217, WT/DS/234.

88 A Chinese trade diplomat was quoted as saying if WTO pressure did not force Europe to change its treatment of banana imports, there would be little hope that Chinese domestic interests would have the resolve to comply with WTO decisions. *See* Gleason, *supra* n. 62, p. 729.

sufficient attention and the Review has received several draft amendments regarding the conflict, which, while not approved and remaining somewhat contentious, provide a useful insight on likely change.[89]

The leading draft amendments mandate Article 21.5 procedures conclude prior to requesting an Article 22 authorization to suspend concessions, but restrict the Article 21.5 review to involve substantially less than 'regular' dispute settlement procedures. In a disagreement over compliance, the amendments require the complaining party request a review within 10 to 20 days *prior* to the expiry of the reasonable period of time; 10 days later a panel would be established; 90 days beyond that, the panel would circulate its report which would be adopted 10 days later. In addition, if the complaining party prevails, it can request an Article 22 request to authorize the suspension of concessions on the day the panel report is adopted. If arbitration were requested as to the amount, the arbitral decision on damages would be rendered within 45 days of referral.

The draft amendment, therefore, stretches the present Article 22 timetable that currently requires an arbitral decision on damages within 2 months after the date of expiry of the reasonable period to a decision within approximately 5 months following the conclusion of the reasonable period. The United States agreed to the delay in exchange for a guarantee that the Article 21.5 review would not lead to never-ending litigation on minor revisions. The amendments also assure the EC that the winning party, prior to seeking Article 22 recourse, would not make a 'unilateral' determination of non-compliance.

6.4.2 Improving the tools to scrutinizing and inducing prompt compliance

The second large implementation problem (inadequate checks and recourse during the reasonable period, the lack of incentives or sanctions to encourage the prompt compliance and no good-faith implementation standard) desperately needs reform. The issue is crucial to the proper functioning of an effective multilateral trading system. Unfortunately, the issue has received little attention in the DSU Review.

Problems associated with the tools for scrutinizing and inducing prompt compliance are evident at every stage of the implementation process. The *EC–Hormones* and *EC–Bananas* cases demonstrate the problems associated with the losing party receiving long implementation periods even if it is certain from the start that they do not intend to comply with the ruling.

---

[89] *See*, for example Decision Regarding the Understanding on Rules and Procedures Governing the Settlement of Disputes, WT/MIN(99)/8/rev (draft) (2 Dec. 1999); Annex, Amendment to the Understanding on Rules and Procedures Governing the Settlement of Disputes, WT/MIN(99)/ 8/rev (2 December 1999) (draft); Negotiations on Improvement and Clarification of the Dispute Settlement Understanding, WT/MIN(01)/W/6 (14 October 2002), Joint Proposal of Japan, based on an earlier draft submitted by Japan, Bolivia, Canada, Chile, Columbia, Costa Rica, Ecuador, Korea, New Zealand, Norway, Peru, Switzerland, Uruguay, and Venezuela. In addition, proposals have also been submitted by the EC, USA, Ecuador, Korea, Thailand, Australia, and Costa Rica.

Additionally, because Article 22 suspension rights are only granted following the expiration of the reasonable period, the losing party has every incentive to seek the longest possible period possible. During the 'reasonable period', the winning party has no right to initiate a compliance review, even if it is obvious from the start that the losing party will not be in compliance by the expiration of the reasonable period (i.e. its progress reports do not report any implementation issues, only that it is conducting tests to challenge the ruling; or the party publicly states it does not intend to comply). Moreover, there is no penalty for bad-faith application of the reasonable period, even though that period is intended to be used exclusively to ensure full implementation. Thus, the system fundamentally conflicts with Article 21.1 requirement of 'prompt compliance' in that it facilitates prolonged periods of non-compliance.

Some argue that the treatment of a losing party is intended to allow the party to opt out of compliance, thus ensuring its sovereign right of choice. This view is without merit. It is known that nations willingly yield some sovereignty when agreeing to all the provisions of the WTO. In addition, DSU Article 22.1 specifically states the right to opt out of compliance should only be 'temporary' and that 'full implementation' is strongly favoured and encouraged. Any interpretation that allows for non-compliance on a regular basis, whether by a single prominent member or generally within the WTO procedures, would decrease credibility and confidence in the system. This could lead to problems similar to that which caused of the GATT's demise. Accordingly, the procedures must minimize the occasion and duration of non-compliance.

In this respect, the DSU Review draft amendments fail. In fact, they may become more generous than the current DSU language towards the losing party. For example, the draft amendments fail to address the stated reasonable period 'guideline' of 15 months. That, coupled with the fact that the amendments would require the winning party to wait up to an additional 5 months to withdraw concessions in cases of non-compliance (as opposed to the current Article 22 period), unnecessarily lengthens the process with no benefit to the winning party.[90] In addition, Article 22 recourse would continue to apply prospectively upon the conclusion of this period, therefore the losing party would have no incentive to comply quicker than required by the extended timeline. Further, while the amendments give the complaining party a right to seek consultations during the implementation period, they do not grant that party any right to compliance review prior to the expiration of the reasonable period. Moreover, while the losing party would now need to specifically state its intention to implement the DSB rulings to avoid immediate recourse to Article 22, it could easily renege on that intention at the end of its implementation period and not be subject to penalty.

---

90 *Ibid.*, 4–6. The proposed DSU amendments to the 'normal' panel procedures (i.e. a shortened consultation period, the establishment of a panel upon request, the consolidation of the panel's 'descriptive portion' with the interim report, and the elimination of the panel hearing on the interim report) are only anticipated to save on average about 30 days, and thus are not likely to offset the timeline extensions to the implementation procedures that are called for under these amendments. *Ibid.*

Further, in an attempt to discontinue sanctioned retaliation, the draft amendments leniently allow losing parties subject to WTO-sanctioned retaliation an accelerated Article 21.5 panel. While this may be appropriate in theory, in reality this allows the losing party, who have resisted compliance to the point of retaliation, to continue to circumvent its compliance obligations even longer. Moreover, the accelerated review creates the opportunity for losing parties to implement new, subtle non-compliant measures to further delay the imposition of sanctions and may prejudice the winning party, who may not have time to acquire the detailed evidence needed to demonstrate the measures continue to be inconsistent with WTO-obligations. This may allow the losing party to win the case, even though time would eventually prove them non-compliant. Therefore, the process would have to repeat itself before the imposition of sanctions could take effect.

In addition, the EC insists upon an amendment that precludes the winning party from substantively changing its retaliation measures, even if the measures prove ineffective at inducing compliance after an extended period of time.[91] Unsurprisingly, the United States opposes such an amendment. This difference of opinion is a major stumbling block and may keep the draft amendments from being approved and implemented.

One must remember, however, that DSU Review is unfinished and, even though it did not meet its Doha Declaration completion date of May 2003, is still on track to finish its task before the end of the year. While the current proposals will form the foundation of change, they need not represent the end of reform efforts. Members should continue efforts to strengthen the existing rules to help minimize the incidence and duration of non-compliance.

Several scholars have suggested the most favourable way of ensuring timely compliance would be to require compliance, compensation or the withdrawal of concessions on or around the date of the WTO ruling rather than allowing the losing party with a lengthy 'reasonable period' to come into compliance.[92] This approach appears successful in the North American Free Trade Agreement (NAFTA), where the winning party is entitled to rebalance interests if there is no satisfactory settlement reached within 30 days of a NAFTA dispute settlement ruling.[93] While the approach is contrary to the general GATT/WTO practice, it finds support in the GATT 1947 antidumping and countervailing duty context, where numerous panels have recommended retroactive relief.[94] This change, however, would have little hope of gaining support and passage among larger Members, who

---

91 *See Ibid.* (n. 11). The amendment is a response to a Congressional bill requiring the United States government to periodically change WTO-approved retaliation measures against a losing party if that party remained out of compliance (so called carousal approach). *See* Trade and Development Act of 1999 (Engrossed Senate Amendment), H.R. 434, 106th Cong. (1999) (this amended version of the House bill includes Senate amendment S.AMDT.2360, which is the legislation to which the EC responded).

92 *See, e.g.*, S. Frechette, *et al.*, 'Comments: Performance of the System III: Appellate Body' (1998) 32 *International Law 747, 750*; P. Lichtenbaum, 'Procedural Issues in WTO Dispute Resolution' (1998) 19 *Michigan Journal of International Law 1195, 1259*.

93 *See* North American Free Trade Agreement, [1993] H.R. Doc. No. 103–159, at 1274.

94 *See* GATT Panel Report, New Zealand – Imports of Electrical Transformers from Finland, GATT, 32 BISD 55 (1985); GATT Panel Report, Canada – Imposition of Countervailing Duties

have grown accustomed to long implementation periods, as well as developing countries, which, due to economic or political conditions, need long implementation periods as a transition towards compliance.

Another suggestion is to confer upon the DSB the power to fine a Member that has failed to comply with a judgment after the reasonable implementation period. This is the power conferred in the European Union. According to Article 228(2) (formerly 171), an aggrieved Member State may request and the court can grant a lump sum amount or penalty payment it considers appropriate under the circumstances to be paid by the Member State that fails to comply with an ICJ judgment within the Commission-stated timeframe. While the Court is not bound by the Commission's recommendations or guidelines, it is generally understood that the payment amount should reflect the aim of the sanction, securing effective compliance as quickly as possible and shall be based on the seriousness of the infringement, its duration and the deterrent effect of the penalty.

The only instance of the ICJ imposing a penalty occurred in *Commission of the European Communities* v. *Hellenic Republic*, where Greece failed to implement all necessary measures in accordance with an EC Directive, thus failing to fulfil its obligations under Article 171 (now Article 228) of the EC Treaty.[95] The Court ordered a penalty payment of €20,000 for each day of delay in implementing the measures necessary to comply with the judgment from the day of the decision until compliance. Similarly to the above suggestion, this measure would have little hope of gaining support among WTO Members, who would likely not agree to succeeding fine power to an organisation, especially when that Member fundamentally disagrees with the decision. This measure would have great impact and considerably shorten periods of non-compliance, but may be better suited to the EU's close-knit structure.

Modest revisions, however, that discourage implementation delay and bad-faith implementation are possible. For instance, the reasonable-period guideline should codify recent arbitral findings and require the 'shortest possible implementation period, adjusted to the particular circumstances of the case', instead of the current 15-month guideline. Additionally, if the a losing party adopts measures that ensure it will not be in compliance by the end of the reasonable period, the complaining party should be entitled to commence a compliance review before the expiration of the reasonable period. This change corrects the problems associated with *EC–Bananas*, where the EC approved new measures 6 months before the expiration of its period, but repeatedly blocked compliance review until the expiration of the reasonable period. Moreover, if the losing party fails to use the implementation period for purposes of full implementation or compensation,

---

Contd.
on Imports of Manufactured Beef from the EEC, SCM/85 (13 October 1987); GATT Panel Report, US – Imposition of Antidumping Duties on Seamless Stainless Steel Hollow Products from Sweden, ADP/47 (20 August 1990) (unadopted); GATT Panel Report, US – Countervailing Duties on Fresh, Chilled and Frozen Pork from Canada, 38 BISD 30 (1991); GATT Panel Report, US – Measures Affecting Imports of Softwood Lumber from Canada, 40 BISD 358 (1993).

95 Case C-387/97, Court of Justice of the EC, p. I-5047, 2000 ECJ CELEX LEXIS 2906 (4 July 2000) (Directives 75/442/EEC and 78/319/EEC).

that party should be subject to penalties or further retaliation, thereby discouraging the use of the reasonable period for purposes other than full implementation. In addition, the additional penalties would assist in redressing the injustice of an additional year or more of injury that the losing member inflicted upon the winning party. These changes represent an attempt to modestly improve the system without changing the entire structure of the system. If members are serious about improving the DSU to effectuate prompt and full compliance, these modifications, both feasible and practicable, will be discussed and implemented.

6.5 Conclusion

The successful functioning of the WTO, and effectively its survival, depends not only upon the membership and consent of nations, but also the level of engagement and cooperation that Member nations lend to the organization. Even basic reform or implementation proposals spark debate on the basic legitimacy of the institution. This rarely happens in domestic institutions, but is a central consideration whenever speaking of reforming an international institution. This fundamental difference with domestic institutions means that the WTO depends on domestic policy makers, who rarely have a full-grasp of how the system functions and almost always allow domestic pressure to influence policy, for support and legitimacy.

The value, effectiveness, and worthiness of the WTO is constantly being debated, not only by member governments, but also in the media and even in streets full of ill-informed rioting protesters. The costs and benefits of WTO Membership are now subject to increased scrutiny. Without changes to the implementation system, WTO advocates will be pressed to defend the benefits of a system perceived to be flawed or ineffective. Even though the system induces compliance in a vast majority of cases, cases of non-compliance gain significant public attention and can negatively effect the stability and success of the WTO. In addition, the incidence of non-compliance is on the rise and will likely increase even further. Moreover, some of the larger Members are passing domestic legislation to resolve compliance issues unilaterally; measures which show the system is facing a vote of confidence similar to that which the GATT faced in the 1980s.

Effective modifications can help quash the growing discontent. While comprehensive change may not be feasible, even simple changes to discourage undue delay and bad-faith use of the reasonable period will likely reduce the occurrence and duration of non-compliance. The changes proposed in this chapter will improve the efficiency and effectiveness of the DSU. The changes will not only aid in the implementation of decisions for frequent users (such as the United States and European Union), but would also assist developing nations in gaining compliance from larger members. Moreover, the changes would assist DSU Article 22.1, which provides that compensation and the suspension of concessions or other obligations are *temporary measures* and neither compensation nor the suspension of concessions or other obligations is preferred to *full implementation* of a recommendation to bring a measure into conformity with WTO agreements, in providing efficient full implementation of DSB rulings.

For the most part, the WTO has successfully established an effective, viable multilateral trading system. It has gained the respect of many nations and others queue to join the substantial benefits of Membership. However, if the WTO does not adhere to the Doha Declaration mandate and address the textual shortcomings of its implementation process, it could join the ill-fated GATT as a superior idea that subsequently failed due to its own shortcomings. Members need to put aside disputes and come together for the betterment of the system. The system is a vast improvement over the GATT and is successful at resolving most disputes, however, recent cases have exposed shortcomings in the text of the DSU that, left unresolved, will significantly harm the institution. The DSU clearly needs reform to remain successful. It is now up to Members to maintain the WTO's status as an effective and successful multilateral trading system.

7. 'It's Not Easy Being Green': Trade and Environment Linkages beyond Doha

Jan McDonald

7.1 Introduction

The Uruguay Round dramatically expanded the traditional portfolio of trade interests. The World Trade Organization (WTO) regime now extends to services, intellectual property, investment, national subsidies policies, and domestic regulation of product standards, food safety, and quarantine. The WTO Agreements take free trade beyond its original project of trade 'free from discrimination', towards 'trade free from any regulatory burden'.[1] This expanded agenda has blurred the boundaries between trade and other subjects of national and international policy, creating the potential for tensions between competing policy goals. The blurred edges or trade 'linkages' include environmental protection, competition policy, human rights, consumer rights, and labour standards.

The WTO Appellate Body (AB) has made impressive progress in reducing friction between trade and environmental policies in several high-profile trade disputes. Despite developments in legal interpretation, however, this chapter argues that the 'environmental evolution' of WTO texts is still not reflected in the institutional mindset of WTO Members. Developing country Members are disillusioned by slow progress on WTO implementation and by rich Members' failure to meet their Agenda 21 commitments to fund sustainable development. Growing economic inequities mean that economic, not environmental, imperatives dominate the modern concept of sustainable development, even in fora whose purported objectives are environmental protection. This chapter argues that the environmental evolution in WTO interpretation should continue to enhance the relationship between environment and trade policy, but that legal refinement of WTO texts alone cannot address the urgent need for mutually reinforcing trade and environment

---

[1] D. Driesen, 'What is Free Trade?: The Real Issue Lurking Behind the Trade and Environment Debate' (2001) 41 *Va. J. Int'l L.* 279; S. Gaines, 'Processes and Production Methods: How to Produce Sound Policy for Environmental PPM-Based Trade Measures?' in Symposium: Trade, Sustainability and Global Governance (2002) *Columbia Journal of Environmental Law* 383, at 391.

policies. Whether it meets as the WTO or the United Nations, the international community must renew its commitment to protecting and conserving the global environment. This can only occur when it takes seriously its commitment to sharing the benefits of economic globalization. As a matter of political necessity, the WTO will have to earn the confidence of developing country Members by delivering real economic benefits before environmental protection can resume a central role international diplomacy.

This chapter organizes its argument into six sections. For followers of the trade linkage issue, Sections 7.2 and 7.3 traverse familiar terrain. Section 7.2 traces the emergence of the trade–environment linkage and outlines the main sources of contention. Section 7.3 explains the ways in which the AB has 'greened' WTO Agreements, particularly the GATT, summarizing the status of the trade and environment linkage at the time of the Doha Ministerial. Section 7.4 assesses the institutional response to the AB's approach and handling of the environment linkage, including the 'environment' provisions of the Doha Ministerial Declaration. It is argued that the conservatism of the Doha environmental mandate and the WTO Committee on Trade and Environment (CTE) negotiations evidences the Membership's continued resistance to linking trade and environment. Section 7.5 suggests that this resistance is also clear from developments in non-trade fora, in particular the outcomes of the UN World Summit on Sustainable Development (WSSD). Deference to the imperatives of world trade and economic development in these political fora show that real progress on promoting mutually supportive trade and environment policies remains elusive. The WTO's failure to deliver on the promises of liberalization for developing countries lie at the centre of this stalemate. Section 7.6 presents the conclusions of this chapter.

7.2 The Trade–Environment Linkage

The trade–environment linkage is both strategic and substantive.[2] Strategic linkages include the suspension of trade concessions for poor environmental performers, or the promise of trade returns to encourage sound policy. They generally enjoy little support: sanctions are regarded as a blunt and unacceptably punitive means of securing environmental commitments.[3] Instead, most analyses and diplomatic efforts have focussed on the substantive relationship between economic liberalization and efforts to promote environmentally sustainable development. A reminder of the historical rise of sustainable development in international discourse will help illuminate the close relationship between the two bodies of principle and policy.

---

[2] D. Leebron, 'Linkages, Symposium: The Boundaries of the WTO' (2002) *American Journal of International Law* 6–14.

[3] S. Charnovitz, 'GATT and the Environment: Examining the Issues' (1992) 4 *International Environmental Affairs* 203; L. Jenkins, 'Trade Sanctions: Effective Enforcement Tools,' in J. Cameron, J. Werksman, and P. Roderick (eds), *Improving Compliance with International Environmental Law* (Earthscan, London, 1996), p. 221.

The ideas underlying the concept of sustainable development were first articulated in the 1972 *Stockholm Declaration on the Human Environment*[4] and developed in the 1982 *World Charter for Nature*.[5] The principles of 'sustainable development' gained international currency with the release in 1987 of the *Report of the World Commission on Environment and Development* (the Bruntland Report).[6] The Bruntland Report defined sustainable development as 'development that meets the needs of present generations in a manner that does not compromise the ability of future generations to meet their needs'.[7] It contemplated a re-fashioning of economic policy development, so that environmental costs and social justice considerations inform and underpin all major economic decisions.

The Bruntland Report laid the foundation for the *Rio Declaration on Environment and Development*[8] and *Agenda 21*,[9] agreed to at the 1992 United Nations Conference on Environment and Development (UNCED). The UNCED documents are by far the best-known international statements elucidating the concept of sustainable development. They articulate the key principles of sustainable development, including inter- and intra-generational equity,[10] the precautionary principle,[11] the polluter pays principle,[12] and the full-cost pricing of environmental resources.[13]

A key aspect of the UNCED compact was the recognition that rich and poor countries owe common-but-differentiated responsibilities (CDR) in respect of environmental protection.[14] It was estimated that implementation of the Agenda 21 framework would cost about US$600 billion and developing countries agreed to the Rio undertakings on the expectation that developed countries would improve their terms of trade, under the auspices of the new WTO, as well as increasing development assistance and addressing debt relief.[15] In addition to financial assistance for developing countries, the

---

4 *Declaration of the United Nations Conference on the Human Environment*, United Nations Conference on the Human Environment, 5–16 June 1972, UN Doc. A/Conf. 48/14 and Corr. 1 (1973), reprinted in (1972) 11 *International Legal Materials* 1416 (*Stockholm Declaration*).

5 *World Charter for Nature*, Adopted by the UN General Assembly, 28 October 1982, G.A.Res 37/7 (Annex), UN GAOR 37th Sess. Supp. No. 51, at 17, UN Doc. A/37/51, reprinted in (1983) 22 *International Legal Materials* 455 (*World Charter for Nature*). 111 States supported the resolution, the United States alone voted against it, and 18 states abstained.

6 World Commission on Environment and Development (WCED), *Our Common Future* (1987) Oxford, Oxford University Press (approved by General Resolution of the United Nations General Assembly in 1987: GA Res 187, 42 UN GAOR (96th plen mtg), UN Doc. A/42/821Add.5 (1987).

7 *Ibid.*, at 8, 46.

8 *Rio Declaration on Environment and Development*, adopted 14 June 1992, *Report of the United Nations Conference on Environment and Development* 3, Rio de Janeiro, 3–14 June 1992, UN Doc. A/Conf. 151/51 Rev.1, Vol I, United Nations Publication Sales No.E.93.I.8, New York (1993), reprinted in (1992) 31 *International Legal Materials* 874, at 878, (the *Rio Declaration*).

9 *Agenda 21*, *Report of the United Nations Conference on Environment and Development* 9, Rio de Jainero, 3–14 June 1992, UN Doc. A/Conf.151/26/Rev.1 (*Agenda 21*).

10 *Rio Declaration*, Principle 3.

11 *Ibid.*, Principle 15.

12 *Ibid.*, Principle 16.

13 *Ibid.*, Principle 4.

14 *Ibid.*, Principle 7.

15 ICTSD, *Bridges Trade BioRes Special WSSD Update No1*, 22 August 2002: <www.ictsd.org>.

CDR principle also acknowledged that rich countries would have to curb their consumption of a disproportionate share of the world's resources. The need to alter patterns of production and consumption that were beyond the planet's absorptive and regenerative capacities has been made more explicit in recent times: the 2002 WSSD emphasises this imperative in both the Political Declaration and the Plan of Implementation.[16]

The Uruguay Round negotiations were in their final stages when the Earth Summit took place. It is not surprising, therefore, that while UNCED marked a significant step forward in international environmental law, it was also the first occasion on which trade interests actively intervened in international environmental negotiations. The GATT Secretariat's influence is directly reflected in Principle 12 of the Rio Declaration, which provides, that:

> ... Trade policy measures for environmental purposes should not constitute a means of arbitrary or unjustifiable discrimination or a disguised restriction on international trade. Unilateral actions to deal with environmental challenges outside the jurisdiction of the importing country should be avoided. Environmental measures addressing transboundary or global environmental problems should, as far as possible, be based on international consensus.[17]

Agenda 21 para. 39.3(d) mirrors and elaborates on this language. It provides that domestic initiatives may need trade measures to render them effective, and that the formulation of such trade measures should be guided by the principles of non-discrimination, least-trade-restrictiveness, transparency and adequate notification, and special consideration for developing countries.

Such that it was,[18] the momentum created by UNCED was not maintained over the following decade. Global environmental quality has deteriorated:

> The global environment continues to suffer. Loss of biodiversity continues, fish stocks continue to be depleted, desertification claims more

---

16 *The Johannesburg Declaration on Sustainable Development*, 4 September 2002, Principle 11 (the Johannesburg Declaration); *World Summit on Sustainable Development Plan of Implementation*, Article 2 and Part III, both located on the WSSD website: <www.johannesburgsummit.org/documents> (20 December 2002).

17 This language mirrors that contained in GATT Article XX and Article 36 of the *Treaty Establishing the European Economic Community as Amended by Subsequent Treaties*, opened for signature 25 March 1957, 298 UNTS 3. It is also contained in Article 3(5) of the *United Nations Framework Convention on Climate Change*, concluded at Rio de Janeiro, 1992. Entered into force 21 March 1994, reprinted in (1992) 31 *International Legal Materials* 849 and the *Non-Legally Binding Authoritative Statement of Principles for a Global Consensus on the Management, Conservation and Sustainable Development of All Types of Forests*, Report of the United Nations Conference on Environment and Development, Rio de Janeiro, 3–14 June 1992.

18 It should be noted, however, that many regarded the UNCED outcomes as a failure for the environment, because they focused too heavily on human priorities, including the need to improve conditions for the world's poor, rather than urgent environmental problems. *See* R. Falk, 'Environmental Protection in an Era of Globalization' (1996) 6 *Yearbook International Environmental Law* 1; L. Campiglio, L. Pineschi, D. Siniscalco, and T. Treves (eds), *The Environment After Rio* (Graham & Trotman, Martinus Nijhoff, London, 1994).

> and more fertile land, the adverse effects of climate change are already evident, natural disasters are more frequent and more devastating and developing countries more vulnerable, and air, water and marine pollution continue to rob millions of a decent life.[19]

The slow pace of environmental reform was exacerbated by the extraordinary rise of the WTO: economic liberalization dominated international relations, and a dynamic body of international economic law emerged. As the WTO regime consolidated its legal status, it exposed two principal sets of trade–environment tensions. The first are those environmental impacts occasioned by the expansion of trade in goods that underpins the WTO's objectives. These impacts include the increased scale of resource depletion and pollution through production of more goods; increased energy use; greenhouse gas emissions; and pollution from international transport of goods; and the creation of opportunities to trade in harmful goods.[20] The impacts of new markets for environmentally unfriendly goods can be avoided provided strong environmental policies are in place when markets are opened, and provided the economic gains are translated into higher environmental standards.[21] But the consistent expansion of trade volumes must eventually confront global biophysical constraints.[22] Greater attention to qualitative development, rather than quantitative expansion, could provide a solution to resource constraints, but there is no sign that such a fundamental shift in dominant economic analysis will take place in the foreseeable future.

The second set of linkages relates to the effects on environmental policy of the WTO's trade disciplines. This includes the potential for environmental benefits from the removal of inefficient and environmentally harmful subsidies and from the promotion of trade in environmental goods and services. It also includes the potential constraints that WTO rules impose on Members in introducing international or domestic environmental policies that have direct or indirect trade effects, especially those aimed at altering unsustainable patterns of production and consumption.

Resistance to the use of trade measures as instruments of environmental policy has focussed on international agreements that ban trade in harmful products, or goods produced in harmful ways, either outright or with countries who are not parties to the agreement.[23] Indeed, the fear that the gains of liberalization will be lost to 'environmental protectionism' has prompted states to ensure the participation of trade diplomats, as well as environmental

---

19 Johannesburg Declaration, *supra* n. 16, Article 13.

20 This categorization is adapted from OECD, *The Environmental Effects of Trade* (OECD, Paris, 1994).

21 Indeed, it is central to economic theory on the benefits of trade that increased competition from liberalization should promote efficient production and resource use. It should also provide the wealth for improved funding for environmental restoration and protection. Nordström and Vaughan, *WTO Special Series 4, Trade and Environment*, (WTO, Geneva, 1999), 58.

22 H. Daly, *Beyond Growth* (Beacon Press Boston, 1996); H. Daly, 'Sustainable Growth? No Thank You', in G. Mander, and E. Goldsmith (eds), *The Case Against the Global Economy* (Sierra Club Books, 1996) 193.

23 Oxley's criticisms are typical of this group. *See*, for example, A. Oxley, 'Poor Environmental Policy – the fundamental problem in the "trade and environment" debate', paper presented to the *Trade and Environment Roundtable* (Environment Australia, Canberra, August 1999).

negotiators at most international environmental negotiations over the decade since UNCED, most notably the Cartagena Protocol on Biosafety and the Kyoto Protocol.

One of the most difficult trade–environment linkages is the concern that environmental protection will be used to justify local laws that purport to alter unsustainable consumption. It will be recalled that sustainable development requires states to not only alter the way that they produce goods and services, but also to change unsustainable consumption patterns. Sovereign states can determine what production techniques may be employed within their territory or by their nationals without interfering with trade. Achieving changes to consumption necessarily involves some restriction on consumer behaviour, either by limiting choice to products that are produced sustainably, raising the price for unsustainably produced goods, or enabling consumers to make informed choices.[24] Consumption of imported goods may be regulated in a potentially discriminatory manner by:

- imposing domestic environmental standards on imported goods, for example, by banning products that fail to meet specified physical, performance or production standards;
- imposing countervailing duties on imports produced under poor environmental standards and border tax adjustment for environmental taxes;
- requiring that certain products bear a label that advises consumers of the environmental impacts of their production, consumption, or disposal.

Environmental policy-makers fear that governments will refrain from introducing high domestic standards unless they can demand comparable standards of their trading partners,[25] but local measures risk conflict with WTO Agreements whenever they affect market access for imported goods.

These interfaces between WTO rules and environmental policy have occupied the minds of trade diplomats, non-governmental organizations, legal scholars, and the pages of scholarly journals for the past decade or so. Indeed, the WTO-consistency of market access restrictions on goods produced in an environmentally harmful way – either unilaterally or pursuant to a multilateral environmental agreement – is the most contentious linkage question. It has profound implications for the debate over trade and human rights and labour standards.

---

24 OECD, *Processes and Production Methods (PPMs): Conceptual Framework and Considerations on Use of PPM-based Trade Measures* (1997) OECD OCDE/GD (97) 137.

25 Little evidence exists that national governments lower environmental or human health standards in order to encourage trade-related investment or protect domestic producers. Since existing environmental laws are already inadequate in many nations, the fear of regulatory paralysis or 'chill' is far more relevant. The chilling effect of competition is extremely difficult to prove because it requires evidence of why investment *did not* occur. Anecdotally, however, evidence of such pressure features in public debate on virtually a daily basis. Australian industry routinely draws upon competitiveness arguments to repel the introduction of new environmental responsibilities in respect of both export commodities and domestic production. Similarly, the United States' abandonment of the Kyoto Protocol to the UNFCCC was justified in large part by the unacceptable impact it would have on domestic industry.

There are a variety of ways in which trade–environment linkages can be handled.[26] The WTO Committee on Trade and Environment has spent the past eight years pondering the scope of, and responses to, several key questions, with no concrete results. In the meantime, the WTO has adopted a default of resolving linkage questions by interpretation.[27] This has involved interpretation of the WTO texts and their place within the wider corpus of international law.

So far, the disputes that have raised environmental or health considerations have concerned the second set of linkages outlined above, namely unilateral import restrictions or taxes on products, based either on their physical properties or on their environmentally harmful production or processing method (PPM). It is worthwhile briefly retracing the significant developments that the WTO AB has made in interpreting trade and environmental obligations, in order to understand where deficiencies remain.

7.3 The Environmental Evolution in WTO Interpretation

The harmonization of trade rules with environmental considerations had very poor beginnings in the *Tuna–Dolphin* disputes of the early 1990s.[28] In those unadopted decisions, two GATT panels rejected the United States' claim that it could comply with GATT obligations while distinguishing between physically identical fish products based on the way in which those products were harvested. They also rejected the United States' attempt to justify its import ban on dolphin–deadly tuna, under the GATT Article XX environmental exceptions.[29] The exceptions were rejected first because Article XX could not condone measures with 'extra-jurisdictional' application,[30] then because the terms of Article XX could never be satisfied by measures that forced trading partners to change domestic laws and policies.[31]

The trade regime endured considerable 'bad press' in the period after *Tuna–Dolphin*.[32] WTO jurisprudence has responded to the organization's need

---

26 A theoretical approach to linkage analysis is set out in Leebron, *supra* n. 2.

27 Leebron, *supra* n. 2, at 22.

28 *United States – Restriction on Imports of Tuna*, 13 September 1991, not adopted, DS29/R (Tuna–Dolphin 1); *United States – Restriction on Imports of Tuna*, 16 June 1994, not adopted, DS31/R (Tuna–Dolphin 2).

29 Readers will recall that Article XX(b) permits measures that are 'necessary for the protection of human, animal or plant life or health' and Article XX(g) permits measures 'relating to the conservation of exhaustible natural resources' provided the measures are not applied to constitute arbitrary or unjustifiable discrimination or manner a disguised restriction on trade.

30 *Tuna–Dolphin 1*, at paras 5.26–5.27, 5.31.

31 *Tuna–Dolphin 2*, at paras 5.25–5.27, 5.38.

32 Full page advertisements were taken out in the New York Times, Washington Post, London Times, and Le Monde featuring 'GATTzilla', the trade monster who crushed a dolphin in one hand and spilled a can of DDT with the other, while chewing on the planet and trampling the US Capital Building. Towards the end of negotiations on the WTO, advertisements featured a full page of suited men with the faces removed, warning that 'faceless bureaucrats' at the GATT in Geneva were controlling US food safety and environmental standards.

to 'be seen to be green', with an 'environmental evolution' in the interpretation of the trade agreements. The AB has observed the general rules of treaty application and interpretation contained in the *Vienna Convention on the Law of Treaties*.[33] In so doing, it has recognized the relevance of international environmental law principles, and the need for WTO agreements to be interpreted in an evolutionary way that keeps pace with emerging legal norms.[34]

The scope and operation of the basic most-favoured nation and national treatment obligations remains relatively unchanged. Members are obliged not to discriminate between 'like products' and the AB has reaffirmed a definition of 'like product' that focuses on physical or market characteristics. Preferential treatment of functionally similar products based on physical qualities that affect product safety or performance will be consistent with Articles I and III.[35] Distinctions between products based on the characteristics of the producer or PPMs that are not reflected in a product's physical composition are inconsistent with basic GATT obligations.[36]

The real interpretive gains have been made in the operation of GATT Article XX(b) and (g) environmental exceptions. The AB has made the test for provisional justification under paragraphs (b) and (g) less demanding, while affirming the important role of the Article XX Preamble or *chapeau* in preventing abuse of the exceptions.[37] In order to obtain provisional justification, a member must first demonstrate that the impugned trade measure advanced a policy that was necessary to protect human, animal or plant life or health, or related to the conservation of exhaustible natural resources. In scrutinizing a measure, WTO panels will not second-guess the policy objective or the level of protection, provided there is some evidence to show that the policy is justified.[38]

Showing that a particular measure is justified under paragraph (b) will require proof that it is 'necessary'. This originally required proof that there was no less-inconsistent measure reasonably available, an interpretation

---

33 Article 30 sets out rules of treaty application, which Article 31 sets out rules of treaty interpretation. Article 31(3)(c) provides that treaties are to be understood in light of 'any relevant rules of international law applicable in the relations between the parties'.

34 *United States – Import Prohibition on Certain Shrimp and Shrimp Products*, Appellate Body Report, 1998, WT/DS58/AB, adopted 6 November 1998, para. 130 (*Shrimp-Turtle AB*).

35 *European Communities – Measures Affecting Asbestos and Asbestos-Containing Products*, Report of the Appellate Body, WT/DS135/AB/R, adopted 5 April 2001 (*Asbestos AB*), at 115. The AB held that recognition of physical properties as a basis for distinguishing between similar products would not undermine the effectiveness of Article XX exceptions for human health and environmental protection; it would merely reduce the number of measures that might require justification under that clause.

36 *United States – Standards for Reformulated and Conventional Gasoline*, Report of the Appellate Body, WT/DS2/AB/R, adopted 20 May 1996 (*Reformulated Gasoline AB*) (producer characteristics); *Shrimp Turtle AB*, para. 120 (harvesting methods).

37 *Reformulated* Gasoline, *supra* n. 36, at 25; *Shrimp Turtle AB*, *supra* n. 34, at para. 158.

38 *European Communities – Measures Affecting Asbestos and Asbestos-Containing Products*, Report of the Panel, WT/DS135/R, adopted 5 April 2001 (*Asbestos Panel*), at 115. paras 8.193–8.194. This conclusion was upheld by the AB. *Asbestos AB*, *supra* n. 35, at para. 161–2. In the *Asbestos* dispute, the Panel had to make a judgment about the health risk posed by chrysotile-cement products, because Canada disputed the extent of the risk. The Panel seemed to require proof to the standard of a *prima facie* case, and was ultimately satisfied that such products did pose a threat to human health.

heavily criticized for ignoring precautionary environmental measures.[39] The AB has relaxed this approach in recent disputes. It may now be satisfied even in cases where other measures are available, following a weighing and balancing of a series of factors that includes:

- the contribution made by the compliance measure to the environmental or health objective;
- the importance of the common interests or values protected;
- the size of the impact on imports or exports.[40]

The necessity requirement has therefore evolved from a 'least trade-restrictive' to a 'less trade-restrictive' test, that is subject to an overriding assessment of proportionality.[41] The more important or urgent the health or environmental objective, the easier it will be to demonstrate proportionality.[42]

Article XX(g) permits measures aimed at protection of living species as 'exhaustible natural resources', regardless of whether they are on the brink of extinction.[43] The AB's standard for measures taken pursuant to paragraph (g) requires only that they be 'primarily aimed at' conservation.[44] Less restrictive measures do not need to be attempted first, provided there is a substantial and not merely incidental relationship between the measure and the conservation objective.[45] The requirement that measures be imposed 'in conjunction with restrictions on domestic production or consumption' has also been interpreted liberally, requiring 'even handedness in the imposition of restrictions, in the name of conservation', rather than an empirical test of whether domestic measures have equivalent efficacy.[46]

One of the most contentious aspects of the trade–environment linkage is the concern that Members will enforce their own domestic environmental priorities on their trading partners, thus engaging in 'green unilateralism'. Many Members resent the prospect of having domestic environmental policy dictated to them by powerful trading partners, who can refuse market access for goods produced in a damaging way. They are also suspicious of the 'green-blue' alliance: the use of environmental policy as a new form of industry protectionism. In both *Tuna–Dolphin* disputes, the GATT panels denied a party's right to restrict imports based on harm caused beyond the importing Member's territory. The WTO AB has taken a more generous approach to the issue of extra-jurisdictional measures. It has concluded that paragraphs (b) and (g) both expect some 'territorial nexus' between the

---

39 *Thailand – Restriction on Importation of and Internal Taxes on Cigarettes*, Report of the Panel, 7 November 1990, BISD 37S/200 (*Thai Cigarettes*), at para. 74; *Korea – Measures Affecting Imports of Fresh, Chilled and Frozen Beef*, Report of the Appellate Body, WT/DS161/AB/R, WT/DS169/AB/R, adopted 10 January 2001 (*Korea Beef AB*).

40 *Korea Beef AB*, at para. 164.

41 WTO CTE Secretariat, *GATT/WTO Dispute Settlement Practice Relation to GATT Article XX, Paragraphs (b), (d), and (g), Note by the Secretariat*, WT/CTE/W/203, 8 March 2002, para. 41.

42 *Asbestos AB*, *supra* n. 35, at para. 172.

43 *Shrimp–Turtle AB*, *supra* n. 34, at para. 128.

44 *Reformulated Gasoline AB*, *supra* n. 36, at 18.

45 *Ibid.*

46 *Ibid.*, at 19–20; *Shrimp–Turtle AB*, *supra* n. 34, at paras 143–145.

object of protection or conservation and the party imposing the trade measure, but that species or resources need not be permanently located within the territory of the party imposing the measure.[47] Evidence of migration or a pelagic species visiting territorial regions will suffice to bring a measure within the scope of paragraph (g).[48]

It remains unclear whether some physical relationship or presence will prove essential to reliance on Article XX in all cases. If the WTO is to promote sustainable development, as its Preamble contemplates,[49] it must find ways of allowing Members to alter unsustainable consumption patterns. Consumption of goods whose production damages the environment either globally or within the producer's jurisdiction is necessarily unsustainable. The location of damage within the political borders of the consuming state is ecologically irrelevant.

No dispute has raised a claim based on a purely philosophical nexus with the object of its protective measure, for example, by arguing that damage is being caused to a species which forms part of the 'common concern of mankind'. Nor has the economic nexus – the incentive of domestic consumption to continue the extra-jurisdictional environmental problem – been argued before the AB. If it were, the AB may well make an incremental extension of its current approach, subject to the measure satisfying the other aspects of Article XX outlined below. It would involve only a modest development of existing reasoning: the AB already permits restrictions on market access for goods which are themselves environmentally damaging, even though these restrictions are also likely to prompt changes in production practices in exporting states.[50] Nevertheless, the doctrinal conservativeness of such a development would be overshadowed by the political storm it would create.

As the AB clarified the operation of paragraphs (b) and (g) in affording provisional justification for environmental measures, it emphasized the important role played by the Article XX Preamble or *chapeau*. It has confirmed that the preamble operates as a safeguard against protectionist abuse of the Article XX exceptions and demarcates the 'line of equilibrium' between GATT rights and obligations.[51] Rather than focussing on the measure *per se*, the chapeau disciplines the means by which a measure is applied: application of a measure must not constitute a means of arbitrary or unjustifiable discrimination, or a disguised restriction on trade, where the same conditions prevail.[52]

Discrimination will be considered unjustifiable where it was not merely inadvertent,[53] and when the Member imposing the measure has not made any 'serious effort' to negotiate a multilateral solution to the conservation

---

[47] *Ibid.*, at para. 121.
[48] *Ibid.*, at para. 133.
[49] *Agreement Establishing the World Trade Organization, Final Act Embodying the Results of the Uruguay Round of Multilateral Trade Negotiations*, 15 April 1994, Preamble.
[50] Charnovitz C, 'The Law of Environmental "PPMs" in the WTO: Debunking the Myth of Illegality' (2002) 27 *Yale Journal of International Law* 59, at 74.
[51] *Shrimp–Turtle AB*, *supra* n. 34, at para. 159.
[52] *Reformulated Gasoline AB*, *supra* n. 36, at 21.
[53] *Ibid.*, at 25.

or environmental problem.[54] The AB has confirmed that the obligation to attempt negotiation does not require the conclusion of an agreement; it requires only that 'serious good faith efforts to reach agreement' are made before resorting to unilateral measures.[55] Measures that are applied inflexibly, requiring exporters to adopt 'essentially the same' regulatory program as importers,[56] will also constitute both arbitrary and unjustifiable discrimination.[57] The AB will scrutinize measures that are not overtly discriminatory to ensure that their 'design, architecture and revealing structure' do not disclose a discriminatory intent.[58]

The AB's broader interpretation of Article XX has resulted in it upholding a unilateral, discriminatory non-product-related harvesting method as a condition of access to the United States' market. In the *Shrimp–Turtle (Article 21.5)* proceedings, the AB decided that the United States' import ban on wild shrimp not caught using techniques that could be certified as turtle-friendly was WTO-consistent. Even though the trawling did not take pace within US territory and had no effect on the physical characteristics of the shrimp, and even though no multilateral agreement had been reached. This decision – unthinkable 10 years ago after the first *Tuna–Dolphin* decision – should dispel doubts over the WTO's capacity to accommodate unilateral PPM trade measures.

The *Shrimp–Turtle (Article 21.5)* AB decision shows that the WTO is capable of accommodating some of the most delicate and politically loaded aspects of the trade–environment linkage. The progress made in 'greening' the GATT provisions does not, however, fully dispel concerns over the WTO's likely impact on domestic environmental and health regulations. The GATT provisions outlined above are not invoked in disputes involving food safety or quarantine measures, or technical product standards. These measures are scrutinized for consistency with the more demanding obligations of the *Agreement on the Application of Sanitary and Phytosanitary Measures* (SPSA) and the *Agreement on Technical Barriers to Trade* (TBTA). Since the SPSA's and TBTA's substantive and procedural obligations are stricter than the GATT, the AB has had less scope to develop sympathetic readings of the texts.[59] It is beyond the scope of this chapter to rehearse the AB's interpretation of the TBTA and SPSA obligations, but their demanding obligations make it likely

---

54 *Shrimp–Turtle AB*, *supra* n. 34, at para. 166.

55 *United States – Import Prohibition of Certain Shrimp and Shrimp Products, Recourse to Article 21.5 by Malaysia*, Report of the Panel, WT/DS58/RW (*Shrimp–Turtle (Article 21.5) Panel*), at para. 5.67.

56 *United States – Import Prohibition of Certain Shrimp and Shrimp Products, Recourse to Article 21.5 by Malaysia*, Report of the Appellate Body, WT/DS58/AB/RW, adopted 21 November 2001 (*Shrimp–Turtle (Article 21.5) AB*), at para. 141.

57 *Shrimp–Turtle AB*, *supra* n. 34, at paras 161–164.

58 *Japan – Taxes on Alcoholic Beverages*, Report of the Appellate Body, WT/DS8, 10, 11/AB/R, adopted 1 November 1996, reported in WTO Dispute Settlement Reports 1996, Geneva (1998), 108, at 121; *Asbestos Panel*, *supra* n. 38, at para. 8.236; *Shrimp–Turtle (Article 21.5) Panel*, *supra* n. 55, at para. 5.142.

59 The AB has considered application of the SPSA on three occasions. In the first dispute, it rejected the direct application of the precautionary principle to the risk assessment provisions of the SPSA as a principle of customary international law, but did suggest that Members

that they will become the primary basis of legal challenge of domestic health and environmental measures wherever possible, especially where Members object to the AB's approach to GATT environmental exceptions.[60] This will test the AB's willingness and capacity to bridge the policy divide.

7.4 Responses to the Greening of WTO Agreements

The principal benefit of an interpretive approach to the trade–environment linkage is its conservatism; it need only address real conflicts. It modifies and interprets WTO agreements incrementally, on an as-needs basis. The relatively small number of disputes over environmental trade measures supports the view that much of the criticism of WTO disciplines is illusory.[61] Yet even the conservative interpretive approach to resolving trade–environment tensions has been resisted by many WTO members. The expected gains from WTO accession for many developing countries have not been realised, and there is deep suspicion of any change to WTO rights and obligations that might undermine future benefits.[62]

The AB has received strident criticism for altering the GATT's balance of rights and obligations.[63] In the original *Shrimp–Turtle* dispute, 14 Members

---

Contd.
should be entitled to set health objectives from a 'position of caution'. *European Communities – Measures Concerning Meat and Meat Products (Hormones)*, Report of the Panels, Complaint by the United States, WT/DS26/R/USA and Complaint by Canada, WT/DS48/R/CAN. In the second dispute, it made clear that Members were permitted to set a zero-risk level of protection for specified threats, provided it took a consistent approach to its treatment of various imports or activities posing equivalent risk. *Australia – Measures Affecting the Importation of Salmon*, Report of the Appellate Body, WT/DS18/AB/R. In the third dispute, the AB made clear that the SPSA can accommodate scientific uncertainty by permitting Members to introduce measures provisionally. It added, however, that provisional measures could only be maintained if scientific evidence was obtained within a 'reasonable period' following their introduction. *Japan – Measures Affecting Agricultural Products*, Report of the Appellate Body, WT/DS76/AB/R.

The substantive provisions of the TBTA have only been considered once. In *European Communities – Trade Description of Sardines*, Report of the Appellate Body, WT/DS135/AB/R, the AB decided that the TBT Agreement's obligation to base domestic measures on relevant international standards required Members to re-examine existing measures whenever new international standards come into effect.

60 This argument is explored further in J. McDonald, 'Retrofitting environmental regulation?: Harmonization and environmental sovereignty under the WTO Agreement on Technical Barriers to Trade', *A-G's International Trade Law Conference*, Canberra, 9 October 2002.

61 Environmental advocates argue that it reveals the chilling effect of the WTO's dominance, discouraging Members from introducing new measures for fear that they will be taken to WTO dispute settlement.

62 It is now estimated that 14% of the world's population control 75% of exports, while the poorest 40% are responsible for only 3%. Watkins K, 'Trade and Sustainable Development: Time for a Fresh Start in Johannesburg' (2002) 6(5) *Bridges*, 1, citing a report of the Inter-American Development Bank.

63 C. Raghavan, 'WTO Appellate Body assailed for usurping jurisdiction' (1998) 198 *Third World Economics* 2; Government of India, *India – Position Paper to the High Level Symposium on Trade and Environment*, March 1999; Anon, 'BOP ruling calls into question dispute settlement system' (1999) 13 *Third World Economics* 207–208.

supported Malaysia's complaint against the United States' ban.[64] No Member made third party submissions on the United States' behalf.[65] Even during the enforcement proceedings, Australia, Japan, Mexico, and Thailand all argued that the flexible modified ban could not be justified under Article XX.[66] Australia submitted that good faith multilateral negotiations may not be enough to avoid 'unjustifiable discrimination' under the Article XX Preamble, because it would impair the GATT's balance of rights of obligations.[67] Japan proposed a 'back to the future' interpretation of Article XX, arguing – in strains of *Tuna–Dolphin* – that Article XX should be interpreted strictly as an 'exception' to GATT obligations.[68] It proposed that a measure could only avoid being 'arbitrary or unjustifiably discriminative', if there was 'common recognition by other negotiating countries of the necessity of the measure in question'.[69] Thailand argued that the fact that the legislation banned shrimp from non-certified nations was *necessarily inconsistent* with GATT obligations, regardless of the revised guidelines' new flexibility.[70] All of these approaches are substantially narrower than the AB's approach to Article XX's Preamble and would add to the obligations arising from a purposive reading of the text. Their significance lies not in their potential for adoption, but as evidence of the strong resistance to the AB's green revolution.

The Membership's resistance to the AB's attempts to reduce tensions with environmental policy is also evidenced in the public documents available on the WTO website, principally the Secretariat's introduction to the WTO, *Trading into the Future*. [71] Revised in March 2001, before the *Shrimp–Turtle (Article 21.5)* decision, but after the first *Shrimp–Turtle* AB decision, the section dealing with trade–environment issues states that:

> The WTO agreements are interpreted to say two important things. First, trade restrictions cannot be imposed on a product purely because

---

64 India, Pakistan and Thailand were co-complaining parties, while Australia, Ecuador, El Salvador, Guatemala, Hong Kong, Japan, Nigeria, the Philippines, and Singapore made third party submissions.

65 Although the European Communities' submission sympathized with the United States' policy objectives, it faulted the discriminatory means by which the ban had been implemented. *See Shrimp–Turtle (Article 21.5) Panel, supra* n. 55, at paras 4.26 – 4.35.

66 The EC submitted that the Malaysian complaint was premature, because it had not applied for certification under the US' revised certification regime, and had therefore not been denied access to the US market under the new scheme. *Shrimp–Turtle (Article 21.5)* AB, *supra* n. 56, at paras 54–59.

67 *Ibid.*, at para. 47–50.

68 This approach was rejected in the first *Shrimp–Turtle AB* report, the AB preferring an interpretation that identified the 'line of equilibrium' and prevention of abuse functions of Article XX. *Shrimp–Turtle AB, supra* n. 34, at para. 159.

69 *Shrimp–Turtle (Article 21.5) AB, supra* n. 56, at paras 67–68. Japan's approach was clearly flawed: it attempted to insert a new 'necessity' test into the Article XX chapeau where none exists, and where present interpretations of Article XX(g) would require only that a policy objective or means of implementation be primarily aimed at conservation.

70 *Ibid.*, at paras 71–74.

71 WTO Secretariat, *Trading into the Future: The Introduction to the WTO* (2nd edn, 1999), located on the WTO website: <www.wto.org/english/thewto_e/whatis_e/tif_e/tif_e.htm>.

> of the way it has been produced. Second, one country cannot reach out beyond its own territory and impose its standards on another country.[72]

Even in March 2001, this statement was misleading. By then, the AB in *Shrimp–Turtle* had recognized that there may be cases where it is appropriate to focus on a product's method of harvesting or production, or to reach out beyond national territory.[73] Following the AB's approval of the United States' modified shrimp import ban, the explanation is simply wrong.[74] While the AB's environmental evolution in GATT interpretation continues to be either disregarded or resisted, its capacity to progress the 'greening' of the WTO remains unrealized. Even if the AB's approach were fully embraced, an incremental approach that tests the WTO-consistency of environmental measures will perpetuate the fear that environmental policy occupies a lower rung in the hierarchy of legal obligations and policy priorities than trade disciplines. What is therefore required is reform at the WTO Ministerial level and in other non-trade fora. The potential for progress on these fronts is discussed in the next two parts.

7.4.1 The Doha agenda

The Doha Declaration reaffirmed the WTO's commitment to the objective of sustainable development,[75] although just as it was in the Preamble to the Final Act Establishing the WTO, the term remains undefined. The Declaration also boosted the potential for harmony between trade liberalization and environmental protection, stating that the two 'can *and must*' be mutually supportive.[76] It restated the language of GATT Article XX(b) and (g) and encouraged greater cooperation between the WTO and international environmental and developmental organizations.[77] In furtherance of these objectives, the Doha Ministerial agreed to negotiations on three discrete aspects of the trade–environment linkage:

(i) the relationship between existing WTO rules and specific trade obligations set out in multilateral environmental agreements (MEAs), as among parties to the MEA;
(ii) procedures for regular information exchange between MEA Secretariats and WTO committees, and the criteria for the granting of observer status;

---

72 *Ibid.*, at 47.
73 *Shrimp-Turtle AB*, *supra* n. 34, at paras 132–133. The note to readers on the document's contents page warns that some aspects of the WTO regime have had to be simplified for a general readership, but it is difficult to put the emphatic tone of the quoted statement down to a need for stylistic elegance or simplicity.
74 This point is also made by Charnovitz, *supra* n. 50, at 95.
75 *Fourth WTO Ministerial Declaration*, Adopted on 14 November 2001, Doha, Qatar, WTO Document WT/MIN(01)/DEC/1, Preamble (the Doha Declaration).
76 *Ibid.*, para. 6 (emphasis added).
77 *Ibid.*, Preamble.

(iii) the reduction of tariff and non-tariff barriers to environmental goods and services.[78]

These topics are conservative, in that they are restricted to issues where substantive entitlements are unlikely to be altered or where there is an opportunity for environmental gains from trade. The Doha Declaration is nonetheless the first time that environmental issues have been included in the formal negotiating agenda and form part of the single undertaking to be concluded by 2005.[79] This, in itself, is a step towards better accommodation of the trade--environment linkage within the WTO and is a positive sign for the future.

7.4.1.1 Measures pursuant to MEAs

Of the three Doha trade–environment priorities, the WTO–MEA relationship has been the subject of most diplomatic and scholarly consideration to date. The WTO CTE has discussed the WTO–MEA relationship since the Committee was first established in 1995. Since then, a variety of solutions have been suggested, ranging from retention of the status quo, to interpretation or amendment of Article XX.[80] Despite the debate generated by this topic within the WTO, multilateral environment agencies, the academy, and civil society, no progress has been made towards diplomatic resolution. Negotiation of the Doha agenda item is likely to be equally cautious: a majority of CTE special session Members are still attempting simply to define the scope of work item (i), not yet having agreed on what constitutes an 'MEA' and a 'specific trade obligation'[81] and to suggest how negotiations should proceed.[82] Only a small

---

78 *Ibid.*, para. 31.

79 The other topics included in the single undertaking are implementation, agriculture, services, industrial tariffs, subsidies, antidumping, and regional trade agreements.

80 These include:

- retention of the status quo (i.e. an interpretive linkage approach);
- granting MEA-specific waivers;
- various models for amendment of Article XX;
- introduction of a 'Coherence Clause' providing that in WTO disputes involving an MEA-mandated trade measure, only the application of the measure will be assessed, it being presumed to be provisionally justified under Article XX(b) or (g);
- developing principles and criteria by which to assess the validity of trade measures taken pursuant to MEAs;
- reversing the burden of proof under GATT Article XX in cases involving specifically mandated trade measures;
- developing non-binding interpretive guidelines to be used as a reference in the negotiation of future MEAs, and to assess the WTO-compatability of MEA trade measures;
- developing an Understanding to apply across the entire WTO Agreement, regarding differentiated treatment for trade measures applied pursuant to MEAs;
- developing and implementing a voluntary consultative mechanism.

Committee on Trade and Environment Special Session, Note by the Secretariat, 'Multilateral Environmental Agreements (MEAs) and WTO rules; Proposals made in the Committee on Trade and Environment (CTE) from 1995–2002' WTO Doc. TN/TE/S/1, 23 May 2002, at 2.

81 Submission by Argentina, TN/TE/W/2.

82 Submission by Australia, TN/TE/W/7. Australia proposes a first phase during which specific trade obligations and WTO rules are identified; a second phase in which to consider

handful of Members are already proposing how the relationship should be clarified.[83] The most notable is the European Union, which advocates clarification of the wider MEA–WTO relationship, including cases where the complaining Member is not a party to the MEA.[84] In the EU's view, clarifying the WTO–MEA issue would advance the debate over other linkage questions:[85]

> In this sense, the EU views the MEA/WTO relationship as an international governance issue, i.e. relating to the functioning of the global governance system and, in particular, to the necessary links between bodies of law dealing with international trade and environment which both form part of a global system.[86]

The terms of the mandate contained in Paragraph 31(i) are very narrow indeed. The Doha Declaration makes clear that it is concerned only with 'specific trade obligations' and states that negotiations shall not prejudice the WTO rights of any Member that is not a party to the MEA in question.[87] Yet clarification of specific trade obligations in respect of members of both the MEA and WTO is probably superfluous in any event. The AB has already emphasized that WTO Agreements are not to be read in 'clinical isolation' from wider international legal principles and that Article XX will require Members to engage in international negotiations.[88] Where Members are giving effect to specific treaty obligations *vis-à-vis* other Members of the WTO and the MEA, the prospects of a clash are extremely low. In any event, it is highly likely that the WTO AB would interpret WTO obligations in light of other relevant international principles, and to construe WTO obligations *inter partes* accordingly. It seems extraordinary that some participants in the CTE still resist the linking of MEA and WTO obligations between parties to both agreement, in light of recent AB decisions.[89] This resistance must therefore be understood as further evidence that they reject the AB's expansive interpretation of Article XX. If this resistance is real, a formal clarification of the WTO–MEA relationship may actually prove counter-productive: it might claw back some of the AB's 'environmental evolution' in WTO

Contd.
whether implementation problems have arisen; and a third phase to discuss the issues. Australia's staged approach is supported by the United States, Brazil, China, India, South Korea, and Taiwan.

83 For example, Switzerland has proposed the adoption of an interpretive statement to clarify the relationship, based on criteria of no hierarchy, mutual supportiveness, and deference. TN/TE/W/4; CTE/W/168.

84 Submission by the European Communities, *Multilateral Environmental Agreements (MEAs): Implementation of the Doha Development Agenda*, TN/TE/W/1, 21 March 2002, at paras 19, 30.

85 *Ibid.*, at para. 14.

86 *Ibid.*

87 It is understood that the United States, a non-party to several major MEAs including the Convention on Biodiversity and the Kyoto Protocol, was instrumental in confining the scope of the Doha mandate on this issue. Anon, 'Going Nowhere Fast: Environmental Negotiations in the Doha Round' (2002) 6(7) *Bridges* 13.

88 *Reformulated Gasoline AB*, *supra* n. 36, at 17; *Shrimp–Turtle AB*, *supra* n. 34, at paras 166–168, 171–172.

89 WTO Secretariat, 'Committee on Trade and Environment Special Session, 11–12 June 2002', *Trade and Environment Bulletin*, Press/TE/039, 27 June 2002, at 3.

jurisprudence, and introduce an interpretation of Article XX that fetters the AB's ability to develop trade and environment linkages in the future.

Paragraph 31(ii) of the Doha Declaration involves enhancing the procedural aspects of the trade–environment linkage. Progress has already been made in improving collaboration between the various intergovernmental organizations: the CTE has held several joint sessions with MEA secretariats and has developed a closer working relationship with UNEP. Reform of the transparency, accountability, and coherence of the major international institutions, including the United Nations, IMF, World Bank, and WTO has been emphasized in several recent multilateral statements. The Preamble to the Doha Declaration itself reiterates the need for better institutional cooperation. In addition, the UN Millennium Declaration, the 2002 Monterrey Consensus and the WSSD all refer to the need to improve coordination between economic, environmental and development agencies.[90]

Implementation of the Doha mandate thus seems likely proceed at two levels. There is likely to be greater consultation with the MEA secretariats in the work of the CTE generally, and more particularly in addressing the substantive aspects of the WTO–MEA relationship. It is also likely that the WTO will engage with these secretariats and other environment agencies within the broader process of reforming international governance arrangements.

7.4.1.2 Environmental goods and services

The third item specifically included in the Doha 'environment' agenda is liberalization of environmental goods and services.[91] Along with subsidies reform, improving opportunities for trade in environmental goods and services is the 'low hanging fruit' in the orchard of mutually supportive trade and environmental policies. Liberalization can increase the adoption of environmentally beneficial services and technologies by lowering their cost and removing regulatory barriers to market access.[92]

In the early stages of negotiation on this issue, debate has focused on what constitutes 'environmental goods and services'. A narrow definition would see the mandate apply only to pollution control, water purification, and other specific technologies and services, whose environmental benefits can be specifically identified. A broader definition – better described as 'environmentally friendly goods and services' – would comprehend any good or service that can claim environmental benefits, for example, because

---

[90] United Nations Millennium Declaration GA/Res 55/2: <www.un.org/millennium/declaration>, para. 30; Draft Outcome of the International Conference on Financing for Development – Monterrey Consensus, A/Conf.198/1, 1 March 2002 (Monterrey Consensus): <www.un.org/esa/ffd/0302finalMonterreyConsensus.pdf>, para. 71; Johannesburg Declaration, *supra* n. 16, Principles 31; WSSD Plan of Implementation, *supra* n. 16, para. 122(b). The Johannesburg Declaration, Principle 32, also calls for enhanced cooperation between international environmental agencies.

[91] Doha Declaration, *supra* n. 75, Article 31(iii).

[92] The potential for trade and environment/development gains from liberalizing trade in environmental goods and services has been discussed in OECD, *Environmental Services: The win–win role of trade liberalisation in promoting environmental protection and economic development* (2000) COM/TD/ENV(99)93/FINAL, Paris, OECD.

of the manner of production. This could include organic products and sustainably harvested forest products. If Members' attitudes towards discriminatory PPM measures canvassed in Section 7.3 serve as a guide, however, this interpretation is highly unlikely.[93]

The real area of concern will be in relation to services which cannot demonstrate any environmental benefit, but which might still constitute 'environmental services' according to the WTO system of goods and services classification. For example, the EU advocates inclusion of water supply in the definition. While clean drinking water is obviously an objective of sustainable development, liberalizing market access in water services *per se*, without any qualification as to the source and delivery modes falls well below the goal of environmental benefit set by Article 31(iii).[94] Similarly, removal of regulatory barriers in respect of sewerage, sanitation, and hazardous waste disposal[95] may actually compromise Members' ability to safeguard environmental and public health. Permitting foreign competition will not necessarily ensure that these services are delivered with environmental protection in mind. In addition, there remain questions about the extent to which the General Agreement on Trade in Services is capable of removing public services from private competition. If these questions are resolved by restricting liberalization to goods and services that can demonstrate a clear environmental benefit, the trade–environment linkage will be enhanced. If not, the WTO can expect criticism that the environment agenda has been used as a guise for liberalization of economically valuable services.

7.4.1.3 Subsidies

The removal of subsidies that are both environmentally harmful and trade distorting has long been recognized as the 'poster girl' for mutually supportive trade liberalization and environmental policies. In addition to the specific environment items identified above, the Doha Declaration restated the need to eliminate trade-distorting subsidies. Subsidies reform is likely to dominate negotiations on agriculture,[96] but the Doha Declaration also specifically identified fisheries subsidies as needing attention.[97] Building on the Doha Ministerial, the commitment to remove subsidies that exacerbate over-fishing and threaten global fisheries was made more explicit in the

---

93 ICTSD, 'Liberalising Environmental Services: the Ultimate Win–Win?' (2002) 6(1) *Bridges* 7. It is worth noting, however, that paras 18(c) and 93(b) the Plan of Implementation for the World Summit on Sustainable Development support the creation and expansion of markets for 'environmentally friendly goods and services'.

94 ICTSD, *supra* n. 93.

95 All of which are contained in the APEC and OECD lists set out in WTO Secretariat, *List of Environmental Goods, Note by the Secretariat*, TN/MA/S/6, 7 September 2002.

96 *See* Williams B, this volume.

97 Doha Declaration, *supra* n. 75, at para. 28.

98 WSSD Plan of Implementation, *supra* n. 16, para. 30 provides that:

To achieve sustainable fisheries, the following actions are required at all levels:
… (f) Eliminate subsidies that contribute to illegal, unreported and unregulated fishing and to over-capacity, while completing the efforts undertaken at WTO to clarify and improve its disciplines on fisheries subsidies, taking into account the importance of this sector to developing countries …

Plan of Implementation of the WSSD, albeit with an 'escape clause' for developing countries.[98]

The fisheries subsidies issue is the pre-eminent example of reform that can deliver wins for trade, environmental protection, and development in poorer countries. It should be the litmus test for whether the international community has a genuine commitment to development that removes perverse incentives for over-exploitation of natural resources. This issue will require wealthier members to commit to removing all support for their own fleets, while affording some special and differential treatment to developing countries. At the time of writing, it was impossible to predict how these negotiations would progress.

7.4.1.4 CTE Work Program

The Doha Declaration gave the CTE Work Program greater focus. Having removed the MEA issue and the issue of market access for environmental goods and services from the regular CTE Work Program, Ministers called on the CTE to consider whether there was a need to clarify existing WTO rules in respect of:

- the effect of environmental measures on market access (the issue on which the AB has made most progress);
- the relevant provisions of the Agreement on Trade-Related Aspects of Intellectual Property Rights;
- labelling requirements for environmental purposes.[99]

The Doha Declaration repeats the language contained in the first two environment agenda items, to the effect that the CTE's work on these issues must not add to, diminish, or alter the balance between existing rights and obligations of Members under existing WTO agreements. With this proviso included to constrain its progress, the CTE seems destined to spend another 3 years deliberating on issues without reaching any conclusions, especially since priority will be given to the three specific agenda items. The Doha Declaration also included an overarching mandate to the CTE and Committee on Trade and Development to identify and debate developmental and environmental aspects of the Doha negotiations, so that sustainable development objectives are appropriately reflected.[100]

7.5 Ecological Sustainability in a Globalizing World

So far, this chapter has mapped the trade–environment linkage, outlined the progress made by the WTO AB in reducing tensions between economic and environmental policies, and sketched the WTO's responses to trade–environment linkage questions. But the influence of trade liberalization on environmental protection extends far beyond the WTO. This part therefore moves from the WTO's handling of the trade–environment interface to a

99 Doha Declaration, *supra* n. 75, para. 32.
100 *Ibid.*, at para. 51.

brief consideration of the effects of economic liberalization – powered by the WTO – on the international environmental agenda. It does not attempt a detailed analysis of how trade interests have affected specific environmental initiatives. Rather, it argues that the objective of sustainable development has been compromised by the WTO's dominance.

Shortly after the debacle of the WTO Seattle Ministerial, the UN General Assembly passed the Millennium Declaration. The Declaration reaffirmed Members' commitment to the UN's Charter, then stated that the central challenge for the new century was to ensure that globalization becomes a positive force for all, since its benefits were unevenly shared, and its costs unevenly distributed.[101] This theme has since pervaded international economic and environmental diplomacy, including the 'development' agenda of the WTO Doha Ministerial.

Two major international meetings took place in the year after Doha – the UN Conference on Finance for Development, at Monterrey in March 2002, and the WSSD in September 2002. Building upon the Millennium and Doha Declarations, the Monterrey Conference was to develop financing mechanisms for development, including trade, aid, debt-relief, loans and a host of other options. The over-arching objective of the resulting 17-page Monterrey Consensus was 'to eradicate poverty, achieve sustained economic growth, and promote sustainable development as we advance to a fully inclusive and equitable global economic system'.[102] While the Consensus was long on rhetoric, however, the final statement lacked any concrete funding commitments. The North's failure in Monterrey to take seriously the economic divide that perpetuates abject poverty in the developing world made harder the task of negotiating binding environmental commitments at the WSSD.[103]

The WSSD offered states an opportunity to identify solutions to the problems of environmental degradation outside the international economic regime. Unlike the Doha Ministerial meeting, whose agenda concerned the future of international trade, the WSSD was to be a stocktake of progress in the implementation of UNCED's Agenda 21 and a plan for future action. Yet disillusionment with the global economic order pervaded negotiations at Johannesburg.[104] Poor countries wanted to re-open the paltry gains of Doha and Monterrey, but the economic north, especially the United States, Canada, Australia, and Japan, made clear that these agreements would not be re-visited.[105] Stalemate over the economic North–South divide pervades the resulting Johannesburg Declaration and Plan of Implementation, taking environmental priorities further down the international agenda. Paragraph 14 of

---

[101] Millennium Declaration, *supra* n. 90, Article 5.

[102] Monterrey Consensus, *supra* n. 90, Article 1.

[103] ICTSD, 'The Monterrey Consensus: A Minor Contribution to Development Financing' (2002) 6(1) *Bridges* 2.

[104] Developing countries' disillusionment with the Doha Declaration's undertakings on implementation are outlined in ICTSD, 'Implementation: What, Where and When?' (2001) 5(9) *Bridges* 7.

[105] ICTSD, 'Stark Differences Emerge on the Value Added of the Johannesburg Summit' (2002) 6(4) *Bridges* 1.

the Johannesburg Declaration recorded the developing world's ambivalence towards progress on economic reform:

> Globalization has added a new dimension to these challenges [of poverty and natural resource management]. The rapid integration of markets, mobility of capital and significant increases in investment flows around the world have opened new challenges and opportunities for the pursuit of sustainable development. But the benefits and costs of globalization are unevenly distributed, with developing countries facing special difficulties in meeting this challenge.

It was recognized that there must be changes to unsustainable patterns of consumption and production and that the natural resource base must be managed for economic and social development.[106] But the over-arching sentiment was that no progress can be made on environmental protection until economic inequities are addressed.[107] The principal objective of WSSD, like the Millennium Declaration, was thus poverty eradication through economic growth.[108] The Johannesburg Declaration implicitly acknowledges the changed focus of sustainable development: Para. 8 observed that at UNCED, 'we agreed that the protection of the environment, and social and economic development are fundamental to sustainable development, based on the Rio Principles'.[109] At Johannesburg, the order of these pillars of sustainable development was reversed, with parties assuming a collective responsibility:

> to advance and strengthen the interdependent and mutually reinforcing pillars of sustainable development – economic development, social development and environmental protection – at local, national, regional and global levels.[110]

---

106 Johannesburg Declaration, *supra* n. 16, Principle 11.

107 In the lead-up to Johannesburg, there had been considerable disagreement over what the focus of the WSSD should be. In its hand-over of the UNCED agenda, Brazil made clear that it regarded development as the principal mandate for Rio + 10. Bridges Trade BioRes, 27 June–August 2002, <www.ictsd.org/biores/02-06-27/inbiref.htm>. At the final PrepCom before Johannesburg, the G77 resisted extensive reference to the Doha Declaration and Monterrey Consensus, but they also resisted language that could increase or add to environmental obligations, or to justify trade protectionism. Bridges Trade BioRes, Special WSSD Update No. 4, 2 September 2002, 1. Para. 93 of the Johannesburg Plan of Implementation calls on states to 'support the Doha Ministerial Declaration and the Monterrey Consensus by undertaking further action … to enhance the benefits, in particular for developing countries as well as for countries with economies in transition, of trade liberalization …'

108 Johannesburg Declaration, *supra* n. 16, para. 11.

109 *Ibid.*, para. 8.

110 *Ibid.*, para. 5. So profound was the domination of the environment agenda by economic issues, that para. 9 included this extraordinary statement:

> Between Rio and Johannesburg the world's nations met in several major conferences under the guidance of the United Nations, including the Monterrey Conference on Finance for Development, as well as the Doha Ministerial Conference. These conferences defined for the world a *comprehensive vision for the future of humanity* [emphasis added].

The second reference to 'these conferences' obviously refers to the many United Nations Conferences held since Rio concerning social development, desertification, developing countries, small island states, women, climate change, and biodiversity. Nonetheless, Article 9's

Negotiations over the WSSD Plan of Implementation deadlocked on its economic elements, rather than environmental commitments. By June 2002, much of the Draft Plan of Implementation was complete – only 3 per cent of the objectives on health, 12 per cent of the objectives on natural resources, and 20 per cent on altering unsustainable production and consumption remained bracketed.[111] At the same time, 93 per cent of the section dealing with globalization, 89 per cent of the section containing financing commitments, and 85 per cent of the trade component remained bracketed.[112] In the final text, numerous references to the need for consistency with the WTO Agreements were dropped, although two paragraphs still oblige states to comply with WTO disciplines regardless of whether they are WTO Members.[113]

Environmental civil society failed in its attempt to have MEAs recognized in the WSSD Plan of Implementation as presumptively consistent with international trade rules. Para. 92 encourages states to promote mutual supportiveness in the WTO–MEA interface, in support of the Doha agenda. Deference to WTO negotiations on this issue is offset only by recognition that promotion of mutual supportiveness should be done 'while recognizing the importance of maintaining the integrity of both sets of instruments'.[114]

What emerges from the outcomes of these international meetings is a new form of strategic trade–environment linkage. Instead of conditioning trade concessions on good environmental practice, resolution of the substantive linkages between trade liberalization and environmental policy can only proceed once improved market access and trade opportunities deliver benefits to the world's poor. Regardless of whether one subscribes to the economic theories upon which WTO disciplines are premised, it is now politically imperative that the Doha Development Agenda delivers on the promised benefits of liberalized trade. The WTO must ensure success of its economic project, or its wealthier members must take seriously their obligations to provide development assistance, debt relief and capacity building opportunities outside of the trading system. The real challenge for the WTO's 'grow now, pay later' philosophy, apart from its potential ecological impossibility, is to find acceptable means by which to prevent irreversible or irreparable environmental harm occurring through its execution.

Contd.
explicit reference to the Doha Ministerial meeting of trade Ministers and the Monterrey meeting on financing development as defining a 'vision for the future of humanity' represents an alarming new stage in the evisceration of sustainable development.

111 Commission on Sustainable Development acting as the preparatory committee for the World Summit on Sustainable Development, *Draft Plan of Implementation Summary of Elements (sub-paragraphs) containing brackets*, 28 June 2002.

112 *Ibid.*

113 WSSD Plan of Implementation, *supra* n. 16, para. 15(b) still requires parties to avoid trade distorting measures inconsistent with WTO rules. Para. 93(b) contemplates national, regional and international actions to complement Doha and Monterrey initiatives. Other references are expressed to apply only to WTO Members.

114 ICTSD, 'Stark differences', *supra* n. 105.

7.6 Conclusions

This chapter has questioned the future of global environmental stability in an international political environment dominated by economic growth and liberalization and increasingly preoccupied with security issues. Writing before the WSSD, Watkins described the WTO as 'the cuckoo that pushed sustainable development out of the nest'.[115] The tone at Johannesburg suggests, however, that it is the economic failure of the WTO, rather that its success, that has created such disenchantment with environmental undertakings.

The WTO has made significant progress in addressing trade–environment tensions. The AB has given GATT Article XX exceptions the potential to permit trade restrictions to protect natural resources, human health and environmental quality, provided the measures are even-handed, do not conceal a protectionist intent. While WTO Members may resist the AB's approach, the Doha Ministerial shows that environmental protection has now been formally recognised as a trade issue.

It is somewhat ironic that the most notable progress on harmonizing trade and environmental linkages and the WTO's relationship with the wider corpus of international law has come from within the WTO itself. The WTO is greener now than the GATT ever was, yet the global commitment to ecologically sustainable development continues to decline. The emergence of global security concerns has hastened its demise. The dominance of economic and developmental issues over ecological sustainability is likely to continue until globalization yields improvement in the desperate conditions facing the world's poor. Let us hope that the planet's life support systems can wait that long.

---

115 Watkins, *supra* n. 62, 1.

8. Dreaming of Red Mansions: Rights, China, and the WTO

*Angus Francis**

8.1 Introduction

The classic Qing text, *Hong-lou meng*,[1] begins with a myth of a flaw in the universe: something less than the perceived problems with the multilateral trading system: a mere hole in heaven. A goddess is given the task of mending the hole. The novel's protagonist, Jia Baoyu, an earthly reincarnation of a stone discarded by the goddess during repairs, symbolizes both desire and enlightenment. Baoyu spends much of his earthly days fashioning a dream-like garden as an illusory and symbolic extension of his own personality. It all ends for Baoyu and his garden in chapter 73 when his mother, Madame Wang, expels Baoyu's maids from the garden after the discovery of a sachet embroidered with a pornographic image. The garden, now tainted, becomes desolate.

Flaws – and repair jobs – abound in the early literature on the new international economic order. Writing in the mid-1980s, Thomas Oppermann referred to 'the foundering of the radical plans regarding the "New International Economic Order" in the style of the 1970s'.[2] At the time, Oppermann called for a 'renewed search [for solutions] in a spirit of improved mutual understanding'.[3] Today, various theories have been advanced to explain how well the World Trade Organization (WTO) and other institutions are answering the challenge of international economic reform.

A growing number of international trade scholars are concentrating on the issue of the 'constitutionalization' or 'boundaries' of international trade

---

* Thanks to Jenny Fu for research and translation assistance, funded by the National Centre for Corporate Law & Policy Research at the School of Law, University of Canberra. My thanks to Ross Buckley and Ernst-Ulrich Petersmann for their comments. Needless to say, any errors in this chapter are my own doing.

1 Cao Xueqin, *A Dream of Red Mansions (Hong-lou meng)*, sometimes called A Dream of Red Towers or The Story of the Stone.

2 T. Oppermann, 'Ideas and Initiatives on Legal Reform of the International Economic Order, within the Framework of the International Law Association since 1978 in particular – German Participation in this Field', in T. Oppermann and E.U. Petersmann (eds), *Reforming the International Economic Order: German Legal Comments* (Duncker and Humblot, Berlin, 1987), p. 11.

3 *Ibid.*

regulation.[4] The malleability of at least one of these terms, remarked Deborah Cass in a recent article, permits analysis of international trade at the institutional level, at the broader structural level, and also at a deeper symbolic and political level.[5] The interest in the future make-up of the world trading system reflects a wider interest in the academic community of reflecting critically on the adequacy, direction, and legitimacy of changes in the notions and practice of constitutionalism and democracy at all levels of governance.[6]

China's accession to the WTO on 11 December 2001 comes at a time when there is a growing perception that 'old and new constitutions – local, national, supranational, regional, global – are in transition ....[7] While there are considerable differences in the terminology employed to describe this movement in the context of international trade, the perception that the international economic order has reached another cross-roads is evident. It is trite to observe that China's accession marked an important milestone in the development of the multilateral trading system. As such, it seems worthwhile to consider what lessons can be learnt about the nature of the international trading system and its future from China's accession.

The purpose of this chapter, then, is to consider what insights can be gleaned from China's accession to the WTO, particularly, what can be learnt from China's accession in relation to the debate over the place of rights in the international trading system. In this limited respect, this chapter takes its lead from the literature which has focused on what China's accession

---

[4] D.Z. Cass, 'The "Constitutionalization" of International Trade Law: Judicial Norm-Generation as the Engine of Constitutional Development in International Trade' (2001) 12 *European Journal of International Law* 39, p. 41 (arguing that one meaning which can be ascribed to constitutionalization in the international trade law context is the traditional characterization of constitution-making by judicial interpretation); J.H. Jackson, *The World Trade Organization: Constitution and Jurisprudence* (Royal Institute of International Affairs, London, 1998) (using the term to describe the institutions, rules and procedures which have developed to administer the multilateral trading system); E.U. Petersmann, *The GATT/WTO Dispute Settlement System: International Law, International Organizations, and Dispute* (Kluwer Law International, London, 1997), Petersmann, n. 25, 26 (including in the term a rights-based notion of constitutionalism: *see* 3 below). Also see, for example, the articles and comments from the recent symposium on The Boundaries of the WTO (collected in 96 *American Journal of International Law*): J.E. Alvarez, 'The WTO as Linkage Machine' (2002) 96 *American Journal of International Law* 146; J. Bhagwati, 'The Question of Linkage' (2002) 96 *American Journal of International Law* 126; S. Charnovitz, 'Triangulating the World Trade Organization' (2002) 96 *American Journal of International Law* 28; R. Howse, 'From Politics to Technocracy – and Back Again: The Fate of the Multilateral Trading Regime' (2002) 96 *American Journal of International Law* 94; J.H. Jackson, 'The Linkage Problem – Comments on Five Texts' (2002) 96 *American Journal of International Law* 118; D.W. Leebron, 'Linkages' (2002) 96 *American Journal of International Law* 5; K.Bagwell, P.C. Mavroidis, R.W. Staiger, 'It's a Question of Market Access' (2002) 96 *American Journal of International Law* 56; D.P. Steger, 'The "Trade and ... " Conundrum – A Commentary' (2002) 96 *American Journal of International Law* 135; J.P. Trachtman, 'Institutional Linkage: Transcending "Trade and ..." ' (2002) 96 *American Journal of International Law* 77.

[5] Cass, n. 4, p. 41.

[6] James Tully, for example, surveys the response of political philosophers reflecting on principles of legitimacy of constitutional democracy in light of what he characterizes as the rapid change in constitutions at the 'local, national, supranational, regional, and global' levels: J. Tully, 'The Unfreedom of the Moderns in Comparison to their Ideals of Constitutional Democracy' (2002) 65 *Modern Law Review* 204, p. 204.

[7] *Ibid.*

means for international trade regulation. This chapter may also be viewed in the context of the so-called 'trade and ... ' or 'linkages' debate which has ranged over the relationship between trade and rights, trade and the environment, trade and social policies, and trade and health.[8] Each area raises similar issues central to the nature of international trade regulation and the place of trade regulation in the wider scheme of international institutions, norms, and agreements.

The chapter starts with what can be learnt about the relationship between rights and trade from China's accession process. In particular, consideration is given to the market forces at play during the Sino–US bilateral accession negotiations. What were the positions, for example, taken by different sectors within US industry toward China's accession? What was the attitude toward the issue of rights taken by the pro- and anti-accession lobbies? At this point it should be noted that it is *not* the intention to investigate the legitimacy or otherwise of concerns regarding China's human rights record. This chapter is merely intended to consider the approaches sectors of the political economy took regarding rights during the Sino–US accession negotiations.

The next section of this chapter focuses on the work of Ernst-Ulrich Petersmann as representing the most comprehensive theoretical argument for the full realization of rights in an integrated international economic order. Two aspects of Petersmann's theory are highlighted. First, Petersmann's early work reflected a time when scholars and practitioners interested in the operation of the GATT, and the international economic order in general, were looking for ways to encourage protectionist inclined states to adopt domestic constitutional and foreign trade-related policies suitable to the maximization of economic theories of comparative advantage and economies of scale. However, it is interesting to query how far Petersmann's later work shifts the focus from this principal concern of early trade law scholarship.

The second aspect of Petersmann's theory to be considered is the progression in his writings towards a cosmopolitan international economic order. This aspect of Petersmann's work displays a steady move away from early state-centered GATT scholarship. While commencing with an integrated economic order based on the constitutionalization of free trade rights in domestic constitutions, Petersmann ends at a normative international economic order less reliant on Member States for its direction.

The concluding part of this chapter focuses on what the Sino–US accession negotiations may mean for proposals to integrate rights into the WTO. It ends with the suggestion that any proposal for the integration of rights

[8] A selection of literature from the 'linkage' debate includes: Jan McDonald, 'It's Not Easy Being Green – Trade and Environment Linkages Beyond Doha', Chapter Seven of this volume; S. Charnovitz, 'Rethinking WTO Trade Sanctions' (2001) 95 *American Journal of International Law* 792; F.J. Garcia, 'Global Trade Issues in the New Millenium: Building a Just Trade Order for a New Millenium' (2001) 33 *Geo. Wash. Int'l. Rev.* 1015; H. Lim, 'Trade and Human Rights: What's at Issue?' (2001) 35 *Journal of World Trade* 275; G. Marceau, 'WTO Dispute Settlement and Human Rights' (2002) 13 *European Journal of International Law* 753; I. Sandford, 'Hormonal imbalance? Balancing free trade and SPS measures after the decision in Hormones' (1999) 29 *Victoria University of Wellington Law Review* 389; R. Howse and M.J. Trebilcock, 'The Fair Trade – Free Trade Debate: Trade, Labour and the Environment' (1996) 16 *International Review of Law and Economics* 61.

and trade would benefit from the accommodation of the reality of the political economy and what use may be made of the linkage between trade and rights, as evidenced during China's accession negotiations. Arguably, any reform process should be open to input from *all* the WTO membership on whether, and how, this should be done.

8.2 The Role of Rights in China's Accession Negotiations

China was one of the 23 original contracting parties of the GATT. In December 1946 the Chinese Nationalist Government was invited to participate in tariff concession negotiations. In October 1947 the Nationalist Government signed the GATT, followed by the signing in April 1948 of the Protocol of the Provisional Application of the GATT. After the establishment of the People's Republic of China in 1949, the Nationalists on Taiwan unilaterally declared the Chinese withdrawal from the GATT in 1950.

The PRC commenced formal moves to resume its membership of the GATT in 1986. The delay in seeking resumption of membership was due to a combination of factors: non-recognition by Western countries; 10 years of the Cultural Revolution; economic underdevelopment; and a simple lack of knowledge about the GATT and the opportunities it offered. A number of issues delayed the resumption of membership following formal application in 1986. They included: economic and trade issues (transparency; uniformity; high tariff levels; a high level of non-tariff barriers; China's developing country status; the application of WTO rules to formerly centrally planned economies; coming to terms with the expected competition from China as it affected import-competing firms and third-country competing suppliers, especially of textiles and clothing; negotiations over the extent and conditions of market access into China); legal factors (prevalence of policies rather than laws; GATT-inconsistent laws and policies; lack of independent judicial review); political factors (the political unrest in 1989; Tibet; Taiwan); and poor bilateral trade relations with the United States (trade deficit; anti-dumping measures; IP protection; forced labour products).

Weighed against these many factors was the growing empirical evidence of the positive economic effects of China's accession to the WTO. At the time of the accession negotiations economists were predicting that the PRC and Taiwans' accession to the WTO would accentuate many of the beneficial effects of the Uruguay Round.[9] This included boosts to the estimated

9 K. Anderson, 'On the Complexities of China's WTO Accession' (1997) 20 *The World Economy* 749. According to Yang at the time, 'the economics of China's WTO accession seem to be unambiguous': Y. Yang, 'China's WTO accession: Why has it taken so long?' Asia Pacific School of Economics and Management, Working Papers, CEPOO-2, Asia Pacific Press 2000, p. 10. *See* also Y. Yang, 'China's WTO Membership: What's at Stake?' (1996) 19 *The World Economy* 661; Y. Yang, 'Completing the WTO Accession Negotiations: Issues and Challenges' (1999) 22 *The World Economy* 513. Yang estimated the benefits for China would include: greater consumer choice, industry expansion, more efficient use of resources, increased skills in the service industries, greater transparency in the trade regime, reduction of corruption, increased access to overseas markets: Yang, 2000, *Ibid.*, pp. 10–12.

global welfare gain from the Round by 40 per cent. It was estimated that China's trading partners would receive more than half of that extra gain. On the other hand, if China did not join the WTO and the impetus for economic reform in China slowed this would adversely affect not only China's economy but also the economies of its trading partners and even its competitors.[10]

Given that economists perceived economic benefits for both China and its trading partners, it is interesting to look in more detail at some of the stumbling blocks to China's WTO accession. A particular concern of certain sectors in advanced economies and in other developing countries was the prospect of competing with China, especially in textiles. During the Uruguay Round advanced economies had agreed to gradually expand textile and clothing import quotas for WTO members over the period to 2005 and then replace the MFA with a tariff-only regime. The expectation during China's accession negotiations was that China would also be expecting greater access upon entry to the WTO. China's accession would, it was envisaged, increase the structural adjustment pressures on declining industries in advanced economies, while at the same time reducing the quota rents to other developing economy suppliers. Hence, as Kym Anderson observed, 'it is understandable that they oppose their government's efforts to get China into the WTO, arguing that China is an "unfair" competitor because its state-owned enterprises are often subsidised'.[11]

Anderson argued that the answer was to give China's trading partners greater assurances of access to China's market 'to compensate for the loss of political support from these adversely affected groups'.[12] This is a pragmatic spin on the conventional economic position that multilateral trading rules can help governments ward off domestic interest groups seeking special favours, sometimes referred to as the 'Ulysses effect' – it helped prevent governments from being tempted to favour certain sectors at the expense of the rest of the economy. On the other side of the coin, Yang concludes that without the phase-in periods evident in the Sino–US agreement on accession the domestic political resistance in China to accession would have been much stronger.[13]

We can see the underlying forces of the political economy at work in the Sino–US accession negotiations. On 15 November 1999 the United States reached an agreement with the PRC both to support the PRC's accession to the WTO and to begin the process of establishing permanent normal trade relations with the PRC. President Clinton subsequently recommended in

---

10 Anderson, n. 9, pp. 760–763. This was consistent with standard economic theory whereby most gains from liberalization are to the liberalizing country, although trading partners also gain from increased market access: C.F. Bach, W. Martin, and J. Stevens, 'China and the WTO: Tariff Offers, Exemptions, and Welfare Implications' (1996) 132 *Weltwirtschaftliches Archiv* 409.

11 Anderson, n. 9, p. 765. Although Yang points out that it will take China many years before it moves into capital and skill intensive goods at a scale that would threaten the dominance of industrial countries in these industries: Yang, 2000, n. 9, p. 13.

12 *Ibid.*

13 Yang, 2000, n. 9, p. 7. Although, as Yang notes, 'the danger of this approach is, of course, that implementation could be delayed if political resistance grows': *Ibid.*

March 2000 that Congress enact legislation granting permanent normal trade relations (PNTR) status to the PRC.[14] On 10 October 2000 President Clinton signed the legislation into law after considerable debate in both houses of parliament.

The Sino–US agreement eventuated only after considerable delays in the negotiation process. Yang Yongzheng examined the approaches of sectors within the US economy to the issue of China's accession to the WTO.[15] Yang observed that the delay in concluding Sino–US agreement on Chinese accession was due, partly, to the influence of interest groups in the 'political economy'.[16] The influence of anti-accession sectors of the US economy, said Yang, helped undermine the signing of the agreement earlier, in April 1999.[17] According to Yang, labour-intensive industries in the United States, such as the textiles sector, were most opposed to China's WTO accession.[18] On the other hand, industries that saw direct benefits from China's WTO accession, such as US hi-tech industries (e.g. aircraft manufacturing), generally supported China's accession.[19] Different approaches toward China's accession also existed within sectors, such as the aerospace industry.[20]

The difference between the stance of the pro-accession and anti-accession lobby groups within the United States during the accession negotiations and the PNTR debate was pronounced. Pro-accession lobby groups, such as the United States–China Business Council, lobbied on the platform that accession and PNTR would improve human rights in China by suppressing conservative economic and political forces (in the form of state-owned enterprises), creating a new entrepreneurial class that would support new economic and political freedoms, liberalizing access to the internet and telecommunications, establishing procedures for judicial review of trade measures, and by sharing American values through 'islands of freedom', that is, joint ventures.[21]

Compare this position to that taken by anti-PNTR lobby groups before the House Committee on Ways and Means, Hearing on Accession of China to the

---

14 Message to the Congress on Permanent Normal Trade Relations Status for China, 36 WeeklyComp. Pres. Doc. 493, 493–94 (13 March 2000). For a detailed account *see*: Sean D. Murphy, 'Contemporary Practice of the United States' (2000) 94 *American Journal of International Law* 373.

15 Yang, 2000, n. 9, pp. 13–14.

16 *Ibid.*, p. 13.

17 *Ibid.*, p. 14. Yang goes so far as to claim that tactics employed by anti-China sectors of United States industry against imports from China in the past included 'allegations of illegal transhipment and customs fraud by Chinese exporters and exports of products made by prisoners and the People's Liberation Army (PLA)': *Ibid.*, p. 13. Yang believes that this campaign was joined by human rights groups and traditionally climaxed each year before the US Congress votes on renewal of China's MFN status: *Ibid.*, p. 13.

18 *Ibid.*, p. 13.

19 *Ibid.*

20 Consider the different attitudes among companies, and between manufacturers and unions, in the aerospace industry evident from the statements of unions during the debate over extending PNTR to the PRC: Reuther, 2000, n. 22.

21 'Questions and Answers: US–China WTO Agreement', 1 December 1999; 'PNTR: Advancing American Values', 26 April 2000; 'The Case for Permanent Normal Trade Relations with China', 6 September 2000.

WTO, 3 May 2000. They argued that the Sino–US accession agreement failed to sufficiently protect American workers employed in various manufacturing industries. For example, they said the agreement failed to protect American workers in industries such as the aerospace industry where 'offset' deals between Chinese and American companies had resulted in the transfer of technology (and production) to China in return for market access. In regard to human rights, the UAW stated that it was 'distressed by the total silence of the WTO accession agreement on issues relating to worker and human rights'.[22] It went on:

> Child labor, prison labor, repression of independent unions, the lengthy imprisonment of independent union activists are all too common occurrences in China. In our judgment, trade and investment that takes place under these conditions cannot be considered as 'fair'. The fact that many American companies have invested in China to take advantage of these conditions, and that the massive U.S. trade deficit with China is fed by these injustices, makes the exclusion of worker rights issues from the WTO accession agreement all the more abhorrent.[23]

Without remarking on the veracity of the claims of either the pro-accession/PNTR or anti-accession/PNTR lobbies within US industry, it is clear that industry groups are willing to use the issue of rights in another country as a tool in obtaining their own trade objectives. The next section of this chapter looks at approaches to the integration of rights and trade, particularly that of Ernst-Ulrich Petersmann. To what extent does his theory take account of the potential use of the link between trade and human rights for protectionist purposes? To what extent does his theory allow for input from those in the WTO membership who may reasonably apprehend this occurring?

8.3 Theory Linking Trade and Rights

A growing number of scholars argue that the lack of formal recognition given to the importance and priority of rights is a flaw in the multilateral trading system. On the other hand, there are concerns that proposals to integrate rights, and other 'non-trade' subjects, with trade regulation contributed to the derailment of the WTO Third Ministerial Conference in Seattle in late 1999, posed problems for the Fourth Ministerial Conference in Doha, Qatar, in November of 2001, and threatened to undermine the function of the WTO itself.[24]

---

22 Statement of Alan Reuther, Legislative Director, International Union, United Automobile, Aerospace and Agricultural Implement Workers of America (UAW), Testimony Before the House Committee on Ways and Means, Hearing on Accession of China to the WTO, 3 May 2000, p. 4.

23 *Ibid.*, p. 5.

24 John Jackson notes the importance of this debate in the context of the future operation of the WTO: Jackson, 2002, *Supra* n. 4 p.118. *See* also J.H. Jackson, 'The WTO "Constitution" and Proposed Reforms: Seven "Mantras" Revisited' (2001) 4 *Journal of International Economic Law* 67.

The discussion is wide-ranging. The general academic interest in reflecting on the nature of all levels of governance, together with the nature of rights themselves, and the malleability of many of the terms employed, mean that scholars involved in this discussion analyse international trade at the institutional level, but also at deeper structural, political, and symbolic levels. So merely repeating the mechanics of proposals for institutional reform by, for example, focusing on GATT 1994 Article XX, risks missing much of the deeper nuance in the debate. It is at the deeper level that this chapter is focused.

Discussion in this section concentrates on the work of Ernst-Ulrich Petersmann because of the comprehensive nature of his theory and because it continues to provoke thoughtful and interesting debate on this issue.[25] Petersmann's theory also provides a useful counterpoint to other approaches, as well as acting as a guide to the different trends that have emerged in the literature in relation to reform of the international economic order since he began to widely expound his ideas in the 1980s. A very brief overview of his theory follows.

Petersmann's early work revolved around developing an integrated constitutional solution to what he saw as the 'government failure' inherent in protectionist trade policies.[26] Writing in the mid-1980s, Petersmann posed what he considered to be a number of important questions regarding trade policy as a constitutional problem. In particular, he asked to what extent 'constitutional techniques' of national law – in which he included the recognition of individual rights, principles of equal and non-discriminatory treatment, limited delegation of powers, procedural requirements for transparent policymaking, and judicial review – could be used to ensure due process in decision-making about trade. Petersmann voiced this question in the context

---

[25] A principal exchange in this debate takes place between Petersmann and his critics in 13 *European Journal of International Law*: E.U. Petersmann, 'Time for a United Nations 'Global Compact' for Integrating Human Rights into the Law of Worldwide Organizations: Lessons from European Integration' (2002) 13 *European Journal of International Law* 621; R. Howse, 'Human Rights in the WTO, Whose Rights, What Humanity? Comment on Petersmann' (2002) 13 *European Journal of International Law* 651; P. Alston, 'Resisting the Merger and Acquisition of Human Rights by Trade Law: A Reply to Petersmann' (2002) 13 *European Journal of International Law* 815; E.U. Petersmann, 'Taking Human Dignity, Poverty and Empowerment of Individuals More Seriously: Rejoinder to Alston' (2002) 13 *European Journal of International Law* 845. This debate is supplemented by a more comprehensive record of the exchange at the *European Journal of International Law* website and Petersmann's longer response to his critics in E.U. Petersmann, 'Time for Integrating Human Rights into the Worldwide Organizations' Jean Monnet Working Paper 7/2001, Harvard Law School. Given it is the more comprehensive version, I rely more on Petersmann's paper published as part of the Jean Monnet series rather than his rejoinder found in the *European Journal of International Law*.

[26] E.U. Petersmann, *Constitutional Functions and Constitutional Problems of International Economic Law* (University Press of Fribourg, Switzerland, 1991), pp. 6, 26, and Chapters V and VI. Petersmann has developed his theory through a long line of writings on the topic. I have relied principally upon: E.U. Petersmann, 'International Trade Order and International Trade Law', in T. Oppermann and E.U. Petersmann (eds), *Reforming the International Economic Order: German legal comments* (Duncker and Humblot, Berlin, 1987); E.U. Petersmann, *Constitutional Functions and Constitutional Problems of International Economic Law* (University Press of Fribourg, Switzerland, 1991); E.U. Petersmann, 'National Constitutions and International Economic Law', in M. Hilf and E.U. Petersmann (eds), *National Constitutions and International Economic Law* (Kluwer Law and Taxation Publishers, Deventer, 1993); Petersmann, 2002, p. 621, n. 25; Petersmann, 2001, n. 25.

of his concerns that states should be encouraged to move from protectionist trade policies to liberal, non-discriminatory ones.[27] In essence, Petersmann was searching for a normative constitutional principle to support what he saw as the economic sense of trade liberalization as a means of making better use of domestic resources in the national interest.

Reform of the international trade system to take greater advantage of the economic theories of comparative advantage and economies of scale had been a basic goal of international trade scholars since the Bretton Woods Conference at the end of the Second World War. The issue for scholars and practitioners was how to make more effective the policies leading towards this aim.[28] At the time Petersmann began systematically expounding his theory the drive toward this goal had been given added impetus by the international debt crisis and the dangers of the 'new protectionism' in the 1980s. While other scholars were also seeking ways to ensure meaningful international and domestic reform, Petersmann differed from many of his colleagues in the way he infused the basis of the economic theory underlying the GATT with strong notions of individual rights and freedoms.

His starting point was Hayek's notion of the individual's desire to maximize his or her wealth.[29] Central to Petersmann's idea of rights was the protection of property rights that in his view went hand in hand with the individual's search for more utility. As the purpose of trade according to Petersmann 'is to exchange property rights relating to the goods and services that are exchanged', trade liberalization needed a regime that could guarantee such rights.[30]

Petersmann's ideal regime rested on the notion of an integrated liberal constitutionalism. The law of the 'international economic order', according to Petersmann, was a three-tiered regulatory structure on the levels of private law, national public law, and international public law.[31] The idea of a strong link between international law and national constitutional systems was not a new proposition in international trade scholarship when Petersmann was first systematically expounding his theory.[32] What was novel in Petersmann's account was his representation of this linkage as the potential expression of a cosmopolitan liberal normative order based on individual rights and freedoms.

---

27 Petersmann, 1987, n. 26, pp. 201–209, 233. Petersmann thought government failure to translate into practice the liberal GATT rules was due less to a lack of appropriate international rules than to deficiencies in domestic and regional trade laws.

28 J.H. Jackson, 'National Constitutions, Transnational Economic Policy and International Law: Some Summary Reflections', in M. Hilf and E.U. Petersmann (eds), *National Constitutions and International Economic Law* (Kluwer Law and Taxation Publishers, Deventer, 1993), p. 571.

29 Petersmann, 1991, n. 26, Chapter I. According to John Jackson, Petersmann 'emphasizes that the "constitutional value" of a constitutional guarantee of freedom of trade does not derive from trade or economic theory, but from individual liberty as a constitutional value and from the need to protect transnational exercises of individual liberty no less than purely *domestic* freedoms ... ': Jackson, n. 28, p. 574. Robert Howse, on the other hand, argues that Petersmann's theory is an extension of the 'embedded liberalism' in the GATT: Howse, nn. 61–66.

30 *Ibid.*, pp. 8–9, 29–30.

31 *Ibid.*, p. 53.

32 By the early 1990s the inter-linkage between international law and national constitutional law in the area of international trade was a generally accepted proposition among international

Petersmann believed that because the purpose of this integrated law was the reconciliation of individual freedoms its rules were applicable to private citizens, as Kant had emphasized in his essay 'Towards eternal peace'.[33] Individual freedom was coupled with the basic elements of Rawlsian 'justice' – the distribution of rights and duties and, especially in Petersmann's opinion, the distribution of scarce resources. Petersmann, therefore, didn't see any contradictions in concluding that 'a pluralistic international economic order must be based on liberal principles'.[34]

In Petersmann's opinion, the principles of the GATT (where Petersmann was a legal officer in the early 1980s) provided states with the appropriate constitutional principles to avoid conflicts among themselves and as a means of 'escaping the siren-like pressure groups within their countries'.[35] As alluded to earlier, Petersmann here was grappling with what other scholars saw as the major obstacles to the proper realisation of trade liberalization principles: national political and legal structures. Petersmann departed from conventional thinking by asserting that properly constituted, these negative trade-related restrictions could – and should – become positive substantive individual rights and freedoms in domestic systems.[36] And so, for instance, Petersmann wrote:

> [T]he principles of non-discriminatory foreign trade competition have "constitutional functions" not only for an international trading system that is capable of securing compatibility and mutual profitability of investment decisions in all participating countries, but also for the domestic foreign trade laws and national trade administrations of countries. By providing precise and justiciable standards for the proper delegation of discretionary trade policy powers to the executive branch and by enabling an effective parliamentary and judicial control of their exercise, they can serve as a "second line of constitutional entrenchment" (*J. Tumlir*) of national foreign trade laws and individuals rights.[37]

Despite his integrated vision of the international economic order, Petersmann recognised in his earlier work that it was still states that must confirm these overarching constitutional principles in domestic laws. He was of the opinion that a working international economic order was dependent on the 'constitutionalization' of the domestic system of trading countries.[38] States were therefore preserved in Petersmann's theory as instruments of a cosmopolitan

---

Contd.
trade scholars: Jackson, n. 28, p. 570. So for example, the inter-linkage between national and international systems was one of the central themes in J.H. Jackson, *The World Trading System: Law and Policy of International Economic Relations* (The MIT Press, Cambridge, Massachusetts, 1989).

33 Petersmann, 1991, n. 26, p. 62.

34 *Ibid.*, pp. 69, 85–86.

35 *Ibid.*, pp. 221, 222–244. Petersmann also includes the constitutional functions of the liberal monetary and financial rules in his integrated constitutional structure: *Ibid.*, pp. 245–279.

36 Petersmann, 1993, n. 26, pp. 25–28.

37 Petersmann thought government failure to translate into practice the liberal GATT rules was due less to a lack of appropriate international rules than to deficiencies in domestic and regional trade laws: Petersmann, 1987, n. 26, p. 236.

38 Petersmann, 1991, n. 26, p. 279, Chapter VIII.

liberal eco-political order. Necessarily, he refuted what he saw as the traditional liberal notion that rule of law and democracy were incompatible with foreign policy. The warring states model, according to Petersmann, was no longer adequate for the modern 'age of integration'.[39] His approach in this regard reflected the widely held view of scholars and practitioners working to reform the international economic order in the early 1990s that the international trade system must be based on rules rather than power.[40]

Later, Petersmann would observe that the 'age of integration' was characterized by the 'increasing *transnational* exercise of individual rights by domestic citizens and by the increasing regulation of their transnational freedoms and property rights through international agreements'.[41] Petersmann considered that the EC model illustrated that far-reaching constitutional reforms of the basic rules of society (what he called its 'material constitution') could be brought about without amendment of the formal written constitution of Member States. What was required, he said, was an adjustment of constitutional traditions and concepts to modern international integration.[42]

However, Petersmann at that time was reasonably sceptical of the ability of the GATT or regional models to give effect to the constitutionalization of international trade principles and rights. As a result, Petersmann argued that 'the most effective and most democratic means of constitutionalizing discretionary trade policy powers is to incorporate international trade prohibitions of trade barriers into domestic laws and to enable private traders, producers, and consumers to enforce these rules through domestic courts'.[43] Central to this process was the integration of the principles of the GATT with existing national measures to establish enforceable individual freedoms and property rights of domestic citizens across frontiers. At the same time, Petersmann argued that a rights-based approach was one of the main reasons for the success of European integration.[44] Petersmann particularly focused on what he saw as the fundamental right of freedom of trade that was embedded in the EEC Treaty, the foreign regulations adopted by the EC Council, and the judgments of the EC Court of Justice. Although he also recognized this right was not unlimited.[45]

At this stage in Petersmann's theory it would appear that his principal aim was to integrate GATT principles into domestic legal systems as a buttress for existing individual rights and freedoms. In more recent work, Petersmann has turned his attention to the integration of human rights into what he calls 'the law of worldwide organizations', including the WTO.[46] This is not so great a shift in emphasis as might appear at first glance. Petersmann's underlying philosophical position has consistently been based on the Kantian notion of an overarching liberal norm of individual

---

39 *Ibid.*, pp. 288–292; Petersmann, 1993, n. 26, pp. 28–30, 291.
40 Jackson, n. 28, p. 572.
41 Petersmann, 1993, n. 26, p. 3.
42 *Ibid.*, p. 8.
43 *Ibid.*, p. 49.
44 *Ibid.*, p. 13.
45 *Ibid.*, pp. 18–25.
46 Petersmann, 2002, p. 621, n. 25; Petersmann, 2001, n. 25.

rights and freedoms. As stated, his stress on the role of domestic constitutions in his earlier work was primarily because he saw them as the most effective instruments for the implementation of this vision. However, implicit in his position was the understanding that international or regional organizations may also legitimately take up the task.

Petersmann has been encouraged in this endeavour by what he sees as indications of a new 'integration paradigm' evident in regional integration law, such as the use of 'human rights clauses' in the EU Treaty and in the EU's Cotonou Agreement with African, Caribbean, and Pacific states. Petersmann has argued that protection of human rights at the national, regional, and international level requires 'a new human rights culture and a citizen-oriented national and international constitutional framework different from the previously prevailing state-centered conceptions and functionalism'.[47] National constitutional law and human rights, says Petersmann, need to be supplemented by international constitutional law and 'by effective protection of human rights in the economy no less than in the polity'.[48]

The European experience of 'multi-level governance', says Petersmann, has given rise to 'multi-level constitutionalism', including a separation of powers. This has, in Petersmann's words, 'succeeded in overcoming Europe's history of periodic wars and of "constitutional failures" of nation states to protect human rights and peaceful division of labor across frontiers'.[49] Petersmann's account of the role of governance in overcoming political and economic conflict in Europe is influenced by the general structure of Kant's own work.[50]

Anthony Pagden highlights what he sees as the link between modern notions of governance and Kant's notion of a cosmopolitan right (*ius cosmopoliticum*).[51] Kant employed the notion of *ius cosmopoliticum* as part of a moral, political, and legal theory aimed at offering a solution to the conflicts between European states in the sixteenth and seventeenth centuries. Kant's intention, it would seem, was to model a new world order on an overarching moral imperative (rather than a 'world government', as is sometimes claimed). This may explain, to a certain extent, the strongly teleological (and European) nature of Petersmann's own 'categorical imperative'.

Unlike Kant, however, Petersmann has the modern experiences of European political and economic integration to refer to as a counterweight to his normative project. His favourable account of the European integration of rights into political and economic discourse within the membership

---

47 Petersmann, 2001, n. 25, p. 45.

48 *Ibid.*

49 *Ibid.* Deborah Cass notes that recent international relations studies also view the changes in the WTO as the development of a system of governance: Cass, n. 4, p. 40.

50 Although Petersmann's specific reading of Kant has been called into question. Robert Howse, for example, agrees with Petersmann that 'free trade and human rights are both the intellectual progeny of the Enlightenment' (as represented by Petersmann in the figure of Kant), but adds that Kant realised 'the connection of the commercial spirit of his age not only with democratic republicanism but also with horrific imperialistic violence': Howse, 2002, n. 25, p. 652.

51 Many modern accounts of 'governance', Anthony Pagden notes, argue for a world governed, not by governments, but by government. Pagden traces these accounts to Kant's notion of *ius cosmopoliticum*, arguing that they are teleological accounts grounded in a European

and also as a principle of the European Union's foreign policy is not without controversy.[52] According to Petersmann:

> European integration confirms the insight of 'functional theories', namely, that citizen-driven market integration can provide strong incentives for transforming 'market freedoms' into 'fundamental rights' which – if directly enforceable by producers, investors, workers, traders and consumers through courts (as in the EC) – can reinforce and extend the protection of basic human rights (e.g. to liberty, property, food and health).[53]

He seeks to ground this order in 'a moral "categorical imperative" of maximising personal autonomy and equal liberties across frontiers'.[54] Petersmann espouses his market-oriented ideal partially at the expense of the Covenant on Economic, Social and Cultural Rights, which he sees as an incident of anti-market bias. He sees reduced scope for the usefulness of the Covenant as a benchmark for a rights-based market economy in WTO dispute settlement practice. It is not surprising, then, that Petersmann also distinguishes the current drive toward a 'Global Human Rights Compact' in the United Nations from earlier UN recommendations to reform the international economic order (e.g. the Charter of Economic Rights and Duties of States). He considers these earlier recommendations to share the same anti-market bias as the ICESCR.[55]

At the institutional level, Petersmann calls for the integration of human rights into the WTO via the 'legal and judicial balancing processes' available in the general exception provisions in WTO law (e.g. GATT 1994 Article XX), and in the interpretation of 'basic WTO guarantees of freedom, non-discrimination, property rights and the rule of law'.[56] Petersmann argues for the integration of 'participatory' rights of individuals into regional and international organizations 'so as to enable, for example, "UN citizens" and "WTO citizens" to invoke international guarantees of freedom before domestic courts and to participate more actively in parliamentary and civil society institutions at national and international levels'.[57]

The emergence of deliberative democratic principles in Petersmann's later writings may be a response to criticisms that alluded to the undemocratic

---

Contd.
notion of the political good: A. Pagden, 'The genesis of "governance" and Enlightenment conceptions of the cosmopolitan world order' (1998) 50 *International Social Science Journal* 7.

52 *See*, for example, the criticisms put forward on this point in Alston, 2002, n. 25. Alston argues: 'Human rights were, on virtually all accounts of the evolution of European integration through the common market, an afterthought. They were not mentioned at all in the Treaty of Rome of 1957, which specifically eschewed the strategy of its failed forerunner, the proposed European Political Community, that would have incorporated the ECHR. Even when limited human rights provisions were included in the Treaty on European Union they were far from reflecting an integrated human rights vision for the Community' (citations omitted): *Ibid.*, p. 821.

53 Petersmann, 2002, n. 25, p. 629.

54 *Ibid.*, p. 630.

55 Contrasting the anti-market bias of earlier UN recommendations for a 'New International Economic Order' with the UN Secretary-General's report on Globalization and its Impact on the Full Enjoyment of All Human Rights: *Ibid.*, pp. 628–629, 641.

56 *Ibid.*, p. 645.

57 *Ibid.*, p. 650.

appearance of using national legal systems to reinforce an international liberal approach to trade. According to Jackson, '[i]t is placing in the constitution a rule which may not suit democratic constituencies over a long period of time. It advances liberal trade by imposing this approach as a matter of constitutional law, rather than by persuading the democratic constituencies of the correctness of the approach …'[58] Petersmann's answer – to stress democratic participation at the regional and international levels – fits well with his underlying cosmopolitan philosophy.

Petersmann's work in this respect shadows what Richard Falk recently described as 'the multifaceted focus on democracy – as project, as norm, and as the foundation of present and future world order' that has strongly emerged since the early 1990s in the work of Thomas Franck, David Held, Susan Marks, Fernando Tesón, and Richard Falk himself.[59] Advocates for this movement also see their work as falling under the philosophical rubric of Kantian cosmopolitanism.[60]

Petersmann is not alone in the importance he places on principles of deliberative democracy in regional and international economic organizations. Robert Howse would go further.[61] Howse's answer to the issue whether rights should be integrated into the WTO, and how, is to force the 'insiders' in the WTO, who have been in the grip of 'embedded liberalism' to open up the WTO to the 'outsiders'. He contrasts this with a new order of distributive justice and deliberative democracy. As Howse admits, precisely because the process for answering these questions will be deliberative, what the result will be is unclear.[62]

Howse identifies 'embedded liberalism' with the economics of the GATT, and the economics with ideology – an ideology of free trade.[63] In Howse's view, Petersmann's theory represents a new form of this 'embedded liberalism'. His main criticism of Petersmann's theory is that it merely finds, in Howse's view, a new justification for the ideology of free trade – this time as a 'right'. But Howse considers that Petersmann's theory is unclear on whether the trading system has the legitimacy to strike the balance between

---

58 Jackson, n. 28, p. 575.

59 R. Falk, Book Review: The Riddle of All Constitutions: International Law, Democracy, and the Critique of Ideology: by Susan Marks (2002) 96 *American Journal of International Law* 264. *See* also: T.M. Franck,'The Emerging Right to Democratic Governance' (1992) 86 *American Journal of International Law* 46; T.M. Franck, *Fairness in International Law and Institutions* (Clarendon Press, Oxford, 1995); D. Held, *Democracy and the Global Order: From the Modern State to Cosmopolitan Governance* (Stanford University Press, Stanford, 1995); S. Marks, *The Riddle of All Constitutions: International Law, Democracy and the Critique of Ideology* (Oxford University Press, Oxford, 2000); F.R. Tesón, *A Philosophy of International Law* (Westview Press, Boulder, CO, 1998); R. Falk, *On Humane Governance: Toward a New Global Politics* (Polity Press, Oxford, 1995); R. Falk, *Law in An Emerging Global Village: A Post-Westphalian Perspective* (Transnational Publishers, Ardsley, New York, 1998).

60 David Held, for instance, argues for a form of cosmopolitan democratic law which Kant – 'the foremost interpreter of the idea of a cosmopolitan law' – believed was required to transform national and international law into a 'public law of humanity': Held, n. 59, p. 227.

61 Howse, n. 4, p. 105.

62 *Ibid.*, p. 117.

63 *Ibid.*, p. 99.

trade and non-trade rights.[64] Howse instead talks of 'transnational democratic deliberation' which is 'not above, or autonomous from, deliberation within domestic polities, but deeply intertwined with the domestic and the local'.[65] At the heart of Howse's approach is the idea that human rights are just politics – albeit, 'a new, legitimate transnational politics'.[66]

Other calls for democratic legitimacy within the WTO tend to focus on the participation of civil society in the WTO dispute settlement or policy-making processes.[67] The more inclusive view of 'outsider' participation in the WTO is a natural consequence of the claim that deliberative democracy attaches to the individual, not the State, and seeks to guarantee direct participatory rights of individuals at the national, regional, and international level. The idea that disputes under the GATT/WTO belong to governments, according to Joseph Weiler, represents what he calls the 'classical Government-is-the-State fallacy' in which 'international law and international organizations condition a belief in the equation of the State with its Government'.[68]

Petersmann's and Howse's respective approaches are far removed from Thomas Oppermann's description of the basic model of the then international economic order *circa* 1987, namely, 'the voluntary, binding, agreed decisions of states – even if these are occasionally predetermined by a certain degree of economic or political compulsion.'[69] According to Oppermann at that time, 'the treaty remains the primary, if not the only formative instrument *vis-à-vis* the economic cooperation and integration within the world regions.'[70]

This traditional perception lives on. Debra Steger, former Director, Appellate Body Secretariat, for example, draws a distinction between the participatory scope of the WTO and the linkage between norms within the agreements. She writes:

> Rewriting the rules, reestablishing the intricate balance between the principles of nondiscrimination and the general exceptions, is a task that only the governments, the members of the WTO, can legitimately perform.
>
> Some "trade and ..." conundrums, I would argue, can be resolved only by the membership. The pressing ones, I believe, relate to the "other" areas of human rights and labor rights, in particular ...

---

64 *Ibid.*, p.105.

65 *Ibid.*, p. 117.

66 *Ibid.*

67 S. Charnovitz, 'Participation of Nongovernmental Organizations in the World Trade Organization' (1996) 17 *U. Pa. J. Int'l Econ. L.* 331 (arguing for rights of participation of NGOs in WTO policy development and decision making); D.C. Esty, 'Linkages and Governance: NGOs at the World Trade Organization' (1998) 19 *U. Pa. J. Int'l Econ. L.* 709 (arguing that inclusion of NGOs in the WTO will enhance the legitimacy, authority and effectiveness of the organization).

68 J.H.H. Weiler, 'The Rule of Lawyers and the Ethos of Diplomats: Reflections on the Internal and External Legitimacy of WTO Dispute Settlement', Harvard Jean Monnet Working Paper 9/2000, p. 6. At the same time, Weiler acknowledges that to allow participation of NGOs (mostly Western) in the WTO will 'skew the system' even more than it is – noting the unequal access of private actors (notably multinationals) to governments: *Ibid.*

69 T. Oppermann, 'On the Present International Economic Order', in T. Oppermann and E.U. Petersmann (eds), *Reforming the International Economic Order: German Legal Comments* (Duncker and Humblot, Berlin, 1987), p. 194.

70 *Ibid.*

> I believe it is time to revise the paragraphs in Article XX to make them reflect present-day shared values and norms. A place to start would be to look to certain widely accepted international conventions on human rights and labor rights to identify certain fundamental values that all WTO members could agree should be contained in the list of general exceptions in Article XX.[71]

Steger places her emphasis on the equal participation of the WTO membership. One way of characterizing the different approaches of Steger and Petersmann could be to see them as different views of liberalism in international relations. The one stresses the equal participation of the individual in international affairs, the other (what Gerry Simpson refers to as 'Charter' liberalism[72]) stresses the equal footing of Sovereign States. Now is not the time to examine the accuracy of this depiction nor the merits of either of the two characterizations of the international system. Suffice it to say that there seems to be merit in engaging the State membership of the WTO in dialogue on the proper role of rights within the organization – at least while this *is* the membership of the WTO.

In concluding this part, it may be useful to draw out two observations concerning Petersmann's theory. An early focus of Petersmann's work – overcoming the protectionist policies of States – is assumed in his later work by his cosmopolitan project. Protectionism will, of course, be eradicated by the very existence of a rights-based order. An international order above the state provides the impetus and justification for non-discriminatory competition, not just an excuse for protectionism.

Although still an integrated transnational order, it no longer relies on the *primacy* of national constitutions or the states constituents of the international economic order for its implementation. Rather, it leans more towards new models of international governance also put forward by Robert Howse and other scholars more widely (Richard Falk, Susan Marks, David Held). In this respect, Petersmann's later work may appear on one reading to be less state-centered than his earlier work.

The strength of Petersmann's theory lies in the vividness of his cosmopolitan vision. However, in opposition, there may be the worry that such an approach necessarily tends to move away from the concerns of the WTO state membership. It is placing the international economic order in a normative zone which beckons it forward while, perhaps, not entering into reciprocal dialogue with those states who fear the linkage of trade and rights as an avenue for protectionist manoeuvres in the political economy.

8.4 Conclusion

Petersmann's original concerns, as expressed in his work in the mid-1980s and early 1990s, focused on seeking constitutional solutions to overcoming

---

71 Steger, n. 4, p. 144.

72 G. Simpson, 'Two Liberalisms' (2001) 12 *European Journal of International Law* 537.

the 'political market for protection' that in his opinion marked a distorting aspect of the political economy.[73] Later he would write that 'international economic law and practice cannot be understood without taking into account the political processes from which they result.'[74]

Ironically, an objection of some members of the WTO to the idea of the integration of rights into the WTO is precisely their potential misuse by other governments in the thralls of the political economy. The Sino–US accession negotiations indicate that sectors within an economy will tend to use the linkage between trade and rights to further their competitive objectives. It is suggested that visions of an integrated rights and trade regime should take into account the presence of this reality of the political economy.

Arguably, this cannot happen effectively unless proper consideration is given to the concerns of member economies of the WTO who may be targets of protectionism.[75] While individual participation in regional and international forums may be a laudable objective, due regard continues to need to be given to the importance of equal participation of the WTO membership in this dialogue. China, as a powerful developing country concerned with these issues, surely has a role to play in any dialogue on this issue.

Yang sees the 'potential longer-term benefits' of Chinese accession as including the 'more balanced treatment of environmental and social issues (such as labour standards) in future WTO rounds'.[76] Yang believes 'the deep division at the failed Seattle WTO meeting between developing and developed countries over the labour and environmental issues highlights the importance of China's participation in future WTO negotiations'.[77] In this respect, it is hoped that China can move beyond the standard line on the separation of rights and trade delivered by its government.[78] Already

---

73 Petersmann, 1987, n. 26, p. 209. Trade protectionism, said Petersmann, is an incident of what he termed 'government failure', ie government decision-making on the basis of maximizing political support and minimising political opposition, including via the shielding of inefficient industries to gain political support: *Ibid.*, p. 207.

74 Petersmann, 1991, n. 26, p. XXVIII. According to Petersmann, 'Neoclassical economics and traditional legal analyses have for a long time ignored the political constraints of economic and legal policies. These analyses have then often produced economic and legal policy recommendations which – because they were based upon the politically unrealistic assumption of "benevolent, omnipotent governments" seeking "public goods" presumed to exist independently of the individual freedom to express one's individual preferences – promoted at best support for liberal trade and for rule of law without addressing the underlying "constitutional problems" and the political hindrances for the actual implementation of liberal policies': *Ibid.*, p. XXVIII.

75 Kai Chang, for instance, refers to 'several factors [that] have led to the claim for "social clauses" by Western countries'. These include: weakening the comparative advantage of developing countries; labour organisations concerned with the effects of globalization on labour standards worldwide; and a desire to change the political structure of developing countries: K. Chang, 'WTO, Labour Standard and Labour Interests Safeguard' (*WTO, Lao Gong Biao Zhun Yu Lao Gong Quan Yi Bao Hu*) (2002) 1. *China Social Science* (*Zhou Guo She Hui Ke Xue*) pp. 126, 129.

76 Yang, 2000, n. 9, p. 19.

77 *Ibid.*

78 Zhu Bangzao, Spokesman of the Foreign Affairs Department, On China's accession to WTO and the Human Rights Issue <http://www.ahetc.gov.cn/wto/luentan/21-15.htm> (accessed 1 November 2002). Further general and academic comment reinforcing the government's position can be found in: B. Duan, 'The Entry of WTO and the Construction of the Democratic Political System' (*Jia Ru Shi Mao Zu Zhi Yu Jian She Min Zhu Zheng Zhi*) (2002) The

there are indications that dialogue within China on labour standards, for example, is looking forward to a time when such standards are integrated into the international trade regime.[79]

Recalling images of flaws, illusions, unwholesome realities, and Madame Wang that, perhaps strangely, commenced this chapter, it may be a good place to end with a more down to earth passage written by Thomas Oppermann in the mid-1980s:

> The disillusionment phase should act as a starting point for a renewed search in a spirit of improved mutual understanding, for the many compromises, big and small, which are necessary for the emergence of a peaceful change in international economic relations. What is needed is not a "revolutionary" approach to a New International Economic Order but rather a restrained approach with all interests being taken into account in the reform.[80]

Contd.
Frontline (*Qian Xian*) March, p. 16; Y. Liu, 'A Comparative Study on the Chinese and Foreign Human Rights Theories' (*Zhong Wai Ren Quan Li Lun Bi Jiao Yan Jiu*) (2001) 19 *Journal of the Adult Education College, HuBei University* (*Hubei Da Xue Cheng Ren Jiao Yu Xue Yuan Xue Bao*) pp. 3–5, 16; Y. Li, 'The Different Views on Human Rights between China and America' (*Lun Zhong Mei Liang Guo Bu Tong De Ren Quan Guan*) (2001) 3 *Journal of Liaoning Teachers College (Social Science Edition)* (*Liao Ning Shi Zhuan Xue Bao, She Hui Ke Xue Ban*) p. 17; M. Qiu and S. Ni, 'Culture and Politics, A Preliminary Analysis of the Human Rights Issues in the China–America Relations' (*Wen Hua Yu Zheng Zhi, Qian Xi Zhong Mei Guan Xi Zhong De Ren Quan Wen Ti*) (2002) 1 *International Observation* (*Guo Ji Guan Cha*), p. 33.

79 Chang, n. 75 (arguing that saying 'no' to a social clause in the WTO is not the right response for China). In particular, Chang argues: '[I]nternational trade will inevitably involve labour standards. Social development shall keep pace with the development of the economy. Secondly, the formulation of the WTO agreements so far are influenced or determined by the major developed countries. The social clauses are not only advocated by the government and labour organizations, but also accepted by the employers of these countries. Meanwhile, they have been recognized by various international organizations including UN and ILO. Therefore, the linkage between labour standards and international trade is an inevitable requirement and trend': *Ibid.*, p. 129. Furthermore, 'As a representative of the developing countries, China, as a new WTO member, is against linking labour standards with international trade because this won't directly safeguard the interests of the laborers. However, the important role of labour standards in international trade should not be ignored. In the market economy, the separation between economic rights and social rights and political rights are not clear-cut. The International Convention on Economic, Social and Cultural rights has been ratified by China, which means, it has taken legal effect in China and has become an important source of Chinese labour law. The ratification of this Convention, in fact, is a recognition of the Core Labour Convention (?) adopted by the ILO, as this Convention has embodied the basic content of the Core Labour Convention. The fulfilment of the obligations under the Convention is in line with the recognition and enforcement of international labour standards: *Ibid.*, p. 129.

80 Oppermann, n. 2, p. 12.

9. Towards Post-establishment National Treatment of Foreign Investment Enterprises in China – From BITs to TRIMs

*Chen Xuebin**

9.1 Introduction

In December 1978, the 3rd Plenary Session of 11th Central Committee of the Communist Party of China resolved to open China to the world. China focused on economic development by opening itself to the outside world and integrating itself into the world market system. Prudent macroeconomic policies were adopted. Legislation followed. The term 'socialist market economy' formally appeared on 29 March 1993 in an amendment to the Constitution.[1]

China has made great efforts to create a sound market economy to expand foreign trade and investment. In order to encourage foreign direct investment (FDI) in China, China promulgated a number of laws and regulations, including three basic laws: Chinese-Foreign Equity Joint Venture Law (EJV Law), Chinese-Foreign Contractual Joint Venture Law (CJV Law) and Wholly Foreign-Owned Enterprise Law (WFOE Law), and their respective implementing regulations. As part of improving the external environment for foreign investment, China negotiated and concluded a number of bilateral investment treaties (BITs) with other countries to enhance cooperation in economic and technological areas. Meanwhile, China became a member of some international institutions. China made a formal application to rejoin General Agreement on Tariffs and Trades (GATT) in 1986, and negotiations on the terms of World Trade Organization (WTO) membership commenced

---

* The author is grateful to Professor Mary Hiscock, Bond Law School, Chairperson of the International Law Section of the Law Council of Australia, for her constructive discussion and contribution to the paper. Thanks also to Professor Ross Buckley, Executive Director of the Tim Fischer Center of Global Trade and Finance, Bond University, for his help. All views are mine.

1 *The Amendment of the Constitution of PRC (1993)*, the revised preamble addressed 'to develop the socialist market economy'; Article 15 used 'China exercises the socialist market economy' instead of 'China exercises the socialist planned commodity economy'. Other Articles changed accordingly.

in 1995.[2] On 11 December 2001, China formally became a full member of the WTO. WTO membership is the crowning achievement of the efforts the country has made since 1978 to integrate into the world economy.[3]

The multilateral trading system includes several components of an investment regime, such as the WTO Agreement on Trade-Related Investment Measures (the TRIMs Agreement) as well as those of the international trade regime. The TRIMs Agreement is mainly based on the principle of National Treatment.

Treatment for investors is a broad term, which refers to the legal regime that applies to investments once they are admitted by the host country.[4] After being admitted and established in China, a foreign investment enterprise (FIE) normally becomes a limited liability company, that is, a Chinese legal person. Should an FIE be treated the same as a domestic enterprise? It is important the answer is yes, and this will be achieved now granting post-establishment National Treatment to FIEs in China. This chapter analyses the steps still required to achieve this in the external legal framework for FDI in China.

9.2 China's Efforts to Create a Sound External Climate for Foreign Investment

9.2.1 The first stage: China's BITs

Since 1978 when China opened its door to the outside world, China has had a profound increase in foreign investment. At present, some 400 of the world's top 500 transnational corporations have invested in China. By October 2002, overseas investors from more than 180 countries and regions had established over 390,000 ventures in China, injecting more than US$400 billion of the over US$800 billion promised capital. China has received most foreign funds among developing countries since 1993, and has received the largest overall amount of foreign investment after the United States.[5] With its dynamic economic growth, China has made a great contribution to world economic growth.

The last two decades have seen intensive law and treaty-making activity in the field of foreign investment. In an effort to make their legal environments more hospitable to such investment, many developing countries

---

2 China was a founding father of the GATT in 1947, but the Jiang Jieshi government withdrew from the Agreement on 6 March 1950. *See* Yang Guohua and Chen Jin, 'The Process of China's Accession to the WTO' (June 2001) 4 *Journal of International Economic Law* 2.

3 Hiddo Houben, 'China's Economic Reforms & Integration into the World Trading System' (June 1999) 33 *Journal of World Trade* 3 (June 1999) 1–18, at 2.

4 J. Leviec, *Protection et promotion des investissements* (1985) at 79; *see also* Rudolf Dolzer and Margrete Syevens, *Bilateral Investment Treaties* (Martinus Nijhoff Publishers, The Hague, Boston, London, 1995), at 58.

5 *China Ranked No. 2 in Absorbing FDI during 1979–99* <http://www.chinaonline.com/wto/c0010102.asp>.

enacted new investment laws or 'codes'[6] and reached bilateral or multilateral treaties with other countries. China is no exception.

Great efforts have been made to encourage foreign investment during the last two decades. BITs are one channel and China has negotiated and signed over 100 BITs with other countries – the first with Sweden in 1982. Among BITs, some of the European contracting countries are Germany, the United Kingdom, France, Italy, Romania, Sweden, the Belgium–Luxembourg Economic Union, Finland, Norway, Spain, and Austria. China has also signed BITs with 10 APEC Members. They are Thailand, Singapore, Australia, Japan, Malaysia, Indonesia, Chile, New Zealand, the Republic of Korea, and the Philippines.

Under China's BITs, the general standards of the treatment of FDI include fair and equitable treatment, full protection and security, non-discrimination as well as most-favoured nation (MFN) treatment. The principle of National Treatment was adopted in China's BITs with a few countries only, like the United Kingdom (1986), Japan (1988), the Republic of Korea (1992), and Morocco (1995).

In addition, China has concluded a number of bilateral agreements for avoidance of double taxation with other countries.

These bilateral agreements demonstrate the significant progress that has been made in China but vigilance remains needed to ensure China's policies and practices are consistent with existing bilateral agreements and international rules.[7]

9.2.2 Second stage: China's participation in multinational conventions other than GATT/WTO

For many years, reciprocity has been the norm in China's bilateral trade relations, and China had less interest in participating in multilateral activities. Being kept outside the mainstream of the multilateral trading system, China had to work under extremely harsh conditions of economic blockade, embargo, and trade sanctions, the vestiges of the cold war era.[8]

Nowadays international conventions and practices strive to make almost all of the world internationalized. A market economy needs to operate according to the rules of the game. Gradually the Chinese have realized the importance of international standards as China tries to write the rules of the game with other countries. During the last two decades, besides BITs, the Chinese government positively participated in many regional activities, like APEC, and international institutions, like UNCITRAL, UNCTAD, IMF,

---

[6] Antonio R. Parra, 'The Scope of New Investment Laws and International Instruments', in Robert Pritchard (ed.), *Economic Development, Foreign Investment and the Law: Issues of Private Sector Involvement, Foreign Investment and the Rule of Law in a New Era* (Kluwer Law International & International Bar Association, London, 1996), at 27.

[7] *Inventory of Foreign Trade Barriers 1998: China*, <http://www.ustr.gov/reports/nte/1998/contents.html>.

[8] Li Zhongzhou, *China's Accession on to the WTO and the Impact on its External Trade Law*, Presentation at the German–Chinese Colloquy, Hamburg, 11–12 June, 1998.

and WIPO, even though these activities meant, to some extent, a limitation on national sovereignty. To date, China has signed over 230 multinational treaties.

China signed and approved the 1965 *Convention on the Settlement of Investment Disputes Between States and Nationals of Other States* (ICSID) in July 1992. It is important to note that ICSID provides a voluntary mechanism and forum for the peaceful settlement of investment disputes between a contracting State and nationals of other contracting States.[9] Among others, if there were a dispute concerning the amount of the compensation from nationalization or expropriation between foreign investors and the Chinese Government, the investors may bring the case to the ICSID for resolution.

Another example in the international investment area is the *Multilateral Investment Guarantee Agency* (MIGA) set up through a multilateral convention of 11 October 1985, which came into effect on 12 April 1988. MIGA serves a dual purpose: (a) an insurance mechanism to encourage the flow of FDI to developing countries by alleviating non-commercial political risks; and (b) a forum for policy co-ordination for investment.[10] China signed, examined and approved MIGA in 1988.

After China becomes a signatory party to a bilateral or multinational treaty and ratifies it, the treaty constitutes an integral part of the Chinese legal system, except for articles over which China makes a reservation. For instance, China declared reservations to Articles 1(1) and 11 when it participated in the *United Nations Convention on Contracts for International Sale of Goods* (1980 Sales Convention).

Chinese who engage in transnational transactions or activities must conform to international treaties. Bilateral or multinational treaties entered into by China, like the *1980 Sales Convention*, are effective in China. Judges of the People's Courts can quote the provisions of the treaty directly in dealing with a specific case. This is quite different from practice in Australia, and other common law countries. An example is where the American copyright holder, Walt Disney Productions won a lawsuit[11] against the Chinese infringers by basing its claim on a bilateral treaty entered into between the governments of China and the United States, namely the 1992 Memorandum of Understanding between the Government of the People's Republic of China and the Government of the United States of America on the Protection of Intellectual Property (1992 MOU).[12]

---

9 John Mo, 'Some Aspects of the Australia-China Investment Protection Treaty' (June 1991) 25 *Journal of World Trade* 3, 43–80, at 45.

10 M. Rafiqul Islam, *International Trade Law* (LBC Information Services, Pyrmont, NSW 1999), at 255.

11 *Walt Disney Productions* v. *Beijing Publisher and Co.* (1995), *see* Zheng Chengsi, *Case Six: The First Major Copyright Case Involving a Foreign Party – Walt Disney Productions* v. *Beijing Publisher and Co.*, in 'Intellectual Property Enforcement in China: Leading Cases and Commentary' (1997), at 48.

12 Kui Hua Wang, 'Protection of Intellectual Property', in K.C.D.M. Wilde (ed.), *China's International Transactions: Trade & Investment* (LBC Information Services, North Ryde, NSW 2000), at 100.

An international treaty in the commercial area acceded to by China is superior even to Chinese domestic law. In the arbitration commission or the People's Courts, if the Chinese law applicable to the specific case is different from an international convention to which China has acceded, the provisions of the international convention normally prevail.

9.2.3 The highest stage: China's WTO accession

From 1986, China applied to rejoin the GATT. During the accession negotiations, there were many hurdles. One which made the access talks particularly arduous was the deficiencies in China's legal system.

Both in China and beyond there was recognition that the next steps of the reform process and the WTO membership would be linked. But an outward-looking China cannot afford to stand on the sidelines while others write the rules of the game; a China with growing export interests cannot afford to be left without secure and expanding access to global markets – security which only the multilateral system provides. And perhaps most important, a China dependent upon technology and modernization cannot afford to fall behind the fast-moving pace of globalization.[13] This is one reason China made such great endeavours to join the GATT/WTO.

In general, there has been unanimous international support for bringing China into the fold of the WTO. A number of WTO Members pushed for China's entry into the WTO, including Australia, which gave China great help to become a WTO member. As Tim Fischer said at the 1999 APEC Meeting:

> China was unfairly outside the World Trade Organization ... allowing Beijing into the fold would open up export prospects for many nations. Specifically among the WTO benefits are improved market access via lower trade barriers, greater transparency of trade and investment regimes; and lower business costs.[14]

Negotiations to bring China into the WTO, as with every acceding country, had included both bilateral and multilateral components. First, China was required to negotiate a market access package with interested WTO members bilaterally; second, it had to negotiate a multilateral 'protocol of accession'.[15]

Fortunately, China managed to overcome these difficulties. All 37 interested WTO members reached a substantial number of bilateral agreements with China, including the Sino–USA Agreement of 15 November 1999 and the Sino–EU Agreement of 19 May 2000. To China, these agreements with the United States and the European Union are crucial. Without them, there

---

13 Speech by WTO Ex-Direct-General, Renato Ruggiero, *China and the World Trading System*, Address to Beijing University, China, 21 April 1997, <http://www.wto.org/wto/speeches/china.html>.

14 Tim Fischer, Australia's retired Deputy Prime-Minister and Trade Minister and instigator of a historical China–Australia trade deal, Asia Newsweek, October 1999, at 5.

15 Timothy C. Brightbill, David B. Calabrese, Neil R. Ellis, Jennifer L. Haworth, Matthew R. Nicely, and Carrie L. Owens, 'International Trade', *The International Lawyer: Business Regulation* at 407–8.

would have been no possibility of entry into the WTO. These agreements were major steps towards WTO membership.

Substantive discussions between China and the WTO working group began in mid-2000 with the text and annexes of the draft Protocol of Accession, and on certain issues. Finally the key hurdles were overcome in the process of China's accession, especially after the United States and European Union reached the consensus with China in late June and early July 2001. The WTO finally opened its door, on 10 November 2001, to China. On 11 December 2001, 30 days after it notified the WTO of the legislature's approval of the document, China formally became a full member. After 15 years of long arduous negotiations between China and its trading partners, China's dream of WTO membership had become a reality.

9.3. Limitations on the Scope of the Former Stages of China's External Framework

9.3.1 China's BITs bind only the contracting parties

9.3.1.1 BITs bind only the contracting parties

BITs are essentially bilateral, concluded for the mutual benefit and common interest of the parties in relation to FDI-related activities in their territories. Through their BITs, the parties purport to create safe conditions with legal and political assurances under which their nationals can invest in each other's territory.[16] While developed parties endeavour to maximize protection for FDI, developing parties seek to exert maximum-possible control on FDI to ensure compliance with their domestic laws and national economic interests.[17]

BITs contain major substantive issues on investment. In the absence of reliable and creditable international law governing FDI, BITs provide rules that regulate FDI only between their contracting parties and provide investors from the contracting parties with standard treatment. Among China's BITs, most cover Fair and Equitable Treatment, and MFN Treatment.

An example is the provision on 'Treatment of Investments' in the Sino–Australian BIT signed in 1988:

A Contracting Party shall at all times:

(a) ensure fair and equitable treatment in its own territory to investments and activities associated with such investments;
(b) accord within its territory protection and security to investments and activities associated with investments and, without prejudice to its law, shall not impair by unreasonable or discriminatory measures the management, maintenance, use, enjoyment, or disposal of investments;

---

16 *Op. cit.*, n. 11, at 254.
17 *Ibid.* at 244.

(c) treat investments and activities associated with investments in its own territory, including compensation under Article VIII and transfers under Article X, on a basis *no less favourable than that accorded to investments and activities associated with investments of nationals of any third country*, provided that a Contracting Party shall not be obliged to extend to investments and activities associated with investments any treatment, preference or privilege resulting from:
   (i) any customs union, economic union, free trade area, or regional economic integration agreement to which the Contracting Party belongs; or
   (ii) the provisions of a double taxation agreement with a third country.[18]

Here, except for National Treatment, the Agreement adopts international basic principles, such as Fair and Equitable Treatment, Non-discriminatory Treatment and MFN, in dealing with issues of the treatment to investment. Under Paragraph (c), Australian and Chinese governments have obligations to treat each other's nationals 'on a basis no less favourable than that accorded to investment and activities associated with investments of nationals of any third country', although there is a limitation. This means MFN treatment, that is, if the country grants preferential treatment to investments from a third country, the former should grant such treatment to the investments from nationals of the contracting nation.

China's BITs can create binding obligations only for the contracting parties in relation to their treatment of FDI. If disputes cannot be settled within a certain period of time at first stage through conciliation or negotiation, the investor may choose certain means for resolution, including application to ICSID.

9.3.1.2 *The legal status uncertain*

Normally, a China's BIT is entitled an 'Agreement', like the *Agreement between the Government of Australia and the Government of the People's Republic of China on Reciprocal Encouragement & Protection of Investment (1988)*. Such a bilateral agreement is usually effective as of the signature day or the day of exchange of the approval instruments. For instance, Article 14 of the Sino–Australia BIT stipulates that 'this Agreement shall enter into force on signature'.

It needs noting that the Constitution of PRC differentiates 'agreements' (Xie Ding) from 'treaties' (Tiao Yue). The legal status of 'agreements' is not certain. Under the Chinese legal system, bilateral or multinational treaties need to be ratified by the Standing Committee of NPC, and then become an integral part of Chinese legal system. However, as to bilateral or multinational agreements, those that are not 'important' are not subject to ratification

---

18 *Agreement between the Government of Australia and the Government of the People's Republic of China on Reciprocal Encouragement & Protection of Investment* (11 July 1988), at Article 3, emphasis added.

by the NPC Standing Committee. Only those 'important agreements' would be ratified by the NPC Standing Committee.[19]

Whether or not a Chinese BIT falls within the category of 'important agreement' is unclear. *The Law of the People's Republic of China on the Procedures of Conclusion of Treaties* provides six circumstances concerning interpretation of the term of 'the treaties and important agreements',[20] but none of them covers that concerning the bilateral investment agreement.

As their legal status is uncertain, China's BITs may be regarded as contracts between the contracting countries, which bind the governments of contracting parties. Despite this, most BITs confer MFN treatment on foreign investment only after establishment and do not grant national treatment for their establishment. [21]

9.3.1.3 A minimal role in attracting FDI

BITs can send positive signals to investors by providing certain standards of treatment, protection against expropriation, and settlement of disputes. But they are only one factor in attracting FDI along with, *inter alia*, the size of the market, infrastructure quality, local skills, and political and economic stability. In addition, BITs do not generally address development issues such as restrictive business practices, environmental standards, and social responsibilities of investors, which some experts think should be covered in a multilateral treaty. [22]

Although the aim of BITs is to promote and protect FDI, it has to be accepted that BITs play a 'minimal role' in attracting FDI. Many African countries have signed investment treaties but have not got any or very little

---

[19] *Ibid*. Article 67(4) provides that the NPC Standing Committee has the power to 'decide on the ratification or abrogation of treaties and important agreements concluded with foreign countries'.

[20] *The Law of the People's Republic of China on the Procedure of Conclusion of Treaties (1990)*, Article 7 provides:

The ratification of treaties and important agreements shall be decided upon by the Standing Committee of the National People's Congress.

The treaties and important agreements referred to in the preceding paragraph are as follows:

(1) Treaties of friendship and cooperation, treaties of peace and other treaties of a political nature;
(2) Treaties and agreements concerning territory and delimitation of boundary lines;
(3) Treaties and agreements relating to judicial assistance and extradition;
(4) Treaties and agreements which contain stipulations inconsistent with the laws of the People's Republic of China;
(5) Treaties and agreements which are subject to ratification as agreed by the contracting parties;
(6) Other treaties and agreements subject to ratification.

[21] Tan Wee Cheng, *China: Investment Climate Statement for 1997*, Tan Wee Cheng's China page, US and Foreign Commercial Cervice (us&fcs) <http://www.tradeport.org/ts/countries/China/climate.htm>.

[22] *UNCTAD Debates: Globalization, LDCs and Africa*, Trade and Development Board Holds 44th Session, NGLS Roundup, November 1997, <http://ngls.tad.ch/english/pubs/ru/ru21.txt>.

foreign investments. In the words of Ms Li Ling:

> There is no evidence to show that the investors would deem the host country unsafe if that country did not conclude a BIT with their home country and would therefore refrain from investing in that country .... In the case of China, the US is the biggest investor behind Hong Kong, Japan and Taiwan, although a Sino–US BIT has not been concluded yet.[23]

The delegate from Japan agreed that BITs have a 'very limited role' in promoting FDI to developing countries. Japan has concluded BITs with only four countries. The major recipients of Japanese FDI are the Southeast Asia region and China. Yet Japan has no BIT with Southeast Asian countries, only with China. So the delegate suggested that a stable political and social condition is the most important investment factor.[24] Investment flows are determined by access to markets, social, and political conditions. 'Therefore, for developing countries, economic growth and development should be put at first place according to their own needs and strategy', said Ms Li.[25]

9.3.2 Regional or multilateral cooperation is insufficient

The main objective typically proposed at the regional level is the liberalization of restrictions to entry and establishment of FDI, followed by the elimination of discriminatory operational conditions. Most regional instruments, like ASEAN, NAFTA, and CER, are legally binding, although there are exceptions,[26] like the OECD Guidelines and the APEC Principles.

9.3.2.1 ASEAN

ASEAN was established to respond to the influence of China, its big neighbour to the north. In 1987, ASEAN established the Investment Agreement. Although the Agreement intented to provide for investors national treatment and MFN, it seems difficult to ascertain the extent of such treatment and protection to which the Agreement has contributed or could contribute to increasing FDI inflows in ASEAN economies.[27]

There are economic links between China and the ASEAN and they each need trade and investment. Some countries and China attempted to enter into dialogue with each other in the mid-1980s. Since China became an ASEAN full dialogue partner in July 1996, the relationship between the two sides has improved,[28] even though China is not an ASEAN member.

---

23 Ms Li Ling, Deputy Director-General, Treaty and Law Department, MOFTEC, China, see *Bilateral investment agreements play only a minor role in attracting FDI* <http://www.worldbank.com/icsid/bilateralinvestmenttreaty/bil_cn.htm>.

24 *Ibid.*

25 *Ibid.*

26 *Overview of Investment-Related Multilateral and Bilateral Agreements*, The Asia–Europe Investment Promotion Action Plan (IPAP), Annex 3 <http://europe.eu.int/comm/external_relations/asem_ipap_vie/ipap_text_annex_3.htm>.

27 Overview of Foreign Direct Investment in ASEAN <http://www.asean.or.id/ov_fd.htm>.

28 China's Diplomacy Since Its Reform and Opening-up, By Tang Jiaxuan, Minister of Foreign Affairs. China and ASEAN established in 1997 the China–ASEAN Joint Committee, defining an

9.3.2.2 APEC

As a member, China joins in APEC's activities positively.

APEC built up a set of Investment Principles in the Bogor Declaration of 17 November 1994. These principles apply to the entire APEC liberalization and facilitation process to achieve the long-term goal of free and open trade and investment no later than the year 2010 in the case of industrialized economies and the year 2020 in the case of developing economies.[29]

The APEC Principles contain National Treatment and MFN obligations but are non-binding. They are an excellent example of the changed patterns of law making – the Principles are best described as 'soft' or 'fuzzy' law – a set of commonly agreed skeletal principles, stated in broad terms, establishing a minimum standard of treatment for foreign investors. [30]

9.3.2.3 OECD

Realizing the shortage of regional cooperation, APEC has been making efforts to enhance regionalism. The OECD does so as well. Open regionalism leads to trade creation by freeing up trade within the region.

The OECD in the mid-1990s attempted to establish a Multinational Agreement on Investment (MAI), which aimed to set high standards of liberalization. It would create strong obligations and commitments on national treatment, MFN, non-discrimination, etc. But there was another side to the MAI that imposed particularly draconian legal constraints on states.

The MAI was a failure for many reasons – its content, its process, and its attempt to impose obligations on non-members. The OECD Ministers announced on 3 December 1998 that the OECD had ceased all negotiations on the MAI.[31]

China is not a member of the OECD, and prefers to join the WTO rather than be an OECD member.

9.4 The WTO Agreement on TRIMs binds All Members

9.4.1 National treatment under the WTO agreement on TRIMs

Although the WTO does not deal directly with many investment issues, the TRIMs Agreement is start. It prohibits members from imposing trade-related investment measures that violate national treatment standards or general elimination of quantitative restrictions.

Contd.

all-directional and all-embracing dialogue framework on mutual relations for the establishment of good-neighbourly partnership of mutual trust orientated toward the 21st century. All this marked that China–ASEAN relationship entered a new stage.

[29] *Op. cit.*, n. 22. <http://www.fmprc.gov.cn/READ.ASP>.

[30] Mary E. Hiscock, Changing Patterns of Regional Law Making in Southeast Asia, 39 St. Louis University Law Journal 1 (1995), at 1.7. 8–9.

[31] RS20448: Foreign Investment Issues in the WTO, James K. Jackson, Specialist in International Trade and Finance, January 27, 2000, <http://www.cnie.org/nle/inter-45.html>.

Paragraph 1 of Article 2 of the TRIMs Agreement invokes an obligation of National Treatment under Article III GATT 1994[32] which expresses that not only internal taxation but also internal laws and regulations are factors influencing trade. The second limb is under Article III, paragraph 4, the obligation of National Treatment on internal laws and regulations, which uses the following words:

> The products of the territory of any contracting party imported into the territory of any other contracting party shall be accorded treatment no less favourable than that accorded to like products of national origin in respect of all laws, regulations and requirements affecting their internal sale, offering for sale, purchase, transportation, distribution, or use.

The test for whether an investment measure violates the principle of National Treatment is to see whether the treatment accorded to an imported product is less favourable than that accorded to a domestic product, no matter whether it resorts to internal taxation or internal laws and regulations, and whether it has caused or would cause a restrictive and disorderly effect on trade in goods.

In a specialized provision, Article 2.2 of the TRIMs Agreement goes on to prohibit some TRIMs listed in the Annex to the Agreement. Here, the obligation of National Treatment is limited in its scope of application under paragraph 4 of Article III of GATT 1994. That is to say, the TRIMs Agreement relates the obligation of National Treatment to internal laws and regulations, but not internal taxation or other matters. So the Canadian *Foreign Investment Review Act* purchase undertaking was inconsistent with Article III(4) of the GATT 1947 according to which contracting parties should accord to imported products treatment no less favourable than that accorded to like products of national origin in respect of all internal requirements affecting their purchase.[33]

In addition, the TRIMs Agreement treats Article XI(1) of GATT 1994 as supplementary to National Treatment. In John Mo's view, Article XI of GATT 1994 may grant the TRIMs Agreement more reliable and unambiguous support than Article III, and Article XI non-discriminatorily eliminates the use of quantitative restrictions, unless the restrictions fall under the exceptions to the provision.[34]

The TRIMs Agreement contains a variety of procedural and substantive obligations. Article 2 of the Agreement, formally, lays down an obligation

[32] Article 2.1 of the TRIMs Agreement states: 'Without prejudice to other rights and obligations under GATT 1994, no Member shall apply any TRIM that is inconsistent with the provisions of Article III or Article XI of GATT 1994'. Article III of GATT 1994 is a clause of National Treatment. For further discussion, please also *see* the author's paper <The Operation of Chinese Foreign Investment Law under the TRIMs Agreement> presented at the China and the WTO Conference at Australian National University, Australia on 16–17 March 2001.

[33] Canada – Administration of the Foreign Investment Review Act, Report of the Panel, 7 February 1984, GATT L/5504–30S/140, para. 6.1.

[34] John Mo, China, the WTO Trade Organization, and the Agreement on TRIMs (1996) 30 *Journal of World Trade* 5, 89–113, at 99.

which is distinct from the obligation contained in GATT III.[35] So the Panel Report noted in *Indonesian Car Programmes*, the Agreement is not an 'Understanding to GATT 1994', unlike the six Understandings which form part of the GATT 1994. If the purpose of the TRIMs Agreement were to refer to Article III as applied in the light of other (non-Article III) GATT rules, there would be no need in Article 3 to refer to such general exceptions. Moreover, it has to be recognized that the TRIMs Agreement in Articles 4 and 5, in addition to interpreting and clarifying the provisions of GATT Article III where TRIMs are concerned, has introduced special transitional provisions, and notification requirements.[36] This reinforces the conclusion that the TRIMs Agreement has an autonomous legal existence, independent from that of Article III GATT 1994.[37] So the assertion of Indonesia that the Agreement was not *lex specialis* to any dispute was rejected. The Panel concluded the TRIMs Agreement applied to the case.

9.4.2 Dispute settlement procedures available

As stated in the Report of the Working Party on the Accession of China, the WTO Agreement falls within the category of 'important international agreements' subject to the ratification by the NPC Standing Committee according to the Constitution and the Law on the Procedures of Conclusion of Treaties.[38] So WTO agreements bind China.

The TRIMs Agreement is binding on all Members since the WTO is a rule-based, global trading system multilateral system. Under WTO's dispute settlement mechanism, once there is a dispute between China and another Member, access to the Dispute Settlement Understanding of the WTO is available. The provisions of Articles XXII and XXIII of GATT 1994, as elaborated and applied by the DSU, shall apply to consultations and the settlement of disputes under the TRIMs Agreement.

The stages of dispute settlement foreseen under the DSU are:

(a) consultations between Members (i.e. State-to-State arbitration);
(b) establishment of a panel;
(c) first and second panel hearings based on the exchange of written submissions;

---

35 Indonesia – Certain Measures Affecting the Automobile Industry, Report of the Panel, WT/DS54/R, WT/DS55/R, WT/DS59/R, WT/DS64/R, 2 July 1998, para. 6.84.

36 In Indonesia Car Programme, Indonesia put emphasis on a particular statement of the Bananas III panel concerning the relationship between Article III of GATT and the TRIMs Agreement. The Panel considered that that statement had to be understood in the particular context of that dispute between two developed countries (no transition period was therefore applicable) where the panel had already reached a conclusion that the measure at issue violated Article III:4 of GATT. Therefore there was no need to further discuss the TRIMs Agreement since any action to remedy the inconsistency found under Article III:4 of GATT would necessarily remedy inconsistencies under the TRIMs Agreement. In the present case, the Panel addressed the legal relationship between these two agreements.

37 *Op. cit.*, n. 36, para. 14.62.

38 The Working Party on the Accession of China, *Report of the Working Party on the Accession of China*, WT/ACC/CHN/49, 1 October 2001, Restricted, para. 67, section I, part III.

(d) circulation and adoption of the panel report;
(e) on request, review of the Appellate Review Body.

Each stage of the procedure for settling disputes is subject to strict time-limits.[39]

According to the DSU, where a panel or the Appellate Body concludes that a measure adopted by China is inconsistent with a WTO Agreement, it shall recommend that China bring the measure into conformity with that agreement and China must do so.

9.4.3 Trade Policy Review Mechanism (TPRM)

Another feature of rule-based WTO system is predictability. The multilateral trading system requires Members' regulations and policies related to trade be transparent. In the WTO, this is achieved in two ways: one is that Member governments have to inform the WTO and fellow-members of specific measures, policies, or laws through regular 'notifications'; and the other is by regular 'reviews' of individual countries' trade policies through the TPRM.[40]

Therefore, with notification and TPRM, the TRIMs Agreement binds all Members:

- Members, within 90 days of the date of entry into force of the WTO Agreement, must notify the Council for Trade in Goods of all TRIMs they are applying that are not in conformity with the provisions of this Agreement. TRIMs of general or specific application must be notified, along with their principal features.
- With respect to their commitment to transparency and notification under the relevant WTO Agreement, each Member must notify the Secretariat of the publications in which TRIMs may be found, including those applied by regional and local governments and authorities within their territories.
- The Committee on Trade-related Investment Measures must carry out responsibilities assigned to it by the Council for Trade in Goods and must afford Members the opportunity to consult on any matters relating to the operation and implementation of the Agreement.[41]

Having acceded to the WTO, China must now comply with the TRIMs Agreement to eliminate illegal local content requirements and trade balancing requirements, but without recourse to the provisions of Article 5.[42] That

---

39 Pierre Sauve, 'A First Look at Investment in the Final Act of the Uruguay Round' (October 1994) 28 *Journal of World Trade* 5 5–16, at 14–15.

40 Trade policy reviews: ensuring transparency <http://www.wto.org/english/thewto_e/whatis_e/tif_e/agrm10_e.htm>.

41 The Agreement on TRIMs, Articles 5–7.

42 *The Protocol on the Accession of the People's Republic of China*, accepted by the Ministerial Conference, Decision of November 2001 Doha, WT/L/432, 23 Nov. 2001, para. 3, Section 7, Part I.

means there is no resort to the 180-day notification period or the 5-year transitional period due to other commitments by China's representatives, and China cannot enjoy the rights of a developing country under the TRIMs Agreement.[43] Furthermore, China must accept the review and supervision by the Trade Policy Review Body on Chinese FDI regulations and policies.

9.5 Towards Post-establishment National Treatment of FIEs in China

In order to comply with the WTO Agreement and its commitments, China has started to revise its FDI Law.[44] However, the revision process is still in its early stages. A number of TRIMs remain in administrative regulations and local regulations, such as local content requirements and trade balancing requirements. China needs to continue to justify all TRIMs in Chinese FDI Law.

Among issues related to further adjustment, the treatment of foreign investment is most important. Consistent with China's rights and obligations under the WTO Agreement and the Protocol, China must provide non-discriminatory treatment to all WTO Members, including Members of the WTO that are separate customs territories.[45]

---

[43] *Ibid.* para. 3, Section 7 Non-Tariff Measures, Part I and Section 2(c) Transparency, Part I; also see *the Report of the Working Party on the Accession of China, op. cit.*, n. 39, paras 8 and 9, Part I; at 2. As to China's status as a developing country Member, some members of the Working Party indicated, in para. 9, that a pragmatic approach should be taken in determining China's need for recourse to transitional periods and other special provisions in the WTO Agreement available to developing country WTO Members. Each agreement and China's situation should be carefully considered and specifically addressed. In this regard it was stressed that this pragmatic approach would be tailored to fit the specific cases of China's accession in a few areas, which were reflected in the relevant provisions set forth in China's Protocol and Working Party Report.

[44] They are the Law of the People's Republic of China on Chinese-Foreign Equity Joint Ventures (enacted by NPC in 1 July 1979, and amended in 1990); the Law of the People's Republic of China on Chinese-Foreign Contractual Joint Ventures (promulgated on 13 April 1988); the Law of the People's Republic of China on Wholly Foreign-owned Enterprises (promulgated on 12 April 1986); and the Regulations for the Implementation of the Law of the People's Republic of China on Chinese-Foreign Equity Joint Ventures (promulgated by the State Council on 20 September 1983); the Detailed Rules on the Implementation of the Law of the People's Republic of China on Chinese-Foreign Contractual Joint Ventures (approved by the State Council on 7 August 1995); the Detailed Rules for the Implementation of the Law of the People's Republic of China on Wholly Foreign-Owned Enterprises in China (approved by the State Council on 28 October 1990). China amended its CJV Law and WFOE Law on 30 October 2000 and its EJV Law on 15 March 2001; revised its WFOE Implementation Rules on 12 April 2001 and EJV Implementation Regulations on 22 July 2001. In these revisions, China removed local content requirement, trade balancing requirement, and foreign exchange balancing of earnings and expenditures.

[45] *Op. cit.*, n. 39, The Working Party on the Accession of China, *Report of the Working Party on the Accession of China*, WT/ACC/CHN/49, 1 October 2001, Restricted, para. 19, Section 1 Non-discrimination (including national treatment), Part II.

Favour one, favour all. MFN is a main principle of non-discrimination under the WTO, but MFN treatment alone is not enough, for investors need to be treated the same as nationals. National Treatment is stressed by the TRIMs Agreement as well as the GATT. China must accept the principle of Post-establishment National Treatment of FIEs in China, at the least. To further adjust Chinese FDI Law to comply with the Agreement, the first and most fundamental step required is to establish a uniform principle of National Treatment in Chinese FDI Law.

9.5.1 Demand for non-discrimination

It is generally accepted that international law requires a minimum of non-discrimination in the treatment of foreigners and foreign investment. However, TRIMs cause different treatment between foreign investors and nationals, and different treatment makes market competition unfair and uneven. So TRIMs result in distortions and restrictions affecting trade. Thus both foreign investors and domestic enterprises request non-discrimination. A lot of cases arising in China show that complaints come from foreigners because of different treatment, and from domestic enterprises as well.

An example is income tax treatment. The Chinese government adopted preferential income taxes on foreign investment, so the treatment of FIEs is superior to domestic enterprises, that is, super-national treatment.

Under the income tax laws, the rate of national income tax on FIEs, including EJVs, CJVs, and WFOEs, is 30 per cent, with rates of 24 per cent, 15 per cent and 10 per cent available on special conditions.[46] However, for the State-owned enterprises (SOEs) or other domestic enterprises, the rate of income tax was up to 55 per cent and has been 35 per cent since tax reform in 1994. There has been different treatment for FIEs and SOEs.

Preferential tax treatment has played a role in attracting FDI inflow to China, but does not always make a major contribution to the Chinese market economy. It is necessary to treat foreign investors in the same way as nationals. In general, income and other taxes should be imposed on domestic enterprises in the same way as on FIEs.

Another issue domestic enterprises have complained about is the right to trade, that is, the right to import and export goods. An FIE gets its right to import and export when it is approved by the examination authority and receives the business licence for its operation. That is to say, the FIE is qualified automatically to import and export. Although there are some other requirements, like local purchase, export requirement and foreign exchange balancing requirement, FIEs may purchase raw materials and sell their own products directly in the international market. They are encouraged to export their products and can also be allowed to sell the products in domestic market. However, a domestic enterprise could not do so even if it has

[46] *Income Tax Law of the People's Republic of China for Enterprises with Foreign Investments and Foreign Enterprises* (Adopted on 9 April 1991 at the fourth Session of Seventh National People's Congress).

operated for a long time and has enough experience in business, just because it is an internal entity, and has no right to run an import and export business. If it wishes to have the export right, there are two ways to seek it. One approach is to apply for the qualification through a strict and complicated procedure to get approval, but only a few larger enterprises are able to pass the assessment; another approach is to borrow the foreign trade right from another enterprise with the right to import and export. But the latter has caused a lot of legal troubles these past years.

On the other hand, foreign investors also complain about differentiated forms of TRIMs. They might be in the form of procedure, decision, administrative action, or any other form as well as law, regulation, and administrative rule. It is seen that official Chinese policy welcomes foreign investment, but the government servants at different levels have been maintaining barriers and controls on FDI, by channeling it in certain directions. Except for the laws and regulations, there are certain requirements used as administrative measures to govern FIEs' businesses and activities. These 'requirements' clearly imply government action involving the imposition of a condition. Sometimes these 'requirements' are negotiated privately by the government and the foreign investor, rather than defined explicitly in a statute. Sometimes they use the form of 'red-head documents', that is, inner documents only for government servants. This is a frequent complaint about China's legal system, that it has been internal rules and practices, which are unavailable to foreigners.[47]

Government officials at different levels are likely to protect favoured sectors or firms. This protection usually takes two forms: local content requirements, and local judicial protection. Local content requirements are barriers that do not allow foreign products into the local market, or make customers only purchase and use local products or accept local services. Such intangible barriers to trade abound in China. For example, local governments can apply a range of fees and other charges to protect an automobile manufacturer within their province or city.[48]

Local protectionism, local judicial protection in particular, often happens due to interference by local government officials in the court decision-making as well. Thus for many companies, the highly personalized nature of business in China and the limited number of suppliers and customers often make arbitration or other legal remedies impractical. Even when they have a strong case, foreign investors often decide against using legal means to resolve problems out of fear of permanently alienating critical business associates or government authorities. The lack of recourse to an impartial legal system that is not susceptible to Chinese Government pressure further undermines investor confidence.[49]

In addition, foreigners also face the problem of the right to trade internationally. In practice, however, China's restrictive foreign trade and investment

---

47 *Op. cit.*, n. 8.

48 Mark W. Frazier, Coming to Terms with the 'WTO EFFECT' on US–China Trade and China's Economic Growth, NBR Briefing, September 1999, <http://www.nbr.org/briefing.htm>.

49 *Op. cit.*, n. 8.

regulations denied foreign companies National Treatment in some service and key industrial sectors.[50] China has restricted the types and numbers of entities within China, which have the legal right to engage in international trade. Only those firms with import trading rights may bring goods into China.[51]

Overall, FIEs have a significantly greater degree of managerial autonomy than typical Chinese enterprises, SOEs in particular. However, domestic enterprises may enjoy certain advantages because local governments frequently provide special advantages to local SOEs. For instance, many local companies are able to obtain preferential treatment in local financing, marketing, price setting, and purchasing of raw materials.[52] In addition, some goods that are of great commercial value to both China and its trading partners, such as grains, cotton, vegetable oils, petroleum, and certain related-products may principally be imported only through state trading enterprises.[53]

Not only multinational enterprises but also some WTO members are concerned about the application of the principle of non-discriminatory treatment to all foreign individuals, enterprises, and FIEs. So in bilateral and multilateral negotiations on China's accession, they expressed their concern regarding certain provisions of Chinese laws, regulations, administrative notices, and other requirements which could, directly or indirectly, result in less favourable treatment of import products in contravention of Article III of GATT 1994.[54]

9.5.2 National treatment in legal documentation

Up to now, there has been no particular provision relating to National Treatment in Chinese FDI Law. Neither the EJV Law, the CJV Law nor the WFOE Law, grants national treatment to foreign investors or FIEs. Even in the *Regulations on Direction Guide to Foreign Investment*, renewed in 2002, there are still no articles covering the issue.

Are there any stipulations in legislation with respect to National Treatment?

First, there is a provision on National Treatment in respect of Statutes, such as the *Foreign Trade Law of the People's Republic of China* promulgated on 12 May 1994. Article 6 of the Law provides for extension of National Treatment, on a reciprocal basis, to contracting parties of international treaties to which China is a party. Article 23 provides for extension of market access and national treatment in services under similar conditions.

As for turnover taxation, the original situation with different tax rates imposed on different types of taxpayers and incentives according to different ownership was changed. To meet the needs of a developing socialist

---

50 *China: investment climate statement*, Trade Port, Trade Directory, US and Foreign Commercial Service (us&fcs), <http://www.tradeport.org/ts/countries/China/climate.htm>.
51 *Op. cit.*, n.8.
52 *Ibid.*
53 *Ibid.*
54 *Op. cit.*, n. 39. para. 20, Section 1 Non-discrimination (including national treatment), Part II.

market economy, China exerted efforts to further reform its industrial and commercial tax system and adopted a revenue-sharing tax system from 1994, in tandem with the blueprint of the reform of Chinese economic system. It was a comprehensive structural reform directed at 'consolidation of tax laws, fairness of tax liabilities, simplification of tax systems, and reasonable delegation of power'.[55] After the 1994 reform, FIEs, foreign enterprises, and foreign nationals have been entitled to the same treatment as Chinese enterprises and nationals with regard to taxes except enterprise income tax and some local taxes. In this regard, the differential tax treatment between domestic enterprises and FIEs disappeared and FIEs have been able to compete fairly with domestic enterprises.[56] The reform has been welcome domestically and internationally. As regards the reform of Personal Income Tax, a unified personal income tax is applied to Chinese as well as foreign nationals working within the territory of China.[57]

Second, there are some BITs containing National Treatment obligations, like the China–United Kingdom BIT in 1986. The contracting party grants treatment to the investors and their investments from the other contracting party on a basis 'as the same favourable as'[58] or 'not less favourable than'[59] that accorded to nationals. Some conditions remain in the clauses, for example, 'to the extent possible',[60] and 'in accordance with its laws and regulations'.[61] However, China has also provided National Treatment without any qualification, such as in the China–Korea BIT.[62]

In addition, China is a member of APEC, which requires the reform of domestic policies to make them more consistent with the principle of National treatment. Although APEC's work on investment remains to be completed, the APEC's Non-Binding Investment Principles adopted in November 1994 are not meaningless, and entail real commitments.[63] Consistently with open regionalism, non-discrimination provides equal opportunity for all foreign investors from within and without APEC economies and all must be on an equal footing with domestic investors under the National Treatment of APEC's Principles.[64]

Finally, multilateral negotiations on China's accession encouraged China to grant unconditional National Treatment as part of its accession to the WTO.

---

55 *Tax incentives for foreign investment*, by Mr. Cheng Faguang Deputy Director General, State Administration of Taxation, People's Republic of China <http://www.chinamarket.com.cn/E/invest/tzzn.html>.

56 *The Impact of the New Sales Taxes on Foreign Investment in China*, Tax Notes INT'L (BNA) No. 94, at 24 (18 April 1994), available at LEXIS, INTLAW Library, TNL File.

57 *Op. cit.*, n. 56.

58 *See* China-UK BIT (1986), Article 3(3).

59 *See* China-Japan BIT (1988), Article 3(2).

60 *See* China-UK BIT (1986), Article 3(3).

61 *See* China-Morocco BIT (1995), Article 3(1).

62 *See* China-Korea BIT (1992), Article 3(2).

63 M. Rafiqul Islam, *International Trade Law* (LBC 1999), at 147–48.

64 *Ibid.* at 147.

There is a provision under the Protocol on China's Accession as follows:

> Except as otherwise provided for in this protocol, foreign individuals and enterprises and foreign-funded enterprises shall be accorded treatment no less favourable than that accorded to *other individuals and enterprises* in respect of:
>
> (a) the procurement of imputs and goods and services necessary for production and the conditions under which their goods are produced, marketed or sold, in the domestic market and for export; and
> (b) the prices and availability of goods and services ...[65]

It is interesting that the term 'other individuals and enterprises' is used here instead of the term 'other individuals and enterprises from any third country Member' or 'other individuals and enterprises from China'. Does such a version mean MFN treatment, National Treatment or both? It may include MFN and National Treatment if compared with other sections in the Protocol. However, the provision, in general, establishes a principle of non-discrimination. The Protocol stresses the commitment that China will grant National Treatment to foreign investments and their investors. The promise of Premier Zhu Rongji at the opening ceremony of the China–EU Business Dialogue in 2000 was that China would faithfully carry out its commitments. Zhu said, 'once China enters the WTO, we will further open up the domestic market, and gradually grant foreign investment "national status" '.[66]

9.5.3 Discussion on post-establishment National Treatment to FIEs

It is noted that the Chinese Government prefers undertaking commitments on non-discrimination. In respect of distribution of import and export licences and quotas, and the provision of border tax adjustments, the Protocol stipulates, foreign individuals and enterprises and FIEs shall be accorded treatment no less favourable than that accorded to other individuals and enterprises.[67] Similar to Section 3, the provision is non-discriminatory as well.

China has, however, insisted on some reservations to National Treatment, in particular, for trade in finance services. In response to some members' concerns, China has noted that any commitment to provide non-discriminatory treatment to Chinese enterprises, including foreign-funded enterprises, and foreign enterprises and individuals in China, would be subject to other provisions of the Protocol and, in particular, would not prejudice China's right under the GATS, China's Schedule of Specific Commitments or commitments undertaken in relation to trade-related investment measures.[68]

---

[65] *Op. cit.*, n. 43, Section 3 Non-discrimination, Part I. Emphasis added.

[66] *Nation to carry out pledges faithfully*, China Daily, 24 October 2000, <http://www.chinadaily. com.cn/nationtowto.html>.

[67] *Op. cit.*, n. 39, para. 2, Section 8, Import and Export Licensing, Part I and para. 4, Section 11, Taxes and Charges Levied on Import and Export, Part I.

[68] *Op. cit.*, n. 39, para. 17, Section 1, Non-discrimination (including National Treatment), Part II.

Nonetheless, China cannot stick only with offering MFN treatment but must grant National Treatment to foreign investments and their investors. This is required by the WTO Members, and by the WTO Agreements, the TRIMs Agreement in particular.

National treatment under the GATT 1994 is invoked by Article 2 of the TRIMs Agreement.

It may be seen that GATT Article I, MFN, merely prevents discrimination among foreigners from different countries. This does not solve the problem whether a complete ban on imports offends an MFN obligation where all foreign exporters are not treated as equally as nationals, albeit badly. So there is a need for the TRIMs Agreement to limit the ways under which adverse trade-related investment measures should be prohibited, based upon the provisions of Articles III and XI of GATT 1994. Article XI indicates that with certain exceptions, no prohibitions or restrictions other than duties, taxes or other charges, whether through quotas, licences or other measures, shall be maintained on the importation or exportation of any product,[69] whereas Article III provides National Treatment between imports and domestic goods. One of the basic purposes of Article III was to ensure that the contracting parties' internal charges and regulations were not such as to frustrate the effect of tariff concessions granted under Article II.[70] The MFN requirement under Article I, with binding tariffs under Article II, would become ineffective if there is no complementary prohibition in Article III on the use of internal taxation and regulation as a discriminatory non-tariff trade barrier.[71] And without invoking Article III, and further Article XI, it would be easy to promulgate domestic investment measures, which impose restrictive and distorting effects on trade.[72]

In fact, before WTO Accession, China could only obtain National Treatment from some countries through BITs. This kind of treatment is on the basis of reciprocity. It may be unstable, and easily broken. It might cause many limitations in the development of bilateral trade and investment.

Critics may insist that the National Treatment principle – especially when extended beyond industrial manufactured goods to farm products, investment, and services (such as financial services) – restricts a nation's economic development options and hurts infant industries.[73]

It could be argued that the National Treatment standard might sometimes lead to unsatifactory results. For instance, in the event that relevant laws of the respective countries differ in a material respect, the standard may give investors from one country access to a wide spectrum of privileges, while

---

69 Michael Oryles, Jeff Waincymer and Martin Davies, *International Trade Law: Commentary and Materials* (LBC Information Services, North Ryde, NSW, 1996), at 747.

70 *Canada – Import, Distribution and Sale of Certain Alcoholic Drinks by Provincial Marketing Agencies*, Report of the Panel, adopted on 18 February 1992, BISD 39S/27, paras 5.30–5.31.

71 *United States – Measures Affecting Alcoholic and Malt Beverage*, Report of the Panel, adopted on 19 June 1992, BISD 39S/206, para. 5.9 (the '1992 Malt Beverages' report).

72 *Op. cit.*, n. 70, at 747.

73 Tom Barry, *What's This Organization(WTO): An Annotated Glossary of Terms & Concepts about the World Trade Organization*, Foreign Policy in Focus, New Series of Policy Briefs & Reports on Trade, <http://www.igc.org/infocus/wto_structure.html>.

investors from the other State would only benefit from limited rights. It is also possible that domestic legislation that governs national investments may fall well below acceptable international standards.[74]

In the international investment area, up to now, there has been no particular international investment treaty concluded to require that a country treat aliens as favourably as its nationals, apart from the TRIMs Agreement. Such treatment of foreign investment stems entirely from treaty or domestic law and States have therefore consistently incorporated these standards in their investment treaties.[75]

In spite of the possible objections, the National Treatment standard has the merit of helping to minimize the extent to which foreign investors will be put at a competitive disadvantage in comparison with national investors.[76] This point of principle was one reason for the incorporation of the standard into the World Bank Group Guidelines.[77] As well, National Treatment obligations now feature prominently not only in BITs but also in a multilateral treaty, like the WTO.

The rationale for undertaking negotiations on this issue, above all, is that investors are looking for uniform and predictable rules pertaining to their investments abroad. They need to reduce their risks on the basis of non-discrimination between them and nationals of the target country. The WTO provides such a principle of non-discrimination, even if it is the only international body dealing with the rules of trade between nations.[78]

Generally speaking, some developing countries have traditionally been reluctant to grant National Treatment to foreign investors, as National Treatment curtails developing countries' ability to control their domestic economies.[79] This concern has led some developing countries to seek a limitation on the application of the principle by including a developmental clause, which makes the obligation to accord National Treatment subject to the economic policies of the host country.[80] They prefer requiring foreign corporations to purchase some of their materials locally. Even in the WTO, developing country members defend the use of local content measures. In 1999, India on behalf of Cuba, the Dominican Republic, Egypt, El Salvador, Honduras, Indonesia, Malaysia, Nigeria, Pakistan, Sri Lanka, and Uganda, proposed that the TRIMs provisions 'relating to local-content

---

74 Rudolf Dolzer and Margrete Syevens, *Bilateral Investment Treaties* (Martinus Nijhoff Publishers, The Hague, Boston, London, 1995), at 63–5.

75 *Ibid.*, at 58.

76 *Ibid.*, at 63–5.

77 *Report to the Development Committee on the Legal Framework for the Treatment of Foreign Investment*, 7 ICSID Rev. –FILJ 295 (1992), at 20.

78 *What is the World Trade Organization?* <http://www.wto.org/english/thewto_e/whatis_e/tif_e/fact1_e.htm>.

79 Asante, *The Concept of the Good Corporate Citizen in International Business*, 4 ICSID Review. FILJ 31 (1989). Also *See* UNCTC Bilateral Investment Treaties (1988), at 33.

80 *Report on Outstanding Issues in the Draft Code of Conduct on Transnational Corporations*, para. 59, reprinted in UNCTC BIT, at 173. As noted in the Report, the concept of preferential treatment of developing countries has been accepted in a number of multilateral agreements including the GATT and the Lome Convention.

requirements... should be revised to allow for accelerating the industrialization process in developing countries'.[81]

Even in China, some scholars rejected the extension of National Treatment to services and to investment, or limited its application to FDI in particular.[82] They argued there were still some differences between National Treatment of foreign investors and their investment and National Treatment under the TRIMs Agreement. That is because the Agreement applies to investment measures related to trade in goods only, and clarifies that only five types of illegal investment measures, which can cause restrictive and distorting effects on trade in goods, appear on an Illustrative List.[83] So entry into the WTO just means China should grant National Treatment to those in relation to trade in goods but not to foreign investors and their investment.[84]

Such views may be understandable, but are not appropriate. It might be that there remains a legal hole between the foreign investment law and 'investment measures in relation to trade in goods'. However, just as a 'measure' should be interpreted broadly under the WTO regime,[85] the term 'investment measures in relation to trade in goods' under Article 1 of the TRIMs Agreement should be interpreted appropriately in a similar way.

As usual, investment relates to goods, otherwise it relates to services. Investment measures relating to trade in services is governed under the GATS, and investment measures relating to trade in goods falls within the governance of the TRIMs Agreement. So in *Indonesian Car Programmes*, obviously National Treatment under the TRIMs Agreement was applied to assess the matter of investment, no matter if it was a domestic or foreign investment.[86] Under the TRIMs Agreement, there is an 'Effect Test'[87] to assess whether an investment measure falls within a TRIM in the Illustrative List. To look at the original version of Article III (4) of GATT, there is the word 'affecting'. It is really meaningful. The word 'affecting' in Article III(4) implies a measure that has 'an effect on' the 'internal sale,... or use' of products and thus indicates a broad scope of application.[88] The term of a measure

---

81 The Ecumenical Coalition for Economic Justice, *Development & Democracy: The WTO Fails to Deliver*, XI. Economic Justice Report, (May 2000).

82 Xu Congli, *On Extension of National Treatment to Foreign Investment*, Li Wanqiang, *The Treatment to FDI and the Transition of Chinese FDI Law*, Shan Wenhua, *Basic Issues on National Treatment to FDI*, in Chen An (ed.), 'Journal of International Economic Law', Vol. 1, Law Press, Beijing, 1998, at 175–267.

83 The Agreement on Trade-related Investment Measures, Preamble, Articles 1, 2, and Illustrative List of Annex.

84 Zhang Zhiyong and Wang Hui *<Agreement on Trade-related Investment Measures> and Chinese Foreign Investment Law*, Law Journal, 3 (1999), at 22.

85 *Op. cit.*, n. 36, Japan supported such view, for example, Article XXVIII (a) in the GATS, a '"measure" means any measure by a Member, whether in the form of law, regulation, rule, procedure, decision, administrative action, or any other form'.

86 *Op. cit.*, n. 36, para. 14.73.

87 'Effect Test', proposed by US in the Uruguay Round to create a broad concept of TRIMs. This approach was agreed by the Ministers in the Punta del Este Declaration and at last incorporated in the TRIMs Agreement.

88 *EC – Banana III*, Report of Appellate Body, 25 September, WT/DS27/AB/R, para. 216; *Canada – Automobile*, Report of the Panel, WT/DS139/AR/R, WT/DS142/AB/R, 11 February 2000, para. 10.80.

'in relation to trade in goods' is and should be interpreted as the measure may be 'affecting' trade in goods under the 'Effect Test'. Thus in *Parts and Components*, the Panel considered that the comprehensive coverage of 'all laws, regulations or requirements affecting' the internal sale, etc. of imported products, and suggested that the requirements EEC had taken constituted 'requirements' within the meaning of that provision[89] of GATT Article III(4). From another approach, to see whether a measure is a TRIM is to see whether a measure violates Article 2 of the TRIMs Agreement. If it is not consistent with GATT Article III(4) invoked by Article 2 of the TRIMs Agreement, it is a TRIM, no matter whether it has caused districting impact on trade in goods or would cause adverse effect. Hence in *FIRA*, a breach of a rule was presumed to have an adverse impact on the other contracting party, and the Panel proceeded on this assumption.[90]

Thus the TRIMs Agreement provides an international minimum standard for trade-related investment measures. As well, National Treatment, which forms the basis of the TRIMs Agreement, has been incorporated into another two agreements of the WTO: the GATS and the TRIPs. Article XVII of the GATS on National Treatment is modeled on paragraph 4, GATT Article III. In accordance with Article XVII of the GATS 'each member shall accord to services and service suppliers of any other member, in respect of all measures affecting the supply of services, treatment no less favourable than that it accords its own like services and services suppliers'. It is essentially designed to ensure that the foreign services and service suppliers are not subject to discriminatory treatment under an importing country's internal taxes, laws, and regulations.[91]

As a WTO Member, China must provide National Treatment whether under the TRIMs Agreement or other WTO Agreements, like the TRIPs and the GATS. China now must repeal and cease to apply all existing laws, regulations and other measures the effect of which is inconsistent with WTO rules on National Treatment. This commitment was made in relation to final or interim laws, administrative measures, rules and notices, or any other form of stipulation or guideline.[92] China must eliminate any TRIMs including local content, export performance, trade balancing, foreign exchange balancing, and prior experience in importing and exporting as a criteria for obtaining or maintaining the right to import and export.[93]

An FIE set up in China is, as usual, a Chinese legal person. After being admitted by the host country and established in the country, foreign investments are governed under the Chinese FDI Law. Under the Chinese law, China must provide the same treatment to domestic enterprises and FIEs in China. China should eliminate differences in treatment accorded to goods

---

89 *EEC – Regulation on Imports of Parts and Components*, Report of the Panel, BISD 37S/132, 16 May 1990, para. 5.21.

90 *Canada – Administration of the Foreign Investment Review Act*, Report of the Panel, 7 February 1984, GATT L/5504–30S/140, para. 6.4.

91 Mary E. Footer, The International Regulation of Trade in Services Following Completion of the Uruguay Round 29 *The International Lawer* 2, at 473.

92 *Op. cit.*, n. 39, para. 22, Section 1 Non-discrimination (including National Treatment), Part II.

93 *Ibid.*, para. 83(a), Section A.1, Part IV.

produced for sale in China in comparison to those produced for export.[94] Even where TRIMs existed in relation to domestically produced goods, any *de facto* or *de jure* less favourable treatment of imported goods should be eliminated in order to ensure full conformity with the principle of National Treatment.[95]

Even if those FIEs have no status as Chinese legal persons, their investments are established and operated in China under the Chinese laws, and they are still Chinese enterprises. The words used in the Working Party's Report 'to provide non-discriminatory treatment to *Chinese enterprises, including foreign-funded enterprises*, and foreign enterprises and individuals in China'[96] reflect this. Such foreign-funded enterprises are FIEs, including ones without the status of Chinese legal persons, and the investments and their investors should be treated no less favourably than nationals.

With respect to FIEs' right to trade, except as otherwise provided for in the Protocol, all foreign individuals and enterprises, including those not invested or registered in China, should be accorded treatment no less favourable than that accorded to enterprises in China.[97] All trade in goods of FIEs shall be accorded National Treatment under Article III of the GATT 1994, especially paragraph 4 thereof, in respect of their internal sale, offering for sale, purchase, transportation, distribution or use, including their direct access to end-users.[98]

Even if no changes took place in Implementation Rules of CJV Law, fortunately, there has been an article that grants the post-establishment EJV National Treatment in the revised Implementation Regulation of EJV Law (July 2001). The previous Article 65 was amended to 'where the EJV needs to pay the price of purchasing goods in China and charges for water, electronic, gas and heating supply, for services of transportation of goods, labour, project design, consultation and advertisement, etc., it should be accorded the same treatment as that accorded to other domestic enterprises'. This is a start to the process of establishing the principle of National Treatment in Chinese Legislation.

9.6 Conclusion

Since the early 1990s, China has developed its socialist market economy. Marching towards the WTO has meant that China is prepared to play a multinational 'game', not only a domestic one. Such a global 'game' must be played under international rules.

BITs bind the contracting parties, but the WTO binds all Members, including China, the 143rd member. Chinese FDI Law must comply with

---

94 *Ibid.*, para. 18, Section 1, Non-discrimination (including national treatment), Part II.
95 *Ibid.*, para. 20, Section 1, Non-discrimination (including national treatment), Part II.
96 *Ibid.*, para. 17, Section 1, Non-discrimination (including national treatment), Part II. Emphasis added.
97 *Op. cit.*, n. 43, para. 2, Section 5 Right to Trade, Part I.
98 *Ibid.*, para. 1, Section 5 Right to Trade, Part I.

the WTO Agreement, including the TRIMs Agreement, and the Protocol on China's Accession.

Although the TRIMs Agreement cannot be regarded as perfect, within its framework, Members are obliged to abolish and remove the use of harmful trade-related investment measures in the Illustrative List, opening more opportunities for foreign investment. The TRIMs Agreement is one of the most important pieces of international trade law in the world right now. Even if the present TRIMs Agreement cannot resolve all the problems of international investment, it is unlikely to be replaced by a MAI or other international instrument soon.

Now that adjustment of Chinese Law has started, China should set up a principle of post-establishment national treatment of FIEs in its FDI Law in order to conform to the TRIMs Agreement. MFN treatment alone is not enough. Since FIEs funded partly or wholly by foreign investors are Chinese enterprises, they cannot be discriminated against. FIEs, including EJVs, CJVs, and WFOEs, and their foreign investors should be treated no less favourably than domestic enterprises and nationals. It is high time to establish the National Treatment principle in Chinese FDI Law and provide FIEs with post-establishment National Treatment. This is required by the TRIMs Agreement, which aims to facilitate investment across international frontiers so as to increase the economic growth of all trading partners.[99]

---

[99] *See* Preamble of the TRIMs Agreement.

10. Cultural and Political Contexts for the Future of World Trade

Rosita Dellios

10.1 Introduction: The Global Potter

Yesterday in the market stood a potter
Pounding relentlessly his batch of clay.
My inner ear could hear it sigh and groan:
'Brother, I was once like you. Treat me gently![1]

It is no revelation to suggest that the cultural and political contours of the early decades of the twenty-first century will be shaped by that great potter of our times – globalization.[2] However, it is not always clear why this might be so. Among the causes three are especially noteworthy: globalization's unprecedented scope; its multidimensionality; and its propagation. In discussing these attributes, the contexts for the future of world trade become more readily discernible, especially under the guidance of an Asian regional case study. The selection of this region for understanding the cultural and political contexts for the future of world trade hinges on China's steady rise in global influence. Goods (and, increasingly, services) will not only be made *in* China but made *for* China. This does not imply a new cultural hegemony. Like Europe, which is not only 'European', China is not only 'Chinese'. Multiple traditions continue to express themselves in *mandalas* of their own syncretic design. This Sanskrit word which means circle is especially pertinent

---

1 *The Rubayiat of Omar Khayyam* (quatrain 37)

2 There are many definitions for this umbrella term. The following two are representative of the meanings ascribed to globalization:

- The cluster of technological, economic, and political innovations that have drastically reduced the barriers to economic, political, and cultural exchange – Daniel W. Drezner, 'Globalization and Policy Convergence' (2001) 3, (1) *International Studies Review*, 53.
- A marked *reduction in the barriers* between societies and states, an *increasing homogeneity* of societies and states and an *increase in the volume of interactions* between societies – F. Halliday, *The World at 2000: Perils and Promises* (Palgrave, Houndmills, 2001), p. 61.

to the future of world trade.[3] As the Chinese trade *mandala* grows, it does so by absorbing tributaries of difference, thereby enriching itself and, in turn, further regionalizing – even globalizing – that composite (more-than-material) wealth. The West is becoming as much a part of contemporary China, and the East more generally, as the 'Other' is permeating the West. This, as stressed above, is not homogeneity. These are *mandalized* globalizations with Centres of cultural orientation, acting as ideational sources,[4] rather than Wallestianian Centres of industrial power dominating a dependent Periphery.[5]

10.2 Globalization's Scope

Like God, globalization is often considered omnipresent, even omnipotent. Mimicking the evolution of thought which proposes that the divine centre is everywhere and circumference nowhere, globalization in its financial guise may be said to be 'located everywhere but regulated nowhere'.[6] Global economic integration has been driven by market capitalism and assisted by the opening of new electronic trade routes. In a broader historical sense, globalization's scope pertains to the universal extension of the European world order. In 'a world defined by pervasive Western influence and power',[7] it may not even be possible in the current period to find an authentic non-Western mediated perspective, let alone a fully-fledged 'culture'.

This is why *syncretism* – the fusion or synthesis of encountered traditions – has become a catchword in efforts to characterize the globalization of

---

3 On the contemporary use of the *mandala* metaphor, see select articles in *The Culture Mandala*, The Centre for East–West Cultural and Economic Studies, Bond University. A number of issues appear electronically on <www.international-relations.com>.

4 This term derives from the constructivist theoretical framework in International Relations, discussed in K.C. Chwee, 'The Ideational Sources of Chinese Foreign Policy: A Framework for Analysis' (2001) 3(2) *Journal of Diplomacy and International Relations* (Kuala Lumpur) 21–44. *See also* J.M. Hobson, *The State and International Relations* (Cambridge University Press, Cambridge, 2000), Ch. 5.

5 Immanuel Wallerstein's world system theory forms a recognised part of the theoretical debates in International Relations. *See* I. Wallerstein, *The Modern World System* (Academic Press, London, 1974).

6 This is the language used by an American investigator of the Bank of Credit and Commerce International (BCCI) which lost US$15 billion – R. Wilson, 'Blue Hawaii', in A. Dirlik (ed.), *What is in a Rim? Critical Perspectives on the Pacific Region Idea* (2nd edn, Rowman & Littlefield, New York, 1998), p. 330, citing Robert Jackson, 'BCCI's Shadowy Web Aided Noreiga in "Shell Game"', *Honolulu Advertiser*, 12 August 1991, p. D2. On transnational banks (TNBs), *see* C.W. Kegley, Jr. and E.R. Wittkopf, *World Politics: Trend and Transformation* 8th edn (St. Martin's, New York, 2001), pp. 227–228.

7 R.L. Euben, 'Contingent Borders, Syncretic Perspectives: Globalization, Political Theory, and Islamizing Knowledge' (2002) 4(1) *International Studies Review* 27. On the 'complete Europeanization of the earth and of humankind', *see* M. Heidegger, 'A Dialogue on Language', in *On the Way to Language*, trans. P.D. Hertz (Harper & Row, San Franscisco, 1971), pp. 15–16; and discussion of this in F.R. Dallmayr, 'Globalization and Inequality' (2002) 4(2) *International Studies Review* 148–153.

culture.[8] Even Swaziland's King Mswati III is not immune to late modernity's claims on his sovereign traditions. 'It is our culture that I should marry as many wives as I can,' he proclaimed to a global media intrigued by the abduction of an 18-year-old to be his 10th wife. 'I cannot allow myself to be forced to follow the Western culture'. Yet his right to practise traditional culture needs to be viewed in the context of his purchase of a luxury jet for the purported purpose of another modern practice: to travel in search of foreign aid for alleviating poverty in his country.[9] Moreover, it can be argued that poverty itself has become a Western mediated concept. It serves to justify Western-style development, despite this very development having destroyed people's support structures causing widespread destitution.[10] Sometimes poor people are not destitute but simply 'underdeveloped', to quote the president of a comparatively overdeveloped country, the United States, back in 1949.[11] It was then that the United States became the prime defender of the European Enlightenment-inspired system, and in doing so acquired a clear preponderance of wealth and power – so much so it became known as a superpower. Such was its worldwide projection of power, in all its forms – hard and soft, coercive and attractive – that it lent its name to a precursor of globalization: *Americanization.*

Americanization relates to the 'cultural imperialism thesis' which was popular from the late 1960s through to the 1980s. It held that American cultural dominance over more vulnerable societies occurred through the practice of corporate capitalism symbolized by Coca-Cola, Disneyland, Hollywood, and other such icons.[12] Indeed, the *American Dream* became synonymous with the 'soft power' of attraction associated with US hegemony.[13] Out of this notion came the more widely recognised 'thesis of global cultural convergence'.[14]

When as few as 20 media/entertainment multinational corporations, such as Time Warner-America Online, Disney and Universal, account for 95 per cent of the global entertainment market, and almost all of the most visited Web sites are located in the USA,[15] it leaves very little scope for

---

8 On syncretism, *see* J. Clifford, *The Predicament of Culture: Twentieth-Century Ethnography, Literature and Art* (Harvard University Press, Cambridge, 1988); and Euben, 'Contingent Borders ...', p. 26.

9 M. Dynes, 'Starving Nation's King Pays $79m for His Own Jet', *The Australian*, 14 November 2002, p. 8.

10 A. Nandy, 'The Beautiful, Expanding Future of Poverty: Popular Economics as a Psychological Defense' (2002) 4(2) *International Studies Review* 107–121.

11 President Truman, in his inaugural address before Congress in 1949, defined much of the world as 'underdeveloped areas'.

12 *See* Tomlinson, *Globalization and Culture*, pp. 79–97.

13 US *soft power* may generally be said to comprise 'cultural attraction, ideology, and international institutions'. J. Nye, Jr., *Bound to Lead* (Basic Books, New York, 1990), p. 72. *See* also, R.O. Keohane, *After Hegemony* (Princeton University Press, Princeton, 1984) on American hegemony.

14 Tomlinson, *Globalization and Culture*, p. 83. The convergence theory is also discussed widely in the globalization literature, including F. Jameson, 'Notes on Globalization as a Philosophical Issue', in F. Jameson and M. Miyoshi (eds), *The Cultures of Globalization* (Duke University Press, Durham, 1998), pp. 56–57; and Kegley and Wittkopf, *World Politics*, pp. 298–302.

15 Kegley and Wittkopf, *ibid.*, pp. 298–300.

non-American culture to be propagated. With the opening of trade though the World Trade Organization (WTO), especially now that the People's Republic of China (PRC) is a member, it is reasonable to expect an even more extensive diffusion of Western contemporary culture through the transnational entertainment industries. However, there is also a less obvious way in which commercial cultural products are transmitted. Moreover, these products need not be Euro-American. For example, the diffusion of Japanese dramas into China through pirated video compact disks (VCDs) indicates that technological globalization can serve – even if in unauthorized ways – an inflow of culture initiated by regional markets, and not only corporate outflows 'pushed from the economic centre', be it New York or Tokyo.[16]

In business practice, too, Western corporate culture has modified Chinese, Arab, Malay, Indian, and other ritualized business cultures in which elaborate etiquette systems for relationship-building are being replaced by profit-directed efficiencies. These include coolly professional 'transparency' of relations and an inordinate emphasis on interventionist practices, finite projects, quantifiable outcomes, and strategic planning. Conversely, the Chinese *guanxi* (cultivation of networks) system favours friends and relatives as trusted associates.[17] A stranger can only be trusted once he or she becomes a friend, even if not a relative. This reflects the traditional diplomacy of Europeans as well as other civilizations, when national alliances were made through intermarriage and hence the formation of family relationships. Despite the immediate challenge of assimilating the new MBA business habits – or 'international best practice' – as a growing trend in Chinese business, 'banquet diplomacy' has yet to be jettisoned in favour of impersonal transactions. Not only do Chinese and Japanese, members as they are of the Confucian culture area, engage in these ritualised business practices, but so do culturally engaged Westerners. For example, Australian negotiators secured a US$12.5 billion natural gas agreement with China in 2002 after extensive 'banquet diplomacy' and the prestige 'face-giving' measure of having the Australian prime minister as a key negotiator.

With regard to the *global cultural convergence* thesis, it may be concluded that, as Appadurai puts it, the 'globalization of culture is not the same as its homogenization', but homogenizating mechanisms such as media, advertising, language and dress do exist.[18] They become part of the socio–economic profile of many countries. This, in turn, could enhance a liberal–democratic–free market culture; but equally, reaction to Western-system pervasiveness may manifest as unexpected innovation (e.g. capitalism in Communist China); violent backlash (anti-globalization protests since 1999); and/or

---

16 Y. Nakano, 'Who Initiates a Global Flow? Japanese Culture in Asia' (2002) 1(2) *Visual Communication* 25 pp.

17 *See* J.J. Schiro, *The New Silk Road: Secrets of Business Success in China Today* (Wiley & Sons, New York, 2000).

18 A. Appadurai, *Modernity at Large: Cultural Dimensions of Globalization* (Oxford University Press, Delhi, 1997), p. 42.

fundamentalism (most disturbingly, the global terrorist networks of al-Qa'ida and allied regional groups).

It comes as no surprise, then, that where *cultural convergence* dominated debates up to the 1980s, the *divergence thesis* become popular in the 1990s. Questions arose as to the implied unilinear transmission of culture – from strong to weak, North to South, Centre to Periphery, America to the rest of the world. Tomlinson summarizes the position well when he points out:

> Movement between cultural/geographical areas always involves interpretation, translation, mutation, adaptation, and 'indigenization' as the receiving culture brings its own cultural resources to bear, in dialectical fashion, upon 'cultural imports'.[19]

Even Coca-Cola has been rendered in some parts of the world into a 'native product', people being unaware of its American origins.[20] Again, the syncretic dimension arises, calling for a closer consideration of the second attribute of globalization, its multidimensionality.

10.3 Globalization's Multidimensionality

The non-linearity of cultural transmission indicates that the scope of globalization is not merely a matter of breadth. The global exceeds the worldwide. It extends to a multidimensionality that befits the global potter, but strives rather awkwardly when deprived of metaphor. Thus, to assist matters, Robertson introduced *glocalization* – an amalgam of globalization and localization – to convey the 'interpenetrating' principles of 'the particular and the universal'.[21] He appropriated the term from global marketing discourse,[22] whereby mass products were modified to suit local tastes (e.g. *halal* chicken for KFC outlets in Muslim communities). Another neologism, Rosenau's *fragmegration*,[23] combines fragmentation and integration to denote a similar situation pertaining to the predicament of the state. On the one hand, it is absorbed by global forces into larger networks; on the other, it is simultaneously threatened by secessionist-prone identity politics. More ambitious, perhaps, in finding words for the scope of globalization's multidimensionality is Jameson. He thinks of globalization as 'the multiple structural possibilities and combinations made available by this most ambiguous ideological concept and its alternating contents'.[24] Beyond the labyrinthine,

---

[19] D. Howes (ed.), *Cross-Cultural Consumption: Global Markets, Local Realities* (Routledge, London, 1996), cited in Tomlinson, *Globalization and Culture*, p. 84.

[20] Tomlinson, *ibid.*

[21] R. Robertson, 'Glocalization: Time-Space and Homogeneity-Heterogeneity', in M. Fetherstone, S. Lash and R. Robertson (eds), *Global Modernities* (Sage, London, 1995), p. 30.

[22] Tomlinson, *Globalization and Culture*, pp. 195–196.

[23] J.N. Rosenau, *Along the Domestic-Foreign Frontier: Exploring Governance in a Turbulent World* (Cambridge University Press, Cambridge, UK, 1997), p. 38.

[24] Jameson, 'Notes on Globalization ...', p. 58.

and reminiscent of Tomlinson (quoted above with regard to 'indigenization'), lies an essentially dialectical process: globalization's omnipresence has been syncretized to the point where that which appears to derive from European culture is no longer necessarily 'owned' – let alone driven – by the West, in some neo-imperialist fashion. 'For the first time in the two centuries of Western-dominated industrialization,' concurs Castells, 'West and East… are deeply integrated in a pattern that does not reflect overwhelming Western domination'.[25]

Interestingly, this is not necessarily a divergence from the basic aims of the liberal European system which 'is one that deliberately eschews centralized power and tries to maximize local centers of power as much as possible and in as many hands as possible'.[26] Thus, like the emanating Godhead that could no longer be conceptually contained, the West is being 'de-centred'.[27] This is not to say that its power – ideational and otherwise – has diminished, but that it manifests at different levels and through diverse expressions. The different levels, moreover, can be interpenetrating, and syncretically inclined. Thus the model which maximizes 'local centers of power' might yet prove to be the most robust in a widespread system of global governance. This is where *subsidiarity* could increasingly define political relations in a one-world future.

Subsidiarity entails decisions taken at the most basic level. *Paternalistic* relations – the hegemonic face of 'imposing' a European liberal order – can transform to *enabling* ones through the mechanism of subsidiarity. The European Union (EU) has enshrined subsidiarity as a principle that allows subnational regions political representation within the supranational organisation. Historically, the notion of subsidiarity may be found in the Roman Empire and imperial China's tributary system. The Romans encouraged municipal self-government and extended citizenship to subject peoples. This conferred status and a sense of familial relations. The inhabitants of 'free states' proudly served as local senators or magistrates, ensuring their names were thus recorded.[28] By the third century, Roman citizenship had become 'virtually universal' in the empire; the Romans, evidently, ruled by consent.[29]

A similar volunteerism obtained through the tributary system of imperial China. It modelled itself on Confucian family relations (discussed above in terms of *guanxi*) with the Chinese emperor at the head of an international household. Those who wished to partake of the Chinese world order, be it for reasons of trade, protection and/or prestige, were obliged to *kowtow* to the emperor, the 'Son of Heaven'. Tributary kingdoms were brothers, cousins, sons-in-law but never strangers or enemies. Further cementing the relationship, as shown in *The Malay Annals*, was the perception that they shared a

---

25 M. Castells, *The Rise of the Network Society* (Blackwell, Oxford, 1996), p. 309, quoted in J. Tomlinson, *Globalization and Culture* (Polity Press, Cambridge, 1999), p. 93.

26 V. Ferraro, 'The "Seed of Enlightenment" and Humanity's Future', Reviews (2002) 4(1) *International Studies Review* 148.

27 Tomlinson, *Globalization and Culture*, p. 94.

28 J. Ferguson, *Utopias of the Classical World* (Thames and Hudson, London, 1975), p. 168.

29 *Ibid*. It should be noted, however, that the rights of these citizens were at the same time deflated, with high v. low status groups.

common ancestor, Iskandar (Alexander the Great).[30] This was a particularly fitting appropriation in view of Alexander's one-world vision.[31] It is also an example of syncretic cultural incorporation which, in Alexander's case as in many others, continues today on a global scale through the auspices of Hollywood.[32]

It should be remembered that China, too, held a one-world philosophy in the form of *datong* ('all under Heaven are one'). Its world explorer during the Ming dynasty, Zheng He, is similarly rendered relevant in the twenty-first century, in this instance through the global reach of the bestseller. For Admiral Zheng He it came in the form of *1491: The Year China Discovered the World*.[33] Indeed, it was Zheng He who, during his voyages on behalf of the emperor, enrolled many a tributary state with gifts and promises of trade and protection. Local rulers enhanced their legitimacy through the Chinese emperor's official appointment and seal, as well as confirmation of the ruling succession.[34] The system was at its strongest in the Ming dynasty (1368–1644) and included as many as 100 kingdoms. This structure of Chinese control was not rigid, nor did it imply absorption. Moreover, it was not necessary to be of Confucian culture to be part of the tributary system. An example of a tributary state which prospered under the Chinese regionalism of the time was Srivijaya. Lasting some six centuries (from the seventh to the thirteenth centuries), this Sumatran-based empire – or *mandala*, as classical Indian and Southeast Asian polities were termed[35] – was the greatest

---

30 The following excerpt is illustrative:

> This letter is dispatched from beneath the sandals of the feet of the King of Heaven [the Chinese emeperor], to be placed above the diadem of the Raja of Malaca [sic]. Verily we have heard that the Raja of Malaca is a great raja, for which reason we have desired his friendship and attachment, because we are also descended from Raja Secander [Iskandar] Zulkarneini, and of the same extraction as the Raja of Malaca. There is no raja in the universal world greater than me…

The Malay Annals, trans. J. Leyden (The Malaysian Branch of the Royal Asiatic Society, MBRAS Reprint 20, Selangor, Malaysia), pp. 173–174. *See also*, J.J. Ras, Hikajat Bandjar: *A Study in Malay Historiography* (Martinus nijhoff, The Hague, 1968), pp. 84–85; M.T. Osman, *Bunga Rampai: Aspects of Malay Culture* (Dewan Bahasa Dan Pustaka, Kuala Lumpur, 1988), pp. 132–133; and J. Drakard, *A Kingdom of Words: Language and Power in Sumatra* (Oxford University Press, Shah Alam, 1999), p. 149. I am grateful to Dr Paulette Dellios (personal communication, Gold Coast, Australia, November 2002) for drawing to my attention the Iskandar connection.

31 As Ferguson (*Utopias of the Classical World*, p. 101) remarked: 'He changed a narrow vision to a broad one, partly because he expanded the Greek world geographically, partly because he came to ignore racial distinctions'.

32 'Alexander the Great Conquers Hollywood: Why an Ancient Hero is Tomorrow's Golden Boy', cover story, *The Weekend Australian Magazine*, 23–24 November 2002.

33 G. Menzies, *1491: The Year China Discovered the World* (Bantam Press, New York, 2002).

34 E.O. Reischauer and J.K. Fairbank, *East Asia: The Great Tradition* (Houghton Mifflin, Boston, 1962), p. 319.

35 G. Coedès, *The Indianized States of Southeast Asia* (Australian National University Press, Canberra, 1968); I.W. Mabbett, 'Kingship at Angkor' (1978) 66(2) *Journal of the Siam Society* 58 pp.; O.W. Wolters, *History, Culture and Religion in Southeast Asian Perspectives* (Institute of Southeast Asian Studies, Singapore, 1982); C. Higham, *The Archaeology of Mainland Southeast Asia* (Cambridge University Press, Cambridge, 1989), Ch. 5; C. Mackerras (ed.), *Eastern Asia: An*

and most durable maritime trading power in the Southeast Asian region. It was well adapted to its environment, making use of the sea and its strategic location for trade between China and India – and even further to Persia. As a tributary state of China, Srivijava had the right to trade with China and so surpassed its rivals as a maritime power. Chinese suzerainty proved vital to Srivijaya in boosting its capacities as a trading nation.[36]

A twenty-first century version of this is being re-enacted in the form of a regional free trade agreement between China and the Association of Southeast Asian Nations (ASEAN) to form what will become the world's largest free trade zone in terms of population by 2010. Tariffs are to be reduced to between 5 per cent and zero and investment barriers removed. This trade region will create an integrated market of 1.7 billion people, account for an estimated total GDP of US$2 trillion (10 per cent of world GDP), a trade volume of US$1.2 trillion per annum, and 40 per cent of global foreign exchange reserves.[37] The old Srivijayan *mandala* now lives through its modern descendants along the strategic Malacca Strait: namely, Malaysia, Singapore, and Indonesia. A past regionalism is being resurrected under modern trade conditions but with equally decentralized units of cooperation. The rule of non-subjugation remains as before. Regionalism then, as now and in the foreseeable future, relies on its sovereign parts to cohere. The most advanced form of this expression is a 'pooled sovereignty'[38] agreed upon in the European Union. Such an arrangement may well reach the China-East Asian region in the next phase of global politico-economic integration, though at present it is not a favoured development. Decolonization and nation-building are still within recent historical memory in East Asia. Hence any suggestion of 'pooled sovereignty' is not likely to prove acceptable in the near future – though increased cooperation is.

Surveying the temporal expanse of regional formations, from the classical past to the projected future, certain observations may be made about subsidiarity as a context in the future in global affairs. While the Roman and Chinese empires operated a form of subsidiarity in their multi-ethnic domains, and Europe today has enshrined it within its new supranational body, the European Union, its appearance at the global level is still formative. One may speculate that subsidiarity is also a phenomenon of contemporary globalization in that traditionally rendered Centre–Periphery, North– South relations need to be rebalanced if such vital concerns as development

---

Contd.
Introductory History (3rd edn, Longman Cheshire, Melbourne, 2000), Ch. 8; and D. Kingsbury, *South-East Asia: A Political Profile* (Oxford University Press, New York, 2001), pp. 14–17.

36 M. Osborne, *Southeast Asia: An Illustrated Introductory History* (8th edn, Allen & Unwin, Sydney, 2000), pp. 27–30.

37 *China Daily*, 'ASEAN Begins Negotiations on Free Trade Zone' 14 May 2002; *Businessline*, 'Meeting the Chinese Challenge, Asean Way', 27 June 2002; and Stephen Lunn, 'ASEAN Snubs Canberra and Tokyo on Ties', *The Australian*, 6 November 2002, p. 8.

38 This refers to legal authority given by the member states to their supranational organization to make decisions on public policy questions. Such decisions were previously made only at the sovereign state level. *See* R.O. Keohane and S. Hoffmann (eds), *The New European Community: Decisionmaking and Institutional Change* (Westview Press, Boulder, CO, 1991).

assistance from donor countries can be taken seriously by both sides.[39] Otherwise, corruption and *bad faith* intervene, evaporating any goodwill or practical improvements to people's quality of life. Worsening levels of corruption are only one negative scenario. Another is that of globalized guerilla warfare, conducted by largely unrepresentative political activists. This method of warfare was popularized during the revolutionary decolonization period of the previous century, most memorably in China, Vietnam and Cuba. Political terror under secular left-wing identity continued into the twenty-first century as witnessed in South America and the Himalayan Kingdom of Nepal. Guerilla warfare with its hit-and-run tactics that seek to destabilize the enemy over a prolonged period, but not take territory, is part of a broader 'people's war', as Mao Zedong called it. The final phase of people's war is to fight for territory by more conventional means in order to effect a change of regime.[40] This was clearly demonstrated by the Vietnamese defeating the French colonial power, culminating in the Battle of Dien Bien Phu in 1954.

Today's globalized terrorism differs in many ways from the national liberation struggles of the past, but still operates in a deterritorialized context. It relies on guerilla terrorist strikes as the prelude to overthrowing existing regimes of power and replacing them with an alternative world order: a particular brand of Islamic hegemony, perhaps, under a council-elected caliphate.[41] At a local level it would entail the creation of 'Islamic states governed by Sharia law'.[42] Certainly, there is evidence of disgruntled populations in existing Muslim countries, such as Uzbekistan, supporting more extreme measures to realise greater social equity.[43] Meanwhile, the 2002 Bali bombings have suggested an objective to build an Islamic state spanning Southeast Asia.[44] The current 'guerilla' phase of global terrorism resembles not only aspects of Mao's revolutionary people's war, but also transnational corporations (TNCs) establishing branches across the world. Just as TNCs shift their manufacturing bases to the most competitive labour markets, global terrorism activates different theatres of operations in accordance with better opportunities. As the war-on-terror led by the USA was taken to Afghanistan, al-Qa'ida, through its system of decentralized 'sleeper cells', easily shifted focus to Southeast Asia where some 3,000 local (Malaysian, Indonesian, and

---

39 This is because over 50 years of development assistance has failed to produce 'development'. To quote Nandy, 'The Beautiful, Expanding Future of Poverty …': 'The underlying myth of development, that it will remove all poverty forever from all corners of the world, now lies shattered' (p. 108).

40 *See Selected Military Writings of Mao Tze-Tung* (Foreign Languages Press, Peking, 1966); and R. Dellios, *Modern Chinese Defence Strategy: Present Developments, Future Directions* (Macmillan, Basingstoke, 1989).

41 John Stapleton, 'Zealots' Quest for Purity', *The Australian*, 19 November 2002, p. 13.

42 Zachary Abuza, 'Tentacles of Terror – al-Qa'ida's Southeast Asian Network', quoted in Martin Chulov, '3,000 Southeast Asian Sleeper Cells Trained in Terror', *The Australian*, 27 November 2002, p. 1.

43 Stapleton, 'Zealots' Quest for Purity'.

44 *See* Cameron Stewart, 'Days of Living Dangerously' and P. Kelly, 'The Islamic Front is at Our Back Door', *The Weekend Australian*, 19–20 October 2002, pp. 19, 30.

Filipino) Islamic radicals had received training in Afghanistan.[45] This region had been rendered vulnerable by the Asian Crisis that began with dramatic currency devaluations in 1997. In Indonesia's case, the financial crisis led to social and political crises, climaxing in President Suharto's resignation in 1998 after three decades of authoritarian rule. With the success of the *reformasi* movement in allowing greater political freedoms came less stringent controls on radical Islamic organizations. This, combined with populations still suffering from the depredations inflicted by the Asian financial crisis, and a government more concerned with avoiding fragmentation than tracking terrorists, rendered Indonesia a more hospitable environment for criminal operations. There was even a certain glamour associated with Osama bin Laden, as demonstrated by the name 'Osama' emblazoned on the rear window of a minibus in Jakarta in 2002.[46] Nearby Singapore and Malaysia were also used by terrorist conspirators, though operations there were foiled through a more focused security apparatus in a less dispersed geography.

Having examined the negative scenario of subsidiarity, that is, a countercultural approach – or a fanatical Islamist Cultural Revolution – it is worth switching back to development and a positive scenario of subsidiarity. Recent thinking in development studies suggests that communities' *capacity to concert* – meaning a people's 'capacity to orchestrate their own development' – may also have important macro socio-economic implications that will drive global institution-building.[47] This form of subsidiarity indicates that globalized culture as it manifests today may be said to have gone beyond mere Americanization and entered the domain of postcolonial cosmopolitanism. Such a movement takes for granted Western influence, indeed incorporates it as a platform from which to build a global society. This entails the 'democratization of the global structure itself' through 'self-development and self-participation'.[48] These features for a cosmopolitical system are conducive to social justice which, in turn, would deprive terrorists, like the communists a generation before them, of the grievances which fuel their cause. However, unlike an orchestrated strategy with a US 'coalition of the willing', cosmopolitics is not concerned with micro-management. Subsidiarity allows for the localization of global life through its own perceptual prism. This often results in a recurring theme of future cultural and political life, that of syncretism.

At this point it is worth returning to Alexander the Great. It is said of him in the national newspaper of a former Chinese tributary region, now the Federation of Malaysia, that he was 'the first exponent of globalization'. Moreover,

> since it was impossible to micromanage all the territories that had been conquered, synrectism or the adaptation of Greek to local practices,

[45] Zachary Abuza, 'Tentacles of Terror – al-Qa'ida's Southeast Asian Network', quoted in Martin Chulov, '3,000 Southeast Asian Sleeper Cells Trained in Terror', *The Australian*, 27 November 2002, p. 1.

[46] Seen and photographed by this writer in June 2002.

[47] R.E. Daubon and H.H. Saunders, 'Operationalizing Social Capital: A Strategy to Enhance Communities' "Capacity to Concert" ' (2002) 3(2) *International Studies Perspectives* 15 pp.

[48] Dallmayr, 'Globalization and Inequality', pp. 153, 155.

> customs and religions became the norm. That it survived as a force was a result of the many accommodations made. Had the Greeks strived for ideological purity, it is doubtful that it would have survived.[49]

Malaysia – with its multi-ethnic, multi-religious citizenry – can well relate to the message of its incorporated ancestor. Iskandar forms part of the Malay world's mosaic,[50] a work-in-progress that has been put to the test by financial crisis, terrorist connections, and the bypassing of *kampong* (village) life via the construction of a 'multimedia supercorridor' (a global icon). Still, at the start of the twenty-first century, Malaysia, like neighbouring Singapore, continues to sit solidly at the crossroads of transnational flows. The Straits of Malacca littoral states, Malaysia, Singapore, and Indonesia, share to varying degrees the condition of global trader in an East–West fusion, just as they had in a previous incarnation when they operated under the maritime trading empire of Srivijaya.

Indonesia is syncretically more complex in that it retains its villages not for museumized nostalgia, as Malaysia and Singapore tend to do,[51] but out of habit and as habitat. The above-mentioned globally networked religious extremists use the countryside to surround the cities, as occurred in commercialized Bali, while nostalgia remains the preserve of an urban-based Occidentalism. The latter is well illustrated by the following newspaper item. On 11 November 2002, a month after the Bali bombings in which some 200 tourists, many of them Australian, lost their lives, *The Australian* published a photo of Indonesians not as terrorist suspects or as Muslims praying but as a people of unexpected personas. In this case, they were enacting the culture of the American West. The caption read:

> Studio audiences in cowboy outfits take part in line dancing at the Indonesian state television's weekly prime-time *Country Road* program in Jakarta. The program features a parade of Indonesian groups and singers, who play old US hits in the original English to appreciative studio audience members clad in check shirts, jeans and boots.[52]

---

49 S.C.M. Wong, 'Limits of Language and Culture in Social Cohesion', *New Straits Times* (Malaysia), 30 September 2002, p. 10. Classical archeology academic, Lesley Beaumont, concurs:

> Alexander married a Bactrian princess, Roxane, and many of his men married Persian women. His method was not to force Greek culture on subjugated people but to initiate an exchange between the cultures of East and West.

Quoted in L. Slattery, 'The Alexander Technique', *The Weekend Australian Magazine*, 23–24 November 2002, p. 20.

50 'Mosaic' is a deliberately chosen metaphor in view of the popularity of mosaics in Greek antiquity and, according to Irvine, some Javanese scholars' preference for 'Mosaicism' as a term instead of 'Syncretism' to describe the Javanese ability to assimilate new religio-cultural influences into their existing traditions – D. Irvine, *Leather Gods and Wooden Heroes: Java's Classical Wayang* (Times Editions, Singapore, 1996), p. 12.

51 *See* P. Dellios, 'The Museumification of the Village: Cultural Subversion in the 21st Century', *The Culture Mandala* (2002) 5(1), available on <www.international_relations.com>.

52 'In Focus', *The Australian*, 11 November 2002, p. 15.

American Wild West 'nostalgia' extends even to the night markets of Java's cultural capital, Yogyakarta, where Native American paraphernalia were being sold in 2002. Street markets which combine a range of products, from the locally produced, to the mass manufactured, and to the fashionably foreign, may be found from Yogya to Kunming. This is an indication that the 'developing world' accounts for consumer tastes across the entire spectrum of traditional, modern and postmodern. Those parts of the developing world that are themselves composed of numerous ethnicities and cross-temporal traditions, such as the above examples of Kunming, capital of China's multi-ethnic Yunnan Province, and the contemporary descendants of the trading kingdoms (*mandalas*) of old, may well reflect a greater sophistication in syncretic culture formation.

This is not to say that the task is an untroubled one. Indonesia's self-described 'unity-in-diversity' appears to house a wide spectrum of identities, from *abangan* (these being 'Animist–Hindu–Buddhist Javanese Muslim'),[53] Islamist militants, the nationalist intelligensia, contemporary Occidentalists, in addition to the numerous nationalities such as Bataks, Sundanese, Buginese, and Madurese. With a backdrop of environmental concerns, especially the seasonal forest fires that produce the notorious cross-border 'haze', Indonesia has yet to *mandalize* its prevailing diversities under conditions of accelerated globalization. Syncretic cultures seek integration of the parts into unified identity, which is what a *mandala* does. In Javanese terms it has traditionally been expressed thus:

> Over time the integration of indigenous and foreign cultures and beliefs came to have its own ordered pattern. This pattern has been likened to the *mandala* design of the Borobodur temple or the traditional Javanese ceremonial rice cone, in which various elements and stages are integrated into a single design to create the symbol of Sangkan Paran, the Cycle of Life according to which all life springs from and eventually returns to the Supreme Consciousness.[54]

It is pertinent to note that the *mandala* has exhibited two contexts of meaning thus far. One is the political, in relation to Sriviyaya as a political system derived from Hindu statecraft;[55] the other is the psycho-cultural, in which a spiritual tradition of syncretism is expressed. Parallels may be found in the contemporary phenomenon of what Appadurai calls 'diasporic public spheres', created via the 'mass media (both interactive and expressive) and the movement of refugees, activists, students, and laborers'.[56] Quite apart from the political and psycho-cultural, there are regional integrational implications in this diasporic syncretism that do not await the 'pooled sovereignty'

---

[53] Irvine, Leather Gods ..., p. 12. See also website: *Javanese Mystical Movements*, last revised 16 September 2002 <http://www.xs4all.nl/~wichm/javmys1.html>.

[54] *Ibid.*, p. 13, footnote 54, citing A. Ciptoprawiro, *Filsawat Jawa* (Balai Pustaka, Jakarta, 1986), p. 27.

[55] Kautilya, *Arthasastra*, trans. R. Shamasastry (Mysore Printing and Publishing House, Mysore, 1967).

[56] A. Appadurai, *Modernity at Large: Cultural Dimensions of Globalization* (Oxford University Press, Delhi, 1997), pp. 22–23.

(or orchestrated) regionalism of the EU model. As Dirlik observes, 'the result of the Asian and Pacific diaspora is to enhance the structural integration of the region (albeit bringing with it, dialectically, previously unknown structural tensions)'.[57] While an organic, diaspora-assisted, regionalism is flourishing in the Asia-Pacific region, China's growing influence can be expected to inject a certain controlled orchestration of regional development, as evidenced in the above-mentioned China–ASEAN FTA agreement, as well as China's own intra-regional development policy.[58] Taken to the broader dimension of the West and Non-West, one may observe that they are not necessarily undergoing monocultural convergence – a system as much out of step with ecologically favoured farming practices as sociological developments – but may well be giving way to a syncretic culture with – to borrow Indonesia's ambivalent term – *reformasi* characteristics. This somewhat menacing shadow to an otherwise enabling *mandala* needs to be viewed under the third distinguishing feature of globalization, that of its propagation.

10.4 Globalization's Propagation

The Macquarie Dictionary definition of 'propaganda' is as follows:

> 1. systematic spreading of a religion or doctrine. 2. (spreading of) ideas, arguments or facts used to persuade people to think well or badly about some person, cause, or movement.

The word comes from the Latin and was used in the name of a papal committee established in 1622 for the propagation of the faith. Globalization, too, is subject to propagation. Its continued development is vital to the prevailing paradigm of the neoliberal economic order, also known as the capitalist world economy. Free market principles via non-discriminatory trade are an ideal seen to be advanced by the 'borderless' scope of globalization. The World Bank, itself an agency of this neoliberal economic system, has reported globalization (in the form of 'increased integration into the world economy') to be a strong predictor of wealth creation in developing countries.[59]

Globalization has its prophets and proselytizers, from corporate elites and international financial institutions to influential columnists like Thomas Friedman who admits that while globalization is 'homogenizing

---

57 A. Dirik, 'The Asia-Pacific Idea: Reality and Representation in the Invention of a Regional Structure', in A. Dirlik (ed.), *What is in a Rim? Critical Perspectives on the Pacific Region Idea* (2nd edn, Rowman & Littlefield, New York, 1998), p. 26.

58 *See* R. Dellios, 'Chinese Forms of Regionalism: Organic and Orchestrated', Centre for the Study of Globalisation and Regionalisation, Warwick University, UK, 1999 <www.warwick.ac.uk/fac/soc/CSGR/conf99/Dellios.PDF>.

59 World Bank, *Globalization, Growth and Poverty: Building an Inclusive World Economy*, 2002, on <http://econ.worldbank.org>.

cultures',[60]

> it is also enabling people to share their unique individuality farther and wider. It makes us want to chase after the Lexus [the car] more intensely than ever and cling to our olive trees [traditions] more tightly than ever. It enables us to reach into the world as never before and it enables the world to reach into each of us as never before.[61]

Yet, as the Sufi poem opening this chapter suggests, there is cause for calling upon its compassion. The forces of globalization, like those of the Chinese Heaven (*tien*) and Earth, are capable of treating humans like straw dogs blown away in the wind.[62] The present historical era has been described as one when 'extreme individualism' and 'market societies shape our views of what is natural'.[63] In a profits-driven globalized economy, the richest 20 per cent of the world accounts for 86 per cent of global consumption while the remainder (80 per cent) survive on 14 per cent of consumption spending.[64] Disparities in wealth occur *intra*nationally as much as internationally. Latham notes that the upper 20 per cent of households in Australia hold 65 per cent of the country's wealth, while the lower 20 per cent 'owns nothing at all'.[65] Nandy, cited above in relation to the manipulation of poverty for Western developmental agendas, sees a direct link between globalization and poverty: 'The presently trendy slogan of globalization can be read as the newest effort to disguise both the declining political clout of the historically disadvantaged and an interest in poverty'.[66]

Thus the subsidiarity depicted above could, in a *yin–yang* alternation, become fragmentation; cosmopolitanism might be charged with the propagation of privileged elitism. How is it, then, that greater caution has not been exercised in the way in which societies and their governments deal with the rise of globalization? Malaysia, for one, did impose currency controls, and hence an impediment to free flows of capital, but on the whole globalization is an untethered 'beast'.[67]

---

60 Contra Appadurai, above, who speaks of homogenizing mechanisms, like the media and fashion.

61 T. Friedman, *The Lexus and the Olive Tree* (Harper Collins, London, 1999), p. 331.

62 The Daoist classic, *Daodejing (Book of the Way and Its Power)* states that 'Heaven and earth are ruthless, and treat the myriad creatures as straw dogs' (Bk 1, V). Straw dogs were used by the ancient Chinese as divine offerings and were therefore treated with reverence while serving this function. Thereafter they were discarded as useless, often trampled upon. *See* translators note in *Lao Tzu, Tao Te Ching [Daodejing]*, trans. D.C. Lau (Penguin, London, 1963) p. 9.

63 M. Lerner, *The Politics of Meaning* (Addison-Wesley Publishing Co., New York, 1996), p. 19.

64 UN Development Program, cited in K. Danaher, 'The New Protest Movement: It's About Demanding a Say in the Future of the Planet', *The Observer*, London, 29 April 2001. *Common Dreams News Center*, online: <www.commondreams.org/views01/0429-07.htm>.

65 M. Latham, 'Let's Rattle the Cage of Insider Power', *The Australian*, 21 November 2002, p. 11.

66 A. Nandy, 'The Beautiful, Expanding Future of Poverty: Popular Economics as a Psychological Defense' (2002) 4(2) *International Studies Review*, p. 107.

67 Or, as Friedman, *The Lexus and the Olive Tree*, refers to its financial dimension, the 'Electronic Herd'. He uses the term to describe the stampede of which the global marketplace is capable. The Electronic Herd consists of 'often anonymous stock, bond, currency, and multinational investors, connected by screens and networks' (p. 94).

Hooper helps answer this question when she identifies the propagandistic dimension to globalization. After examining the content of *The Economist*, from 1989 to 1996, she argues that globalization has been presented 'as a glamorous process at the cutting edge of progressive capitalist development'.[68] Her study reveals a certain masculinity about globalization. This is not a traditional patriarchy but a 'sexy, sci-fi' masculinity (in a world of technology, business, speed) which treats 'the whole globe as its playground'.[69] Such an image of globalization must appear attractive to those in the so-called Business Class economy.[70] If globalization is viewed as a trend, then there will be those who will seek to exploit it, as exemplified by Naisbitt[71] who is probably the USA's best-known 'trend-chaser'. The danger inherent in this approach, however, is that trend-chasing amounts to 'worshipping the conqueror of the present moment',[72] rather than reflecting on the conqueror's credentials.

A more critical approach to the globalization 'trend' has in fact begun. It was proclaimed most graphically by the 'Battle for Seattle' anti-globalization protest of 1999. Though more like a millenarian movement than a systematic critique, it nonetheless opened debate on the merits and demerits of globalization to the broader public. With a sharpening competition between philosophies of *globalization-from-above*, which is seen as exclusionary and elitist, v. *globalization-from-below* which promises to be more participatory, the world's security in the early twenty-first century now seems to rest on the 'clash of globalizations',[73] overtaking Huntington's late twentieth century 'clash of civilizations'[74] thesis. Dialectically speaking, it would not be unrealistic to expect the clash of globalizations to yield to a switch in civilizational *mandalas* for the purpose of harmonizing the two extremities. Eschewing the adversarial politics of street marches versus international financial institutions in favour of a syncretic system of accommodation, the global potter might appear once again in the *agora*.

Here China, with its growing economic and political influence, has a conceptual contribution to the Greek foundations of Western participatory politics. Of particular interest is the Daoist philosopher Zhuangzi's approach of

---

68 C. Hooper, *Manly States: Masculinities, International Relations and Gender Politics* (Columbia University Press, New York, 2001), p. 158.

69 *Ibid*., p. 193. *See also* the book review of Hooper: M. Zalewski, 'Old Wine in New Bottles?' (2002) 4(1) *International Studies Review* 161–165.

70 A term used in Indian business circles to differentiate the privileged economic elite from the 'Bike Economy' (the rising middle class who can afford a motorcycle but not a car), and the vast majority of the population who exist in the 'Bullock Economy' (they rely on bullocks and not bikes). *Asia Business Report*, BBC World News, 26 November 2002.

71 J. Naisbitt, *Megatrends: Ten New Directions Transforming Our Lives* (2nd edn, Warner Books, New York, 1984); J. Naisbitt, *Megatrends Asia: The Eight Asian Megatrends that are Changing the World* (Nicholas Brealey Publishing, London, 1995).

72 Max Dublin, *Futurehype* (Viking, Markham, Ontario, 1989), p. 5.

73 S. Gill, 'Constitutionalizing Inequality and the Clash of Globalizations' (2002) 4(2) *International Studies Review* 20 pp.

74 S.P. Huntington, *The Clash of Civilizations and the Remaking of the World Order* (Simon and Schuster, New York, 1996).

liang xing,[75] meaning to follow two courses simultaneously. This has been applied to the PRC's own policy of 'one country' (China), 'two systems' (socialism and capitalism) that led to the successful reunification of socialist China with capitalist Hong Kong and Macao, as well as the establishment of capitalist zones within the mainland itself. Such a *liang xing* logic accords with the *yin–yang* principle of interpenetrating polarities. The Chinese Communist Party (CCP) would never have survived to its 16th Congress in November 2002 had it not invoked market economics to enrich the nation. Indeed, capitalists are now permitted to join the CCP.[76] Similar dynamics may be found in the family-based business traditions using new technology, for example, internet cafes in family homes. This process is also underway in another Socialist Confucian state, Vietnam, whose *doi moi* or *renovation* policy is yielding results reflective of China's. Vietnam, like the other ASEAN states, comprised the wider Chinese tribute-trade system which, as has been noted above, is now reimagining itself through an ASEAN–China regionalism.

10.5 Conclusion: The World City

That trade in the twenty-first century will be shaped by the diversity of styles and meanings emerging out of localizations in the global *mandala* is incontrovertible. The world will see a wider presence of cultural market niches, particularly in the form of fusions between traditions and across the postmodern, modern and the traditional spectrum. What is not so clear is whether this diversity will inform a more compassionate potter than the one which is currently feared. Here is where the role of governments and governance are needed if exploitation is to be curtailed. Without mechanisms of self-monitoring, even the winners in the global game will lose. In the wider world of concerted civic efforts, cultural resources abound. For every Islamic extremist a Sufi may be found, for all of Washington's unilateralism it must operate in a multipolar world of multilateral thought. The integrative properties of globalization describe the global city with its square. Herein lies the opportunity to create, in Dallmayr's words, 'the required democratization of the global structure itself, that is, the need to render global power legitimate and hence to hold global hegemons democratically accountable'.[77] Beyond the global city lies the circle of the environmental life-support system that infuses the Centre with a *yin–yang* process of 'world making'. This, in turn, depends on diversified as well as concerted human action.

---

75 *Chuang-Tsu* [*Zhuangzi*], trans. Fung Yu-lan (Foreign Languages Press, Beijing, 1989). *See* M. Lu and R. Dellios, '"One Culture, Two Systems": A Cultural Approach to Inter-Chinese Politics' (1998) 3(1) *The Culture Mandala*, 22 pp.
76 C. Armitage, 'Jiang Pushes Accelerated Market Reform', *The Weekend Australian*, 9–10 November 2002, p. 9.
77 Dallmayr, 'Globalization and Inequality', 153.

11. Lessons for the WTO from Recent EFTA Bilateral Free Trade Agreements

*Andreas R. Ziegler**

11.1 Summary

Despite the successful launch of a new world trade round at the Ministerial Conference in Doha in November 2001, there is a continuous and increasing tendency of (newly) industrialized countries to conclude bilateral free trade agreements. This chapter examines the motives and basic structures of the existing free trade agreements, taking as an example the agreements the European Free Trade Association (EFTA) has concluded with numerous States since 1991.[1] The objective is to identify WTO-plus elements and developments in areas that are crucial for the current WTO-negotiations.

The most recent agreements of the EFTA States with Mexico and Singapore go significantly further than the traditional agreements which mainly abolished customs duties and non-tariff barriers for industrial goods. They are typical so-called second or third generation agreements. They carry on the liberalization of trade in services as achieved within the WTO framework (GATS), as well as the liberalization in areas such as public procurement or protection of intellectual property rights (IPR). Furthermore, they partly include new areas such as foreign direct investment (FDI) or competition law, areas on which so far no consensus exists within the WTO. The strong increase in very comprehensive bilateral agreements can lead to opportunities but also to potential conflicts within the global trading system. In particular, the regional developments in areas where no global consensus has been achieved, such as competition and investment, could help to advance the debate in the WTO.

---

* The views expressed here are purely personal. I would like to thank my assistants Michel Mitzicos and Jane Mulder for the invaluable assistance.

[1] As of the time of writing, the Members of EFTA are Norway, Switzerland, Iceland, and Liechtenstein. Denmark and the United Kingdom were founding members of EFTA but joined the European Community (EC) as early as 1973. Of the other earlier members, Portugal became an EC Member State in 1986 and Sweden, Austria, and Finland left EFTA in 1995 to become Members of the European Union (EU).

11.2 Historical Evolution of Bilateral and Multilateral Trade Negotiations

11.2.1 First generation agreements (1850–1910)

Bilateral agreements are significantly older than the global trading system. The General Agreement on Tariffs and Trade (GATT)[2] came into effect in 1947/8.[3] The first modern bilateral trade agreements were concluded in the middle of the 19th century. At that time, as a result of initiatives of the United Kingdom and the United States of America in particular, a large number of bilateral agreements, known as 'Commerce, Establishment and Friendship Treaties', were concluded. Between seafaring nations these agreements were usually concluded as 'Friendship, Navigation and Commerce Treaties'.[4] Switzerland concluded such a treaty with the United Kingdom in 1855. It remains – at least partly – in force today.[5] Because of the euphoria of that period relating to trade expansion and the liberal attitude of those States, these first general free trade agreements included an advanced framework not only for the free movement of goods[6] but also for the free movement and establishment of persons in each Party. Towards the end of the 19th century, the necessity to finance wars (e.g. between France and Germany) and civil wars (e.g. in the United States of America) with income from customs duties, as well as the general movement towards 'protectionist nationalism' contributed to the turning away from free trade.

11.2.2 Second generation agreements (1960s and 1970s)

After the economic tensions of the 1920s and 1930s and the creation of war economies during the Second World War, it was only in the 1940s that ideas for a liberal trade order (at least in basic terms) were also formulated internationally.[7] While the immediate post-war period was influenced by

---

2 *See* Swiss Official Collection of Laws and Treaties, SR 0.632.21, available on the Internet: <www.admin.ch>.

3 International Trade Organization, *see* also John Odell, 'The United States, the ITO, and the WTO', in Anne O. Krueger (ed.), *The WTO as an International Organization*, (Chicago, 1998), pp. 181–209 and Howard S. Piquet, *The Havana Charter for an International Trade Organization*. U.S. Government Pr. Office, Washington 1950).

4 For the United States, *see* The Avalon Project at Yale Law School: American Diplomacy to the Present – Treaties, Agreements and Correspondence, on the Internet: <http://www.yale.edu/lawweb/avalon/amerdipl.htm>.

5 *Friendship Commerce, and Establishment Treaty*, between the Swiss Confederation and the Majesty the Queen of the United kingdom of Great Britain and Ireland, concluded on 6th September 1855, ratified by the Swiss Parliament on 7th February 1856; Exchange of Ratification Documents on 6 March 1856; entry into force on 6 March 1856, SR 0.142.113.67, *see* n. 2.

6 *See also* Article VIII/IX/X (MFN Principle) and Article VII/XI (National Treatment) in the *Friendship Commerce, and Establishment Treaty*, between the Swiss Confederation and the Majesty the Queen of the United Kingdom of Great Britain and Ireland (1856), n. 4.

7 They had been brought forward in the United States domestically already as from 1934; *see*, for instance, Kevin O'Rourke and Jeffrey Williamson, '*Globalisation and History: The Evolution of a Nineteenth-Century Atlantic Economy*' (MIT, Cambridge MA, 2000).

the idea of bringing about global economic liberalization, this ambitious project was quickly completed or partly replaced by regional integration agreements. After failing to create the International Trade Organization (ITO) as conceived in the Havana Charter (1948), the legal basis for world trade remained solely the General Agreement on Trade and Tariffs (1947).[8] Since the 1950s several regional free trade area agreements came into force in parallel with the GATT. Actually, such regional preferential agreements were provided for through Article XXIV GATT, allowing for the deviation from the general most-favoured-nation (MFN) clause (Article III GATT). In Europe, these were the European Economic Community (EEC, now EC) on the basis of the Treaty of Rome (1957)[9] and the EFTA on the basis of the Stockholm Convention (1960).[10] In the 1960s and 1970s, the EC and the EFTA began to integrate their trade through agreements and expanded such agreements to other European States.[11] In addition, the trade relations of the European Community in relation to the African, Caribbean, and Pacific (ACP) States were also regulated on a preferential basis as a consequence of their status as former colonies.[12]

Outside Europe, besides a few isolated bilateral trade agreements, the most important initiatives were the Latin American Free Trade Area (LAFTA) of 1960[13] and CARICOM (1973)[14] in the South American, as well as the Bangkok Agreement (1975)[15] and ASEAN (1977)[16] in Asia.

11.2.3 Third generation agreements (since the 1990s)

11.2.3.1 Regional integration

In the 1980s less effort was placed on bilateral and regional free trade agreements. Priority focused on multilateral efforts in the Uruguay-Round of

---

8 *See*, for example, Andreas Lowenfeld, *International Economic Law* (OUP, Oxford, 2002), pp. 22–26.

9 Hereafter EC; *see*, <http://www.europa.eu.int/>.

10 Agreement of 4 January 1960 for the creation of the European Free Trade Association (EFTA) for Switzerland reprinted in SR 0.632.31 (*supra* n. 2). About the Swiss considerations on this subject *see* Roland Maurhofer, The quest for the lesser evil: Great Britain, Switzerland and the decision to create EFTA, Working Paper 286, Institut für Politikwissenschaft, Universität. St. Gallen, 2000.

11 With the exception of Turkey, which has already been associated 1963 and Algeria (1976). *See* also the Free Trade Agreement of 22 July 1972 between the Swiss Confederation and the EEC (with Annexes and exchange of letters), for Switzerland *see* SR 0.632.401 (see *supra* n. 2).

12 *See*, for instance, the Agreement of Jaunde (1963 and 1969) and thereafter the Agreement of Lomé (1975). Currently, the Lomé Agreement of 20 June 2000 is in force. *See* <http://europa.eu.int/scadplus/leg/de/lvb/r12100.htm>.

13 The Latin American Free Trade Association (LAFTA) became LAIA/ALADI in 1980; *see* <http://www.aladi.org/>.

14 Known as the 'Caribbean Community'; *see* <http://www.caricom.org/expframes2.htm>.

15 *See* also <http://www.unescap.org/itid/bkkagr.htm>; the Member States are Bangladesh, India, the Republic of Korea, Laos, Sri Lanka, and since 2000 China.

16 *See* <http://www.aseansec.org/>. The tariff abolishment was only accomplished in 2002/03.

trade negotiations from roughly 1986 until 1994, leading to the establishment of the WTO on 1 January 1995.[17]

However, even whilst concluding the Uruguay Round, but in particular afterwards, there were substantial efforts from both industrialized countries and emerging nations to advance trade liberalization regionally or bilaterally. In the beginning, the achievement of the EC Internal Market Programme (1992) and the free trade agreement between the USA and Canada (CUSFTA)[18] played an important role in this respect. The CUSFTA was intended to serve as a model for the multilateral system, supported by the United States of America during the Uruguay Round.[19] Before the conclusion of the Uruguay Round, this agreement between the United States of America and Canada was expanded to include Mexico within the framework of the North American Free Trade Agreement (NAFTA).[20] It came into force on 1 January 1994. The enlarged Internal Market between the EC and the EFTA-States creating the European Economic Area (EEA) also came into force on 1 January 1994.[21] As the third most important regional free trade area with at least theoretically a great potential and with analogous political significance, mention should be made of the Mercosur/Mercosul Agreement between Brazil, Argentina, Uruguay, and Paraguay, which came into force on 29 November 1991.[22]

11.2.3.2 New bilateral agreements

Besides the so-called regional integration agreements, another phenomenon strongly affirmed itself during this period and still does so today: purely bilateral free trade agreements. While this approach had been followed at a regional level by the EC and EFTA since their creation, it expanded after the end of the Cold War, first to Central and Eastern Europe[23] and later to the Mediterranean countries.[24]

---

17 All the Agreements of the Uruguay Round can be found on the internet: <http://www.wto.org>.
18 *See* International Legal Materials, 1988, p. 281.
19 This is very obvious in the dispute settlement rules: *see* for instance, Marceau, Gabrielle, 'NAFTA and WTO Dispute Settlement Rules – A Thematic Comparison' (1997) *Journal of World Trade*, 1997, pp. 25–81 and William A. Kerr, 'Greener Multilateral Pastures for Canada and Mexico – Dispute Settlement in the North American Trade Agreements' (2001) *Journal of World Trade* 1169–1181.
20 *See* <http://www.nafta-sec-alena.org/english/index.htm>.
21 *See* <http://secretariat.efta.int/euroeco/ECProg/>. Meanwhile the character of this Agreement has been strongly changed because of the absence of Switzerland (due to a negative referendum) and the entry of some important EFTA-States into the EU.
22 The Treaty of Asunciòn (Spanish: Tratado de Asunciòn) of 26 March 1991, on the Internet in Spanish at <http://www.mercosur-comisec.gub.uy/DOCUMENT/TRATADOA/Asuncion.htm>.
23 *See* the EU-Association Agreements with these States and the efforts of some of these States to become full members. To this point, Philippe G. Nell, 'Extension of the European Union/EFTA Regional Trading Bloc to Central and Eastern Europe' (1997) *World Competition – Law and Economics Review* 131–150.
24 *See* the Agreements and negotiations with Morocco, Egypt and Tunisia; *see* 'Die Mühsal des zweiten Zugs – Die Schweizer Textilindustrie will nicht nur der EU nachrennen' in: Neue Zürcher Zeitung, Nr. 49, 28 February 2000, p. 15. So far, it has been necessary that all these

At the end of 1990s, extra-regional agreements, the existence of which could no longer be justified by pure regional integration efforts, became more prominent such as the agreements negotiated between the EC and Mexico or between Canada and the EFTA-States. In fact, after the conclusion of the Uruguay Round, a certain vacuum appeared, which some countries attempted to overcome through bilateral agreements. Besides the EC and EFTA these were most importantly Canada, Mexico, Chile, Singapore, New Zealand, Australia, South Korea, Japan, South Africa, Israel, and very recently the United States of America. Mercosur/Mercosul is currently negotiating for a Pan-American free trade area[25] and for an agreement with the EC, although the recent economic problems in Argentina have slowed down these efforts. Meanwhile, a network of agreements has been created between all these States, similar to the network of bilateral friendship, navigation and commerce treaties of the 19th century.[26] The failure of the WTO Ministers' conference in Seattle (1999) had an important influence on the activities of Asian States in this respect.

Among the treaties already concluded and in force, the following agreements are worth mentioning: United States–Israel (19 August 1985), Canada–Israel (1 January 1997), Canada–Chile (7 June 1997), Chile–Mexico (1 August 1999), European Community–South Africa (1 January 2000), Mexico–Israel (1 July 2000), European Community–Mexico (1 July 2000), New Zealand–Singapore (1 January 2001), EFTA–Mexico (1 July 2001). An agreement has been signed between Japan and Singapore (13 January 2002) as well as between the EFTA-States and Singapore on 13 July 2002. Another agreement between the EC and Chile was approved by the European Commission on 3 October 2002 and Korea and Chile agreed in principle on a free trade agreement on 24 October 2002. Finally, on 4 November 2002 Australia and Singapore announced that they had concluded free trade negotiations.[27]

These new bilateral agreements are not only increasing in number and dynamism, but also in scope. Because of their broad coverage of trade in goods, services, and investment these are often referred to as third generation agreements. The European Community started by including into its agreements with the Central and Eastern European candidate States rules relating to the other freedoms besides the free movement of goods, as it had done in the EEA Agreement. The inclusion of rules regarding trade in services, investment, competition, public procurement, etc. was considered a preparatory step to membership. It was in particular the NAFTA Agreement and the expansion of the disciplines covered by the WTO in the Uruguay Round, which lead to the inclusion of trade in services, investment, and public procurement in bilateral free trade agreements aiming purely at economic

---

Contd.
EU trade partners conclude free trade agreements among each other, in order to create the Pan-European Cumulation System (for rules of origin). *See* <http://www.osec.ch/osec/glossar-aw/paneurop-kumul;internal&action=buildframes.action>. The expansion of this system to the Mediterranean States is under preparation (EUROMED cumulation system).

25 FTAA – Free Trade Area of the Americas, on the Internet: <www.ftaa-alca.org/>.

26 *See* to this point Section 11.2.1.

27 *See* Neue Zürcher Zeitung, 5 November 2002, Nr. 257, p. 21.

integration. Indeed the provisions on intellectual property and competition law in most third-generation agreements are as of today substantially more comprehensive than those of classical trade agreements (even of the early nineties).[28]

11.2.3.3 The motives for bilateral agreements: The case of EFTA

Explanations for the strong increase in extra-regional free trade agreements and for why certain States chose this path while others remained sceptical, often amount to little more than speculation. It is interesting to note, however, that even Japan and the United States of America, long-time strong critics of the EC and its preferential agreements, have recently changed their attitude and negotiated bilateral agreements themselves. In the case of the United States of America, this development first appeared in relation to the expansion of its existing agreements to other states in the Western hemisphere only, but recently, the new administration has announced efforts to use the trade promotion authority received by the Senate in Autumn 2002[29] to negotiate bilateral trade agreements with states such as Australia and Singapore.[30]

The agreements so far concluded between the United States of America and Vietnam, Jordan, and Israel were based more on development and security consideration than on an economic rationale.[31]

For years, Japan has been known for its strong support of the multilateral trading system and opposition to bilateral agreements. However, the Japanese government readjusted this attitude in 2000 to smooth the way for bilateral negotiations.[32] Japan signed, in a surprisingly short time, a first agreement with Singapore (13 January 2002) and since has started or prepared to start negotiations with South Korea, Mexico, and other countries.

More obvious are the motives of the EFTA-States in concluding bilateral agreements. In the beginning, the EFTA-States tried to keep track with the EC in Europe and the Mediterranean. More recently, the extra-regional free trade agreements of the EC induced them to follow the same path in order to avoid disadvantages for their exporters in these markets.[33] The external commercial policy of the EEA-States (Norway, Iceland, and Liechtenstein) remains unbound under the EEA Agreement. Switzerland has no obligations with regard to its commercial policy *vis-à-vis* the Community. Therefore all EFTA-States considered from the beginning the negotiation and conclusion of agreements with third parties as one trading-block as an advantage. The fact that the EFTA-States concluded parallel agreements

---

28 For details *see* Sections 4 and 5.

29 *See* the Trade Promotion Authority based on the Trade Act of 30 October 2002, <www.tpa.gov>.

30 *See* <http://www.mti.gov.sg/public/FTA>.

31 *See* <http://www.ustr.gov/regions/index.shtml>.

32 *See*, for instance, the White Paper on International Trade 2000 of the International Trade Research Office, Ministry of International Trade and Industry, Japan; available on the Internet: <http://www.meti.go.jp/english/report/>.

33 *See supra* n. 24.

with States in Central and Eastern Europe that had already concluded agreements with the EC allowed for a cumulation of the existing origin requirements for the entire area leading to the creation of the Pan-European Cumulation System.[34]

The efforts – as yet not successful – to conclude an agreement with Canada represent a precedent for the relations between EFTA free trade agreements with third countries and the corresponding negotiations of the EC. This was the first time the EFTA-States had negotiated with a country that was not engaged in parallel negotiations with the European Community. Canada was the first candidate for a bilateral agreement with the EFTA-States where the parallel with the EC could not be invoked to justify the bilateral approach. On the other hand, the successful conclusion of an agreement with Canada could potentially result in a level playing field with competitors from the United States of America and Mexico.

As the negotiations with Canada have not yet been concluded, the agreement with Singapore in 2002 represents the first agreement the EFTA-States have concluded independently from any corresponding negotiations by the EC. Because of the efficient running of the negotiations, this agreement could be signed after few months of negotiations. As of the time of writing, no official negotiations have been launched between Singapore and the EC. The fact that the EFTA-States concluded an agreement with an Asian country without awaiting initiatives by the EC is certainly also related to the often surprising dynamics of bilateralism which has a lot to do with political opportunities and coincidences. For small trading nations like Singapore or the EFTA-States, such agreements can represent important political signals and serve as door openers for defined geographical areas, in spite of their limited economic relevance.

11.3 Relationship between the Global Frameworks and Regional Integration

The relationship between bilateral preferential agreements and multilateral trade liberalization has always been the cause of intense controversies.[35] Basically, it can be said that the unconditional MFN principle, as contained in Article III GATT, is not compatible with regional or bilateral preferential treatment. Simultaneously, the GATT of 1947 already contained Article XXIV allowing for the possibility of further trade liberalization at a regional or bilateral level. At the time of its creation Article XXIV applied most

---

34 *See supra* n. 24.

35 *See* Rodolphe S. Imhoof, Le GATT et les zones de libre échange (thèse Genève) 1979; More recently, Thomas Cottier, and Marion Panizzon 'Die sektoriellen Abkommen und das Recht der WTO: Grundlagen und Spannungsfelder', in Daniel Felder and Christine Kaddous (eds), *Accords bilatéraux Suisse – EU = Bilaterale Abkommen Schweiz – EU (commentaires), Basel*, 2001, pp. 43–76, and Thomas Cottier, 'The Challenge of Regionalization and Preferential Relations in World Trade Law and Policy' (1996) 2 *European Foreign Affairs Review* 149–167.

prominently to the BENELUX Cooperation Agreement between Belgium, the Netherlands, and Luxemburg. Generally speaking, Article XXIV GATT must ensure that the local welfare gains resulting from additional regional liberalization do not (excessively) affect the general welfare effects stemming from multilateral liberalization or even outweigh the total welfare effects.

Finding the balance between safeguarding the multilateral approach and allowing for regional preferential treatment is not easy. The debate on how bilateral agreements should be drafted to not erode multilateral trade liberalization has always been vigorous. This became very obvious in recent years, first in the context of GATT and since 1996 in the WTO Committee on Regional Trade Agreements (CRTA). A fundamental dispute has arisen around the question of whether under Article XXIV GATT it is enough to liberalize a 'substantial part' of the actual trade between the 'free trade partners' or whether 'substantially all products' must be included. While in the first case it is sufficient to cover a 'substantial part of the actual trade volume', the second view usually refers to the 'sufficiently high number of tariff positions' under the harmonized system for the registration of customs positions (HS System) covered by the free trade rules of an agreement.[36] The background for this dispute is the fact that many bilateral agreements exempt agricultural products from free trade. This is especially the case for agreements concluded by European countries. The countries that are most critical to this approach are those disposing of a very competitive and export-oriented agriculture. They are organized in the Cairns-Group.

Article XXIV GATT has never assumed the function it was originally assigned.[37] Its underlying criteria remain unclear and difficult to apply.[38] During the Uruguay Round, Article XXIV GATT was complemented by a more specific 'Understanding on the Interpretation of Article XXIV",[39] but this did not really clarify the situation. In the current Doha Round this discussion continues in the WTO Negotiating Group on Rules. While this discussion already has a long tradition in the context of trade in goods, surprisingly, the discussion concerning the relationship between multilateral and bilateral liberalization in the area of services is so far not very developed, be it with regard to the academic discussion or to the political debates.[40] In principle,

---

36 *See* the 'Harmonized Commodity Description and Coding System', on the Internet at: <http://www.wcoomd.org/ie/En/Conventions/conventions.html>.

37 *See* Thomas Cottier, 'Die Bedeutung des GATT im Prozess der Europäischen Integration', in Olivier Jacot-Guillarmod *et al.* (eds), *EG-Recht und schweizerische Rechtsordnung* (Basel, 1990) pp. 141–185, 164.

38 *See* John Jackson, *World Trade and the Law of GATT* (1969), p. 621. *See* also the unclear result of the dispute in EC – Tariff treatment on Imports of Citrus Products from certain countries in the Mediterranean region, GATT Doc. L/5776, 7 February 1985, Para. 5.1, Section b, at 102.

39 Understanding on the Interpretation of Article XXIV of the General Agreement on Tariffs and Trade 1994, *supra* n. 17.

40 Article V of the General Agreement on Trade in Services (GATS) corresponds systematically and substantially to Article XXIV of the GATT, *see supra* n. 17. *See*, however, Pierre Sauvé, 'Regional versus Multilateral Approaches to Services and Investment Liberalization: Anything to Worry About?', in Paul Demaret, Jean-François Bellis, Gonzalo Garcia Jimenex (eds), *Regionalism and Multilateralism after the Uruguay Round* (European Interuniversity Press, Brussels, 1997), pp. 429–455.

however, Article V GATS[41] foresees a similar solution as is contained in Article XXIV GATT. Maybe, this difference can simply be explained by the modest degree of existing liberalization in international services trade. Another reason could be the limited experience with regional preferential trade in services (at least outside Europe).

11.4 Development and Inventory of the EFTA Third Country Agreements

Since the early 1970s the EFTA-States have concluded free trade agreements with other States or customs areas in tandem with the EC. Nowadays, the conclusion of a Declaration on Co-operation normally precedes the negotiation of such an agreement in Europe or in the Mediterranean Area. The agreements, the EFTA-States concluded with countries that later became EC Members (e.g. Spain 1979) are only important today from a historical perspective. In addition, the free trade agreements individual EFTA-States concluded with the EC at the beginning of the 1970s are today overtaken by the advanced integration efforts of the these countries in the EEA. Only for Switzerland does this agreement remain important and even it is part of a more comprehensive set of bilateral agreements with the EC.[42] However, it is worth noting that the agreements that were concluded in the early 1970s between the EFTA-States and the EC served as models for the agreements the EFTA-States concluded later with third countries. This approach guaranteed a certain homogeneity between the agreements of the EC with these countries and those of EFTA. Legally, this allows for the application of the case law of the European Court of Justice (ECJ) and national courts on *de facto* identical provisions in these agreements for the clarification of the agreements still in force although differences of context and political consideration may have an additional impact leading to a different interpretation depending on the specific agreement concerned.[43]

The agreements in force today in the European or Mediterranean Area are those of the EFTA-States with Turkey (in force since 1992), Israel (1993), Hungary (1993), Bulgaria (1993), Romania (1993), Poland (1994), Latvia (1996), Estonia (1997), Lithuania (1997), Slovenia (1998), Morocco (1999), the PLO (1994), Macedonia (2002), Croatia (2002), and Jordan (2002). The agreement with Czechoslovakia of 1992 has been replaced – after the separation of the two sub-entities – by two separate agreements with the Czech Republic and Slovakia, respectively, by means of an additional Protocol of

---

41 General Agreement on Trade in Services (GATS), *see supra* n. 17.

42 *See supra* n. 10.

43 For the comprehensive case law concerning the Agreement between Turkey and the EC or the case law concerning the Agreement between Switzerland and the EC, *see supra* n. 11. *See* also in the case of Switzerland: Decision of the Swiss Supreme Court (BGE) 105 II 49 (*Bosshard Partners Intertrading AG* v. *Sunlight AG*, so-called Omo Case) or BGE 104 IV 175 (Stanley Adams), all available on the Internet at: <www.bger.ch>.

19 April 1993.[44] Since 1995, free trade agreement negotiations have been under way with Tunisia and Egypt. In 1998, EFTA began negotiations with Malta, but in 2002 these were terminated due to the expected early entry of Malta into the European Union. Declarations of Co-operation for this geographical area, which eventually could lead to the conclusion of free trade agreements, exist with Albania (1992), Lebanon (1997), Ukraine (2000), and Yugoslavia (2002).

In substance, all these virtually identical agreements only regulate trade in goods. Although these agreements contain 'evolutionary clauses' concerning services and investment, no effective legally binding rules exist in this respect as of the time of writing.[45] In more recent agreements the developments in certain areas in the framework of the Organization for Economic Cooperation and Development (OECD) or the WTO are noticeable, as is the case in the areas of subsidies and public procurement where reference is made to existing WTO Agreements. This is also explained by the fact that all these countries have acceded to the WTO or are in the process of doing so.[46]

The initiation of negotiations with Canada, Mexico, and Singapore meant a significant change for EFTA negotiators from a substantive and conceptual point of view. In the case of Canada and Singapore no parallel agreements with the EC existed and in all these cases different conceptions for the structure and organization of a free trade agreement collided. Canada and Mexico were strongly influenced by their agreements with the United States (CUSFTA[47] and NAFTA[48]). Also Singapore had defined conceptions of the ideal form of such an agreement with EFTA as a result of its negotiations with New Zealand and Japan.[49] In the case of Singapore, it was interestingly observed how previous negotiations with other partners affected later negotiations. In particular, its agreement with New Zealand, which itself has a structure with striking similarities to the Agreement between New Zealand and Australia (CER),[50] served as an example that influenced all the agreements entered into by Singapore, including the one with Japan.

In a similar manner, the negotiations of the EFTA-States with Canada and the agreement between the EFTA-States and Mexico resulted in an interesting combination of typical NAFTA-elements and genuine European elements, as they had already appeared in the agreement between Mexico

---

44 For the time frame and the contents of these agreements, *see* the detailed documentation in <http://secretariat.efta.int/thirdcountry/> and Nell, *supra* n. 23.

45 *See*, for instance, Article 30 of the Agreements of 10 December 1992 between the EFTA-States and the Republic of Poland, Reprinted in SR 0.632.316.491 (*see supra* n. 2).

46 *See*, for example, the Agreement with Croatia, as commented in Chapter 9.2.1 of the Swiss Government's Foreign Commercial Policy Report 2000, as well as the Federal Council's Message on Economic Corporation of 10 January 2000, reprinted in the Swiss Official Bulletin (BBl) 2000, p. 261ff.

47 *See supra* n. 18.

48 *See supra* n. 20.

49 *See supra* n. 30.

50 The Australia New Zealand Closer Economic Relations Agreement entered into force in 1983. *See* in this respect <http://www.dfat.gov.au/trade/negotiations/anzcer.html>.

and the EC.[51] An analogous situation could recently be observed in the negotiations between the EC and Chile,[52] after Chile had concluded a NAFTA-inspired agreement with Canada. At the same time, the understanding and the knowledge of the different concepts increase over several rounds of negotiations and are beneficial for future negotiations with other partners.

11.5 WTO-plus Elements in EFTA Third Country Agreements

11.5.1 Does the WTO leave space for the negotiation of WTO plus elements?

11.5.1.1 Quantitative aspects

In principle, free trade agreements are concluded to achieve further liberalisation of barriers to trade and investment flows through preferential treatment. As today's agreements normally also comprise trade in services, investment, public procurement, competition policy, and rules related to intellectual property, they are no longer simple trade agreements but economic integration agreements. The Closer Economic Partnership Agreements between New Zealand and Australia or between New Zealand and Singapore are good examples of this development. Preferential treatment in bilateral agreements is normally chosen if a multilateral solution (in the WTO) seems unlikely to be achieved soon or is economically or politically undesirable due to the application of the unconditional MFN treatment enshrined in the WTO (Article I GATT). Many industrialized countries could very easily abolish their remaining tariffs on industrial goods among each other as they do not rely on the income from this source and no longer have a strong protective interest for most industrial sectors.[53] With regard to developing countries this is different. The fervent discussions regarding the liberalization of trade in textiles, clothing, and footwear is a telling example of this. There are also other isolated sectors like steel[54] and, partly related to this, shipbuilding[55] that remain difficult even among

---

[51] Interestingly, the EC chose with Mexico a structure that is based on a framework agreement establishing organs that adopted the substantive agreements as decisions. *See* on this subject: <http://europa.eu.int/comm/trade/index_en.htm>.

[52] The negotiations were concluded in the summer of 2002. The agreement was accepted by the European Commission on 3 October 2002, *see* <http://europa.eu.int/comm/trade/index_en.htm>.

[53] In particular, one must note that among industrialized countries most tariffs on industrial goods are very low, especially after the conclusion of the Uruguay round. The same holds true with regard to most imports of industrial goods from developing countries as a result of Part IV GATT (GSP).

[54] *See* the current debate on US safeguard measures for steel in the framework of the WTO. *See* <http://www.ustr.gov/sectors/industry/steel.shtml>.

[55] *See* the current debate on EC countervailing measures in respect of South Korean shipbuilding. *See* Directive (EC) No. 1177/2002, Council, 27 June 2002 for the introduction of limited safeguard measures for the shipbuilding sector, OJ EC L 172/1 of 2 July 2002.

developed countries. The same developments are true for newly developed countries in South East Asia and Latin America while most developing countries still rely heavily on tariffs for their revenue and fear foreign competition in many weak sectors. As a result industrialized countries and certain emerging countries are able to agree on the complete dismantling of tariffs and the further elimination of existing non-tariff barriers to trade in bilateral agreements relatively easily. For the newly industrialized countries (and the former Communist countries of Central and Eastern Europe) this is especially the case if they have undertaken internal economic reforms (deregulation and liberalization).[56]

In the area of agriculture the situation is much more difficult. The EFTA-States are perfect examples of countries that have highly protected domestic agricultural sectors. Historically, this is partly due to their agricultural policy during the two world wars and the time between the wars when they relied on their increased domestic production to survive. At the same time the geographic and regional structure of countries such as Norway and Switzerland relies on the existence of small farmers in remote areas. In the WTO the term 'multifunctionality' has been coined to take into account these non-economic considerations.[57] In this situation these countries are only slowly liberalizing their agricultural sectors and are not able at this stage to make major concessions let alone fully open their domestic markets for free trade in agricultural products.[58] As a result the scope of free trade agreements with these countries is limited in the area of agricultural goods, often including processed agricultural products. These problems at the global level also constitute constraints for the conclusion of bilateral agreements with countries that have a strong agricultural sector.[59] Among the latter are currently countries like Chile, South Africa, New Zealand and, more recently, Australia looking for free trade partners worldwide. For these countries, partners like Singapore, with no significant agricultural sector at all, are ideal, which explains the early conclusion of agreements between Singapore and New Zealand and Australia.

In the area of fish and other marine products, however, the situation is fundamentally different for the EFTA-States. Norway and Iceland are among the most competitive suppliers of fish and other marine products globally. Although this sector is treated in the WTO under the heading of industrial products,[60] many countries have similar problems with their fishery sector as with agriculture. A prime example of this situation is the European Community with Member States such as Spain or Portugal.

---

[56] *See* for details Wilfred J. Ethier, Unilateralism in a Multilateral World, Tinbergen Institute Discussion Papers 01–033/2, Tinbergen Institute, 2001 or 'Der heutige Regionalismus ist anders – Ausdruck des Erfolgs, nicht des Versagens des Multilateralismus' (February 2001) 46 *Neue Zürcher Zeitung* 24/25, p. 29.

[57] *See* OECD, Multifunctionality: Towards an Analytical Framework, OECD, Paris 2001.

[58] This can also apply to specific products that can be used for animal feeding but are classified as industrial products.

[59] This simplifies the conclusion of agreements with countries like Singapore which do not have an important agricultural sector.

[60] *See supra* n. 36.

While all EFTA-States have highly protected agricultural sectors, they are highly competitive in the area of fish and other marine products.[61] With large natural resources they have a competitive advantage in this area without having to seek access to other waters outside their own exclusive economic zone. Different in this respect, for example, from the European Union, they thus do not ask for resource sharing when negotiating market access for fish and other marine products.[62] Hence EFTA free trade agreements thus normally include the principle of free trade in fish but have limitations in the area of agricultural products.

11.5.1.2 Qualitative aspects

Besides negotiating better market access through tariff dismantling and improved commitments in the areas not fully liberalized (services, public procurement, etc.), free trade agreements can serve to develop disciplines or improve existing WTO disciplines in areas where no global consensus can yet be reached. Especially in the 1960s and 1970s, when the GATT framework consisted in many areas only of rudimentary rules contained mostly in non-binding codes,[63] this objective of free trade agreements seemed worthwhile. The conclusion of a broad set of agreements under the umbrella of the WTO in the Uruguay Round, however, changed the situation considerably. The density, degree of concreteness, and level of detail achieved in the WTO regime is unprecedented. Many of the bilateral solutions found in agreements like the CUSFTA or the NAFTA were adapted to the global framework and incorporated in to the WTO regime.[64] There is certainly still room for improvement of the existing disciplines and new disciplines to be integrated into the WTO framework, but the task is getting more difficult and politically sensitive. This makes it often difficult even in bilateral agreements to find *WTO-plus elements*[65] for the covered disciplines. A consequence is that in many of the recently concluded agreements these WTO-plus elements are relatively simple or mostly procedural. Examples are the elimination or limitation of anti-dumping measures[66] or general

---

61 Iceland is an exception as it produces only a very limited number of agricultural products due to the existing climate. Some crops, however, are produced with geothermal heat in glasshouses. On the whole, Iceland imports most of its vegetables and fruit.

62 *See* the recently concluded Agreement between Chile and the EC which includes a protocol on access for European fishermen to Chilean waters. On this Riordan Brian, in Samudra Report Online, July 2002, at p. 36 (available on the Internet at: <icsf.net/jsp/samudra/english/issue_32/art8.pdf>).

63 *See* the competition rules or the rules on measures having equivalent effect as quantitative restrictions in the free trade agreement of the EC and the EFTA-States, as contained, for example in the FTA between Switzerland and the EC, Articles 23 and 13. *See supra* n. 10. On this also Borer, Jürg, Massnahmen gleicher Wirkung wie mengenmässige Einfuhrbeschränkungen im Freihandelsabkommen Schweiz – EWG, Diss. St. Gallen 1988.

64 *See* for the area of dispute settlement, *supra* n. 19.

65 The term is often used in the context of specific trade concession going beyond GATT or GATS commitments (*WTO-plus commitments*). With regard to rules the term is sometimes also applied to indicate that rules are more detailed and more liberal than the existing WTO rules.

66 *See* the Agreement between New Zealand and Singapore or the Agreement between Chile and Canada, *supra* Section 2.3.2. This approach can, however, lead to additional problems at

safeguard measures and the introduction of additional consultations for time limits regarding the adoption of certain measures. Most often these agreements include a mere reference to the WTO in areas where satisfactory WTO disciplines exist such as in the areas of subsidies, technical barriers to trade, sanitary, and phytosanitary measures (SPS)[67] or exceptions.[68] In these areas the achievements of the Uruguay Round have sometimes even led to a harmonization of rules in bilateral agreements where traditionally genuine solutions existed, such as regarding the concept of 'measures having equivalent effect as quantitative restrictions' found in many traditional EFTA agreements.[69]

Besides the liberalization of trade in goods, most recently concluded bilateral agreements in this area include also the liberalization of trade in services and access and/or protection for foreign investments and investors.[70] From an economic point of view the liberalization in this area is similar to that of trade in goods but the legal and structural problems related to liberalization of domestic services supply and investment/establishment are highly complex. They involve important issues related to highly regulated sectors of the economy, including such aspects as supervision and liberalization of existing state monopolies.

Apart from the European Community's Internal Market (including its extension to the EEA) and the CER between New Zealand and Australia, the CUSFTA/NAFTA Agreements were the first agreements to approach comprehensively the liberalization of trade in services. The services negotiations under the Uruguay Round led only to very modest results with regard to the liberalization of trade in services.[71] It was therefore no surprise that some countries with an important services sector would try to go further in bilateral agreements. As a matter of fact the bilateral trade agreements concluded in recent years do usually use the conceptual framework developed under the GATS and basically achieve better commitments

---

Contd.
the multilateral level. In particular, it is very controversial whether WTO safeguard measures can be applied on a preferential basis under Article XXIV or whether this constitutes a violation of Article III GATT. *See* most recently the decision of the Appellate Body in United States – Definitive Safeguard Measures on Imports of Circular Welded Quality Line Pipe from Korea, AB-2001–9, WT/DS202/AB/R of 15 February 2002.

67 *See* the WTO-Agreement on Sanitary and Phytosanitary Measures, *supra* n. 17.

68 *See* the Free Trade Agreement between the EFTA-States and Mexico (*see* Message of the Swiss Federal Council regarding the Free Trade Agreement with Mexico = Botschaft zum Freihandelsabkommen zwischen den EFTA-Staaten und Mexiko sowie zum Landwirtschaftsabkommen zwischen der Schweiz und Mexiko, of 14 February 2001, reprinted in BBl. 2001, p. 1850ff) and the Free Trade Agreement between the EFTA-States and Singapore (see Message of the Swiss Federal Council regarding the Free Trade Agreement with Singapore = Botschaft zum Freihandelsabkommen zwischen den EFTA-Staaten und Singapur sowie zum Landwirtschaftsabkommen zwischen der Schweiz und Singapur, 4 September 2002, reprinted in BBl. 2002, p. 6701ff., at 4.1.1. For details *see* Section 11.5.

69 *See* the current solution regarding subsidies in the EFTA Free Trade Agreements with the Central and Eastern European countries or the Mediterranean countries. The approach is now based on the WTO Agreement on Subsidies and Countervailing Duties while the traditional approach was based on Article 92 of the Treaty of Rome (now Article 87).

70 Public procurement rules are also relevant in this context.

71 *See supra* n. 40.

among the bilateral trade partners. Despite this general development, it must be noted that the achievements so far are not very far reaching. Many countries seem reluctant to open services sectors that have been protected from foreign competition for a very long time. They fear strong implications for their regulatory framework. At the same time the economic theory advocating free trade in services seems less clear and stringent than the principles developed with regard to trade in goods. Furthermore, the strong connections between trade in services and investment, lead to a strong interdependence between the opening of services markets and investment rules.[72] In this area there exist so far no comprehensive rules in the framework of the WTO, besides the disciplines related to mode 3 of the GATS and the TRIMs Agreement. The failure of the Multilateral Agreement on Investment (MAI) negotiations under the auspices of the OECD reminds us also of the myriad of problems traditionally related to investment protection. The number of open questions and problems grows when market access in the form of a right to establishment is part of negotiations.[73]

In recently negotiated trade agreements we seldom find extensive rules on investment. Sometimes they are limited to the traditional rules concerning protection (post-establishment) already contained in many bilateral investment protection and promotion agreements (IPPAs). Since even rules concerning protection have become more controversial in recent years, due amongst other things, to a growing number of controversial arbitral awards under the NAFTA Agreement (Chapter 11), negotiations for the inclusion of comprehensive investment rules into bilateral agreements are also getting more difficult.[74] Nevertheless, there are now a growing number of bilateral and regional agreements including market access for foreign investors (*establishment*). The degree of openness of markets for foreign services differs considerably between these agreements if one looks at such agreements as NAFTA, the Agreement between EFTA and Singapore[75] or the recently concluded Agreement between Chile and the European Union. The relationship between the general right to establishment of investors and the specific market access commitments in the services sectors (mode 3) is interesting, as here, two different concepts of liberalizing investments interfere. It is interesting to note that also under the GATS a considerable part of all services commitments is made under mode 3 (establishment). Some observers actually claim that one of the main reasons for many countries to negotiate bilateral free trade agreements is actually to attract more foreign direct investment. In fact, the possibility to export from these countries under the preferential conditions negotiated in bilateral free trade agreements may be an important factor when choosing a location for a production plant abroad.[76]

---

72 *See*, for example, Hauser, Heinz, Kommentar: *Ausbleibende Konvergenz von GATT und GATS*, in: WTO News 7, St. Gallen, 2002, on the Internet at: <http://www.unisg.ch/org/siaw>.

73 *See* Multilateral Agreement on Investment: Documents Relating to the 1995–1998 Negotiations, on the Internet at: <http://www.oecd.org/EN/document/0,,EN-document-92-3-no-6-27308-92,00.html>.

74 *See supra* n. 20.

75 *See* Sections 11.5 and 11.6.

76 *See* Ethier, *supra* n. 56.

11.6 Singapore Issues in EFTA Free Trade Agreements

11.6.1 The Singapore issues: new areas for global liberalization

Despite strong resistance by certain developing countries, the issues of investment, competition policy, transparency in government procurement, and trade facilitation, were for the first time mentioned as possible future areas of WTO negotiations in the Declaration resulting from the Ministerial Meeting in Singapore in 1996.[77] Since then, these new items have normally been referred to as the 'Singapore Issues'. Specific working groups, *inter alia* on trade and competition as well as on trade and investment have since held their meetings in Geneva. In accordance with the Doha Declaration of 2001 these issues have been incorporated into the WTO post-Doha work programme for the next two years.[78] Although a consensus is still necessary before any negotiations can actually be undertaken on these issues, the discussion on what elements could possibly form the starting point for WTO rules in these areas has already achieved a considerable importance. The following remarks concentrate on how the issues of investment and competition have been dealt with in the EFTA free trade agreements and whether this could be of any relevance for future WTO negotiations.

11.6.2 Investment

With regard to investment rules, the Agreements that the EFTA-States have concluded with Mexico and Singapore go considerably further than the traditional agreements with European and Mediterranean countries. It should be noted however, that Norway and Switzerland especially have concluded an important number of bilateral investment protection treaties in the past. The inclusion of investment protection rules together with rules concerning the access of foreign investors and rules governing trade in goods and services in the Agreements with Singapore and Mexico were, however, unprecedented for EFTA-States. The WTO so far only covers some aspects of foreign direct investment: under the GATS with respect to establishment of foreign service providers and in the TRIMs-Agreement[79] with regard to performance requirements (host country measures).

The Agreement between the EFTA-States and Mexico was the first EFTA Agreement to include substantive investment rules.[80] In view of the modest results Mexico had achieved in a similar agreement with the European Community, this Agreement contains only very auxiliary disciplines on

---

77 *See* Ministerial Declaration adopted 13 December 1996 in Singapore, at: <http://www.wto.org/english/thewto_e/minist_e/min96_e/wtodec_e.htm>.

78 *See* Ministerial Declaration adopted 14 November 2001 in Doha, at: <http://www.wto.org / english/thewto_e/minist_e/min01_e/mindecl_e.htm>.

79 *See* Agreement on Trade-Related Investment Measures, *supra* n. 17.

80 *See supra* n. 68.

investment and an evolutionary clause for future negotiations. With regard to substantive rules the Agreement only contains a provision on the free transfer of payments (Article 46). At the same time both the EFTA-States[81] and Mexico are members of the OECD, which allows for a reference to all the obligations the parties have accepted in the OECD investment framework (Article 48). Article 49 provides that the negotiations for a comprehensive liberalization of investment flows shall start no later than three years after the entry into force of the Agreement. The first meeting of the Joint Committee Mexico – EFTA that is in charge of overseeing the administration of the Agreement, on 22 October 2002, has not led to the initiation of negotiations yet.[82]

The Agreement between the EFTA-States and Singapore is the first EFTA Agreement to include a comprehensive chapter on investment. It is important to recall that Singapore is not an OECD Member and thus there was no common basis for the liberalization of investment flows between the Parties.[83] At the same time Switzerland especially is a very important investor in Singapore. Singapore is Switzerland's primary location of investment in Asia and the sixth most important host country for Swiss investments worldwide. Many of the rules contained in the EFTA–Singapore Agreement resemble those already contained in the existing investment Agreements between Switzerland[84] and Singapore and Norway and Singapore. At the same time this agreement contains for the first time a right to establishment for foreign firms from another Party. Article 40 provides for non-discriminatory access for investors. Investors from an EFTA State benefit from national treatment or MFN treatment, whichever is better in a specific situation.[85] The MFN treatment, however, does not apply to agreements with third states that provide for a substantial liberalization of investment flows. Nevertheless, the conclusion of such agreements with third states entitles the parties to this agreement to renegotiate their investors' access if desired.

The establishment right for investors and investments is limited to the goods sector. With regard to investments in the field of services supply, the specific commitments undertaken under the services chapter of this agreement prevail (Article 38). The Agreement thus combines a top-down liberalization in the area of investments in the goods sector with a bottom-up approach in the area of services, as is already contained in the GATS (mode 3, *establishment*). For investments in goods sectors, exceptions are listed in a specific annex. This latter method follows the model of transparent top-down liberalization used in the OECD investment instruments (Article 46).

---

81 Except for Liechtenstein, which is not (yet) an OECD member.

82 *See* EFTA Press Release of 22 October 2002, at <http://secretariat.efta.int/library/Library/dbafile24602.html>.

83 *See* Message by the Swiss Federal Council on the Free Trade Agreement between the EFTA-States and Singapore FHA EFTA-Singapur, *supra* n. 68, at 4.3. Singapore is currently looking at the option of adhering to the OECD Investment Declaration.

84 *See* Bilateral Investment Promotion and Protection Agreement between Switzerland and Singapore of 6 March 1978, reprinted in SR 0.975.268.9 (*see surpa* n. 2).

85 *See* Message by the Swiss Federal Council on the FTA EFTA-Singapore, *supra* n. 68, at 4.3.

In view of the sensitivities regarding access for foreign investors these exceptions can be altered and new areas can be added at any time.

11.6.3 Competition

The EFTA States have included competition rules in their own Convention (1960) as well as in all the free trade agreements they have concluded since the early 1970s. The objective of these rules was to avoid the benefits resulting from the agreement being frustrated by private behaviour. Non-state actors should not be allowed to create new obstacles for market access of foreign producers in situations where state-imposed obstacles (tariffs and non-tariff measures) had been eliminated. An identical idea is contained in the competition regime of the European Community under the Treaty of Rome (formerly Article 85, now Article 81 of the Treaty). While the Community has complemented this basic principle by an extensive enforcement system at Community level and a very comprehensive competence for the Community to maintain competitive market conditions, the EFTA States always relied on very simple rules in their Agreements and left the way in which a State complied with this obligation to the Parties. A good example is Article 17 of the Agreement between the EFTA-States and Turkey of 10 December 1991 on rules of competition concerning undertakings. It reads as follows:

> 1. The following are incompatible with the proper functioning of this Agreement in so far as they may affect trade between an EFTA-State and Turkey:
>   (a) all agreements between undertakings, decisions by associations of undertakings and concerted practices between undertakings which have as their object or effect the prevention, restriction, or distortion of competition;
>   (b) abuse by one or more undertakings of a dominant position in the territories of the States Parties to this Agreement as a whole or in a substantial part thereof.
> 2. These provisions shall also apply to the activities of public undertakings, and undertakings to which the States Parties to this Agreement grant special or exclusive rights, insofar as the application of these provisions does not obstruct the performance, in law or in fact, of their particular public tasks.
> 3. If a State Party to this Agreement considers that a given practice is incompatible with this Article, it may take appropriate measures under the conditions and in accordance with the procedures laid down in Article 23 [safeguard measures].

These rules resemble those contained in the Treaty establishing the European Union but they lack the effects of Community law and are considered classical public international law. At the same time they lack the in-built enforcement system and leave it to the Parties to the Agreement to comply and address each other for non-compliance.[86] This approach is also contained in

---

[86] For a legal analysis of these rules *see* the explanations by the Swiss Federal Government reprinted in BBl 1972 II 661 and 730 as well as Amtsbericht EJPD, act. 415a, as referred to in the Decision by the Swiss Supreme Court (BGE) 104 IV 175 (Urteil des Kassationshofes vom 3. Mai 1978 i.S. Adams gegen Staatsanwaltschaft des Kantons Basel-Stadt). For comments *see* Meyer-Marsilius, Hans Joachim (ed.), *Beziehungen Schweiz-EG: Abkommen* (Gesetze und Richtlinien, Kommentare, Zurich, 1989–1999).

all the agreement the EFTA-States have concluded individually with the European Community and the agreements between the EFTA-States and countries in Central and Eastern Europe as well as the Mediterranean.

In the Agreement between Singapore and the EFTA-States this approach was considered alien to the Asian countries. Therefore, a common basis was looked for in the WTO system. The most adequate point of reference for both sides seemed to be rules contained in Article IX GATS, which led to the inclusion of an Article 50 *Competition* in the Agreement which reads:

1. The Parties recognize that certain business practices, such as anti-competitive agreements or concerted practices, and abuse of a dominant position, may restrict trade between the Parties.
2. A Party shall, at the request of another Party, enter into consultations with a view to eliminating practices referred to in paragraph 1. The Party addressed shall accord full and sympathetic consideration to such a request and shall co-operate through the supply of publicly available non-confidential information of relevance to the matter in question. Subject to its domestic law and the conclusion of a satisfactory agreement safeguarding confidentiality of information, the Party addressed shall also provide any other information available to the requesting Party.
3. No Party may have recourse to arbitration under Chapter IX [Dispute Settlement] with respect to matters arising under this chapter.

With Mexico the EFTA-States have concluded trade-related competition rules that are much closer to the principles for cooperation on competition issues as generally favoured by the United States.[87] This can be explained by the NAFTA experience of the Mexican side and their strong orientation towards the US-system. The United States has also favoured such rules in the existing OECD committees.[88] Thus, the approach used in the Agreement between the EFTA-States and Mexico is based on the recognition of the equivalence of the existing domestic competition laws in all Parties to the Agreement.[89] Furthermore the Agreement contains relatively detailed rules on how the domestic authorities shall co-operate to effectively apply their domestic rules in cases affecting important interests of another Party (Article 52). This concept is also used in the existing OECD-recommendations in this field.[90]

Neither in the Agreement with Mexico nor in the agreement with Singapore the competition rules are subject to binding arbitration. The Parties

---

[87] *See* Eleanor Fox, 'Competition Law', in Andreas Lowenfeld (ed.), *International Economic Law* (OUP, 2002), at 373–79.

[88] *See* the OECD Recommendation of 1998 concerning Effective Action against Hard Core Cartels, on the Internet at: <http://www.oecd.org/pdf/M00018000/M00018135.pdf>.

[89] In the case of Liechtenstein (which does not have a proper domestic competition law in force yet) this has led to a reference to the applicable rules of the Agreement on the European Economic Area (EEA) and thereby indirectly to the relevant legislation of the European Community. *See* Annex XI of the FTA EFTA-Mexico, *supra* n. 68.

[90] *See supra* n. 88.

considered that the character of these rules did not merit making them subject to dispute settlement by a quasi-judicial arbitration panel. In the context of competition cases an arbitration panel might have to assess the decisions by domestic competition authorities and need comprehensive information regarding the business activities of private undertakings. This would involve important issues regarding business secrets and reviewability of competition decisions, which did not seem ripe for arbitration at the time.

In the WTO the only significant reference to competition law as of today can be found in the GATS. There is, however in the Singapore and Doha Ministerial Declarations a reference to the possibility of future negotiations in this field and preparatory work has been undertaken since 1996. As of today the most comprehensive multilateral rules on competition exist in the OECD. But even there the opinions on which elements are desirable for international competition (co-operation) law are split. The EFTA-States have always maintained that in free trade agreements competition rules were appropriate that were related to the elimination of tariffs and non-tariff measures. While co-operation between domestic authorities may be part of this, the main principle should be that private behaviour may affect the trade and investment flows between the parties and that the parties have an obligation to address such 'private obstacles'. While the existing EFTA competition rules may seem very fragmentary and general, they have the advantage of leaving a lot of freedom to the individual States with regard to how they want to address such private behaviour. In particular, States which do not have a fully developed domestic competition law or which have problems in co-operating with highly sophisticated foreign competition authorities may find alternative means to solve a competition-related trade dispute.

11.7 Conclusion

In the consolidation phase the global trading system went through from the conclusion of the Uruguay Round until the Doha Ministerial in November 2001, many countries used this time to conclude bilateral free trade agreements or to foster existing regional arrangements. This is certainly not only due to the fact that many trade diplomats and lawyers had to be kept busy, but related to a genuine desire of certain States to continue their liberalization processes and use the results of domestic reforms undertaken for increased participation in world trade and investment.[91] Whether these bilateral attempts will ultimately harm the negotiation of multilateral solutions is by no means certain. A recent OECD report claims that multilateral and bilateral initiatives can be mutually supportive.[92]

With regard to the substantive issues dealt with in bilateral second or third generation trade agreements one can say that only very few non-WTO

---

[91] *See* Ethier, *supra* n. 56.

[92] *See* OECD, Regional Trade Agreement and the Multilateral Trading System: Consolidated Report, TD/TC(2002)8/FINAL, on the Interent at <www.oecd.org>.

areas are contained in these agreements. Often mere references to existing WTO disciplines must suffice. Thus these agreements normally achieve substantial WTO-plus commitments in the areas of trade in services and trade in goods but contain few WTO-plus elements with regard to rules. This has the positive effect of not leading to a situation where a great number of existing bilateral trade agreements would contain an even bigger number of divergent disciplines applicable in a given field. Such a development could lead to a so-called 'spaghetti bowl-effect', that is an untransparent and unmanageable number of different rules and preference systems that could easily lead to incompatibilities with the WTO system. Over all, most agreements contain WTO commitments allowing use of the existing trade regime for further liberalization of market access for foreign suppliers. Such preferential treatment of specific trading partners often leads to a domino effect, as competing trading partners will try to engage in negotiations giving them equal treatment and avoiding disadvantageous market distortions.[93] As different countries compete in very different sectors this may lead to interesting multiplier effects. The recently concluded agreement between South Korea and Chile[94] has important implications for Norwegian fish exports and car exports from many nations. At the same time there is a limited number of trade-related areas where multilateral coordination and harmonization seems desirable to certain States but not to others. Amongst these are, most prominently, the Singapore issues and, in particular, competition and investment. With regard to these areas, bilateral agreement can serve as laboratories where new approaches are tested and different regional or national approaches can be melted down, refined, and recast.

---

[93] *See* 'Schweizer Kleinfirmen entdecken Mexiko – Positive Bilanz nach einem Jahr EFTA-Abkommen' (September 2002) 212 *Neue Zürcher Zeitung*, p. 23.

[94] As announced in the international press; *see*, for example, Dow Jones, 24 October 2002.

12. The Twin Security Challenges of AIDS and Terrorism: Implications for Flows of Trade, Capital, People, and Knowledge

Bradly Condon

12.1 Introduction

In 2002, a cartoon appeared in the Economist. It depicted two grim reapers mowing down people with their scythes. The smaller one represented terrorism. The larger one represented AIDS. Referring to AIDS, terrorism said, 'That guy scares me'.

At the 2001 World Trade Organization (WTO) ministerial conference in Doha, these two global security issues converged to influence the prospects for successful global trade negotiations. The terrorist attacks of September 11 exerted pressure to succeed in launching a new round of WTO negotiations to counter a global economic slowdown, to show a united political front and to demonstrate that the world could go back to business as usual. The ensuing anthrax attacks prompted Canada and the United States to threaten the patent of Bayer to secure cheaper supplies of the drug Cipro. This in turn ignited a controversy over access to affordable medicine to treat AIDS and other epidemics in the developing world and erupted in a North–South divide that threatened to derail the Doha meeting. AIDS is the first health issue to have been treated as a global security threat by the United Nations. The AIDS issue galvanized developing country members who insisted that a new round of trade negotiations could not be launched until the issue was addressed to their satisfaction.

AIDS and terrorism are global security issues that highlight the difficulties inherent in North–South trade relations. Moreover, both issues make it clear that the concept of 'security' must be viewed in a broader perspective in the twenty-first century. AIDS raises the potentially divisive issue of the distribution of costs and benefits between developed and developing countries in the WTO Agreement on Trade-Related Intellectual Property Rights (TRIPS).[1]

---

[1] Agreement on Trade-Related Aspects of Intellectual Property Rights, 15 April 1994, Final Act Embodying the Results of the Uruguay Round of Multilateral Trade Negotiations, Legal

With respect to terrorism, disparities in institutional and technological development could make it difficult to implement anti-terrorist measures uniformly in developed and developing countries. Both issues have the potential to affect the ability of developing countries to benefit from global capital and trade flows. Moreover, both issues demonstrate the impact that unexpected events can have on trade negotiations.

This chapter examines these issues through the lens of two case studies. The first case looks at the impact of September 11 on North American border management. This case highlights the differences between North–North and North–South border security co-operation. The second case examines the controversy over patents and access to AIDS medicine in Brazil. This case demonstrates how developing countries that have the capacity to manufacture generic drugs benefit from TRIPS exceptions in price negotiations with multinational pharmaceutical firms. However, it also raises the issue of how poor countries that lack such capacity may benefit to the same degree. Both cases show how disparities in economic and institutional development may affect the ability of developing countries to benefit from international trade and investment flows.

12.2 Balancing Acts: Trade and Security in the NAFTA Region

The terrorist attacks on the World Trade Center and the Pentagon made border security a top priority for the countries of the North American Free Trade Agreement (NAFTA).[2] Their efforts to strike a balance between trade and security contain lessons for the global trade community. The NAFTA countries represent a microcosm of the WTO membership, with a major North–South divide along the Mexico–United States border. NAFTA and WTO members face similar challenges when it comes to reconciling trade and security. The central issue is how to deploy resources to minimize the economic costs of doing business across the borders of an increasingly integrated economy. Variations in levels of economic and institutional development mean that a one-size-fits-all approach may not work.

In the aftermath of the attacks, the American level 1 security alert caused serious delays at the southern and northern borders. These delays disrupted production in the highly integrated North American auto industry and other trade-intensive industries that depend on just-in-time delivery.[3]

Contd.
Instruments – Results of the Uruguay Round, Annex 1C, vol. 31 (1994) 33 *International Law Magazine* 1197 [hereinafter TRIPS].

[2] North American Free Trade Agreement between the Government of Canada, the Government of the United Mexican States and the Government of the United States of America, 17 December 1992, Canada–Mexico–United States (1993) 32 *International Law Magazine* 296, and 32 ILM 612 [hereinafter NAFTA].

[3] Greg Keenan, 'Canada auto plants at risk from 'fragile' US border', <www.globeandmail.com>, 20 February 2002.

Border delays and security concerns discouraged cross-border travel, adversely affecting tourism and the economies of border communities.[4] The global movement of goods, people, and capital is at once the lifeblood of global commerce and the primary channel for terrorism. Enhancing security without restricting people, merchandise trade, and capital flows represents a challenge for governments and business alike.

12.3 Border Management Politics: Bridges Over Troubled Waters

Prior to the attacks, the notion of a common security perimeter was widely discussed in Washington and Ottawa, amid security concerns and growing cross-border traffic. In Ottawa, American Ambassador to Canada Paul Cellucci suggested a European-style 'perimeter' that would have Canada, the United States and Mexico jointly manage North America's external border entry points while dismantling internal borders. In Detroit, the Canadian Ambassador to the United States, Michael Kergin, pointed out that the average non-tariff border cost had reached about 5 per cent of the price of products and 10–13 per cent in trade-sensitive industries (in 2000). Somewhat prophetically, he asked whether Canadian and American customs and immigrations rules should be aligned, while improving controls 'to keep undesirable elements away from our common North American space'.[5]

Canada and the United States have a long history of military and security co-operation. They fought together in the First and Second World Wars, the Korean War, the Cold War, the Gulf War, and the Afghan war. They are partners in the North American Aerospace Defense Command (NORAD) and the North Atlantic Treaty Organization (NATO). The Canada–United States Joint Defense Board, which reports to the Prime Minister and the President, has existed for over 50 years.[6] These ties facilitated deeper co-operation in the wake of the September 11 attacks.

Canada has begun harmonizing some of its laws with the United States. New legislation on terrorism, border operations, and immigration procedures resemble their equivalents in the United States. Canadian landed immigrants will get new identification cards with photographs and a magnetic information strip that are similar to the American green card. Canada and the United States formalized co-operation under a 1995 bilateral Border Accord that has since been further enhanced by several bilateral initiatives. These include the Canada–United States Partnership (CUSP), USINC-CIC

---

[4] See Tapen Sinha and Bradly Condon, 'Three's Company: US Borders After September 11' (February 2002) *Texas Business Review* 1.

[5] Alan Toulin, 'Agency Calls for Open Border', *National Post*, 17 July 2001, A1.

[6] Allison Dunfield, 'North American perimeter under scrutiny by joint US–Canada board' <www.globeandmail.com> 11 October 2001.

Border Vision (a strategic planning initiative of the immigration authorities to deal with illegal immigration), and the Cross-Border Crime Forum (co-operation and information sharing on transnational crime).[7]

In November 2001, Canada passed its first anti-terrorism law in history. In December 2001, Canada and the United States signed a new bilateral 'anti-terror action plan' to further integrate border security and immigration.[8] That same month, Canada passed a 5-year budget plan for border infrastructure and security measures worth $7.7 billion Canadian dollars.[9] The FBI gave the RCMP access to its fingerprint database, the first foreign police force to be granted such access.[10] These initiatives are designed to help the two countries improve the passage of commercial traffic on the border while facing the common external threats of international terrorism, transnational crime and drug and people smuggling.

In contrast to Canada, Mexico has had an uneasy relationship with the United States ever since Mexico lost half of its territory in the Mexican–American war over 150 years ago. There is no history of military and security co-operation. Corruption in Mexico has created mistrust in the United States and complicated efforts to co-operate on drug trafficking. Mexican customs officials also have a bad reputation for corruption. An elephant was smuggled into Mexico from Texas in 2000.

Since 2000, co-operation has improved. The Federal Bureau of Investigation (FBI) has begun sending agents to investigate drug-related crimes in Mexico. However, corruption will not be eliminated overnight, and will likely continue to complicate the information sharing and trust required to co-operate closely on security issues. Moreover, some opposition members of the Mexican congress have attacked the Mexican federal government for letting the FBI making arrests in Mexican soil.[11] Between the United States and Mexico, distrust cuts both ways.

In the aftermath of the attacks, public opinion in Mexico sent out mixed signals. A national telephone survey by Mitovsky Consultants found 76 per cent Mexicans condemned the attacks of September 11. The same survey found that 73 per cent of Mexicans were opposed to sending troops to help the Americans. Polls conducted by the newspaper La Reforma showed 62 per cent of Mexicans think that Mexico should be neutral. Many Mexican intellectuals interpreted the events of September 11 as divine justice. Others believed a show of support for the United States would amount to a demonstration of Mexico's submissiveness towards the Americans.

Public opinion in Canada is very different. Following the attacks, a survey found that 85 per cent of Canadians generally favour making the

---

[7] Canada, *Canada–United States Accord on Our Shared Border, Update 2000* (Minister of Public Works and Government Services Canada, Ottawa, 2000).

[8] Jeff Gray, 'Ridge, Manley sign "smart border" declaration' <www.globeandmail.com> 12 December 2001.

[9] Terry Weber, 'Security targeted in budget' <www.globeandmail.com> 10 December 2001.

[10] Jeff Gray, 'Canada, US sign border deal' <www.globeandmail.com> 3 December 2001.

[11] Notimex General, 'Opera Coordinacion Binacional De Seguridad En Frontera Mexico-EU', 19 October 2001.

changes necessary to create a North American security perimeter.[12] Another poll found that 59 per cent of Canadians 'don't mind giving up some of our national sovereignty if it increases the overall security of North America'.[13] In a poll conducted between 27 September and 1 October 2002, 66 per cent of Canadians favoured greater economic integration with the United States. Eighty-seven per cent believe that economic survival requires international integration. A majority also support stronger cultural ties to the United States.[14]

Canada and the United States have been able to work quickly and closely to address the tension between security and trade. Their capacity to do so springs from similar levels of technological, economic, and institutional development, elements that are also in place in other developed countries. Trust and a history of co-operation on security issues are also key components. A similar level of trust and co-operation characterizes North–North co-operation at the global level, particularly among the members of NATO.

The combined effect of illegal immigration, drug smuggling, corruption, and political ambivalence is to make co-operation much more challenging on the US–Mexico border than it is on the US–Canada border. Disparities in economic and institutional development and cultural differences further complicate the situation. Asymmetries in technological development and government resources impede rapid co-ordination on border security. Mexico does not have the financial resources or institutional structure to match Canada's border efforts.

12.4 People Movement: Crossing the Line

Most border issues are handled on a bilateral basis rather than on a trilateral basis among NAFTA members. For example, the United States has a visa requirement for Mexicans but not for Canadians. The United States imposes an annual limit of 5500 NAFTA visas for Mexican professionals but no limit for Canadians.[15] American customs officers are stationed at airports in Canada to pre-clear passengers travelling to the United States, but not at airports in Mexico. These discrepancies reflect differences in the relationships the United States has with its northern and southern neighbours and serve as a microcosm for examining the difficulty of adopting a uniform approach to North–North and North–South management of people flows at the global level.

In terms of purchasing power, Mexican GDP per capita is only 25.7 per cent of the United States (compared to 78.6 per cent for Canada).[16] The

---

12 André Picard, 'Most want PM to cede sovereignty over border' <www.globeandmail.com> 4 October 2001.

13 'Security tops sovereignty, poll finds' <www.globeandmail.com> 4 October 2001.

14 Robert Fife, '66 percent Favour Stronger Ties to U.S.' *National Post*, 21 October 2002, A1.

15 *See* NAFTA, Appendix 1603.D.4. Also see Bradly Condon, 'A Study in Contrasts: Professional Visas under NAFTA' (October 2002) *Texas Business Review* 4. This limit is due to expire 1 January 2004.

16 OECD, 'GDP per capita, 2000, at current prices, in US dollars' <http://www.oecd.org>.

wage gap between Mexico and the United States has resulted in a game of cat and mouse, with massive flows of illegal immigrants from Mexico and ever-increasing border patrols creating a cottage industry of people-smuggling rings in the border zone. As Figure 1 shows, of the top four sources of illegal aliens in the United States, Mexico ranks first, followed by Guatemala and El Salvador (whose people pass through Mexico to get to the United States).

Mexico only began working on a computerized immigration database after September 11, at which point it also began to consider harmonization of immigration policies in order to reduce the attractiveness of Mexico as a gateway for people smugglers whose destination is the United States.[17] The United States has resisted the Mexican campaign to legalize the estimated 3 million undocumented Mexicans working in the United States. It did not help when Republican congressional members visiting Ciudad Juarez (a Mexican border city) were able to find a vendor of fake US entry visas within one minute of asking the first person they approached.[18]

The situation with respect to people movement is dramatically different on the northern border. After September 11, Canada and the United States

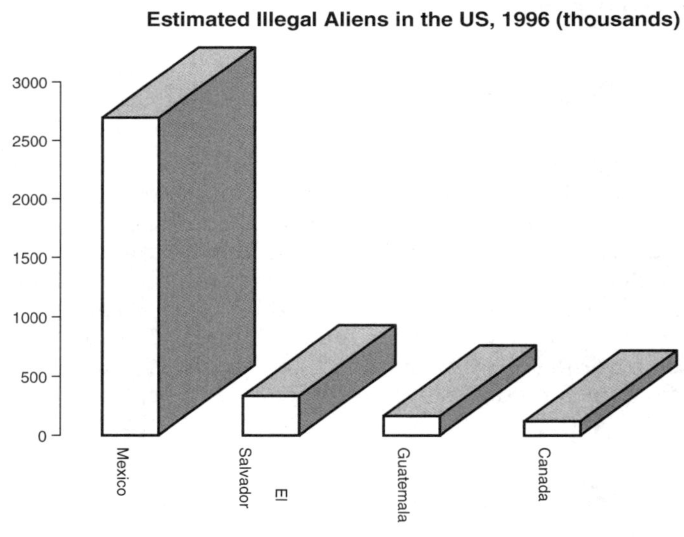

Figure 1 Estimated Illegal Aliens in the United States, 1996 (thousands). (*Source*: INS, 2001.)

[17] James F. Smith, 'Mexico Seeks Shared Border Security Plan Diplomacy: Meetings today in US will weigh uniform visas' <www.latimes.com> 19 November 2001.

[18] Julie Watson, 'US Seeks Safe Border with Mexico', *Associated Press*, 28 December 2001.

decided to expand their Frequent Crosser Border Pass Program (NEXUS). NEXUS is a joint Canada–United States border pass program that harmonizes border-crossing procedures for low-risk travellers. Participants complete a single application form to receive a membership card valid for entry to both Canada and the United States. The card entitles them to use dedicated lanes at the border where they are not subject to normal customs and immigration questioning.

Visa policies in Canada and the United States for citizens of third countries are also converging. As a general rule, citizens of all countries require a visa to enter Canada or the United States. The United States grants visa 'waivers'. Canada grants visa 'exemptions', subject to ongoing reviews. Since December 2001, Canada has eliminated visa exemptions for Dominica, Grenada, Hungary, Kiribati, Malaysia, Nauru, Saudi Arabia, Tuvalu, Vanuatu, and Zimbabwe. These changes were motivated either because a country became a significant source of questionable refugee claimants (e.g. Hungary) or because their passports were subject to abuse (e.g. Saudi Arabia). However, Canada still exempts nineteen more countries from its visa requirement than does the United States (see Table 1).

On 14 May 2002, President George W. Bush signed into law the Enhanced Border Security and Visa Entry Reform Act of 2002.[19] Under Section 307, to participate in the visa waiver program, a country must report to the United States the theft of its blank passports in a timely manner. The US Immigration and Naturalization Service (INS) and State Department must review countries in the visa waiver program every 2 years, rather than every 5 years. Under Section 302, beginning 26 October 2004, the State Department and INS must issue only machine-readable, tamper-resistant

Table 1 Citizens requiring a visa for the United States but not Canada, September 2002

List of Countries	
Antigua and Barbuda	Namibia
Bahamas	Papua New Guinea
Barbados	Saint Kitts and Nevis
Botswana	Saint Lucia
Costa Rica	Saint Vincent and the Grenadines
Cyprus	Samoa
Greece	Solomon Islands
Israel	South Korea
Malta	Swaziland
Mexico	

Sources: US Immigration and Naturalization Service, US State Department, Citizenship and Immigration Canada, United Nations list of member countries.

19 H.R. 3525.

visas, and other travel and entry documents that use biometric identifiers. Likewise, to participate in the visa waiver program, a country must issue its nationals machine-readable, tamper-resistant passports that incorporate biometric and authentication identifiers that satisfy the standards of the International Civil Aviation Organization.

Section 401 requires a feasibility study of a program for foreigners travelling to the United States, Canada, or Mexico to voluntarily submit to preclearance procedures at their point of departure. A similar program already exists inside the region at Canadian airports, where travellers pass through American customs and immigration before boarding flights to the United States. Section 603 requires the state department and the INS to study alternatives for encouraging or requiring Canada, Mexico and countries with visa waivers develop an intergovernmental network of interconnected electronic data systems which would facilitate access to each country's law enforcement and intelligence information. Canada and the United States have already made some progress in this area since September 11, notably with respect to air passenger lists and access to fingerprint databases.

Section 307 indicates that the United States has decided to use its visa waiver program to promote the harmonization of visa requirements, particularly among the NAFTA countries (Table 2 lists countries for which Canada and the United States both waive visa requirements). The United States is likely to pressure Canada to bring its visa waiver policies in line with those of the United States in order to maintain easy access for Canadians entering the United States. Indeed, the Canadian government has debated the idea of issuing special identification cards to Canadians in order to dissuade the American government from imposing visa requirements.[20] Mexico is under less pressure to accommodate the United States, since it does not enjoy visa waiver status.

Table 2 Citizens not requiring a visa for the United States or Canada, September 2002

Andorra	Iceland	Norway
Austria	Ireland	Portugal
Australia	Italy	San Marino
Belgium	Japan	Singapore
Brunei	Liechtenstein	Slovenia
Denmark	Luxembourg	Spain
Finland	Monaco	Sweden
France	Netherlands	Switzerland
Germany	New Zealand	United Kingdom

Sources: US Immigration and Naturalization Service, Citizenship and Immigration Canada.

20 Allison Dunfield, 'ID cards still up for debate, Coderre says' <www.globeandmail.com> 18 November 2002.

The overwhelming majority of countries listed in Table 2 are developed countries. This reflects the reality that North–North people movement is managed differently than South–North people movement, not just in the NAFTA region, but globally. With respect to global trade in services, the terrorism threat may make WTO members less willing to relax immigration measures to facilitate people movement.

12.5 Movement of Goods: Get Me to the Plant on Time

Immediately following September 11, the cost of border delays in North America was high. Commercial traffic delays have since been reduced (Figure 2). The following charts track border delays for commercial vehicles at major border crossings on both American borders.

For commercial vehicles, delays were virtually eliminated in a short period of time after September 11. Eliminating delays costs money. Governments increased manpower at the border and began upgrading border technology and infrastructure. Firms spend time and money implementing government security guidelines, such as the American Customs Trade Partnership Against Terrorism program (CTPAT).[21] Under this program, the

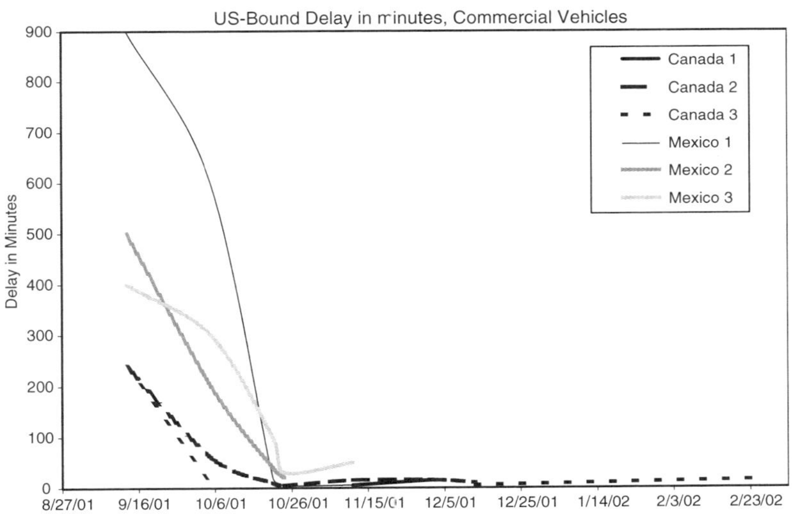

Figure 2 Commercial delays (*Source*: US Customs, Border Wait Times, http://nemo.customs.gov/process/bordertimes/bordertimes-asp).

---

[21] *See* US Customs Service, 'Customs-Trade Partnership Against Terrorism'. <www.customs.gov/enforcm/tpat_fact.htm> and <http://www.customs.gov/enforcm/tpat_security.htm>.

owners of the supply chain (brokers, carriers, importers, warehouse operators, and manufacturers) voluntarily comply with security guidelines in order to reduce border inspections and border costs. However, there is a trade off in terms of the cost to the companies of the added documentation, technology, and personnel requirements involved. In essence, such programs offload a portion of the cost of security to the government onto the private sector. The implication is that firms will face higher security costs where the institutional capacity of governments is lower. This will make government resources a factor in assessing the cost effectiveness of different production locations, which disadvantages developing countries compared to developed countries in the absence of developed country assistance.

Facilitating the movement of goods is less problematic than co-operation on people movement, because the private sector can play a larger role. For example, most of Mexico's exports to the United States originate with some 50 companies, making pre-clearance for electronically sealed containers feasible.[22] Multinational firms can bridge the gap between the institutional capacity of the Mexican government and the security needs of the United States.

The World Customs Organization (WCO) is working on guidelines for new laws and co-operative arrangements between member governments and private industry to improve supply chain security while facilitating international trade flows. However, with 161 members, it will take longer to make progress than it will take to develop such arrangements between the NAFTA countries. Moreover, the WCO program implies a cost to rich country members who are being asked to contribute money and expertise to assist members who lack the resources to introduce new technology and risk management techniques and whose personnel have an 'integrity' problem (a euphemism for corruption).[23] In the NAFTA context, the United States will likely have to subsidize Mexican security measures, just as the richer members of the WCO will have to subsidize the poorer members at the global level.

The different capacities of the United States and Mexico to implement border security measures is repeated at the global level between developed and developing countries. For example, the ability of developing country members to implement obligations regarding border measures has become a significant issue at the WTO.[24] Similarly, constraints on cross-border flows of labour are a continuing source of frustration for many developing countries.[25] Finally, corruption involving public officials is more prevalent in developing countries than in developed countries.

In Transparency International's 2001 ranking of 91 countries, the fifteen least corrupt were all developed countries (see Table 3). Of the 47 countries

---

22 *See* Bradly Condon and Tapen Sinha, *Drawing Lines in Sand and Snow: Border Security and North American Business and Economics* (M.E. Sharpe, Armonk, NY, 2003).

23 World Customs Organization, 'Resolution of the Customs Co-operation Council on Security and Facilitation of the International Trade Supply Chain', June 2002.

24 *See* UNCTAD, *Trade and Development Report, 2002* (United Nations, New York and Geneva, 2002), p. 45.

25 *Ibid.*, p. 40.

Table 3 2001 Corruption ranking of selected countries

Country	Rank	Score
Finland	1	9.9
New Zealand	3	9.4
Canada	7	8.9
Australia	11	8.5
United Kingdom	13	8.3
Hong Kong	14	7.9
United States	16	7.6
Chile	18	7.5
Germany	20	7.4
Japan	21	7.1
Italy	29	5.5
Greece	42	4.2
Korea	42	4.2
Brazil	46	4.0
Mexico	51	3.7
China	57	3.5
India	71	2.7
Indonesia	88	1.9
Nigeria	90	1.0

Source: Transparency International Corruption Perceptions Index 2001.

that scored less than five, all were developing countries with the exception of Greece and Korea.

Corruption represents a serious constraint on border security co-operation between developed and developing countries. Institutional capacity may affect the smooth passage of developing country exports to developed country markets, which will influence the location of global production chains of multinational companies (MNCs). Higher security efforts increase the cost of cross-border movement of goods. This imposes a higher cost of producing goods with production systems spread across borders. However, the differences in institutional capacities between developed and developing countries means that these costs will be unevenly distributed along global production chains.

The cost of eliminating delays will be borne by both government and industry. However, these costs should be viewed as investments that can pay for themselves over the long-term, by reducing the cost of border delays and reducing security risks. Firms can use technology, such as satellite tracking of goods, to increase both efficiency and security in the transportation of goods. Governments can invest in border infrastructure and technologies, such as electronic scanners, to more efficiently process cross-border traffic.

With respect to goods, the cross-border integration of multinational production chains facilitates voluntary compliance with programs such as CTPAT. Such programs give the private sector responsibility for security at the point of departure, in return for special customs treatment. The private sector thus has a big role to play in balancing economic and security needs in the transportation of goods.

12.6 Capital Movements: Doing the Laundry

At the global level, the impact of September 11 on insurance, transportation and security costs may affect trade and capital flows, particularly with respect to exports from developing countries to the United States. In addition to North–South competition for MNC foreign direct investment (FDI), large, emerging-market economies such as Mexico, Brazil, China, and Indonesia compete with each other for FDI in manufacturing and for export markets in labour-intensive goods.[26] Increased insurance, transportation, and security costs, together with the increased uncertainty over disruptions of flows of manufacturing inputs in global supply networks, could affect location decisions of multinational firms. For Mexico, geographic proximity to the United States, NAFTA membership and closer border co-operation with the United States could make it a relatively more attractive location compared to comparable developing countries, particularly for multinationals that use just-in-time manufacturing strategies.

A further impact of September 11 on global capital flows comes in the form of more stringent regulations designed to combat illicit transactions. This may reduce access to private capital for developing countries that have difficulty meeting more transparent reporting requirements.[27] Mexico may stand to benefit at the expense of similar emerging markets. Mexico stands out as an exception to the general downward trend in capital flows to developing countries over the 1997–2001 period.[28] Acquisitions of Mexican financial institutions by developed-country firms has made the proportion of foreign ownership of Mexican financial institutions the highest in the world. The management expertise this brings should facilitate compliance with reporting requirements in Mexico.

Canada, Mexico, and the United States are all members of the Financial Action Task Force on Money Laundering (FATF). FATF is an inter-governmental policy-making body created in 1989 by the G-7 summit in Paris. Forty recommendations provide a policy framework for member and non-member countries.[29] There are currently thirty-one members, which are listed in Table 4, and several international organizations with observer status, which are listed in Table 5.

Since 2000, FATF has published lists of countries that are not co-operative in fighting money laundering. FATF members request their financial institutions

---

26 *See* UNCTAD, *supra*, n. 24.
27 *Ibid.*, p. 15.
28 *Ibid.*, p. 21.
29 FATF, 'More About the FATF and Its Work' <www1.oecd.org/fatf/>, 30 May 2002.

Table 4 Thirty-one members, financial action task force on money laundering (FATF)

Argentina	Greece	Norway
Australia	Gulf Co-operation Council(GCC)	Portugal
Austria	Hong Kong, China	Singapore
Belgium	Iceland	Spain
Brazil	Ireland	Sweden
Canada	Italy	Switzerland
Denmark	Japan	Turkey
European Commission	Luxembourg	United Kingdom
Finland	Mexico	United States
France	Netherlands	
Germany	New Zealand	

Notes: The members of the GCC are Bahrain, Kuwait, Oman, Qatar, Saudi Arabia, and the United Arab Emirates. While the GCC is a member of the FATF, its members countries are not.

Source: OECD <www1.oecd.org/fatf/Members_en.htm>.

Table 5 Observers, financial action task force on money laundering (FATF)

FATF-Style Regional Bodies
Asia/Pacific Group on Money Laundering (APG)
Caribbean Financial Action Task Force (CFATF)
Council of Europe PC-R-EV Committee
Eastern and Southern Africa Anti-Money Laundering Group (ESAAMLG)
Financial Action Task Force on Money Laundering in South America (GAFISUD)

Other International Organizations
African Development Bank
Asia Development Bank
The Commonwealth Secretariat
Egmont Group of Financial Intelligence Units
European Bank for Reconstruction and Development (EBRD)
European Central Bank (ECB)
Europol
Inter-American Development Bank (IDB)
International Monetary Fund (IMF)
Interpol
International Organisation of Securities Commissions (IOSCO)
Organization of American States/Inter-American Drug Abuse Control Commission (OAS/CICAD)
Offshore Group of Banking Supervisors (OGBS)
United Nations Office for Drug Control and Crime Prevention (United Nations ODCCP)
World Bank
World Customs Organization (WCO)

Source: OECD <www1.oecd.org/fatf/Members_en.htm>.

to scrutinize business transactions with individuals, companies, and financial institutions from listed countries. Table 6 lists those countries.

At an extraordinary plenary meeting in October 2001, FATF expanded its mandate beyond money laundering, to include terrorist financing. The group issued a set of international standards for countries to adopt, to criminalize the financing of terrorism, to freeze and confiscate terrorist assets, to enhance international co-operation, and to impose anti-money laundering requirements on alternative remittance systems. They also agreed to identify countries that lack appropriate measures to combat terrorist financing, as they had done with respect to money laundering.[30] In February 2002, FATF asked all jurisdictions to complete a self-assessment questionnaire to determine what further actions were required to combat terrorist financing. As of September 2002, 108 jurisdictions had responded.[31]

National security takes precedence over trade obligations under NAFTA and WTO. The NAFTA national security exception applies to obligations regarding the treatment of foreign investors, obligations that have yet to be negotiated at the WTO. Because it is so broad and discretionary, this exception could be used to restrict capital movements whenever one of the governments considers such restrictions necessary for the protection of its essential security interests. Following the attacks, the NAFTA governments used money-laundering laws to deal with terrorist funds.

As members of FATF, Canada, the United States, and Mexico have comparable laws in place to combat money laundering. In Canada and the United States, FATF estimated that 60–80 per cent of money laundering transactions involved narcotics proceeds. Success in reducing the laundering of illegal proceeds in traditional banking institutions has led to a significant increase in cash smuggling out of the United States, particularly on the border with Mexico. Mexico's money laundering problem stems from its strategic geographic location between the South American drug producers

Table 6 Thirteen countries listed as non-cooperative in fight against money laundering

Cook Islands	Indonesia	Russia
Dominica	Marshall Islands	St. Vincent & the Grenadines
Egypt	Myanmar	Ukraine
Grenada	Niue	
Guatemala	Philippines	

Notes: Cayman Islands, Panama, and Liechtenstein were removed from the list in June 2001. Hungary, Israel, Lebanon, and St. Kitts & Nevis were removed from the list in June 2002.

Source: OECD, Third FATF Review to Identify Non-Cooperative Countries or Territories: Increasing the Worldwide Effectiveness of Anti-Money Laundering Measures <www1.oecd.org/fatf/pdf/NCCT 2002 _en.pdf>, 21 June 2002.

---

30 FATF, 'Terrorist Financing' <www1.oecd.org/fatf/> 30 May 2002.

31 FATF, 'Overview of Steps Taken to Combat Terrorist Financing Since October 2001' <www1.oecd.org/fatf/> September 2002.

and American drug consumers. In Canada, the problem stems from its location next to the United States.[32]

In May 1996, the Mexican Congress modified the Penal Code to make money laundering a punishable offence, independent of other monetary violations (Article 400 bis). Article 400 bis is broad enough to apply to all criminal activities. To combat money laundering, banks, stock brokers, and exchange houses have been required since May 1997 to confidentially report suspicious financial activities involving $10,000 dollars or more. Mexico established a Special Prosecutor's Office for Crimes Against Health under the attorney general in April 1997 to spearhead anti-narcotics investigations. In addition, Mexico has added a Financial Intelligence Unit to the Finance Ministry's Directorate General for the Investigation of Transactions.[33]

Canada introduced new anti-money laundering guidelines in 1996. In May 1997, Canada enacted organized crime legislation that expanded the scope of money laundering offences. All serious crimes are now covered. In June 2000, Canada enacted the Proceeds of Crime (Money Laundering) Act, which established the Financial Transaction and Reports Analysis Centre of Canada (section 41). The Act applies mandatory record-keeping and reporting rules regarding suspicious activity to banks and non-bank financial institutions and sets out new search and seizure and forfeiture laws.[34]

In the United States, money-laundering regulations are issued by the Director of the Financial Crimes Enforcement Network (FinCEN) under the Bank Secrecy Act (BSA), enacted in 1970. More than 220,000 financial institutions are subject to BSA reporting and record-keeping requirements, including banks and non-bank financial institutions. An extensive list of crimes is covered, including terrorism, health care, and immigration offences.

The experience in North America tells us that September 11 will perpetuate the existing asymmetries in North–North and North–South management of cross-border flows of people, goods and capital. The private sector may be able to smooth out the differences with respect to the movement of goods and capital due to cross-border integration in manufacturing and financial services, but has a limited ability to do so for people movement. Despite recent advances in the relationship between Mexico and the United States, the Canadian border remains more open to the movement of people than the Mexican border and can be policed with fewer personnel. However, the tighter security on the Mexican border remains insufficient to stop the passage of 300,000 illegal migrants each year, making it a less than optimal solution over the long term. The migration issue is not going away and will continue to complicate trade in services and security co-operation between Mexico and the United States.[35] Similarly, wage gaps between

---

32 FATF, 'Mutual Evaluations of Canada, United States and Mexico' <www1.oecd.org/fatf/>, 1997–2000.

33 *Ibid.*

34 *Ibid.*, Proceeds of Crime (Money Laundering) Act, 2000, c. 17 <laws.justice.gc.ca/en/P-24.501/text.html>.

35 *See* Bradly Condon and Brad McBride, 'Do you know the way to San José? Resolving the Problem of Illegal Mexican Migration to the United States', *Georgetown Immigration Law Journal* (Spring 2003).

North and South will complicate efforts to achieve comprehensive agreements on the movement of natural persons at the global level.

The twin threats of AIDS and terrorism converge in the area of movement of natural persons. Both terrorism and AIDS travel across borders through the movement of natural persons. Both issues may serve as justifications for stricter screening of visa applicants. In both cases, citizens of developing countries are more likely to be targeted. Finally, restrictions based on either criterion may be justified by general exceptions to trade obligations – namely, health and safety and national security.[36] Thus, the ease with which multinational firms move key personnel from one subsidiary to another could ultimately be affected by both issues.

12.7 Lovers in a Dangerous Time: AIDS and TRIPS

AIDS is a global security issue that highlights the difficulties inherent in North–South trade relations. AIDS raises the potentially divisive issue of the distribution of costs and benefits between developed and developing countries in the WTO the Agreement on Trade-Related Aspects of Intellectual Property Rights (TRIPS).[37] This part examines the controversy over patents and access to AIDS medicine in Brazil.

In 2001, Brazil extracted price concessions from Merck and Roche by threatening to issue compulsory licenses on their patents and to manufacture generic versions of their AIDS drugs. The Brazilian experience serves as a case study on how TRIPS affects the bargaining power of a developing country in negotiations with multinational pharmaceutical companies and the cost of access to AIDS treatment. However, it also raises the issue of whether TRIPS provides a comparable level of bargaining power for developed and least-developed countries that lack the capacity to manufacture generic drugs under compulsory license.

12.8 Brazil's AIDS Program: Ya gotta have HAART

In Latin America, Brazil has the highest number of AIDS cases, with an estimated 610,000 people infected (figures for 2001).[38] However, its 2001 infection rate of 0.65 per cent is much lower than the rates in Sub-Saharan Africa, some of which approach 40 per cent. Brazil's AIDS treatment program has made medications available free of charge to HIV-positive patients. According to the Brazilian Ministry of Health, 100 per cent of the population has access to

---

36 For a more detailed discussion of AIDS, trade policy and the movement of natural persons, *see* Bradly Condon and Tapen Sinha, 'AIDS and Trade Policy in Latin America: TRIPS in Brazil and Mexican Migration' (unpublished).

37 TRIPS, *supra*, n. 1.

38 UNAIDS/WHO, Estimates of Adults and Children Living with AIDS, new infections, and deaths, as of end of 2001 <www.unaids.org>.

health care.[39] Of 227,523 diagnosed cases, 105,150 have initiated highly active antiretroviral therapy (HAART).[40] The difference in estimated infections and diagnosed cases reflects the fact that many people choose not to be tested or are unaware of their infection. The difference between those diagnosed and those receiving HAART reflects the fact that infected individuals may not require treatment for several years while they remain free of symptoms.

In 1992, the World Bank predicted that 1.2 million Brazilians would be infected by 2002.[41] The actual number is half of that figure and demonstrates Brazil's success in tackling the epidemic. Moreover, the epidemic shows signs of stabilization in Brazil, with the incidence of new cases stable for the past 5 years and now decreasing.[42]

Brazil has been manufacturing AIDS drugs in its government laboratory, which make generics for the free drug program. Under the current Industrial Property Law,[43] no compulsory licenses have been issued so far in Brazil. Those AIDS drugs produced by the Government laboratory (called 'Farmanguinhos') are actually not protected by patents in Brazil, as patent protection for pharmaceuticals only began after 1997 with the Industrial Property Law, and those drugs were already on the market before that. Consequently, anyone was free to produce them without a (compulsory or voluntary) license from the patent holders, as they were off-patent.

The program has driven down both drug prices and deaths from AIDS. Brazil's AIDS program has reduced the nation's death rate from AIDS by half. The health ministry spent $444 million on AIDS drugs in 2000, 4 per cent of its health budget. The decline in hospitalizations from opportunistic infections from 1997 to 1999 saved the health ministry $422 million.[44] The money that the government has saved on treatment that would otherwise have been necessary now exceeds the cost of the drugs by 60 per cent.[45]

Since Brazil began making the generic copies of AIDS drugs, it has reduced the price of the patented equivalents. The Brazilian state laboratory makes 8 of the 15 AIDS drugs used in the country.[46] The price of AIDS drugs with no generic competition fell 9 per cent between 1996 and 2000. The price of those that faced generic competition fell 79 per cent. Brazil now produces some triple therapy for $3,000 per year and expects the price to drop to $700 per year in the future. This compares to a cost of $10,000 to $15,000 per year in the United States.[47]

---

39 UNAIDS, Epidemiological Fact Sheets on HIV/AIDS and Sexually Transmitted Infections, Brazil, 2002 Update.

40 <www.aids.gov.br>; UNAIDS, 2002, *Ibid*.

41 'AIDS: Hope for the best. Prepare for the worst', *The Economist*, 13 July 2002, 65.

42 UNAIDS, 2002, *supra*, n. 58.

43 Regula direitos e obrigaçoes relativos a propriedade industrial, Lei N. 9.279, de 14 de mayo de 1996, Diário Oficial, de 15 de maio de 1996, entered in force 15 May 1997 [hereinafter Industrial Property Law].

44 Tina Rosenberg, 'Look at Brazil', *New York Times Magazine* <www.nytimes.com>, 28 January 2001.

45 *Economist*, 2002, *supra*, n. 41.

46 Katherine Baldwin, 'Latin American AIDS Activists Turn on Brazil', *Reuters*, 25 May 2002.

47 Rosenberg, 2001, *supra*, n. 44.

In 1999, Brazil's president decreed that his government could grant compulsory licenses on patents in a national emergency. Brazilian law says a national emergency might arise from a threat to the public's health or nutrition, the environment, or the country's social, economic or technological development.[48] A central purpose of the Brazilian decree (although not written in the text of the Decree) is to ensure affordable access to AIDS medications.

In August, 2001, the Brazilian health minister announced that his government would issue a compulsory license on Roche's AIDS drug Nelfinavir and begin manufacturing a generic copy in government laboratories in 2002. The announcement came after negotiations between the Swiss drug company and Brazil failed to produce an agreement on price reductions. The health minister said that over a quarter of his AIDS program budget was being spent on Nelfinavir alone.[49] Even if the company agreed to reduce its price by an additional 40 per cent, the health minister said that would be insufficient to stop the government from proceeding with its plan.[50] The reason for the Government's refusal of the offer was that it would still be less expensive for the Government laboratory to carry out the local manufacturing of Nelfinavir than to accept Roche's proposal. The Government reasoned that in order to avoid the compulsory license, the price reduction by Roche would have to be as advantageous as the cost of manufacturing in the government laboratory.

The company responded by pointing out it had already reduced the price in Brazil to 50 per cent of the cost in the United States and had donated thousands of doses of the paediatric syrup version to Brazil. The company stated its intention to begin manufacturing Viracept (the brand name of Nelfinavir) in Brazil in 2002 and to continue to provide the medicine free to Brazilian children with AIDS. It sought further negotiations, which the health minister described as an attempt to delay preparations to manufacture the drug in the government's laboratory. Financial analysts said the dispute would affect public relations more than finances, with Roche's overall sales of Viracept rising 5 per cent to US $132.6 million in the first half of 2001.[51]

On August 31, 2001 the Brazilian health minister announced an agreement with Roche to reduce the price by a further 40 per cent, making the Brazilian price 30 per cent of the American price. In March, a similar threat to the patent on two AIDS drugs produced by Merck led to an agreement to reduce the price of Indinavir and Efavirenz by about 60 per cent in Brazil.[52] In both cases, the decision of the Brazilian government to purchase the

---

48 Sabra Chartrand, 'Patents: In Health Emergencies, Brazil Allows the Copying of Drugs' <www.nytimes.com> 19 February 2001.

49 Reuters, 'Brazil plans to ignore patent on AIDS Drug' <www.globeandmail.com> 23 August 2001.

50 Melody Petersen, 'Roche Asks for Meeting With Brazil Health Minister' <www.nytimes.com> 24 August 2001.

51 Michael Shields, 'Drug Maker, Brazil Near Accord on AIDS Drug Price', *Reuters*, 23 August 2001.

52 Jennifer L. Rich, 'Roche Reaches Accord on Drug with Brazil' <www.nytimes.com>, 31 August 2001.

patented drugs, rather than issue compulsory licenses to government laboratories, indicates that the negotiations succeeded in reaching the optimal price for the drugs.

6.8 The Legal Context and Price Negotiations: The Trap of the TRIP

Under TRIPS, WTO members may allow 'other use of the subject matter of the patent', subject to certain conditions.[53] For example, a government may issue a compulsory license to produce generic drugs without the authorization of the patent holder where negotiations fail to obtain authorization on reasonable commercial terms.[54] However, the use of the patent must be predominantly to supply the domestic market and the patent holder must be paid adequate remuneration, based on the economic value of the license.[55] The negotiation requirement may be waived in cases of national emergency, extreme urgency, or non-commercial public use.[56] Members are not obliged to comply with the negotiation requirement nor to predominantly serve the domestic market where the use is permitted to remedy anti-competitive practices.[57]

Brazil, as a developing country that did not provide patent protection when TRIPS came into force, was not required to fully implement its TRIPS obligations until 2005.[58] However, Brazil chose not to use the full transition period that was available.[59] Prior to enacting its 1997 Industrial Property Law, Brazil had incorporated the Uruguay Round Agreements as part of its intellectual property law in 1994.[60]

The TRIPS provisions relating to compulsory licensing strengthened Brazil's position in its price negotiations with the Roche and Merck. Brazil met the necessary conditions to halt negotiations because the generic versions would have served a non-commercial public use and predominantly supplied the domestic market. Since the term 'adequate remuneration' is not defined, the pharmaceutical companies could not predict with certainty what compensation they would have received had Brazil walked away from the negotiations. This gave the companies an added incentive to determine the price through negotiation.

Roche's commitment during the negotiations to begin manufacturing the drug in Brazil reflected another source of bargaining strength for Brazil.

---

53 TRIPS, Article 31.
54 TRIPS, Article 31(b).
55 TRIPS, Article 31(f), (h).
56 TRIPS, Article 31(b).
57 TRIPS, Article 31(k).
58 WHO/WTO, *WTO Agreements and Public Health*, Geneva, 22 August 2002, 47, n. 13 <www.wto.org>.
59 *Ibid.*
60 Promulga a ata final que incorpora os resultados da Rodada Uruguai de Negociaçoes Comerciais Multilaterais do GATT, Decreto N. 1.355, de 30 de Dezembro de 1994, publicado no Diário Oficial, de 31 dezembre de 1994.

Earlier in 2001, the United States had filed a complaint at the WTO over Brazil's requirement that patent owners manufacture their products in Brazil in order to maintain full patent rights.[61] The law makes patents subject to compulsory licensing if the product is not manufactured in Brazil.[62] The United States argued that the Brazilian law violated the TRIPS obligations to make patents available without discrimination as to whether the products are imported or produced locally.[63] However, the United States dropped the case after world leaders and health organizations said the case could hurt Brazil's AIDS program.[64] At the time of writing, it appeared that Roche has not yet complied with this commitment, although the company still maintained its intention to do so.[65]

6.9 What's Sauce for the Goose: North America Copies Brazil

The United States and Canada used Brazilian tactics against Bayer to lower the price of anthrax drugs following incidents of mailed anthrax in the United States.[66] Following the appearance of anthrax in the United States, the Canadian government decided to acquire a stockpile of ciprofloxacin (Cipro) in case the same problem occurred in Canada. Health Canada ordered one million pills of Cipro from Canadian generic drug manufacturer Apotex, even though Bayer's patent would not expire until 2004.[67] Under Section 19 of the Canadian Patent Act, the government is allowed to apply to the Canadian Commissioner of Patents for the right to use a patented product in a case of national emergency or extreme urgency.[68] However, in its haste, the government failed to follow this Patent Act procedure or to seek permission from the patent holder, Bayer.

The Canadian Minister of Health claimed that he had placed the order with the generic manufacturer because Bayer was unable to fill the order. Bayer denied this.[69] Bayer and the Canadian government later reached an agreement in which Bayer agreed not to sue the government and to supply one million Cipro tablets within 48 hours of receiving an order.[70] After the

---

61 WTO, *WTO Annual Report 2002*, <www.wto.org>; Brazil – Measures affecting patent protection, Complaint by the United States, WT/DS199, mutually agreed solution notified 5 July 2001, <www.wto.org>.

62 Industrial Property Law, Article 68(1)(I), *supra*, n. 62.

63 See TRIPS Articles 27 and 28

64 Shasta Darlington, 'Brazil Latest AIDS Drug Battlefield', <www.globeandmail.com>, 24 August 2001.

65 Roche Notícias, 'Roche do Brasil será centro de producao de ampola injetável' <www.roche.com.br> 5 April 2002.

66 Patent protection versus public health, editorial, 358 *The Lancet* 1563.

67 Shawn McCarthy and Leonard Zehr, 'Ottawa weighs paying Bayer after ignoring Cipro patent' <www.globeandmail.com> 20 October 2001.

68 Richard Gold, 'My body, your patent', *Globe and Mail*, 29 October 2001, A13.

69 Jeff Gray, 'MPs grill Rock over drug fumbling' <www.globeandmail.com> 25 October 2001.

70 Jeff Gray, 'Opposition demands Rock's resignation' <www.globeandmail.com> 23 October 2001.

American government negotiated a price discount with Bayer on its purchase of Cipro, Bayer agreed to give Canada the same discount, which lowered the price to the same price charged by the generic manufacturer.[71] Thus, while a compulsory license was actually issued, it was not given effect, in light of Bayer's commitment to supply the Canadian market.

In the United States, the Secretary of Health and Human Services negotiated a price reduction from the American retail price of $4 to $5 per pill (and the $1.75 per pill that Bayer offered to the American government) to just under $1 per pill. The Secretary had said he would consider going to Congress to seek a waiver of the patent and allow production of a generic medication if Bayer did not lower its price.[72] The threat lowered the price.

While negotiations with Bayer were proceeding in North America, trade negotiators in Geneva were preparing for the WTO Ministerial Conference in Doha. In the words of a trade negotiator from Brazil, the Canadian and American moves had provoked 'a lot of talk in the corridors'. A group of developing countries began pushing harder for a waiver to allow them to circumvent patents to protect public health.[73]

Prior to the Doha Ministerial Conference, the United States took the position that there was no need to change TRIPS and was backed by Switzerland, Japan, and Canada on this issue. However, the threats that Canada and the United States had made against Bayer's patent on the anthrax drug, Cipro, weakened their position.[74]

In preparation for the Doha meeting, two competing visions emerged. One version, backed by the United States, proposed to acknowledge a right 'to take measures necessary to address public health crises, in particular to secure affordable access to medicines'.[75] Under this proposal TRIPS would take precedence. The version backed by developing countries reversed the priority, stating that 'nothing in TRIPS shall prevent members from taking measures to protect public health'.[76] Going into the Doha meeting, the Director-General of the WTO, Mike Moore, declared that 'this could well be the deal-breaker at this conference'.[77]

At Doha, Brazil and India used their combined leverage in the WTO to champion the cause of creating a public health exception to the patent rules.[78] By the fourth day of the ministerial meeting, the negotiators had reached a tentative agreement stating that TRIPS 'shall be interpreted and implemented in a manner supportive of WTO members' rights to protect public health and in particular to ensure access to medicines for all'. However, while developing countries were insisting on the word

---

71 Gray, 'MPs grill Rock over drug fumbling', *supra*, n. 69.
72 'US Deal Expected on Cipro Prices', *Associated Press*, 24 October 2001.
73 Elizabeth Olson, 'Drug Issue Casts a Shadow on Trade Talks' <www.nytimes.com> 2 November 2001.
74 *Ibid.*
75 *Ibid.*
76 *Ibid.*
77 Steven Chase, 'Drug patent skirmish threatens WTO talks', *Globe and Mail*, 9 November 2001, B6.
78 *Ibid.*

'shall', some developed countries were insisting on the weaker 'can and should'.[79]

The severity of the AIDS crisis in many parts of the developing world, combined with the duplicitous policy of Canada and the United States regarding patent rights, contributed to a North–South divide at the Doha Ministerial Conference over the issue of drug patents and threatened to derail global trade negotiations. There was also a North–North divide with respect to this issue. The European Commission and Norway took fairly flexible positions regarding the developing countries' positions. In addition, important sectors of civil society within developed countries shared the same concerns as those of developing countries, as abundantly shown in the international public opinion during the pre-Doha debate.

12.10 The TRIPS Declaration: Ambiguous Clarity

The Doha meeting produced the Declaration on the TRIPS Agreement and Public Health (the 'TRIPS Declaration'), which clarified the application of TRIPS provisions to public health crises, including AIDS.[80] The TRIPS Declaration states that TRIPS 'does not and should not prevent Members from taking measures to protect public health … and, in particular, to promote access to medicines for all'.[81] The TRIPS Declaration notes further that TRIPS gives WTO Members 'the right to grant compulsory licenses and the freedom to determine the grounds upon which such licenses are granted'.[82] It also clarifies that Members have 'the right to determine what constitutes a national emergency or other circumstances of extreme urgency, it being understood that public health crises, including those relating to HIV/AIDS, tuberculosis, malaria, and other epidemics, can represent a national emergency or other circumstances of extreme urgency'.[83] Thus, the scope of the Declaration is not limited to a specific number of diseases (such as HIV/AIDS, tuberculosis, or malaria), nor to types of diseases, such as epidemics.[84]

In the context of AIDS, the Declaration clarifies that 'national emergency' and 'extreme urgency' can be interpreted according to the nature of the disease rather than just the number of infections in a particular country. Indeed, the nature of AIDS is such that the United Nations Security Council views AIDS as not only a global health crisis, but a threat to global peace and security, the first health issue to be so characterized.[85] The Declaration eliminates any doubt as to whether countries with low infection rates for AIDS, like Brazil's current rate of 0.65 per cent, could consider AIDS

---

79 Steve Schifferes, 'WTO on brink of drugs deal', *BBC News Online*, 12 November 2001.

80 World Trade Organization, Declaration on the TRIPS agreement and public health, Adopted on 14 November 2001, WT/MIN(01)/DEC/2, 20 November 2001 <www.wto.org>.

81 TRIPS Declaration, para. 4.

82 TRIPS Declaration, para. 5(b).

83 TRIPS Declaration, para. 5(c).

84 A dictionary definition of an epidemic is a rapidly spreading or widely prevalent attack of disease that affects a large number in a community.

85 United Nations, 'Security Council Holds Debate on Impact of AIDS on Peace and Security in Africa', Press Release SC/6781, 10 January 2000.

a national emergency or a situation of extreme urgency. This reinforces the legitimacy of Brazil's application of its 1999 decree to AIDS and thus enhances its bargaining power.

The TRIPS Declaration clarifies the application of TRIPS obligations and exceptions to the AIDS crisis, although it applies to more than just that particular disease. In addition to the portions cited above, the following provisions of the TRIPS Declaration will have a positive effect on the balance struck when interpreting TRIPS obligations and exceptions in the context of the AIDS crisis in countries like Brazil:

> 1. We recognize the gravity of the public health problems afflicting many developing and least-developed countries, especially those resulting from HIV/AIDS, tuberculosis, malaria and other epidemics.
> 2. We stress the need for the WTO Agreement on Trade-Related Aspects of Intellectual Property Rights (TRIPS Agreement) to be part of the wider national and international action to address these problems.
> 3. We recognize that intellectual property protection is important for the development of new medicines. We also recognize the concerns about its effects on prices.
> 4. We agree that the TRIPS Agreement does not and should not prevent members from taking measures to protect public health. Accordingly, while reiterating our commitment to the TRIPS Agreement, we affirm that the Agreement can and should be interpreted and implemented in a manner supportive of WTO members' right to protect public health and, in particular, to promote access to medicines for all.
>
> In this connection, we reaffirm the right of WTO members to use, to the full, the provisions in the TRIPS Agreement, which provide flexibility for this purpose.
>
> 5. Accordingly and in the light of paragraph 4 above, while maintaining our commitments in the TRIPS Agreement, we recognize that these flexibilities include:
>
> a. In applying the customary rules of interpretation of public international law, each provision of the TRIPS Agreement shall be read in the light of the object and purpose of the Agreement as expressed, in particular, in its objectives and principles.
>
> ...

The customary rules of interpretation of public international law, as set out in the Vienna Convention on the Law of Treaties, require an interpretation of TRIPS terms in their context (which includes the preambles of TRIPS and the WTO Agreement) and in light of its object and purpose.[86]

---

[86] Vienna Convention on the Law of Treaties, in Ian Brownlie, ed., *Basic Documents in International Law*, 2nd ed., Oxford University Press, 1972, Article 31. Article 31 provides as follows:

General Rule of Interpretation

A treaty is to be interpreted in good faith in accordance with the ordinary meaning to be given to the terms of the treaty in their context and in the light of its object and purpose.

Subsequent agreements on interpretation, such as those contained in the TRIPS Declaration, may also be taken into account. The WTO Appellate Body has consistently taken the view that the rules of treaty interpretation in Articles 31 and 32 of the Vienna Convention have 'attained the status of a rule of customary or general international law' and form 'part of the "customary rules of interpretation of public international law" '.[87]

The objectives of TRIPS promote 'technological innovation … to the mutual advantage of producers and users … in a manner conducive to social and economic welfare, and to a balance of rights and obligations'.[88] Under TRIPS principles, WTO members may 'adopt measures necessary to protect public health…provided that such measures are consistent with [TRIPS]'.[89] The TRIPS preamble seeks 'effective and adequate protection of intellectual property rights', while recognizing the developmental objectives of intellectual property protection and the special needs of least developed countries for 'maximum flexibility in the domestic implementation of laws'.[90] The WTO Agreement preamble also makes special reference to the needs of developing countries, 'especially the least developed among them'.[91]

The evaluation of the TRIPS consistency of measures taken by countries in the context of the AIDS crisis thus involves balancing the need for the development of new medicine against the need for affordable access to existing treatments. This requires an inquiry into the impact of measures on incentives for patent holders to invest in research on the one hand, and the affordability of medicines in a particular country on the other. With respect to the latter, the balance should favour affordability in cases involving developing countries, especially least developed countries.

Contd.

The context for the purpose of the interpretation of a treaty shall comprise, in addition to the text, including its preamble and annexes…

There shall be taken into account, together with the context:

a) any subsequent agreement between the parties regarding the interpretation of the treaty or the application of its provisions;
b) any subsequent practice in the application of the treaty which establishes the agreement of the parties regarding its interpretation;
c) any relevant rules of international law applicable in the relations between the parties.

[87] *See* Appellate Body Report, United States – Standards for Reformulated and Conventional Gasoline, adopted 20 May 1996, DSR 1996:I, 16. See also Appellate Body Report, Japan – Taxes on Alcoholic Beverages, WT/DS8/AB/R, WT/DS10/AB/R, WT/DS11/AB/R, adopted 1 November 1996, DSR 1996:I, 104; Appellate Body Report, India – Patent Protection for Pharmaceutical and Agricultural Chemical Products, WT/DS50/AB/R, adopted 16 January 1998, DSR 1998:I, para. 46; Appellate Body Report, European Communities – Customs Classification of Certain Computer Equipment, WT/DS62/AB/R, WT/DS67/AB/R, WT/DS68/AB/R, adopted 22 June 1998, DSR 1998:V, para. 84; Appellate Body Report, United States – Import Prohibition of Certain Shrimp and Shrimp Products (Recourse to Article 21.5 of the DSU), adopted on 21 November 2001, 41 *International Law Magazine* 149 (2002), para. 114; and Panel Report, European Communities – Trade Description of Sardines, WT/DS231/R, 29 May 2002, 58, para. 7.12. *See* also John H. Jackson, 'The WTO Dispute Settlement Understanding: misunderstandings on the nature of legal obligation' (1997) 91 *American Journal of International Law* 60.

[88] TRIPS Article 7.

[89] TRIPS Article 8.

[90] TRIPS Preamble.

[91] WTO Agreement Preamble.

The WTO recognizes as least developed countries those countries that have been designated as such by the United Nations.[92] Brazil does not qualify as a least developed country. Nevertheless, the level of development will affect the balance between research incentives and affordable access even in the case of a developing country like Brazil because the value of its market influences the evaluation of the impact of compulsory licenses on research incentives. Moreover, while the rules applying to least-developed countries and developing countries are different, the TRIPS Declaration recognized the severity of the AIDS crisis in both.

The issue of balance is part of the inherent tension that exists in intellectual property rights generally, including patent protection. This tension is not limited to developing and least developed countries. However, in the context of the global AIDS crisis, affordable access to medicine is a problem in developing countries, not developed countries. Moreover, least-developed and developing countries have been hit harder by the disease, in terms of absolute numbers of infections, new infections and deaths. Of the 40 million cases worldwide, over 85 per cent are in Sub-Saharan Africa and South and South-East Asia. In contrast, North America and Western Europe together make up less than 4 per cent of the total.[93] The story is similar with respect to new infections in 2001. Of a total of five million new cases worldwide, 84 per cent were in Sub-Saharan Africa and South and South-East Asia. North America and Western Europe combined had 1.5 per cent of new cases.[94] Of three million deaths in 2001, 90 per cent occurred in Sub-Saharan Africa and South and South-East Asia. North America and Western Europe together had less than 1 per cent of deaths.[95]

12.11 The Declaration, the Decision and the Waiver: The Trilogy of the Ring

As noted above, TRIPS gives patent holders the right to prevent third parties from making, using, selling or importing their product without consent.

---

[92] There are no WTO definitions of 'developed' and 'developing' countries. Members can announce for themselves whether they are developing countries. However, this does not automatically provide rights. Other members can challenge the announcement, and this has sometimes happened in the area of intellectual property. This challenge can then lead to negotiations to clarify the position. For countries that joined the WTO after 1995, their status depends on the terms agreed in the accessions negotiations. The WTO recognizes as least-developed countries those designated as such by the United Nations. There are currently 48 least-developed countries on the UN list, 29 of which to date have become WTO Members. These are: Angola, Bangladesh, Benin, Burkina Faso, Burundi, Central African Republic, Chad, Congo, Democratic Republic of the, Djibouti, Gambia, Guinea, Guinea Bissau, Haiti, Lesotho, Madagascar, Malawi, Maldives, Mali, Mauritania, Mozambique, Myanmar, Niger, Rwanda, Sierra Leone, Solomon Islands, Tanzania, Togo, Uganda, Zambia. Seven additional least-developed countries are in the process of accession to the WTO. They are: Cambodia, Cape Verde, Laos, Nepal, Samoa, Sudan and Vanuatu. See WTO, 'Who are the developing countries' < www.wto.org/english/tratop_e/devel_e/d1who_e.htm>.

[93] Authors' calculations based on figures from UNAIDS/WHO, *supra*, n. 38.

[94] *Ibid.*

[95] *Ibid.*

Under TRIPS Article 31(f), the use of the patent must be predominantly to supply the domestic market, as is the case of compulsory licenses in Brazil. TRIPS is unclear regarding the meaning of 'predominantly'. Nevertheless, when read together, these provisions clearly prohibit large-scale exports of non-authorized generic copies of patented medicines.

The case of Brazil demonstrates that TRIPS, in conjunction with the TRIPS Declaration, provides developing countries with significant bargaining power to extract price concessions for AIDS drugs or to issue compulsory licenses when negotiations fail. However, the case of Brazil applies only to countries that have the capacity to produce generic drugs under compulsory licenses. Many developing countries do not have the capacity to manufacture generic drugs. This weakens their bargaining position substantially unless they can import generic drugs from another country that has issued a compulsory license.

The TRIPS Declaration recognized the need to resolve this issue in stating, 'We recognize that WTO members with insufficient or no manufacturing capacities in the pharmaceutical sector could face difficulties in making effective use of compulsory licensing under the TRIPS Agreement'.[96] The TRIPS Declaration instructed the Council for TRIPS to find an expeditious solution to this problem by the end of 2002.

Seven months after the Doha meeting, the TRIPS Declaration led to a Decision of the Council for TRIPS (the 'Decision')[97] and a WTO Waiver[98] addressing the issue of access to pharmaceuticals in the least-developed countries. The TRIPS Declaration provides, 'We also agree that the least-developed country members will not be obliged, with respect to pharmaceutical products, to implement or apply Sections 5 and 7 of Part II of the TRIPS Agreement or to enforce rights provided for under these Sections until 1 January 2016 …'.[99] Section 5 applies to patents and Section 7 applies to the protection of undisclosed information. The TRIPS Decision formalizes para. 7 of the TRIPS Declaration, using the same language.

TRIPS already allowed least-developed countries and developing countries to delay providing patent protection for pharmaceuticals. Least-developed countries could delay intellectual property protection generally until 2006,[100] while developing countries could do so until 2000.[101] With respect to patents however, developing countries could delay protection until 2005 if they did not provide patent protection for a particular area of technology when TRIPS obligations came into effect in 1995. Less than 20 developing

---

96 TRIPS Declaration, para. 6.

97 World Trade Organization, Decision of the Council for TRIPS of 27 June 2002, 'Extension of the transition period under Article 66.1 of the TRIPS Agreement for least-developed country members for certain obligations with respect to pharmaceutical products' (IP/C/25) <www.wto.org>.

98 World Trade Organization, Draft Waiver, 'Least-developed country members – obligations under article 70.9 of the trips agreement with respect to pharmaceutical products', submitted to the WTO General Council for approval on 8 July 2002 <www.wto.org>.

99 TRIPS Declaration, para. 7.

100 TRIPS Article 66.1.

101 TRIPS Article 65.2.

countries fit this description, but they include Brazil and India.[102] However, the affected WTO members still have to permit patent applications to be submitted during this transition period for pharmaceutical products.[103] If the country then approves the sale of the product, and a patent has been filed and granted in another WTO member after 1 January 1995, the patent applicant must be given 'exclusive marketing rights' for 5 years even though there is no patent.[104] These obligations have been in force since 1 January 1995 and have been applied to India.[105] The TRIPS Waiver provides, 'The obligations of least-developed country Members under paragraph 9 of Article 70 of the TRIPS Agreement shall be waived with respect to pharmaceutical products until 1 January 2016'.[106]

The effect of these provisions, for least-developed countries, is to exempt them from the obligation to provide patents for pharmaceuticals or exclusive marketing rights until 2016, at which point the exemptions may be extended further. Thus, they may manufacture or import generic versions of patented drugs without violating their WTO obligations. The effect of the TRIPS provisions for India, a major producer of generic AIDS drugs, is that Indian law can allow generic production of AIDS drugs that were patented in other WTO members before 1995. However, the Waiver has not changed the obligation of developing countries, such as India, to fully comply with TRIPS in 2005.

Have the TRIPS Declaration, Decision and Waiver resolved the issue of affordable access for developing countries and least developed countries that are unable to manufacture generic medicines? At present, there are at least two examples of circumstances in which TRIPS still may be tested.

(1) When Argentina fell into its economic crisis in 2001–2, patients who relied on the Argentine government to provide medicine were put at risk (including diabetics and HIV-positive patients on drug therapy). Brazil sent emergency supplies of generic AIDS drugs to Argentina. Brazil supplied these drugs to Argentina on a non-commercial basis. On the same basis, Brazil has also supplied small amounts of drugs to a few African countries (such as Kenya) and some Latin-American countries. In principle, such operations seem to be less likely to be challenged by pharmaceutical companies than the substantial price cuts offered by Indian companies, such as in example (2) below.

(2) Cipla Ltd. of India, a major manufacturer of generic drugs, has offered to supply triple-therapy drug 'cocktails' for $350 a year per patient to Doctors Without Borders. The doctors' group, which won the Nobel Peace Prize in 1999, would distribute the Cipla drugs free in Africa. Cipla also offered to sell the drugs to larger government programs for $600 a year per patient, about $400 below the price offered by the companies that hold the patent.

---

102 WHO/WTO, 2002, *supra*, n. 58.
103 TRIPS Article 70.8.
104 TRIPS Article 70.9.
105 India – Patent Protection for Pharmaceutical and Agricultural Chemical Products, Report of the Appellate Body, WT/DS50/AB/R, 19 December 1997 <www.wto.org>.
106 TRIPS Waiver, *supra*, n. 98.

In both examples, the source of the generic drugs is a developing country. In the first example, the destination (Argentina) is a developing country. In the second example, the destination countries are primarily least-developed countries. Clearly, the least-developed countries may import the generic drugs, given the new exemptions under the WTO waiver, at least until 2016. Similarly, Argentina may accept the donations of drugs from Brazil, since its economic crisis qualifies as a situation of national emergency, extreme urgency, or non-commercial public use under TRIPS Article 31. However, in both scenarios the importing nation still requires a source of supply. TRIPS clearly permits WTO members to issue compulsory licenses to serve their domestic markets, subject to the conditions set out in Article 31. In 2005, India can no longer take advantage of the TRIPS transition period to supply generic drugs. Clarifying that least developed countries may import generic drugs and waiving certain TRIPS obligations until 2016 only provides bargaining power in price negotiations if they have a source of supply.

The head of Brazil's AIDS program has stated that the limited capacity of the state laboratory, combined with a limited health budget, puts Brazil in no position to provide generic drugs (in large scale) to other countries.[107] However, Cipla Ltd. of India has offered to supply low-cost generic AIDS drugs to Africa, an offer that has had the effect of motivating patent holders to lower the price of the patented versions in the same markets.[108] In 2005, India's patent laws will have to comply with TRIPS. Where will least-developed countries and developing countries that lack manufacturing capacity find a supply of AIDS drugs after 2005?

As noted earlier, WTO members may adopt measures 'necessary to protect public health'.[109] At this point it is useful to recall the following part of the TRIPS Declaration:

(4) We agree that the TRIPS Agreement does not and should not prevent members from taking measures to protect public health. Accordingly, while reiterating our commitment to the TRIPS Agreement, we affirm that the Agreement can and should be interpreted and implemented in a manner supportive of WTO members' right to protect public health and, in particular, to promote access to medicines for all.

In this connection, we reaffirm the right of WTO members to use, to the full, the provisions in the TRIPS Agreement, which provide flexibility for this purpose.

It is also useful to recall that the TRIPS Declaration calls for an expeditious solution to the fact that 'WTO members with insufficient or no manufacturing capacities in the pharmaceutical sector could face difficulties in making effective use of compulsory licensing under the TRIPS Agreement'.[110]

---

107 Baldwin, *supra*, n. 46.
108 Economist, *supra*, n. 41.
109 TRIPS Article 8.
110 TRIPS Declaration, para. 6.

The TRIPS Declaration stresses the need for TRIPS 'to be part of the wider national and international action' to address the problem of HIV/AIDS.[111] HIV/AIDS 'can represent a national emergency or other circumstances of extreme urgency'.[112] Read together, these provisions emphasize the intention of the WTO membership to allow measures aimed at not just national public health, but international public health crises such as AIDS.

The intention of the WTO membership is clearly to ensure that TRIPS be part of the solution to the AIDS crisis. To achieve that purpose, TRIPS may have to be applied in a manner that permits compulsory licenses issued in a country that has the manufacturing capacity to supply AIDS drugs to members who lack that capacity.

The purpose of giving developing countries that lack manufacturing capacity the right to import generic medicine is to give them the same bargaining power as those whose manufacturing capacity makes the threat of a compulsory license effective. However, the right to import only strengthens their bargaining power if others have the right to export generic drugs produced under compulsory license. In the context of AIDS, the interpretation of TRIPS requires a balance between research incentives and affordable access to medicine. As long as developed country markets are secure, the pharmaceutical industry has sufficient incentives to continue research in this field. Thus, in this context, the application of the rules of interpretation of customary international law to TRIPS should favour affordable access in both developing and least-developed countries by whatever means are necessary to ensure that TRIPS results in a uniform degree of bargaining power in price negotiations with pharmaceutical firms.

Generally speaking, developing countries are in favour of avoiding narrow and overly restrictive solutions based on the mandate of para. 6 of the Declaration. In this context, developing countries have expressed the common view that there should be no exclusion of countries or categories of countries from the solution under para. 6. A decision not to participate – as suppliers or as beneficiaries – should be based on an individual and voluntary basis. Discussions on the establishment of criteria to determine participating countries would only have the effect of narrowing down the purpose of the solution. Given that para. 6 contains no indication of the need to define categories of countries, or criteria to determine participants, developing countries have expressed the position that every WTO member should have the prerogative to determine whether it is in a situation being a beneficiary under para. 6. It is also important to bear in mind that Brazil, in particular, does not envisage the discussions under para. 6 from the perspective of an exporter of drugs, but rather as an importer of the active substance to manufacture drugs in Brazil. Currently, Brazil imports the generic version of these substances from India, at a very low price. This situation demonstrates that discussions on para. 6 are important to further complementarity interests even among bigger developing countries (rather than competition, as some might assume).

---

111 TRIPS Declaration, para. 2.
112 TRIPS Declaration, para. 5(c).

The threat of generic competition has had the effect of dramatically lowering the cost of AIDS drugs in developing countries and least-developed countries. The recent developments at the WTO have sent a strong signal regarding the willingness of its members to ensure that TRIPS plays a positive role in tackling the AIDS epidemic. However, the issue of supply of generic drugs may come to the fore when developing countries with generic manufacturing capacity, notably India, are required to comply fully with TRIPS in 2005. Whether further action is required on the part of the WTO may depend on how patent holders respond to the changing legal environment in their price negotiations. If the threat of generic competition or further WTO action exerts sufficient pressure, the patent holders may prove to be an adequate source of supply of low-cost AIDS drugs in the countries that lack manufacturing capacity, particularly if combined with financing from developed countries through tax incentives to pharmaceutical companies or through government donations.

Brazil has succeeded in containing its epidemic and providing drug treatment, while spending less on the drugs than it would have spent on hospitalizations and palliative care in the absence of universal access to drugs. Brazil's program has been made affordable through a combination of compulsory licensing threats and hard bargaining in price negotiations. Fifteen Caribbean nations, negotiating as a group, have reached an agreement with pharmaceutical companies to buy AIDS drugs at discounts of up to 90 per cent.[113] Thus, there is evidence that price negotiations with patent holders is a viable method of reducing the cost of treatment in developing countries where there exists a balance of bargaining power.

Permitting exports of generics manufactured under compulsory licenses will not deter private investment in AIDS research as long as developed countries preserve the rights of patent holders in their markets by prohibiting the domestic sale of these generic drugs and imports of discounted drugs from developing countries, as they are entitled to do under TRIPS. Pharmaceutical companies cannot make much profit from the developing countries for their drugs or vaccines. Thus, what happens in developing countries is not relevant for their financial decisions as long as these generics are not sold in the developed countries. Under these circumstances, allowing generic exports from countries with manufacturing capacity would achieve the objective of providing access to medicine, by equalizing bargaining power and without undermining incentives to invent new drugs.

For pharmaceutical companies, price discrimination between markets is an important strategy for maximizing profits. When they have a monopoly over certain drugs, they charge the price that will maximize their total profits. As long as they own the patents, the legal protection provided in each market permits them to negotiate the price and seek compensation for their investment. However, if governments allow parallel imports, they have the potential to undermine a firm's price discrimination strategy.

---

113 Bert Wilkinson, 'Caribbean countries announce deal for cheaper AIDS drugs', *Associated Press*, 6 July 2002.

Parallel imports involve products sold by the patent owner in one market that are then imported into another market without the patent owner's approval. Under a system of national exhaustion, a patent holder can prevent parallel importation of his product from a foreign country. Under a system of international exhaustion, as soon as the product is put on the market of any country by the patent holder, he can no longer block the importation of that product into any other country.[114]

During the Uruguay Round, WTO members were unable to reach agreement on how to deal with the issue of exhaustion of intellectual property rights. TRIPS lets patent holders prevent third parties from making, using, selling or importing their product without consent. However, under a system of international exhaustion of patents, the patent owner cannot prevent the importation of his own product from a foreign country once it has been sold there. Exhaustion of patent rights cannot be raised in a WTO dispute, which raises the risk that patented drugs sold at a discount in developing countries could be exported to a developed country market. This could threaten differential pricing strategies used by pharmaceutical companies unless they insist the buyers of discounted drugs not offer them for resale.

As long as developed countries maintain a policy of national exhaustion, the primary source of profits remains secure. Thus the issue is not the price charged in developing countries, but rather the policies maintained in developed countries. Since the patent owners are primarily located in developed countries, their governments have an incentive to support prices through a system of national exhaustion.[115] The issue of parallel imports is thus a North–North issue more than a North–South issue.

There appears to be no immediate need to introduce further reforms at the WTO to solve the issue of bargaining power in countries that lack the manufacturing capacity to make a credible threat of issuing compulsory licenses. Until 2005, Indian generic manufacturers can supply generic drugs. Indeed, the evidence is that Cipla's offer to supply triple-combination therapy has had a significant impact on the price of the patented equivalents in developed and developing countries that lack manufacturing capacity. When compliance with TRIPS prevents India from supplying these generics in 2005 (or if India ceases to do so before then), developed countries can provide WTO-consistent tax incentives to prompt the patent holders to donate drugs where necessary. Patent holders have an added incentive to co-operate in this regard given the clear intention of WTO members to take any action that may be necessary to address the AIDS crisis. Of course, this solution assumes good faith efforts on the part of all countries and the pharmaceutical companies. In the event that such incentives prove inadequate, further WTO action may be required to achieve a long-term solution.

---

114 *See* Claude E. Barfield and Mark A. Groomridge, 'Parallel Trade in the Pharmaceutical Industry: Implications for Innovation, Consumer Welfare and Health Policy' (1999) 10 *Fordham Intellectual Property, Media and Entertainment Journal* 185.

115 *See* Condon and Sinha, *supra*, n. 36.

12.12 Conclusion

AIDS and terrorism are two matters of global security that raise a set of common issues. Both result in the loss of human lives, though AIDS has a far greater impact on this measure (which is the point made in the Economist article mentioned at the beginning of this chapter). Both are relevant to the management of cross-border movements of people. Both issues require solutions that strike the right balance between economic concerns and security concerns. Both raise important questions regarding the best allocation of responsibility among the private sector, national governments, bilateral institutions, and multilateral organizations, including the WTO. Both AIDS and the terrorist threat can have a significant impact on North–South relations and affect the prospects for economic development in developing countries. At the same time, both issues affect North–North relations and have important economic consequences for developed countries. As a result, both issues have the potential to affect global trade negotiations in unforeseeable ways, as demonstrated by their impact at the Doha Ministerial Meeting.

The controversy at Doha over affordable access to AIDS drugs arose because the AIDS crisis affects North and South differently in some respects. In terms of numbers of people affected, AIDS hits the South much harder than the North. Moreover, affordable access to medicine is an issue in the South, not the North. The issue of ensuring adequate profits to provide research incentives is sometimes cast as an issue of greater importance to the North than to the South. However, this is where the interests of North and South coincide. Without adequate incentives to produce effective drug treatments, there would be no issue of access – affordable or otherwise. However, ensuring that parallel imports of cut-rate patented drugs or their generic copies do not threaten research incentives is primarily a North–North issue. As long as the governments of the North ensure generic or cut-rate patented medicines in developing countries do not find their way back to developed-country markets, research incentives will be preserved.

The manner in which the terrorist threat is addressed also highlights the asymmetries along the North–South divide, as well as the issue of incentives for the private sector to dedicate resources to the problem. The experience thus far in the NAFTA region suggests that measures taken to balance trade liberalization and security concerns will result in different measures being applied to developed and developing countries due to differences in technological capabilities, financial resources, and human resources. Moreover, problems stemming from corruption and illegal migration complicate border security co-operation between the North and South to a far greater degree than they do North to North. However, since over half of world trade is dominated by the 500 largest multinational firms,[116] the implementation of voluntary security programs by firms will resolve the issue for a large percentage of merchandise trade flows.

---

116 Alan Rugman, *The End of Globalization: Why Global Strategy is a Myth and How to Profit from the Realities of Regional Markets* (Amacom, New York, 2001).

With respect to both terrorist threats and AIDS, the private sector has a major role to play in striking the right balance between security and economic interests. With respect to terrorism, multinational firms must implement security measures for the transportation of goods and must monitor financial transactions. With respect to AIDS, multinational pharmaceutical firms have a central role to play in providing affordable access to treatment. In both cases, the manner in which multinational companies meet their responsibilities will influence the measures taken by governments and inter-governmental organizations. Similarly, the incentives provided by national governments and the multilateral regulatory framework will influence the contribution the private sector makes to address both border security and access to affordable AIDS treatments.

The issue of allocation of responsibility among the private sector, national governments, bilateral institutions, and multilateral organizations is relevant to the design of solutions to address both AIDS and terrorism. In the NAFTA countries, governments have responded to the threat of terrorism with a mixture of unilateral measures, bilateral co-operation, and multilateral agreements. Unilateral measures, such as decisions on visa requirements, the American CTPAT program, and the freezing of terrorist assets, can be implemented quickly and are justifiable under the security exceptions of trade agreements. Bilateral co-operation between developed countries is a close second in terms of speed of implementation, as demonstrated by Canada–US initiatives. However, bilateral initiatives between developed and developing countries take longer to implement. Similarly, multilateral initiatives can be implemented more quickly in organizations dominated by developed countries (such as the OECD FATF initiatives) than in organizations dominated by developing countries (such as the World Customs Organization). To their own detriment, developing countries are in the slow lane when it comes to balancing security and economic needs, except where MNC compliance with security requirements and financial reporting obligations can overcome the financial, institutional and technological constraints faced by developing country governments.

The financial and institutional capacity of developing country governments affects the allocation of responsibility for both AIDS and border security. Unilateral responses are appropriate to address aspects of both problems and are permitted by the applicable international rules. Governments with generic manufacturing capacity can unilaterally decide to issue compulsory licenses to lower the cost of AIDS drugs and use this threat to enhance their bargaining power. Similarly, governments can take unilateral actions to enhance security in the movement of goods, people and capital. However, unilateral actions alone are insufficient to address either issue. Bilateral and multilateral co-operation are necessary, particularly when developing countries lack the capacity to address AIDS and terrorism on their own. However, bilateral and multilateral initiatives get slowed down when developing countries are involved, to their detriment.

The economic impact of AIDS and terrorism is likely to be more significant for developing countries than developed countries, particularly with respect to their ability to capture global trade and capital flows. Their rates of AIDS prevalence and their ability to meet security requirements influence their attractiveness as destinations for foreign investment and as sources for inputs in global production networks. As such, both issues complicate the development agenda of the WTO. The WTO has a major role to play in balancing the need for affordable access to AIDS medicine against the necessity of preserving research incentives, due to the impact of the TRIPS agreement on these competing goals. However, the WTO mandate is much more limited when it comes to addressing the issue of terrorism. With respect to capital movements, there appears to be no need for the WTO to take action, given the role of the OECD through its FATF initiatives. The same is true with respect to supply chain management, an issue being addressed by the WCO. Finally, WTO exceptions regarding matters of national and international security allocate responsibility to national governments and the United Nations. This limits the ability of the WTO to question both unilateral and bilateral initiatives being taken to balance trade needs against the need to secure borders against the threat of terrorism.

Index

GLOBAL TRADE AND FINANCE SERIES

1. Emmanuel T. Laryea, *Paperless Trade: Opportunities, Challenges and Solutions*. 2002. ISBN 90-411-9897-0

2. Xiang Gao, *The Fraud Rule in the Law of Letters of Credit: A Comparative Study*. 2002. ISBN 90-411-9898-9

3. Yuwa Wei, *Comparative Corporate Governance: A Chinese Perspective*. 2003. ISBN 90-411-9908-X

4. Ross P. Buckley (ed.), *The WTO and the Doha Round: The Changing Face of World Trade*. 2003. ISBN 90-411-9947-0